SIXTY SPOUSES OF RETIRED REFORM RABBIS IN THEIR OWN WORDS

NAOMI PATZ
EDITOR

JUDITH MASLIN
EDITOR

A Project of NAORRR:

NATIONAL ASSOCIATION OF RETIRED REFORM RABBIS

Published by FAITH: The Foundation to Advance Interfaith Trust and Harmony

WE, THE EMERITUS RABBIS AND SPOUSES WHO ARE MEMBERS OF NAORRR, are a distinctive – and, we believe – special collectivity. Despite the fact that our organization is called the National Association of Retired Reform *Rabbis,* rabbis' spouses and the surviving spouses of rabbis of the Reform Movement, are fully equal in NAORRR – together as participants, as seminar and workshop leaders and taking roles in leading worship services, as well as in payment of dues.

Equal, not hierarchical. A united group.

It is because we are equal partners in NAORRR that NAORRR is the perfect venue for publishing *Married to the Rabbi.*

PRAISE FOR *MARRIED TO THE RABBI*

"I'm grateful for having had the opportunity to read the wonderful essays contributed to this collection. They are moving, funny, insightful, and wise, and they include some terrific anecdotes that provide vital texture to what we know about some of the critical moments in American Jewish history over the past seventy years."

Dr. Shuly Rubin Schwartz is the Provost of the Jewish Theological Seminary and Irving Lehrman Research Professor of American Jewish History. She also serves as Dean of the Gershon Kekst Graduate School and is the author of the award-winning The Rabbi's Wife: The Rebbetzin in American Jewish Life.

"*Married to the Rabbi* contains much more than a bouquet of pleasing reminiscences. These essays are primary sources that document the life of the American rabbinate from the 1950s to the present day. They provide personal insights into a facet of modern Jewish life that until now has been understudied. The contributors offer readers a fascinating look behind the scenes at those who dwell in the public limelight and, in doing so, they enrich our understanding of the rabbi's spouse as a significant figure in Jewish life in the voices of those who have lived it.

The American Jewish Archives takes pride in accessioning the entirety of this collection, which will richly benefit future researchers and historians."

Dr. Gary P. Zola, Executive Director, The Jacob Rader Marcus Center of the American Jewish Archives, & The Edward M. Ackerman Family

Distinguished Professor of the American Jewish Experience and Reform Jewish History, Hebrew Union College-Jewish Institute of Religion, Cincinnati, Ohio.

"*Married to the Rabbi* is a sometimes delightful, sometimes upsetting, but always interesting view into the world of the Reform rabbi's spouse and family. (I say "spouse" advisedly, because one of the writers is a man.) That world – and the role rabbinic spouses play in it – too often has been both misunderstood and undervalued. Most of the authors in this volume became rabbis' wives when a majority of women were "stay-at-home" mothers. Some rabbis' wives embraced their special spousal role; others tolerated it. Since that era has largely passed, this volume reflects a period of American Jewish life that is already becoming history. Judith Maslin and Naomi Patz have assembled and edited a fascinating volume."

Rabbi Jeffrey Stiffman is Rabbi Emeritus of Congregation Shaare Emeth in St. Louis, Missouri and immediate past president of NAORRR.

DEDICATION TO OUR DONORS

◆═◆

In honor of
Rabbi Harry and Jeanne Danziger
by Rabbi Micah Greenstein and Temple Israel
Memphis, Tennessee

◆═◆

In honor of
Rabbi Steven and Senator Joyce Foster
by Rabbi Joe Black and Temple Emanuel
Denver, Colorado

◆═◆

In honor of
Rabbi James and Jane Perman
by the Temple Shalom One Family
Naples, Florida

◆═◆

In honor of
Rabbi Merle and Myra Singer
by Rabbi Dan Levin and Temple Beth El
Boca Raton, Florida

◆═◆

In honor of
Rabbi Jeffrey and Dr. Arlene Rubin Stiffman
by Rabbi Jim Bennett and Congregation Shaare Emeth
St. Louis, Missouri

◆═◆

In honor of
Rabbi Alvin and Barbara Sugarman
by Rabbi Peter Berg and The Temple
Atlanta, Georgia

Acknowledgments

To Norman and Shim, our beloved spouses–
without you, we wouldn't be rabbis' wives!
Naomi and Judy

We acknowledge with gratitude the support of NAORRR and our nurturing collective of caring colleagues who enabled *Married to the Rabbi* to happen.

And we especially thank the people named here whose assistance and advice have been invaluable:

On behalf of the NAORRR Board: Rabbi Jeffrey Stiffman, president, and Rabbi Julian Cook and Susie Cook, Co-Executive Vice Presidents.

Rabbi Mark Winer, who has served as indefatigable producer for this project. Mark is president of FAITH: The Foundation to Advance Interfaith Trust and Harmony, publisher of *Married to the Rabbi.*

Our meticulous copy editors/proofreaders: Rabbi Connie Golden, Rabbi Sam Stahl, Helen Wolkow, N.N. Light, and Shana Brodsky.

Pat Bloom, Judy Maslin's energizing initial cochair.

Robert Sturtz, book cover designer.

Shana Brodsky, publishing technical advisor and, with Alexandria Bishop, interior book formatter.

Shoshana Dweck and Hillel Parness, intellectual property advisors.

Rabbi Gary Zola, who has supported and encouraged this project since its inception, and the American Jewish Archives for accepting all of the essays into the Archive collection.

Dr. Shuly Rubin Schwartz, for her encouragement and generous introduction.

Of course, there would be no book without the sixty members of NAORRR whose insights and thoughtful reflections comprise the entries in this volume. Sadly, two of the women whose work appears here – Phyllis Kudan and Eudice Lorge – died during the year before the book was published; essays and poems by several other writers were generously contributed by their surviving spouses and children. These pieces help enrich *Married to the Rabbi*'s breadth and depth.

~Naomi Patz and Judy Maslin, editors

TABLE OF CONTENTS

FOREWORD

IN MARCH 2018, *THE NEW YORK TIMES* LAUNCHED A NEW SERIES, "Overlooked," featuring obituaries for individuals –mostly women – who had not been memorialized in the paper at the time of their deaths. Acknowledging that the vast majority of obituaries had been written about white men, *The Times* is striving to compensate for the earlier narrow focus by adding these new life stories, and fifty years of scholarly research in the field of women's and gender studies has made it possible to do so. This *Times* initiative has begun to enrich the public record immeasurably, at the same time also calling attention to long-standing cultural assumptions that marginalize many, including women, while privileging white Christian men, especially those associated with prestigious activities, professions, and pedigrees.

Despite considerable achievements – both in arenas traditionally ascribed to men and in the domains of family and culture – women's contributions have long been regarded as less valuable than men's political, business, religious, and intellectual attainments. "Overlooked" not only adds the biographies of so many previously omitted women, but in doing so, it also reframes assumptions about what makes a life worthy of recognition. Reading the "Overlooked" obituaries also inspires reflection and increased consciousness regarding the countless underappreciated women in our own communities whose lives merit recording.

Thankfully, the contributors to this volume anticipated the message that the "Overlooked" series strives to convey. Cognizant of the significance of their lives as rabbis' spouses, they have documented their experiences for future generations. What a treat to hear their voices! Their moving, funny, and insightful stories about their lives as rabbis' wives (and one husband) add vital texture to our understanding of the history of American Judaism over the past seventy years, a time of major changes. We are all indebted to them for sharing, and thus preserving, their experiences and reflections in writing for posterity.

As we know, for over a century and a half, rabbis have played a key role in establishing, securing, and enriching Jewish life in America. While rabbis held the most visible Jewish religious leadership roles in their communities, their successes were inexorably intertwined with the achievements of so many others in their communities, including pioneering settlers, wealthy benefactors, energetic volunteers, and often to an underrecognized degree – their wives. These essays portray the many ways in which rabbis' spouses – some of whom are proud to call themselves "rebbetzin" and others who totally reject the title (if not, in fact, the role) – have played a key function in furthering Jewish life. As the essays illustrate, a number of women of this era who wanted to assume a meaningful role in the Jewish community discovered that marrying a rabbi would be the surest avenue toward that end.

Through this volume, we learn about the wide variety of leadership paths that rabbis' wives took from the middle of the last century into at least the first decade of the current one. They have served as school teachers and university professors, writers, hostesses, advisers, administrators, Jewish communal professionals, psychologists and social workers, program managers, accountants, homemakers, public speakers, community advocates, and more. Their stories range from short anecdotes of less than a single page (although most include extended autobiographical information) to fairly lengthy essays. We read poetry, satires, an ethical will, book chapters, and magazine columns. Some of the essayists reflect on their roles as the spouses of career academics, Hillel rabbis, military chaplains, and more.

While all of our writers married Reform rabbis, their Jewish backgrounds vary widely. Some come from traditional Jewish upbringings while others grew up in classical Reform families. Some had Christmas trees in their childhood homes and did not observe Jewish rituals or holidays; others are themselves the children and grandchildren of rabbis.

Similarly, these women traveled diverse paths to the marriage canopy. Some contributors met their spouses as children in Hebrew school or through movement-related Jewish youth groups or summer camps. Many looked forward enthusiastically to being rabbinic spouses. Some of the essayists did graduate work in Jewish studies and/or Jewish education, whether before they met their spouses, while their husbands were in rabbinical school, or later in life. A number of the essayists aspired to be rabbi's wives, some even choosing to attend college in Cincinnati to increase the likelihood of marrying a rabbinical student. Others, including the one male contributor, married ordained rabbis, though that did not necessarily mean that they had aspired to do so. On the contrary, some had consciously determined never to marry a rabbi but then fell in love with one anyway. Some knew what they were getting into, while still others were surprised, believing that they understood the role only to discover they had no clue. Several women married men who were studying for or already embarked on careers in the secular world; this led, in some cases, to an unnerving transition to life as a rabbi's wife, a role for which these women felt woefully unprepared.

Some of the contributors have chosen to reflect on the role their spouse's retirement from the active rabbinate has played in their own identities. Some miss the status they had during their husband's years in the pulpit, while others feel liberated from it. A few have found new venues – such as retirement communities – in which to offer their rebbetzin skills. Some are now widowed, and their essays reflect the effect of that loss on their lives.

Thanks to the intimacy of the essays, we also learn about the similarities and differences among the wives' experiences and the range of emotions the role evoked. For example, we see that whether or not they had formal Jewish education or teacher training, a relatively large number of wives taught in their congregation's religious school. We hear from rabbis' wives who loved the role and others who found a way to make it work, and we see the ways in which the role evolved at different periods of their lives. We are also privy to their thoughts about coping with congregants' unrealistic expectations, insensitivities, and judgments as well as how much they enjoyed and appreciated the unique bonds they formed in their communities as a result of their special status.

Finally, these essays describe how not only the rabbinate but also the role of the rebbetzin changed as a result of post-World War II American history. For example, several essayists reflect on the effect that the leadership roles their spouses held in the civil rights movement had on their lives and the lives of their families. These women share personal accounts of their husbands' and their own public actions and principled stances, speaking to the sometimes-traumatic impact these had on their families. Many contributors also reflect on how Second Wave feminism changed the way they viewed their work at home, in the synagogue, and, increasingly, in professional life.

The single essay by a male spouse describes the lack of expectations imposed on him by the congregation. It serves as the exception that reinforces the gendered norms that for so long circumscribed the lives of the female contributors. But it also buttresses the notion that for women specifically – particularly before women's ordination was an option – the spouse role proved to be a winning path to a supportive religious leadership role together with their husbands.

These essays give us a rich appreciation of both the significant role that Reform rabbis' wives played in the expansion of American Jewish synagogue life and the opportunities marriage to a rabbi provided for women who felt called to religious leadership in the era before they could become rabbis. Consciously or not, these women have modeled female religious leadership for future generations of

American Jewish women and thus paved the way for the talented women rabbis and communal leaders who enrich the Jewish world today.

Dr. Shuly Rubin Schwartz, author of the award - winning The Rabbi's Wife: The Rebbetzin in American Jewish Life is the Provost of the Jewish Theological Seminary and the Irving Lehrman Professor of American Jewish History.

I

How the Book Came About

As I was completing the writing of my own memoir, I realized – and wrote – that the wife of almost any clergyman of my generation could probably write a similar book. So many of my experiences were common to those of other rabbis' and even ministers' wives. I mentioned this to Dr. Gary Zola, Executive Director of the American Jewish Archives, when he told me that my book was one of only a very few that dealt with life in a rabbinic family from the mid- to late-twentieth century. That gap in the Archives gave me the idea for this group project, which Dr. Zola enthusiastically endorsed, promising that the material we amassed would become an important part of the Archives' holdings. I determined that the best way to proceed was to solicit essays from the rabbinic spouses who belong to NAORRR, the National Association of Retired Reform Rabbis. I am most grateful to Pat Bloom who was my initial partner in this endeavor. She helped me get the project underway.

As the essays began to come in, I was delighted to see that although they do reflect many similar experiences, every essay has something different to say. It became increasingly important to me that the range of essays be as broad as possible.

Early in the project, Naomi Patz became my co-editor. She brought with her a deep knowledge of, and vast experience in, writing and editing. Without her expertise and diligence, this book would not have come to fruition. Both of us are very happy with the breadth of the subject matter, the background of the authors, their congregational experiences, their self-identification as rebbetzins or abhorrence of the term, and the scope of their careers. They represent a wide variety of voices.

It was very important to us that the individual style of each writer be maintained. Some wrote short anecdotes, others long essays. Several essays and poems were written years ago by rabbinic spouses now deceased; we are grateful to their family members who generously shared them with us. We are very happy that one male spouse of a rabbi wrote about his experiences, which – as we suspected – have been very different from those of female rabbinic spouses of our era.

With the rabbinate changing so dramatically in the last several decades, we are delighted that this collection represents sixty individual voices of spouses whose rabbinic experiences evoke a rabbinate and a life of rabbinic families very different from what exists today. We will leave the important documentation of our RKs' (rabbis' kids) lives for them to write!

Judith Maslin
co-editor

2

Whither Thou Goest

JUDITH MASLIN

I HAVE OCCASIONALLY TOLD PEOPLE I DID NOT MARRY A RABBI. After graduating from Harvard in 1952, Shim – my husband for more than sixty-five years – came to the University of Pennsylvania to get an M.A. in governmental administration. He was studying to become a city manager. We met six months later, during my first week as a Penn freshman, at a Hillel event welcoming new students. It was toward the end of Shim's studies at Penn the following year that he decided to go to Hebrew Union College – Jewish Institute of Religion in Cincinnati and become a rabbi.

I cannot remember Shim making the decision to go to rabbinical school, but it seemed that suddenly he decided to study for the rabbinate. Perhaps I should have anticipated it because Friday night dates always began or ended by our going to services at one or another Reform congregation in the Philadelphia area. I really had no opinion about it, and at barely eighteen years of age, had no idea of what was involved or what was to come. I was not a part of the decision-making process even though by that time, it also involved me. This was between 1953 and 1954, and many girls like me were simply not as involved as most young women are today. Our wedding took place just a few weeks before he started HUC- JIR.

With all the weddings that Shim performed over the past sixty years, the one thing they have had in common is that none of them has been unflawed. Every bride seems to think that if everything is planned down to the very last detail (as it should be), the wedding of her dreams will be perfect. Yet it is likely that something unforeseen – and undesired –will happen. It can be something as small as the frozen dessert coming out slightly melted, or something more significant. For example, some years back, one of the season's most anticipated weddings in our congregation was that of the daughter of the owner of a brand new, elegant hotel. This was to be the very first wedding in the ballroom. And the ceremony was lovely. But a pipe burst on the floor above the ballroom in the middle of the sumptuous dinner that followed, and water began raining down through the ceiling. It was especially heavy over the large orchestra. I will spare you details of the scramble that followed. My own thoughts were that it was lucky it was not a "paying" customer, who probably would have sued the hotel!

I was there when a bride's younger brother, who had been standing with groomsmen on the opposite side of the pulpit from the bride's family, fainted and dropped to the pulpit steps. As the father of the bride rushed over to his son, he tripped over his daughter's elaborate train and grabbed the pole of the heavily embroidered huppah, which began to wobble dangerously. There was even more... That wedding was a story and a half, so much so that it was actually shown on TV's America's Funniest Videos! At the time, it was not so funny.

I should have anticipated such events at weddings because of what happened at our own. Shim's Orthodox family, embarrassed that he was not becoming either an Orthodox or a Conservative rabbi, had told friends that he was going to be studying in the Midwest. Period. My family, somewhat intimidated by the fact that my husband-to-be not only was becoming a rabbi but also came from a religious background, remembered a distant cousin who was a Reform rabbi and decided to invite him to the wedding to assert our bona fides.

After dinner, my father-in-law, a highly respected hazan in the Boston area, asked a few people to give speeches. First, he called on his own rabbi (who could not pronounce the letter "l") who spoke to us about "yuv" and ended by saying that we would learn more about "yuv" that night than he could begin to tell us.

Then Abba called on my mother's cousin, a rabbi from Brooklyn. He spoke in a booming voice about how happy he was that this young man was entering the Refooooorm ministry. I thought my new mother-in-law would slide under the table.

Lastly, Abba called on his distinguished elderly cousin, Dr. Leon Medalia, who was on the board of the Boston Hebrew Teachers College (as it was called at the time). Basically, Uncle Leon asked the crowd to send wedding gifts in our honor to the college. Shim and I, depending on gifts to live on during our first year in Cincinnati, almost passed out.

It is funny how we all survive these traumatic weddings. Shim and I did get the needed gifts, he did become a Reform "minister," and we have indeed found "yuv" in each other's arms all these years.

After our honeymoon in Maine, we drove to the Hebrew Union College-Jewish Institute of Religion in Cincinnati with our clothes, books, and as many wedding presents as we could stuff into the car. We had been told that we could stay in the dorms at the College-Institute until we found a place to live. Within a day or so, we were invited to go on a tour of the HUC-JIR campus by another student, Joe Glaser. We visited all the buildings, and then as we came back to the dorm, Joe ended the tour by saying the school could be summed up in one word: "Zoo!" As newcomers we did not yet know Joe and his sense of humor. While we were digesting that comment, Joe asked Shim why he wanted to become a rabbi. Shim barely took a breath and said to Joe, "because I married a rebbetzin." That comment took but a couple of seconds, and then we were talking about something else. The rest of the conversation is long gone from my memory, but not Shim's answer. What did he mean? I know that to give Joe a serious response would have been long and complicated. Shim has always said he was just joking, but I've continued to wonder. At the time, it certainly did not feel like a compliment. The title, "rebbetzin," was not my image then – or now – of someone young and sexy! It felt as if my husband was describing another woman, probably someone Orthodox. It wasn't an insult, but it wasn't *me*. At that point, having grown up in a Conservative congregation with a bachelor rabbi, I also most decidedly had no idea what the "job requirements" were.

Because of his excellent Judaic studies background, Shim was able to pass off many classes, and he was ordained in three years instead of five. We therefore only lived in Cincinnati from September 1954 until May 1957 – two years and eight months – minus the three summer months in both 1955 and 1956. I mention the short amount of time we spent there to emphasize how intense and significant those years were. They were jam-packed with school, both for him and for me, the birth of our daughter, Naomi, and many hours spent studying and socializing with classmates and faculty. It was a time to bond with them and to learn the basics of what the job would be: his and, yes, mine as well.

I cherish the many evenings we spent in the homes of HUC-JIR students living near us in Swifton Village, an inexpensive garden apartment compound about twenty minutes from the college. We regularly had evening get-togethers to drink coffee, have a little nibble, and to play games like Dictionary and charades. It was a time to relax and discuss what our future lives would be like. My closeness to rabbinic spouses began at that time and has lasted to this day. For all our personal differences, career aspirations, widespread locations, to some extent we have continued to share common goals, experiences and frustrations. I know that HUC-JIR student life and rabbinic life have certainly changed in the late 20th and early 21st centuries. During the time Shim was still in the active rabbinate, the understanding among us wives was that our primary role was to serve as a huge source of support for our husbands in what were then the expectations of rabbinic life.

Shim had two student pulpits. The first was a monthly in Burlington, Iowa. At the time Shim was their rabbi, Burlington had fifteen Jewish families. They almost all came to every service he conducted. He said that they were always warm and friendly and most hospitable. Our Naomi was born during the time Shim was serving in Burlington. The people there were very eager to meet me and to see the new baby. So, it was arranged that when Naomi was about four months old, we took her on a visit to Iowa.

The Burlington congregation could not do enough for us. They oohed and aahed over baby Naomi and were extremely hospitable. It is what happened that Sunday morning that we can never forget. While I was being entertained, Shim was teaching Sunday School. Someone came into his class and asked for the keys to his car. When school was over and Shim went to the car, it had four brand new tires! The Burlington congregants told him they could not have the rabbi's family traveling in a car with balding tires. In Cincinnati, we were scraping by on salaries from my weekend music teaching jobs and Shim's other part time work. We certainly had no discretionary money for new tires. What a generous act! That tiny congregation remains in my mind and heart as the exemplar of what a congregation could be: thoughtful, kind and caring to its rabbi. It was a benign (and somewhat unrealistic) introduction to what we might later expect from a congregation. Shim's four post-ordination congregations have also been very kind to us over the years, but perhaps what we had in Iowa stands out because of how welcome it was to a very young couple just starting out.

When the time came, in mid-1957, for Shim to decide on a first fulltime congregation, he was offered several positions. We chose a congregation in Monroe, New York, a small town in the foothills of the Catskill Mountains. The location seemed perfect. It was about halfway between Shim's family in Boston and mine in Philadelphia.

The Monroe Temple for Liberal Judaism had about one hundred and twenty families. It was the only synagogue in town and had always tried to meet the needs of the broad spectrum of member families. (In more recent years, the town has changed a great deal, with a major influx of Satmar Hasidim.)

Most of the members of the congregation were the age of my parents and grandparents. There were only a few couples our age. When we arrived, I was pregnant with our second child, David. For the first couple of years there, I did what I thought was expected of me. My main job, of course, was taking care of the house and the children. But I attended services every Friday evening, I went to all sisterhood events, and I was even in charge of the gift shop. We were fortunate to have the same, very reliable woman babysit for all five of our years in Monroe (at fifty cents an hour!).

It was only after a year or two of a very busy child-centered life that I really began to miss playing the piano and teaching music. From the time I was about fourteen, I had been an accompanist and later a music teacher in Sunday schools. In Cincinnati, in addition to taking courses at the University of Cincinnati and HUC-JIR, I studied piano at the Cincinnati Conservatory of Music. When we enrolled Naomi in kindergarten at an excellent, modern Orthodox Hebrew day school in Monsey, about a forty-five-minute drive away, I applied for and was hired to teach music at the day school two days a week. It was both a teaching and learning opportunity for me. I loved the job. It greatly added to my own knowledge of the Hebrew language and Jewish music, and I continued teaching there until our move to Curacao.

It was in Monroe that, as the rabbi's wife, I got to see that what was really involved with Shim's job went far beyond Shabbat and holiday services. There were not many weddings in that congregation because of the age of the members, but there were quite a few funerals. Some were tragic, like the deaths of two children and several younger men. There were several that have stayed with me for various reasons, including an ultimately funny one in which the family car followed the wrong hearse toward the wrong cemetery.

But it is this story that has stuck with me all these years:

We got a call in the middle of the night from a young member of the congregation to tell us his baby son, one of twins, had just died in the hospital. He could not face going home alone to tell his wife, who had stayed at home with the other twin. Shim met him as he pulled his car up to their house and they walked together toward the door. When the baby's mother saw Shim, she began to scream hysterically. She knew immediately what had happened. Shim told me when he returned home just before dawn, he felt as though he himself had personified the angel of death.

That last line stuck with me over the years. What is it like to be a person who, at any time, can feel as though he "personifies" death? And how does a rabbi cope with officiating at tragic funerals or performing the funeral of a close friend? What long range effect does it have? I know, professionals learn to deal with these things, as physicians must do to deal with dying children. But isn't there the risk of becoming inured just to protect oneself? My father-in-law used to officiate at many funerals. Shim remembers from his childhood that, after many a funeral, his father – usually a rather strict and serious person – would play silly games with him or tickle him to make him laugh. Did my father-in-law need to hear that laughter to help *him* cope? I came to admire the strength it took for Shim to perform these difficult duties. It always took hours both before and after the funeral service itself. I think it is an aspect of the rabbinate that the average congregant and, yes, even spouse, rarely thinks about. How much of the pain and frustration of those events does the rabbi bring home in one form or another without realizing it? Weddings and other *simhahs* are perhaps even more time consuming but they are, without doubt, much easier emotionally! Is it the combination of all rabbinic responsibilities that keeps a rabbi in balance?

In 1962, as President Kennedy spoke about the Peace Corps,

Shim and I were considering what to do next. Shim felt he had done as much as he could for the Monroe community, and he was ready to move forward. He had never done any military service. The HUC-JIR class of 1957 had so many married men with children that all of them were exempted from the chaplaincy that year. Now, five years later, we were moved by Kennedy's ideas about service and felt we owed something, some kind of service. After consultations with the World Union for Progressive Judaism placement director in New York, we chose to go to Temple Emanuel in Curacao. Temple Emanuel had broken away from the historic Congregation Mikve Israel in 1864 and – until now – in its one-hundred-year history, had not managed to find a full- time rabbi.

The forty-member congregation was able to afford a rabbi because the Dutch government paid the salaries of all clergy serving historic congregations on the island. Although it was a meager salary, it was just about enough for us to live on. The move felt to us as though we were doing our version of the American Peace Corps.

There were many changes in our lives. I was pregnant for this move, too. In Curacao, I delivered the baby, Eve, by natural childbirth, six weeks after our arrival on the island. The older children were enrolled in Dutch-language schools. Shim learned to preach in what the Voice of America called "special English." And we all, more or less, got used to the year-round heat. There were many other things to which we adapted. It was a challenge, but it was a happy challenge because we quickly grew to love the members of the congregation. They could not have been more helpful or more supportive. Shim worked harder than he had ever worked before. He saw areas that desperately needed attention. He began a religious school, and he started weekly adult education classes. Within a year, talks were underway to reunite the two congregations. It was as if he had a magic touch. Parents were starved for the school, for the adult education and ultimately, for the merger. The oldest congregation in the western world in continuous use, founded in 1651, became

Congregation Mikve Israel-Emanuel.

My role in Curacao was mostly social and supportive. We ran a weekly Saturday afternoon Oneg Shabbat in our home. For the Saturday afternoons with the children, I taught myself how to play the accordion so I could accompany and teach songs. As an American on this Dutch island, I was not permitted to hold a paying job unless there was no one else on the island who could do that work, so I did not work outside the home. We very often entertained Americans and other foreign visitors and dignitaries. It was in Curacao that I really learned to bake... out of necessity. I baked more cupcakes than I could ever imagine or count. I made the hundreds of matzah balls for the chicken soup served at the congregational seder.

Our lives there were very busy, filled with things pertaining to our children and to the congregation and everything that came along with it. There was just so very much happening. Since Shim was a government employee, we were invited to all varieties of official events. We met and spoke with Queen Julianna and with Princess Beatrix, who later became the queen, and then, many years later, on a visit to the island, we met Prince Willem-Alexander, who is now the king. We had not a clue about this kind of life when we decided to go there. Who would have thought that our initial idea of a two-year stint of service out of the country would become so significant to our lives? In my memoir, *Rabbi and Judy,* I wrote more about our lives on the island than in any other congregation. Not only did we stay there for five wonderful years, but we have remained very close with the community to this day. By doing a lot of writing about the island, Shim really made a name for himself – a totally unexpected outcome.

In the fifth year on our now beloved island of Curacao, Shim and I began to talk about the future. We were all very happy, but we realized perhaps it was time to return to the States. Naomi was getting ready for junior high school, David spoke English with a Dutch accent, and Eve was approaching school age. If we were ever to return to the States and Shim not have a foreign career, now was the time to make the move. As a government employee, he was entitled to a month's vacation for every year he had served, and our belongings would be moved to the next location. We found temporary homes for our kids with family and friends, and he and I traveled to Israel and Europe for the first time, using the severance money from the Dutch government.

In May of 1967, we began the process of settling into Chicago, our new home city, and KAM Temple (formally, Kehilath Anshe Ma'arav) in Hyde Park. The change was monumental. From the climate to the size and composition of the congregation to the entire environment, it was quite an adjustment. I personally felt as though my stock had plummeted in one particular area because I had not finished college, and now we were in a highly academic environment. Although it didn't happen instantly, with a lot of determination and professional guidance, I did go back to school and earned an M.A. in art history from the University of Chicago. During our years in the very windy city, I also had great success and fun as a music teacher in both our own congregation and in two Hebrew day schools. I loved living in Chicago!

◆═◆

All rabbinic spouses have stories, vignettes and anecdotes associated with the rabbinate. As I look back over the years, I realize that I have learned a great deal as a result of certain such experiences. I wrote about many events in my memoir, but I especially tried to write about those events that, while they may have been upsetting or funny at the time, allowed me to gain from the experience. I will retell one now that I think taught me *the* most useful piece of knowledge for a rabbi's wife.

After we had been in Chicago for some months, Shim and the officers of KAM Temple decided that a merger with a neighboring congregation, Isaiah Israel, would be to the advantage of both congregations. After a short while, the merger was completed, but ironically, it turned out not to be as simple for the members of the newly-merged synagogue to get along well together. Each of the congregations had a very different personality and relationship with its rabbi. It was like an arranged marriage: it made sense, but it took time for the partners to get to love one another.

Shim and I tried hard to get to know the members from Isaiah Israel, and we were looking forward to a 50th wedding anniversary party at a fancy hotel to which we had been invited by Isaiah Israel members. We were seated with three other couples. All the men at the table, board members of the newly combined temple, had been among those giving Shim a really hard time at board meetings. I barely knew them but had heard their names from Shim. Although table conversation was not easy, we were managing.

Shortly before dessert, I left the dance floor to go to the ladies' room. After passing through the posh lounge, I entered the narrow bathroom and, fortunately, chose the farthest stall in the room. Suddenly, I heard the voices of the three women from our table. They were in the lounge and they were trashing Shim, mostly analyzing who he kissed after services and why: this one had money, or that one was all dolled up. They called him cold and unfeeling. I was furious and stayed in the stall, trying to decide how to confront them politely; after all, they were our new members. Before I could figure out what to say, they began trashing their old rabbi, Shim's partner in the newly merged congregation. They, his friends, were discussing how they hated his wet, sloppy, insincere kisses.

At that moment I realized something that I perhaps should have known already: if people want to talk, they talk. With luck, it does not affect us or change anything important. And, in any case, we can't do anything about it. Eventually, the voices faded out and the room was quiet and still. They were gone. My jumpy gut was slowly calmed by the serenity of the beautiful lounge. By the time I left the lounge, I had a peculiar sense of peace. I no longer felt angry at the women, or guilty for eavesdropping. I had not confronted them or embarrassed them.

I had not done anything I would later regret. In this instance, in good Chicago tradition, less was more.

When I reached the table, everyone was eating the grand dessert. I smiled and sat down. I saw some frantic eye contact among the women as they tried to read my expression. They dared not even ask me where I had been all that time. My God, I thought, this time I won!

This event, initially so upsetting, quickly became a very funny story. It was a good lesson for me. I was just barely beginning to digest the fact that *everything* we or the kids did, whatever decisions we made, could be grist for the gossip mill. It hardly mattered if what was being said was true or not; people, or at least some people, like to talk.

Some years later, I thought of myself on a few occasions as being in the eye of a storm. It can be quiet and peaceful inside, with life just going on as usual. Over the years, I have more than occasionally had to remind myself that what goes on "out there" is not within my control. I cannot let it affect me because there is nothing I can do about it. I cannot remember ever discussing anything like this in the Cincinnati student wives' group... or in "Rebbetzin 101."

In 1980, Shim was named successor to Rabbi Bertram Korn in Elkins Park, Pennsylvania and we returned to the Philadelphia area. I reconnected with old school friends and cousins, and it was as if I had never been away.

We all talk so much about what congregations expect of the rabbi's spouse that I smile when I think back to what Keneseth Israel expected of me when we arrived in 1980. Their only thought – and voiced desire – was that I not embarrass them! Other than that, they expected nothing. In fact, I very quickly learned that they had an unwritten rule that a spouse could not *work* at the temple, a "rule" that was enacted after problems in previous years. I had certainly expected to teach music if there was an opening in the staff. I was tentatively accepted as a volunteer music teacher, and I guess I passed muster because after a while, I did become a member of the faculty. And after working at the Philadelphia Museum of Art as a researcher for several years, I became the director/curator of the newly formed museum at the temple, and even had my own office next to the library. I gave talks on new exhibits and was right in my element, doing for my beloved synagogue the very work I had specialized in for my art history degree.

I worked at the temple. I attended services every Friday night, went to all major events, and occasionally to sisterhood meetings. But I felt as though I was doing what I might have been doing whether married to the rabbi or "just" as a congregant. How lucky for me that my own skills and interests, now very much expanded, were what they had been from my teenage years onward. The one big drawback of working at our own temple was that whatever I did was viewed as the work of the "rabbi's wife," not me as a trained professional in the arts. Someone even suggested when Shim retired that the wife of the next rabbi should be asked to "take care" of the museum, as I had done. What would have been the point of trying to explain that what I had done was to contribute my services as a professional in my field? Many years back, when I complained to Shim that my work at the temple was not appreciated, he told me, "Knowing that you did a good job and that you *enjoyed* it may be all the thanks you will ever get." (Would a rabbi, especially a *male* rabbi, accept that?) In retrospect, I am pleased to realize that my activities at the temple *were* appreciated.

Retirement for both of us has brought all kinds of other fun and excitement. We have been able to travel a great deal. Shim volunteered his services for the High Holy Days in places as far as Perth, Australia and Cape Town, South Africa, which has given us the opportunity to get to know both countries quite well. As a result of his serving as a chaplain on lovely ships, we have seen most of the world. Just before retirement, we bought a little place on the ocean in Maine. We love now spending almost half of each year there. We have been blessed with relatively good health and strength and continue to enjoy life.

Judith Blumberg Maslin, First career: piano accompanist and Hebrew day school music teacher; University of Chicago, M.A. in Art History, 1980. Second career, Jewish Museum curator and director. Married in 1954 to Simeon Maslin, ordained HUC-JIR, Cincinnati, 1957. Three children, Naomi, David and Eve. Ten grandchildren, two great-grandsons, Daniel and Yitzchak.

3

PROFESSOR AND RABBI'S WIFE

ARLENE RUBIN STIFFMAN, PH.D.

I have yet to hear a man ask for advice on how to combine marriage and a career.
– Gloria Steinem

WOULD ANYONE ASK A MAN HOW HIS CAREER CONTRIBUTED TO HIS SPOUSE'S CAREER?

WHEN I FIRST HEARD ABOUT THIS PROJECT FOR A BOOK OF CHAPTERS about the life of a rabbi's spouse, I dismissed it as "not for me," as I like to think that I define myself by my career as a professor. I was taken aback, thinking, "Would anyone ask a man this question?" After thinking about it, I realized that what threw me off is the assumption that a wife's role would be to contribute to the rabbi's career. The truth is that, although I rebel against it, much of my life has been defined as a rabbi's wife.

As I wrote this chapter, I realized how much my life has been a bridge between different types and aspects of spouse behavior, and how much it has evolved over time.

SEEDS OF DISCONTENT AND CHANGE

In the beginning, I assumed that I would have a traditional life as a rabbi's wife and would have to give up any ideas of a personal career. I certainly started that way. In fact, when Jeffrey was first an assistant rabbi, the senior rabbi's wife gave me orders for everything. She chose an apartment with Jeff that I did not even see until we moved in. I hated it. She took us shopping for better furniture, saying ours was too much "student furniture." She told me what I could wear and criticized my hats and gloves (remember those days?). (Note that she also refused to let a president of the congregation sit on the pulpit when he showed up in a brown suit.) She told us whom we could or could not entertain. Thank goodness that only lasted a short time before we moved.

Two years later, when Jeffrey returned to that congregation with the promise of succession, I made every effort to become involved in the volunteer community. However, I felt wasted. I certainly wasn't making the positive impact on the world that I had hoped. There were two personal triggers to my decision to redo my life, and two historical/environmental triggers.

The first personal trigger was a phone call from the Jewish Community Center saying that they wanted me to pour tea at an event. I could not do it, and they said, "but we need a rabbi's wife to pour." To say I felt invisible as a person is putting it mildly. The next personal triggering event was a congregational committee meeting lasting several hours which discussed the color of flowers to be ordered for Confirmation.

The first historical/environmental trigger was the divorce of a friend who had devoted herself fully to being a perfect rabbi's wife in their congregation. When her husband left her, she no longer had a role in the life she had led. The second historical/environmental trigger was the whole movement toward women's liberation that was occurring at the time.

I first decided to move to a career in which I could incorporate the community role I had played as a rabbi's wife. I decided to go for an MSW, thinking, "I might as well get paid for my community work."

When I first decided I wanted to go back to school, I trapped Jeff in the bathroom as he was brushing his teeth and told him about it. He agreed, probably because his mouth was full and he could say little else!

TIME OF PERSONAL AND FAMILY TRANSITION

I must admit that I was frightened of beginning school again, and of juggling a career, motherhood and being a rabbi's wife. Luckily, I loved school, but I soon saw that much of social work was based on unresearched approaches and assumptions. Therefore, I decided to continue for a doctorate in order to do research in the field. Neither Jeff nor I knew the impact these movements and decisions would have on our lives.

We really went through a long period of adaptation, as I was no longer able to be full-time supportive in the role of a rabbi's wife. But I was so much happier and more fulfilled. I was excited about what I was doing and the life that I was developing. That fulfillment even helped me enjoy and value my children more, as time with them became especially precious. A really fortunate part of my studies and my role as Professor was my ability to set my own schedule by coming home early in the afternoons and working evenings and weekends when Jeff and/or the children were out or busy.

TRANSITION FOR THE CONGREGATION

Obviously, I can't really say what the reaction of the congregation as a whole was. Those who spoke with me, by and large, were very supportive. I think they took the cue from Jeff, who never demanded of me or our children anything other than being ourselves. For some congregants, it never even registered that I had a career, as they were focused only on "the rabbi." Others seemed to appreciate more what I did do for the congregation. In many ways, I was lucky, largely because the prior rabbi's wife was widely resented for her interference.

One older lady told me directly that I should confine myself to doing things like being the sisterhood president. Her values were quite different than mine. For example, she always pointed out that she had her bag and shoes dyed to match each of her outfits. When she was young, several rabbis earlier in the congregation's history, she spent every day driving the rabbi on every call (he didn't drive). I never knew what her husband thought as she was a widow by the time I came to know her.

As I obtained my doctorate and advanced in my career, I received many comments of praise for being a role model. A few of the congregants were motivated to go back to school and get advanced degrees themselves, telling me I inspired them.

A NEW LIFE *VIS* THE CONGREGATION

The big question I was asked to address in this chapter was, "How did it effect my relation to the congregation?" The most important thing for me was that it enabled me to say no to things I did not enjoy. I was able to only accept tasks that related to my expertise, or that, for one reason or another, I enjoyed. For example, I did some teaching of interpersonal counseling skills to volunteer home visitors and gave some talks on adolescent problems.

I still tried to attend everything with Jeff. But I felt a real time pressure. As a professor whose colleagues all assumed the central employment role in the family, I was torn. In a career such as mine, it was necessary to work sixty or so hours a week at a minimum. I would unashamedly double dip. For example: I would go to weddings, and as Jeff signed the ketubah, and during the cocktail hour, I would find a place to edit the papers I was writing or read professional articles.

My big weakness was that I would almost always doze for a minute or two at the start of Friday services, as it was my first chance to sit down and relax all day. Luckily the cantor's wife did the same thing. Both our husbands said we were inspirational that way.

Despite my work, I always served dinner at our home to any guest speakers who came to the congregation, and we also always tried to include lonely or isolated members in our family holidays. We always had family Shabbat and holiday meals and celebrations, even if we had to rush off or have them ridiculously early, as family celebrations and meals were central to my concept of what it meant to be a Jewish family.

SOME STORIES ABOUT MY LIFE IN A CAREER

The night before I was to defend my dissertation, Jeff and I were invited to a very fancy dinner party hosted by a key congregant who loved food and wines. I wanted to decline, but Jeff insisted I go despite being nervous, and tried to convince me it would be relaxing. When we arrived, we found that they sat couples apart at tables for six without spouses, and mixed people so that no one at any table knew anyone else at that table very well. The meal was incredible, with course after course of rich French dishes. At the end of the dinner, they had a disco dance exhibition. They then turned all the lights off for a presentation of flaming cherries jubilee for dessert, which was rolled in and around the room on a cart. When they turned the lights back on, we discovered that a guest had slid off his chair and died. The room was quietly hysterical with doctors trying resuscitation, paramedics stomach pumping and everyone in silenced grief. Needless to say, I didn't sleep that night, and plowed my way through my defense in a state of shock. It ended the way I'd automatically agree to put my needs behind Jeff's and the congregation's social needs.

As I started to earn a more substantial income, we were able to increase the amount and objects of our charitable giving. When the JCCA had its first named big givers level, we gave at that level because the children and I regularly used the JCCA (Jeff never did). In the entry to the JCCA, along with the other givers, they put up plaque listing Rabbi and Mrs. Jeffrey Stiffman. I strongly felt that anyone Jeff married would be a Mrs. Stiffman and I asked that the plaque be changed to Rabbi Jeffrey and Dr. Arlene Stiffman as I thought I deserved the same respect for my degree as he got for his. The response was that there was no room on the plaque, so I said, "Then just put Jeffrey and Arlene." They said no because, "We want to advertise that the rabbi gave." I made sure that we stopped giving at that level.

One night we attended a temple fundraising event with a professional auctioneer. When it came time to bid on the right to deliver a sermon, the auctioneer announced: "Here is your chance to finally tell the rabbi what you think. Anyone who has been wanting to talk back to the rabbi should bid on this. Here is your chance!" I shot my hand up, laughing, and gave the first bid of $200.00 as a joke, knowing it would go for more. I got the laugh I was after, and something unexpected. After some wild bidding (that I never upped) a member bought it and publicly announced right there that he was giving it to me. I sat paralyzed in total shock until Jeff nudged me and whispered, "Get up and thank him. You started this!" I used the sermon to discuss women juggling careers with the roles of wife and mother.

I was in a dialogue group of women from different streams of Judaism and became friendly with the rebbetzin of St. Louis' chief Orthodox congregation. She was also a social worker, and over a period of months, we even discussed doing a book together based on interviews of rabbis' wives. We never followed through, but we did have some interesting discussions about how she used the title rebbetzin and I refused to. Every time the chief rabbi saw Jeff, he would ask him how the "Rebbetzin Who Does Not Want to Be Called

Rebbetzin" was doing. (Maybe I was the precursor to "He Who Cannot Be Named" of Harry Potter fame!)

WHAT DID I SEE AS THE BENEFITS?

Although every choice one makes in life has costs and entails regrets, I feel there were real benefits to me in several areas: personal, communal, marital, financial, and the expanding of lived worlds. None of these may apply to others with different personalities and needs.

Personally, I was much happier and more content with my everyday life. It was stimulating and satisfying, albeit stressful. I felt that I could contribute to an area in which I was valued for my own self and my personal abilities and contributions.

In the community, I felt that I became a role model for liberated women at a time when that was just emerging. No small part of this feeling was due to the fact that my career was totally outside the Jewish community in which my husband's role was centered.

Although the time constraints obviously imposed some marital exhaustion, there were many marital benefits. Not least of these was vacation time together. I traveled to many cities to present papers and, if it was an interesting city, Jeff came along and we extended a few extra days to grab a half-paid vacation together. Jeff was very proud of my accomplishments. We often laughed at how strangers at conferences would assume Jeff was the professor. When I went to Japan, our host extended his hand to Jeff and said, "Ah, Professor Stiffman, we are looking forward to hearing your talk." He was totally confused when Jeff said, "No, she is Professor Stiffman." The confusion only accelerated when Jeff said he was a rabbi and our hosts had no idea what a rabbi was.

We traveled for very little cost internationally when Jeff led tours from the congregation to Europe, Israel, Egypt, China, and Russia; and when I presented in Amsterdam, Venice, Florence, Taiwan, Barcelona, Japan and Israel. These adventurous times together would not have been possible without our dual careers.

There were also many financial benefits to us personally and to the community. Obviously, my salary made a difference, but perhaps the biggest benefit was free undergraduate tuition for all three of our children. Adding my salary to Jeff's enabled us to be much more generous to the Jewish community, the congregation, the local day school, the Jewish Federation, Washington University, and other charities. We were able to give at the level where we funded parts of buildings and scholarships, which would not have been possible otherwise.

Because our careers took place in two different (but not opposing) worlds, we each expanded the other's world view through our sharing of interests, issues, colleagues, and information. I appreciated his work as a rabbi more because I could clearly see the different skill sets he had to bring to his work that I did not. He felt the same about my role as a researcher and a professor. At home, we had a full range and variety of things to talk about, as well as different groups of friends, both in and out of the scholarly and the Jewish community, that we shared with each other. We entertained visiting scholars from my work and from his. Each world fed into the other and enhanced it. For example, when my school hired a new dean, Jeff and I invited him to our home for dinner along with some big donors from the Jewish community who had a history of contributing to the university. We served grilled salmon and had a delightful time, except that, in the process of grilling the salmon, Jeff managed to burn our house down. But we will save that tale for another time...

Dr. Stiffman is Barbara A. Bailey Professor Emeritus of Social Work at the George Warren Brown School of Social Work at Washington University in St. Louis. Her areas are at-risk youth, focusing on child and adolescent mental health and addictions, foster care, child welfare, and services. She has been a Principal Investigator on over fifteen research grants from NIDA and NIH. She developed the Gateway Provider model to help explain youths' access to services and developed instruments for evaluating youth behavior (the BRIC), youth environment, and mental health services (the SACA). She has also published on ethical issues in minority research. Over the course of her career she has authored over 100 articles and edited eight books. She is married to Rabbi Jeffrey B. Stiffman, Ph.D., ordained Cincinnati 1965; Rabbi Emeritus, Congregation Shaare Emeth, St. Louis, Missouri. They are the parents of three children and grandparents of eight.

4

JOY AND SORROW—WHERE IS THE BALANCE?

SUE WEISS

SO MY MOTHER SAID, "YOU'RE GOING TO MARRY A WHAT??????" THUS began my realization that I was beginning a new and exciting chapter in my life.

I was raised in the Oakland, California Bay Area in a very secular home. Both my parents worked hard in their jewelry business. We belonged to a classical Reform congregation, the same one my grandparents were a part of when they arrived in 1908 from Riga, Latvia. I went to religious school and was confirmed and married there, as were my older sister and brother. I don't remember ever walking into the temple with my parents for services or other holiday observances until the day I was married. Yet I knew my parents were friendly with the rabbi and his family, and their daughter was in my sister's wedding party. And I loved going to religious school (carpooling with four other temple families each Sunday) and even taking the bus by myself to other temple activities. I was also lucky enough to have a Jewish family living next door, where I enjoyed many Shabbat dinners and Hanukkah celebrations. They became a second family to me, welcoming me and treating me as one of their own. As a teenager, I became very involved in B'nai B'rith and loved my leadership roles.

Then the big event of my life happened. Although I had never been to summer camp, I applied for and was given a job at Camp Saratoga/Swig in 1965 as a girls' counselor. The program director was a young man from Los Angeles studying to be a rabbi, and we developed a friendship that turned into a budding romance. At the end of the summer, he left for Cincinnati to continue rabbinical school and I stayed in California for my senior year at Cal State, Northridge. We wrote endless letters and had a few phone calls (no cell phones in those days). We saw each other in California over winter break, and I flew to Cincinnati in the spring to see what I was getting myself into. Just a few months later, on July 3, 1966, we were married. We had never gone on dates, never had a chance to argue and make up, never really known each other the way couples might if they lived in the same town over the months of their courtship.

But I was lucky. I was marrying Ken Weiss, and as I look back on those days over fifty years ago, I think we each had qualities that enabled us to build a strong, loving, meaningful relationship and marriage.

Our professional life was very, very full, positive and ever-growing. We went from two years at HUC-JIR in Cincinnati, to three years in the Navy at Pearl Harbor, Hawaii. Our first child, Jennifer, was born there. Then we went on to Glendale, California for eight years, where our second daughter, Amy, was born. It was great to be back in California, where our entire family lived. We were also able to get involved in PARR (Pacific Association of Reform Rabbis) – which Ken later served as president) and to head back to Camp Swig for many, many summers.

◆═◆

Then, what I call Ken's "midlife crisis" mode began. He was working on his doctorate and thought he had done as much as possible at our wonderful little congregation in Glendale. He suggested we take our cute little girls (ages eight and five at the time) to Israel, to try something new and different and exciting. Oh my goodness, did this scare me! But off we went, renting an apartment, going to ulpan, sending the girls to school, welcoming lots of family who wanted to visit us while we were there. We returned and faced the prospect of having to interview at congregations in need of a new rabbi. We were most excited and fortunate to find a very warm welcome in El Paso, Texas at Temple Mt. Sinai.

I call it another "midlife crisis," but, in fact, Ken had always wanted a third child, so when Jennifer and Amy were twelve and nine years old, along came Daniel. He got himself three mothers and a congregation that welcomed him with open arms. Our twenty-two-plus years in El Paso were wonderful. The people made it so! We had a baby naming, three b'nei mitzvah, a wedding and many other celebrations that our special friends helped to host. I told Ken I was never moving again – as with each new congregation, I had another baby, and I was done! Ken and I felt very privileged to share in the joys and sorrows of so many people. He especially loved teaching the kids and excelled in life cycle ceremonies. I loved teaching at the JCC, religious school and Hebrew school. We looked forward to hosting a Rosh Hashanah open house at our home every year and having the youth group over for sukkah building and pizza parties. My special love was sisterhood. I always called it my "heart" friend. The sisterhood kitchen was my favorite place, and many days were spent preparing holiday and Shabbat dinners there with my sisterhood friends.

Another "midlife crisis" came along. (I shouldn't have been surprised!) At age sixty-one, Ken decided it was time to retire. He had always advised people to "have something to retire to." But sometimes it is hard to follow your own advice, and after six months of quiet retirement, he was looking to get involved in work again. We were fortunate to return to California and a position at Seacrest Village, a very beautiful and special Jewish senior residence in North San Diego County. Ken and I led services together at three different levels of living. We taught classes and were involved in the "golden" years of many residents. I was absolutely delighted when eight of my ninety-plus year-old students became b'not mitzvah. A standing-room-only sanctuary and even some newspaper reporters were there to enjoy and capture the event.

Life moves along for all of us, and because we had become grandparents during this time, we wanted to share in the life of our children and their children. After four years at Seacrest, we made a most unusual move. My parents were told to "move west." We were moving east! We ended up in the city of Salem, Massachusetts (known for its witch history), on the north shore of Boston. Our daughter, Jennifer, and her husband, Jonathan, who live a stone's throw away, have blessed us with seven beautiful grandchildren. Our daughter Amy and her husband Scott, who live a stone's throw plus fifty minutes away, have blessed us with two beautiful grandchildren. Our son Daniel, who continues to live in San Diego, recently married his bride, Michelle.

So now I get to the difficult part of writing a synopsis of my life. A much larger and sadder crisis befell me and my family when Ken suddenly died just before his seventy-third birthday. He was a healthy, loving, giving man, busy doing many life cycle ceremonies and teaching Torah study at the local synagogue. Both of us enjoyed our children and grandchildren fully. Both of us loved our positions as Executive Directors of NAORRR. It has now been over five years since Ken died, and I would agree with those who have gone through this experience of loss and grieving: It is the most heart-wrenching, overwhelming event I have ever had to face and live through. And grow through.

I hardly know how to put into words the emotions that float to the surface of my consciousness as I put these thoughts on paper. It is all such a big mystery. But I know what Ken would want me to do. He would want me to go on. He would tell me to "walk through the valley" and get to the other side. He would want me to be strong. And if I could talk to him (which, of course, I do in my quiet moments of solitude), I would tell him that I want him to be proud of me, that I am so grateful for what we had – our trips to visit refusniks in 1977, our stay in Minsk, Belarus for a month with the Jewish community in 2009, our twenty-one weekends as leaders for Jewish Marriage Encounter, and all the years of traveling, being close to family, sharing a life that was very well lived.

Ken was always aware of how much I treasured my role as "the rabbi's wife." And he would tell me how important it was for me to be aware that someday I would not be "the rabbi's wife." How did he know that would happen? I would tell him that it hasn't been easy. I am constantly learning and evaluating my identity. I like being a busy and involved and giving person, and although his influence is always there, as if he's sitting on my shoulder, I know, too, that it's okay to just be me, Sue, doing what I believe I can to make the world better. That was always our goal. I would also tell him I know I am not alone. I have felt the support of so many friends and family, and I continue to stay in touch with people from all our congregations. They have been "my rabbis," confirming for me always what a special person Ken was and that his memory will always be for a blessing. My heart sometimes overflows with tears, but it also overflows with gratitude.

So...back to my mother. Why did she say, "You're going to marry a what??????" She told me I would always live in a "glass fishbowl" and would never own a fur coat (the standard measure of economic success in those days). My mother was an absolutely terrific person, but she was wrong. I did own a fur coat for a while. A lovely furrier in our first congregation saw to it that Ken could buy me one for our tenth wedding anniversary. And if we lived in a glass fishbowl, nothing could make me happier or prouder than to live our life the way Ken and I did and represent the joy and blessing of Judaism and Jewish life.

I know that for every human being there is joy and sorrow as life unfolds. My goal now is to find the balance, to look at the glass as "half full," to acknowledge that I have so many blessings, to push through and jump over the hurdles, to cry when I need to cry and laugh whenever possible, and to fill my days with hope and gratitude.

Sue Weiss was born and raised in Oakland, California and graduated from California State University in Northridge. She has spent most of her life teaching in religious school and JCC pre-school and doing volunteer work. Ken was ordained in l968 at HUC-JIR Cincinnati.

5

REFLECTIONS ABOUT OUR CCAR SPOUSE SUPPORT GROUP

PRISCILLA POLLER

I BELIEVE I SHOULD BEGIN BY EXPRESSING OUR COLLECTIVE GRATITUDE to Rabbis Joseph Glaser and Elliot Stevens, both of blessed memory, who were so very supportive of our efforts. Agathe Glaser, Louise Stern and Priscilla Stern, all of whom had wonderful insights, served as our Steering Committee. Sadly, all of them also are no longer with us.

At the time we began our efforts, many spouses already had begun to work outside the home and beyond their volunteer life in the congregation or were just entering the work force. Many expressed feelings of being pulled between their family and home responsibilities and the expectations of congregants. They wanted to talk, to hear about others' experiences and to get help in finding ways to cope.

The opportunities our spouse support group gave each of us to share thoughts and feelings created an openness that I hope still prevails among rabbis' spouses. I am most grateful that, even though we are no longer involved in the "active rabbinate," many of us are still in touch with one another and continue to treasure those friendships.

May it be so for those who are now in the active rabbinate. And, if it is not, then I hope this reminder of the critically important spouse support network that functioned in the CCAR for many years will be the impetus for the creation of a similar group designed to meet the needs of rabbinic spouses today.

Priscilla (Marks) Poller is originally from Winthrop, Massachusetts, and graduated from Burdett College in Boston. She worked in Boston for the Combined Jewish Appeal as Director of the Youth Division, and then at the UAHC in New York for the National Federation of Temple Youth. She married Rabbi H. Leonard Poller in 1957, the year he was ordained from HUC-JIR in Cincinnati. Len spent the majority of his career as the rabbi of Larchmont Temple (Temple Har-Chayim), in Larchmont, New York. This proximity to Manhattan gave Priscilla the opportunity to interact with many rabbinic spouses, and she helped found and became the first chair of the CCAR Spouse Support Group. Len and Priscilla had three daughters – Judith, Sharon and Elyse. Leonard Poller died in 1998.

6

FOUR POEMS

BY PRISCILLA RUDIN STERN

INTRODUCTION

My mom, Priscilla Rudin Stern, was born on August 8, 1934, to Rabbi Jacob Philip Rudin and Elsie Katz Rudin. She grew up in Great Neck, New York, where her father was founding rabbi of Temple Beth El. She went to – and loved – Wellesley College. Mom met dad in Great Neck during his time as my grandfather's assistant. They fell in love and had a secret courtship. My grandfather announced their engagement at my father's farewell party from the congregation. Dad married the boss's daughter and skipped town!

My mother loved reading, especially fiction and poetry. She loved language in all its forms and was the poet laureate of our family. She was a tireless volunteer at the temple and beyond it and was always so proud to have helped start the CCAR Spouse Support Network. She taught us the importance of learning and justice every day. She loved mentoring younger rabbis and their families. She was smart, articulate, passionate, brave, stylish, unfiltered and filled with life during every moment of her own, which was tragically too short. She died from a fast spreading pancreatic cancer in May 2000, at the age of sixty-five. Dad's word for her in those months was "gallant." That says it all. I am pleased that some of her poems are included in her memory in this volume.

- Rabbi David Stern

◆═◆

VOICES

God spoke to Adam
And Adam spoke to Eve
And forever there would be voices in the world.

Voices draw us in;
Debate and dissent
Conversation and consensus.

Raise your voice;
A voice to raise children
A voice to raise money
A voice to raise spirits.

Shout out against the hypocrites
Rage against the bigots.
Raise your voice in song
In praise of God.

And hear, always,
That quiet voice,
That still small voice, of the heart.

SING A NEW SONG

We pray that we may sing a new song –
a song that is as old as our faith itself,
a song that was new for David as he sang Your praise,
a song that rang triumphant from the ram's horn,
a melody of Torah from the lips of every generation,
a chant that ran with blood as our people sang, "I believe," in their darkest hour;
a soaring chorus as a remnant stood once again at the Wall and proclaimed "Shema Yisrael,"
a song of peace and justice in our day,
a song that will be heard by everyone everywhere!

MEDITATION

We reach for You, our God
        from our quiet places.
May we stand still
        for a brief moment and listen to the rain –
Stand still for a brief
moment and watch the play of sunlight
and shadows on the leaves.
For a brief moment –
        listen to the world.
Let us stop the wheels
of everyday to be aware of Shabbat.
Find the stillness of the sanctuary
which the soul cherishes.
Renew the Covenant
        of an ancient people.
We need a quiet
space to test the balance of our days, the weight
of our own needs against the heaviness
of the world's demands.
The balance is
        precarious – steady us with faith.
Quiet places and
stillness – where we will
hear our own best impulses speak.
Quiet places and
        stillness – from which
we will reach out to each other.
We will find strength in silence
and with this strength we will
        turn again to Your service.

WALK WITH ME INTO THE WOODS

Walk with me into the woods.
Leave the edge of the forest behind –

Come deep into the green
until the shafts of
sunlight are lost.
Feel the stillness of the center.

Walk with me to the top
of the hill.
Leave the broad path
behind.
Up – up beyond where
the trees grow.
Hear the quiet of the heights.

Walk with me into
        this New Year –
Into its demands
into its joys
into the clamor of its unfolding.

Walk alone
        each on her own right
        path
With the echoes of the blasts of the shofar
with the stillness of the
        center
with the help of our God.

Priscilla Stern's husband, Rabbi Jack Stern, was ordained by HUC-JIR in Cincinnati in 1952. David Stern, a recent president of the Central Conference of American Rabbis, is the senior rabbi of Temple Emanu-El of Dallas, Texas.

7

THE RABBI'S WIFE

JANICE ROTHSCHILD BLUMBERG

THE MAKING OF A SOUTHERN REBBETZIN

AFTER I MARRIED JACK ROTHSCHILD, PEOPLE CONSTANTLY TOLD ME: "But you don't look like one." I recognized that they intended it as a compliment, but it really bothered me. Why should a rabbi's wife look different from anyone else? And what exactly was it that they expected us to be? Frowzy, of course. Homely, depressed, ill-clothed and over-fed? The implication was so insulting that I failed to be flattered at being judged otherwise. When such remarks were addressed to him, Jack replied, "Rabbis have better taste than rabbis' wives."

Either way, generalizations are unfair and by now most of those have been proven untrue...

◆═◆

I was totally unprepared to marry a rabbi. I even stumbled over the title. It was an advantage to be in my hometown and in the congregation where I grew up because I knew all of the old families and was accustomed to socializing with them. It was also a disadvantage. Friends with complaints (a.k.a. "friendly suggestions") about the rabbi – but not enough chutzpah to tell him – told me instead. One woman, whose husband was president of The Temple at the time, counseled me to tell Jack that it didn't look nice for him to play golf at the club on Saturday afternoon. I didn't have the nerve to ask her how that differed from her husband playing tennis there on the same day. Nor did I have the nerve to inform her that Reform Judaism doesn't restrict leisure activities on the Sabbath. I just bit my tongue and said, "Thanks."

Times have changed, and busy, dedicated rabbis seem to spend more hours with their families than they did in our day. Many of them then had little time for us and even less for our children, which brought far more grief to the kids than to us. We mothers also were frequently absent and rarely took the children with us as parents do today. We chose the life we led. They didn't, and were not equipped to deal with it.

As unsure of myself as I was, I consulted a child psychiatrist to set me on the right track. "Jack and I understand the pressures put on preachers' kids," I told him. "We discussed it even before they were born and agreed not to hold ours up as examples to the other kids. We don't expect them to be role models."

The doctor leaned back in his chair and smiled. "There's where the problem starts," he said. "Do you think that the grocer and his wife have a conversation like that when they are expecting their first child?"

Indeed. Just by anticipating the problem, we initiated it.

Even in bygone days, being a rabbi's wife brought many advantages and much joy, in my case well outweighing the gloom. There were funny incidents such as the time we gave a party for the temple board and found a note on the pillow of our old-fashioned double bed, saying, "My husband couldn't even sleep on a bed this small if he were alone."

The father of a bride, watching ushers escort guests to their seats, responded to my compliment on the beauty of formality even at a very small wedding such as that, by proudly crediting his wife with having made the arrangements. "Before the ceremony," he said, "she laid out a diaphragm for each guest."

Then there was the woman who complimented Jack after a funeral he had conducted, saying "That was a beautiful urology."

The best one of all is too good to withhold, even though I wasn't there to hear it. A local businessman, philanthropist and community leader, was seated on a dais between two rabbis, Jack Rothschild on one side and the newly ordained twenty-something year old Orthodox Emanuel Feldman on the other. Friends who belonged to both congregations had horses, which they made available to both rabbis, avid riders who often rode together. The rabbis were discussing their experiences while waiting for the event to begin, which caused the elderly philanthropist to turn his head back and forth as if at a tennis match. Wearying of this and somewhat surprised by the subject, he pointed his finger in the younger rabbi's face and asked in his inimitable Jewish accent, "You ride?"

"Sure," Feldman replied. "Do you think only Reform rabbis ride horseback?"

"No," said the philanthropist, "but when a Reform rabbi falls off a horse, the people ask, 'Did he get hurt?' When an Orthodox rabbi falls off a horse the people ask, 'What was he doing on a horse?'"

Being the rabbi's wife gave me many advantages that I would not have had otherwise. If I had not been thrust into leadership in the sisterhood, I might never have known I had a talent for writing historical or religious programs and parodied musicals. Later, as a rookie journalist freelancing without professional training, I was unlikely to have been taken seriously by editors had they not known me (and been able to introduce me) as the wife of Rabbi Rothschild.

My first sisterhood production, a parody of Gilbert & Sullivan entitled, "Trial by Jewry," launched me on a series of wider opportunities within Atlanta's Jewish community. A professional dancer and choreographer, Hildegarde Bennett, saw it and spotted me as a potential partner in writing a benefit show that she had been engaged to produce for B'nai B'rith. Thus began an ongoing partnership in which we produced a series of shows for local Jewish organizations and were jokingly known as Atlanta's answer to Rogers and Hammerstein.

At the same time, I was writing and producing for the sisterhood more serious pieces, which Jack thought worthy of repeating as creative services on Shabbat. This was not without its downside, for the task of directing them initially fell to me. On one occasion, adapting the original staging to suit the larger space of the sanctuary involved my giving a direction with which some of the performers disagreed. When I stood firm, one of the women sweetly suggested that they vote on it.

From my experience in acting and in orchestras, I knew it was unheard of to question a director's instruction. Further flabbergasted at the notion of voting on it, I could only blurt out, "Would you have made a suggestion like that to Hildegarde?"

"That's different," came the reply. "She's a professional."

So much for giving of oneself as a volunteer. Thereafter when the sisterhood presented something that I wrote, they had to hire a professional to direct it.

Even before my first visit to Israel and love affair with Zionism, I wrote an inspirational piece for the UJA Women's Campaign that drew high praise and invitations to present it at subsequent events, one of which was a state convention of Hadassah. After the performance, one of the longtime leaders came up to me, gave me a big hug, and with tears in her eyes said, "Don't tell me you're not a Zionist. You couldn't have written that if you weren't one."

In fact, I wasn't a Zionist when I wrote it. I was simply a Jewish woman becoming aware of the need to support a Jewish state. I doubt I would have been sensitive to that had I not married a rabbi.

With each visit to Israel, I felt more attached and more involved in projects designed to help it. I wrote other presentations for UJA campaigns, one of them a documentary produced at WAGA-TV that won a national award. Asked to head the Women's Campaign for Israel Bonds in 1969, I agreed on condition that all of Atlanta's other rebbetzins join as co-chairs. They consented, after which I invited them to our home for a planning session.

The significance of the others joining me as co-chairs was far more than symbolic, for there wasn't enough interest from within our own congregation then to support the event.

In the effort to free Soviet Jewish prisoners of conscience, national Jewish women's organizations held annual protest events in their various cities, each group taking its turn as sponsor. When responsibility fell to the National Federation of Temple Sisterhoods (now, Women of Reform Judaism), I co-chaired it in Atlanta with our sisterhood president. We asked Betty Talmadge, wife of Georgia Senator Herman Talmadge, to be honorary chairwoman, and leaders of our parallel Protestant and Catholic women's organizations to be honorary co-chairs. The program, held in The Temple sanctuary, featured the Spelman College choir singing their spirituals that echo the call for freedom, then also significant to the plight of Soviet Jews. As a climax, the Christian churchwomen walked down the aisles, depositing on the bimah baskets of petitions containing thousands of signatures of Christian women throughout Georgia protesting Soviet treatment of its Jews. The plan was for Betty Talmage and me to deliver them to the Soviet embassy in Washington the following day.

In Washington, on the day after our event, Betty and I met at noon directly across from the Soviet embassy, where B'nai B'rith sponsored a daily vigil protesting the Soviet action. Senator Talmadge had asked Ambassador Anatoly Dobrynin to receive us. When refused, he then asked for Mrs. Dobrynin to receive us, and was told that she would see Mrs. Talmadge, but not Mrs. Rothschild. Nevertheless, Betty and I joined the vigil, and when it ended, we crossed the street with the baskets of petitions to ask admittance to the embassy. We were rebuffed, as expected.

◆═◆

One thing I could never remember was not to speak to people who had stopped speaking to Jack and me. We never knew why they didn't talk to us, of course. We accepted it as one of life's mysteries to which rabbis were especially susceptible. When people asked Jack why two specific women who had originally embraced him suddenly stopped speaking to him, he admitted that he didn't know but conjectured, "I think it's because every time they see me it reminds them that they're Jewish." Alfred Uhry unknowingly corroborated that theory by caricaturing one of those women as the social climbing daughter-in-law in *Driving Miss Daisy*. There were many more, however, who – raised in an earlier era when outward signs of Jewishness were considered déclassé – flinched at our increasing manifestations of cultural acceptance.

THE BOMBING

The most traumatic event of my life with Jack began when the telephone awakened us shortly after seven o'clock on Sunday morning, October 12, 1958. He scurried to my side of the bed to answer. After a long, horrified, "Oh, no!" followed by, "I'll be right there," he put down the receiver and told me, "The Temple's been bombed."

Robert Benton, The Temple's devoted custodian, wept as he spoke. He had discovered the damage when he opened the building for religious school. Dynamite placed against a door on the north side of the building had detonated inward, devastating everything in its path. A massive steel vault in one of the offices protected the sanctuary and rabbi's study.

Jack dressed as he told me about it, grabbing whatever clothes remained out from the night before. I sat upright in bed, trying to focus. As he reached for a sport shirt, I heard myself say, "Wear a coat and tie. There may be reporters."

It was completely out of character. I had never advised him what to wear.

"Don't be ridiculous," he shouted from the bathroom. "This is an emergency, not a fashion show."

Nevertheless, he put on a dress shirt and tie, and reached for a jacket as he raced out, calling back instructions for me to stay home and field telephone calls.

My fashion advice was justified the next morning when we saw a New York newspaper, its front page featuring a picture of him with the mayor captioned, "Mayor Hartsfield and the hatless rabbi." Mayor Hartsfield had been on his way to church and was dressed accordingly when he heard the news.

As I began calling friends to tell them not to bring their children to Sunday school, my own children, obviously awakened, indicated that they also needed attention. I told them what had happened and sent them off on their bicycles to tell Temple members in the neighborhood that there would be no religious school that day.

The news spread quickly. President Dwight Eisenhower mentioned it later in the morning at a largely Jewish political rally in New York. From then on, our telephone rang without pause. I couldn't leave it even long enough to get a cup of coffee.

A friend picked up Bill to spend the day with her son, and another friend came with her seven-year old son to help me. Her husband, as vice president of the congregation and president of the Jewish Community Council, hurried to The Temple to help Jack. Still on automatic, I canceled my Monday morning hair appointment and arranged for someone to pick up from my outdoor freezer the sandwiches I had promised for the Monday night opening reception at Theatre Atlanta.

At supper time, with the phone continuing to ring, Julie heated leftovers as I continued to answer the phone, endlessly repeating, "Thank you. We appreciate your concern."

She had just put the plates of warmed-over spaghetti on the table for herself and the kids and handed me mine at the telephone when the call came that was unlike all the others. "I'm one of them that bombed your church," the caller said, "and I'm callin' to tell you there's a bomb under your house and it's lit and you've got five minutes to get out."

Still in shock, I said, "Thank you," and hung up.

Julie, who was five months pregnant, asked "What was that?" and I automatically repeated it, not thinking how it might affect her and the children. Before I regained common sense, she had scaled the retaining wall behind our garden with the children. With Laffy, the dog, barking and the children yelling for me to get out of the house, I stood at the door dazed, wondering whether to save my fur coat or my violin. I believed the call was a hoax but couldn't risk being wrong.

We called our husbands from our neighbor's house. They soon arrived with police and FBI agents. I found myself wondering who hated us enough to have set the bomb...

Later, as we sat returning phone calls, we suddenly noticed a strange man with a rifle on the other side of our jalousied door. He quickly allayed our fears, identifying himself as a special police agent, called back from his vacation in the North Georgia mountains to protect us. Hence the rifle and casual dress.

Finally, we went to bed. I lay awake, seemingly for hours. I couldn't stop wondering if we would wake up the next morning... Suddenly the telephone rang. I grabbed it, hoping it wouldn't disturb him. The caller was a reporter from New York, asking to speak to the rabbi. I whispered that the rabbi was asleep. It had been a grueling day and I didn't want to disturb him. The reporter persisted, and so did I. Finally, despairing of sleep, Jack reached across me for the telephone.

"This is Rabbi Rothschild," he said. "What can I do for you?"

"Was that Mrs. Rothschild I was talking to?" the reporter asked.

Now thoroughly awake, Jack growled, "If it wasn't Mrs. Rothschild, do you really think I'd tell you?"

His sense of humor helped preserve our sanity. The next day, when people asked him if I was upset by what had happened, he told them, "She sure is. With me. She's been telling me all summer that our downspouts needed painting and I neglected to have it done. Now, she says, our house is on television and the whole world can see how bad it looks."

Jack determined that our life and that of the congregation would proceed as usual. On Monday, the sisterhood held its meeting as scheduled, but at the community center, not The Temple. He transferred his Temple committee meeting on Tuesday night to our house so as to be there with the children while I went to a PTA board meeting at their school. My presence wasn't necessary, but that wasn't the point.

I was accustomed to worrying about his safety, but now I feared for our children. I questioned the advisability of having the police guarding our driveway in a squad car and asked our friend, the child psychiatrist, what I should do.

"I can't predict what might happen to the children physically if you dismiss the police," the doctor told me, "but I do know what harm will occur emotionally if you don't."

I dismissed the police immediately and had the fright of my life that afternoon when Bill didn't come home from school as expected. He showed up in time for dinner, having forgotten to call to say he'd gone home with a friend. He couldn't understand my hysteria.

The night of the bombing, when the FBI questioned me about the call, I replied that it was a man's voice speaking ungrammatically and sounding as if it came from middle Georgia. Since that was more detail than they had expected, Jack explained that acting was my hobby and I could recognize different accents. Ten days later, the FBI asked me to listen to tapes of the five men who had been indicted reading transcripts of the calls reported by all of us who had received them, hoping to get a confession if I identified the right man. I did, and he confessed but later repudiated it, none of which I knew at the time of the trial. I couldn't understand why in cross-examination the defense attorney used every means possible to discredit me, pelting me with rambling questions that included false statements, misleading implications and deprecating asides.

Eventually the defense attorney, Reuben Garland, turned from trying to smear me as a capitalist to what he apparently hoped would reflect on my moral character, peppering his questions with references to my "career" on the stage. I had succeeded in getting a role in *Anne of the Thousand Days*, which was playing then. Each time he suggested that I was an actress I demurred, adding some mitigating detail such the fact that I majored in theater arts at the University of Georgia, or that I volunteered for Theatre Atlanta as a cultural enhancement for the city. Finally, he blurted out angrily, "But you do consider yourself an actress, do you not?"

I certainly did at that point, but I wouldn't admit it to him. As demurely as possible I innocently drawled, "Why, Mr. Garland! That's not for me to say."

He didn't give up easily. It was then that he recalled my alleged ability to identify regional accents, grilled me about the telephone call, and asked me to imitate the accent I had heard. Judge Jephtha Tanksley told me I wasn't required to comply, so I didn't.

"Why not?" asked Garland, gleefully anticipating the kill.

"Because it isn't dignified," I replied.

"Oh?" he questioned with feigned surprise. "You put your dignity above the life of my poor innocent client?"

A divine hand must have been holding cue cards for me. I could never have thought of those answers on my own. "No, Mr. Garland," I said. "I meant the dignity of the court."

After ninety minutes, Garland succeeded in winding me to the breaking point. With his seemingly innocuous question that caused me to think of how the event had affected our children, I choked with emotion and the floodgates opened. Judge Tanksley excused me and directed his clerk to take me to his chambers. The afternoon paper carried the news as its front-page lead, captioned, "Rabbi's Wife Ties Griffin to Threat."

That night, between acts at the theater, our director told me to wait so he could follow me home after the show. He didn't say why, only that Jack had called and asked him to do so. At home I learned our housekeeper had received an anonymous call saying, "You tell Mrs. Rothschild that she identified the wrong man, and she'll pay for it."

The following week I was again summoned to court. This time the defense attorney questioned me in detail about what I did on the day of the bombing. His voice dripping with sarcasm, he asked why I hadn't bothered to go to The Temple to see the damage. Having again been wound into an emotional knot, I broke. "Because I considered it more important to keep people from bringing their children there for Sunday school than it was to satisfy my curiosity!" I retorted between sobs.

Again, the afternoon paper carried the story, this time with the caption, "Tearful Rabbi's Wife Ends Testimony."

Jack predicted that the accused would go free and his attorney go to jail, and that's exactly what happened. George Bright was acquitted and Tanksley sentenced Garland to forty days for contempt of court, mainly because of the way he treated me. He went to jail wearing blue satin pajamas. While in jail he ran for the office of state solicitor and called me to ask my help getting the Jewish vote. "I was just trying to save the life of my poor, innocent client," he cooed. "I don't dislike Jewish people and I'd appreciate it if you'd tell your folks at The Temple so they'd vote for me."

One can't make up such a story. Flabbergasted, I replied, "Mr. Garland, your lack of respect for the American system of jurisprudence is so appalling that whether you are anti-Semitic or not is totally irrelevant."

Jack overheard and told me I should have said, "I wouldn't vote for you even if you were Jewish."

THE KINGS AND I

I was never truly an activist, but I felt a deeply personal anger at southern politicians' reactions to the Supreme Court ruling on public school desegregation, and whenever I saw an opportunity, I tried to contribute in my own way to the struggle for social justice. Sitting at services on the High Holy Days one year, I realized how the Akedah story, the sacrifice of Isaac, related to our own times. Each night, watching television news, we saw six-year old children in other southern cities, dressed in their finest for the first day of school, walking the gauntlet between rows of angry white adults, mean-faced women shouting epithets and even spitting on them because they were entering a school previously restricted for white children only. As I listened to the story of Abraham preparing to obey God even when he thought that meant sacrificing his beloved only son, I thought of those children and their parents who must have anguished much as Abraham did when they faced their own test of faith in following God's way.

With that story in mind, I wrote "The Sacrifice," a dialogue between two fictional parents based on what I knew at that time about Martin and Coretta King, who had just moved from their welcoming surroundings in Boston to the moral "wilderness" of Alabama. At the time, they had only one child. I had not yet met the Kings and could only guess at their feelings from what was reported in the press. "The Sacrifice" was performed in a number of churches as well as on public radio.

In 1954, when the Supreme Court decision outlawing segregation in public schools forced action in Georgia, the local director of the National Conference of Christians and Jews organized a day-long seminar exploring the bases of prejudice. One part of the program was a panel of four mothers representing different races and religions, discussing the subject "Rearing Children of Good Will." The panelists were Eleanor Troutman Bockman, a Catholic; Dorothy Wang, a Protestant; Coretta Scott King, and me. As its planners hoped, the panel spawned ongoing invitations for us to repeat it at churches, PTA meetings, and other all-white groups sincerely trying to adapt to what they feared would be a disastrous situation when schools implemented the court decision. Our program drew so many invitations that we had to get substitutes for ourselves when we were unavailable.

◆═◆

My mother, who was born and raised in Columbus, Georgia, lost her southern mores the year she attended Smith College. To my grandparents' dismay, she absorbed Massachusetts liberalism immediately and permanently. It was at Mother's home that I first met the Kings. In 1960, soon after they moved to Atlanta, she met Martin while having lunch with an African American friend at Paschal's, one of the only two restaurants in town where "mixed dining" was allowed. Upon learning that Coretta was a musician, Mother invited them to dinner, also inviting us and a few close friends. I sought to follow her lead, but both Martin and Jack had such busy schedules that it took some six months to find an evening when both of them were free. Jack quipped that, "With Martin, it was literally true."

In November 1960, while Jack was on a fact-finding trip abroad, I learned that Martin had been arrested during a peaceful attempt by students to be served food at Rich's department store. I called Coretta to offer sympathy, and we continued in our conversation for almost an hour. She told me that she and Martin realized he would undoubtedly go to jail some time, but they were not expecting it so soon and had not yet prepared their children for it.

I knew that they had two children then, younger than ours, but I didn't know how much younger. "I'm not so concerned about Marty," she said referring to Martin Luther III. "He's too young to know what's happened. But Yoki [Yolanda] heard about it on the car radio on her way home from school, and I need to explain it to her."

Coretta shared with me some of the problems that she and other mothers of color encountered trying to raise their children with healthy self-esteem in an overwhelmingly white society. Until then, I hadn't thought of what it meant for newspapers to publish pictures only of Caucasian brides, models and other glamorous women. I'd forgotten that leading roles in movies and on stage also were played by whites only. And I had forgotten how I myself felt as a girl growing up looking Semitic in the days before Sophia Loren and Barbra Streisand showed the Western world that one did not need to have a straight nose and a figure like Twiggy to be considered beautiful.

◆═◆

When we finally did set a date for the Kings to come to dinner, I invited a few others including the president of our congregation and his wife, my mother and several close friends.

A disturbing conversation took place when the Kings first arrived at our house that night, late by more than an hour. Although we assured them that it was okay, Martin insisted on giving a full explanation. There were several causes, but he wanted to be sure that we understood the last and most difficult of them: being unfamiliar with our part of town and unable to read house numbers because our street was so poorly lighted, he and Coretta finally resorted to driving up to one of the houses to inquire. "But I was very careful not to embarrass you with your neighbors," Martin said. "I let Coretta go to the door so they wouldn't recognize me and would figure we were just here to serve a party."

I still choke up when I think about that. It was really so, in those days. People of color, after dark in what is now known as Buckhead, were seen either as servants or suspects.

Coretta amazed me with her ability to entertain at the drop of a hat. With young children and no regular household help, she put together a luncheon for twenty women on one day's notice to honor Xernona Clayton, when the television personality from California relocated in Atlanta. The affair was lovely, but what impressed me even more than the hostess's expertise was the fact that her husband, busy as he was, took time out to help by driving the children's carpool and then coming in to chat with the ladies for a few minutes. In those days, it was most unusual for a father to substitute in what was typically considered women's work.

In 1967, with schools and other public facilities finally open to all by federal law, the fight to end de facto segregation was still by no means over. Although I didn't realize it at the time, the situation for people of color in America was parallel to what we Jews had been experiencing ever since Napoleon gave our ancestors the rights of citizenship in Western Europe. Being legally accepted was only the first step to being actually accepted – and it could take a very long time to reach that next level.

◆═◆

When Martin Luther King, Jr. received the Nobel Prize for Peace, Jack went with a few others to Mayor Ivan Allen to say that the city should honor its first Nobel laureate. The mayor wholeheartedly agreed, and plans proceeded, chaired by the editor, Ralph McGill, Archbishop Paul Hallinan, Morehouse College president Benjamin Mays, and Jack, whom they designated as emcee for the dinner.

The event exceeded anything we could have imagined. The 1,000 places that the committee hoped to fill were sold out a week in advance.

◆═◆

When Martin was assassinated, Jack and I saw it almost immediately on the news. Father Noel Burtenshaw, aide to Archbishop Paul Hallinan who lay in the hospital close to death himself, picked up Jack in a driving rain later that evening to visit Coretta. They wouldn't let me go with them because they expected to encounter violence in the streets. Mercifully, there was none. Jack reported finding Coretta alone, calm, and appreciative of their visit.

We were not invited to Martin's funeral. We didn't make the cut because there were too many others, dignitaries who had to be accommodated in the small church while still leaving room for its members. We understood, but rather than standing in the crowd outside on the street in the broiling sun, we felt we could better honor

Martin in the quiet of our home where we could hear and see the service on television.

Shortly after that, I wrote a story about Coretta for the Atlanta Journal & Constitution Sunday Magazine in which I described her in personal terms as I knew her then. Charlotte Hale Smith, one of the city's top journalists who worked on the paper, read it in manuscript and commended me on it even before it was published. I appreciated that – especially coming from her – and was especially pleased by a note of thanks from Coretta herself.

I also received an anonymous letter saying, "I'm glad I am not a Jew. My Jewish neighbors were deeply hurt after reading your article."

That's the way things were.

LOOKING BACK

Those were scary times. I wouldn't want to relive them, but neither do I regret having experienced them. Although it may seem curious, I look back on them as part of the good side of being married to the rabbi. They fostered growth of spirit, tests of inner strength, broader views and interaction with the community, and they greatly enhanced my life in the long run. Jack's sense of humor saved us from many a difficult situation, especially in severe times such as those.

Developing a thick skin was a primary requisite for my rebbetzinhood. I could not have survived without it. Rabbis' wives come in all shapes, sizes and personalities. Among those I've encountered, some wanted to become rabbis themselves and were born too soon to fulfill that dream. As a result, they shadowed – and in some cases overshadowed – their husbands as unpaid, usually unappreciated assistants. Others reject all vestiges of the role. It's no life for the faint-hearted. To survive the loneliness, the spotlight and the slings and arrows of outrageous circumstances, one needs, above all, a good sense of humor. Of equal importance, in the days before women's liberation, we required a passion for doing something on our own. Whether with a hobby or assisting our husband, we needed to fight for our identity. So did everyone else, but I suspect that we needed to be somewhat more aggressive about it.

My choice was writing. After reading Jacob Marcus' books on American Jewish history, I became increasingly fascinated with the subject and wanted to interpret it for the great majority of my peers who were unlikely to learn it otherwise. In 1955, with The Temple sisterhood as my captive audience and the newly celebrated 300th anniversary of Jewish settlement in America just passed, I wrote and produced a pageant about Jewish women in America from colonial times to our own. Its success led Jack to ask if I'd like to tackle the task of writing our congregation's hundred-year history, due for celebration in 1967.

I couldn't resist the challenge. Unprepared as I was, I began by questioning Dr. Marcus himself, a dear friend since Jack's days as his student and sometimes bridge partner at HUC. He was walking with us to a session of the CCAR at the old Edgewater Beach hotel in Chicago when I seized the opportunity.

"Do you have some sort of tutorial that I could study?" I asked.

He said yes, that he would send it to me. Then he smiled, patted me on the head, and told Jack, "Encourage her, my boy. It will keep her out of trouble."

Wow! He was right, of course, and I wasn't yet liberated enough to resent it.

A decade later, the CCAR commissioned Dr. Theodore Lenn and his associates to do a report on the state of the Reform rabbinate. I was asked to write a critique of the section on the rabbi's wife for the CCAR Journal, and I did not give that portion good grades. In my view, the absence of a breakdown on the age of the respondents rendered the conclusions valueless. "After twenty-five years of attending CCAR hen sessions," I wrote, "I see an entirely new ball game in rebbetzinville than the one I entered. Our generation formed relationships and habits before women's lib, traffic conditions, mobile society, and the disappearance of domestic help changed almost everyone's way of life."

In 1972, Rabbi Malcolm Stern invited me to give a paper on early Atlanta Jewish history at the conference of the American Jewish Historical Society. I was thrilled out of my skin to be asked to speak to historians, and not a little intimidated. It didn't help my self-confidence to receive a telling put-down upon arrival. It was early Saturday afternoon and attendees were still seated for Shabbat lunch at Temple Beth Ahabah. As I edged through the crowd to my table, friends greeted me asking, "Where's Jack? "We're looking forward to hearing his paper tomorrow."

His paper?

Granted, in those days married women were usually deprived of their given names when mentioned in print, and the program did list me as Mrs. Jacob Rothschild, but still...

Now, in the 21st century, when our lives have changed so much more, it may be impossible to visualize the life an average well-meaning, reasonably intelligent "wife of" in those days, regardless of the husband's profession. As to my own, which was by no means pure joy, I must clearly declare that it contained some wonderful moments and rated far above average on the bright side. I recognized my good fortune in being married to a man of extraordinary intelligence, remarkable foresight and impeccable integrity. And I savored the moments of being with him at the vortex of historical change, in the eye of the storm.

I also realized that the unjustified assessment, "But you don't look like one," also contained the even less justified implication, "But you don't act like one," both of which are now, I hope, buried in a dusty archive.

Things have changed, of course, but generations of us walked the line trying to please everyone, and frequently on a very small budget.

Happily, our children survived their dysfunctional environment and became productive, law-abiding adults. Not all our rabbinic friends of that era were so fortunate.

This essay was excerpted and adapted from What's Next? by Janice Rothschild Blumberg,

Janice Rothschild Blumberg is a historian and freelance journalist. Wife of Jacob M. (Jack/ Racky) Rothschild, HUC Cincinnati, 1936, d. 1973; mother of Bill Rothschild, HUC-JIR 1980, Cincinnati. Married David M. Blumberg 1975, (d. 1989). She is a native of Atlanta, Georgia where she currently resides, and lived in Washington, D.C. from 1976 – 2009.

8

WHEN WE PAY HER WHAT WE PAY JIMMY

SHELLEY KESSLER

DURING THE TIME JIMMY AND I WERE DATING, HE TOLD ME ABOUT A speaker who had addressed his senior class at HUC-JIR. The speaker was the wife of the Director of Placement of the CCAR. Her presentation centered on the life of a rabbi and his/her spouse. Jimmy was ordained in 1972, with the first American female rabbi, and Mrs. Stern spoke to the few wives present about their obligation to help make their spouses successful. Mrs. Stern was a lovely woman, and her suggestions were practical advice for the rabbinic spouses of her generation.

Among her recommendations were some related to the home: the house should always be clean and ready for company; there should be cakes and cookies in the freezer, ready to serve to any congregant who just happened to show up. All members of the congregation should be invited over once a year. She should never be her husband's messenger; she should be involved in everything with the congregation, but not its leader.

This is the image of a rabbi's spouse that I grew up with. My dear uncle and aunt, Rabbi Morris and Julia Kertzer, were the quintessential rabbinic couple of their time. Mrs. Stern's presentation could have been made using my aunt as the role model. In my eyes, my Aunt Julia was the perfect rebbetzin, doing everything she was supposed to do to support her husband in his role as rabbi.

However, the problem was that this was not me. I am a child of the rebellious 'sixties and 'seventies. Jimmy told me that, at the end of Mrs. Stern's presentation to the rabbinic spouses on that day in 1972, one of the women stood and declared that she had not gone to rabbinical school and was not going to be her husband's servant nor that of his congregation. Although her statement was harsher than mine would have been, I had somewhat the same feelings, if to a lesser degree. I did want to support Jimmy and the congregation, but I wasn't quite sure how it would all work out.

When Jimmy and I were first married, I was a Claims Representative for the Social Security Administration in Galveston, Texas. I worked five days a week from eight a.m. to five p.m. At one of the first synagogue board meetings, someone asked Jimmy how I was going to do all the duties a rabbi's wife was expected to do when I had a full-time job. Before Jimmy could answer, the first VP of the congregation – who went on to become its first female president – said, "When we pay her what we pay Jimmy."

It put an end to my fears that I wouldn't live up to anyone's expectations, and allowed me to set the tone for what I was comfortable with in my role as rabbinic spouse.

Throughout Jimmy's thirty-two-year tenure at the temple, I was there for all the major services and functions and even chaired the Passover seder for years. However, I only went to Friday night services once a month, when we had our monthly potluck dinners, and never went to Saturday services. I was involved as a parent when our kids were in Sunday school, but never taught. Since I am a CPA, I used my accounting talents to serve as sisterhood treasurer for many years...and, when asked, I happily baked cookies for receptions!

Jimmy began and ended his rabbinic career at Congregation B'nai Israel in Galveston. I was born and raised in Galveston, where I went to the shul – the Conservative congregation in town. My mom was first vice president of the shul. When Jimmy and I got engaged, many people wondered if this would be the beginning of the merger of the two congregations (which, to this day, has yet to happen). I knew many of the congregants at the temple and they knew me as a kid. Jimmy is retired and I will be soon. We plan on remaining in my hometown of Galveston, and feel fortunate to have been here for so many years among the many lifelong friends we have made in the congregation and in the city we both love so much.

Shelley Kessler is now happily retired and living in her beloved Galveston with her husband of forty-one years, Jimmy Kessler. Jimmy was ordained in 1972 from HUC-JIR Cincinnati and is currently the rabbi emeritus of Congregation B'nai Israel in Galveston.

9

FROM RABBI'S SPOUSE TO RABBI

ANN FOLB

I AM THE ONLY MEMBER OF NAORRR, SO FAR, WHO HAS GONE FROM NAORRR to rabbinical school at Hebrew Union College. Since NAORRR has long welcomed surviving spouses of its deceased rabbinical members, it was always an open possibility that such a thing might occur. Perhaps it will be the case for others in the future. Certainly, as a result of my occupying this pioneer role, I have a somewhat different perspective on the rabbinate from other spouses who are sharing stories about their lives.

My thirst for Judaism began at a very young age. My father died when I was six years old, so I believe I started asking life's very basic questions a good deal before many other people do. I did not go to religious school until the third grade – mostly, I think, because my mother could not afford it. I loved it when I went, and I also loved going to services. I wanted to go to Hebrew school as well, but my mother insisted Hebrew school was only for boys so they could become bar mitzvah – something that was clearly not an option for me. Obviously, I later made up for that gap in my education.

I was active in youth group. I also was lucky enough to go to Union Institute, or simply, Oconomowoc, in the late 1950s. It was then that our movement had the insight to realize the benefits the camping experience would have on the development and survival of 20th century Judaism. Herman Schaalman, who would become my mentor and the subject of my rabbinic thesis, convinced a somewhat reluctant UAHC leadership and many of his colleagues in Chicago of the benefits to be had by such an endeavor. The leadership for the Reform movement and the many innovations in worship, practice and music which sprang from our camps were and are still truly formative.

For me, the wonderful rabbis who volunteered their time at Oconomowoc in those summers were a real inspiration. I loved to learn with them and to immerse myself in the richly Jewish environment they created there. It reinforced my desire to learn on a deeper level, and to be part of the leadership which was helping other Jews in the process of making informed Jewish choices.

In short, I wanted to be a rabbi and I was not ready to accept the idea that women didn't have that option open to them. In those days, the Chicago public schools were dealing with the abundance of babies born to soldiers returning from World War II to start their new lives. As one of those children, I was a mid-year high school graduate and went for the first six months of college to Roosevelt University. I was also in the process of informing the Hebrew Union College-Jewish Institute of Religion of my desire to become a rabbi.

At the time, HUC-JIR had a joint undergraduate program with the University of Cincinnati. I was informed that while women were welcome to take classes at the rabbinical school, so far none had gone on to become rabbis. Most had chosen careers in Jewish education. I was accepted into the program with the caveat that it would not mean automatic acceptance into the rabbinic program, which I later discovered was not the case with male applicants. In September 1963, I moved to Cincinnati to continue my education.

The guys were skeptical as to my motivation for entering the program. Many assumed that I would never finish. I was met in the registrar's office by a certain Howard Folb, who wanted to see what such a woman would be like. I was also in correspondence with a prospective student from Cleveland, Ohio, Sally Priesand, who wanted to know about the atmosphere at the school.

As my relationship with Howie became more serious, it became obvious to me that Sally would become the one to make history. It was my opinion then, and remains today, that two rabbis in one family would have a very difficult time career-wise. Sally has more than earned every honor she's received, since in 1972, she became the first American woman to be ordained a rabbi.

Howie and I married in January 1966. Upon completing my undergraduate work at the University of Cincinnati, I entered Ohio State and earned a master's in social work. For the next thirty years, I worked primarily in mental health as I followed my husband's career moves. I also became the mother of two wonderful children and later *sovtah* to a terrific grandson.

On March 4, 1998, the day after we buried his father, Howie had a heart attack and never regained consciousness. He was a month short of his fifty-fifth birthday. We had been married thirty-two years and he had been a rabbi for twenty-eight of them. I am not sure if I was a good rabbinic spouse. I remember asking at Dr. Schwartzman's course for graduating rabbinic couples what I was supposed to do with all my education if congregants didn't want the rabbi's spouse to be well-educated, as we had been told. He recounted the tale of the spouse of a very distinguished rabbi who received negative comments as she returned from the library carrying an armful of books. "Did she think she was better than them?" My impression was that we would just be expected to deal with it.

I believe things have changed in that respect. I know that I loved the man I married, but not always the role of a rabbi's spouse. A large part of what I experienced in regard to the spousal role, I believe, was part of a general societal shift in expectations of both marital partners' obligations to each other.

I worked, because I loved my career in mental health, but also because we needed the money. If the congregation didn't want me to work, they should have paid my husband more. That never happened, so I never had to look at my options. Meanwhile, Howie liked to cook so he didn't mind starting dinner. I taught religious school, because parents were expected to do so, and the rabbi wasn't considered a substitute. Sometimes, I even got paid. And I liked teaching.

Sisterhood was another issue. I have never been good at baking. I usually contributed my share for the oneg or the bar or bat mitzvah reception, but it often came from the local bakery. After my ordination, the problem got more complicated. National Sisterhood does wonderful work and paid for my education. I am very grateful, but contribute now primarily by supporting WRJ projects. It takes some educating of congregations to make the point that the rabbi does not need to provide the oneg because she is a woman, unless it happens to be something she likes to do.

After Howie died, I spent a few years trying to decide what I wanted to do with the rest of my life. I realized that I still wanted to become a rabbi. I was sure I still had things to teach and things to give, both to God and to the Jewish people. On June 2, 2007, I was ordained as a rabbi at the Plum Street Temple. I would like to take this occasion to thank Rabbi Sally Priesand for her support over the years, and for the special trip she made to Cincinnati to attend my ordination.

Some people have suggested that I was finally doing what God wanted of me. I am not always very good at knowing what God's will is. In fact, I am somewhat suspicious of people who do think they know. I have made my share of mistakes, as any beginning rabbi does. However, at my age, it is a little more difficult to pick up and move on. If. indeed, God is pleased with me, I am truly one blessed woman.

I am the widow of Rabbi Howard Folb, who died on March 4,1998. Both he and I attended the Cincinnati campus of HUC-JIR and were ordained at the Plum Street Temple, he, in 1970, and I, in 2007. I presently reside in Arlington, Virginia, quite close to my son and his family. My daughter lives in Florida. My life is rich with opportunities to teach and enjoy a myriad of cultural experiences. I am also involved in the various social and political issues of our day.

10

RABBINIC SPOUSE MEMORIES: THE SILLY STUFF

JUDITH HOLZ

MY FATHER, LEONARD DEVINE, *Z"L*, WAS A REFORM RABBI, AND I'VE been married for more than fifty-one years to Anthony (Tony) Holz, who is also a Reform rabbi, so the only life I've ever known has been in a rabbinic household. Because Tony was born and grew up in Cape Town, he served a congregation for five years in Pretoria. We went to Pretoria with a one-year old, and our other two daughters were born while we were living there. Whether in South Africa or the States, rabbinic life makes unique demands not only on the rabbi, but on the spouse and family. We've had our share of nutty or malign congregants, but an equal or greater share of loving, appreciative and generous congregants. It has been a great joy to be part of people's lives at happy events, and – like all rabbinic families – we've also shared in people's tragedies, and those events have altered our own lives, as well.

I want to concentrate in this short essay on some of the "silly stuff," because it's more fun to laugh than to cry, right? Some odd moments came in phone calls I fielded for Tony:

One man called and, learning that the rabbi was out, said: "Well, maybe you can help me. I wanted to ask: What's the Jewish blood type?" I thought "What a yahoo!" but replied civilly: "There are no special Jewish blood types. Jews have the same blood types as other people: A, B, O, etc."

Another call, again a man with a southern accent: "Ma'am, is it true that if you shine a flashlight on a Jew's forehead, you can see a Star of David appear?" Whack job! I tried to disabuse him of that notion, but probably didn't succeed.

As we all know, people sometimes have trouble seeing the rabbi's family as ordinary human beings. I was sitting during a children's service with a darling second-grader. Tony and the others who would be on the bimah with him entered through the two doors from the "vestry room." As Tony came out, the child turned to me and asked, "Do you live back there?" (Sometimes it felt like we did...)

Tony wore shorts to a temple picnic and beach party. Several people commented with seeming surprise on the fact that the rabbi had knees.

One event that remains ever fresh in my memory happened on an ordinary Friday evening in Charleston. Tony had conducted a lovely Shabbat service. We were all in the social hall for the oneg, and I was circulating, talking to people, when one of the sisterhood women came running up to me, grabbed my arm, and burbled:

"Judy, I just realized something!"

"What is it, [Nameless]?" I asked.

"You get to see the rabbi NAKED!"

And having dropped her bomb, she pranced off, leaving me in a rare state of speechlessness. I had absolutely no response. At 3:00 A.M., I thought of several things I could have said:

"Oh yeah, baby, whenever I get the chance!"

Or taking the opposite tack: "Why would I want to do that?"

Or even, embellishing my husband's new status as sex symbol: "Yeah, just me and Jennifer Aniston!"

So perhaps it's just as well I didn't respond, and that she had flitted off. Aside from being gobsmacked, I did and do see the humor in it. But it's also true that the rabbi (if male) is the alpha male in the congregation, and we rabbinic spouses probably all have to face the somewhat queasy fact that other congregants are picturing our husbands in less than their rabbinic robes...

Judith (Judy) Devine Holz is an RK, the daughter of Rabbi Leonard (C'48) and Anne Devine. She grew up in Chicago and met Anthony D. (Tony) Holz (C'70) at Olin-Sang-Ruby Union Institute camp in the summer of 1965. They were married in November 1966. Judy earned B.A. and M.A. degrees in English from the University of Cincinnati, and served as editor for the College of Science and Engineering at the University of Minnesota-Duluth during Tony's stint as rabbi there and as Executive Assistant to the President of the Medical University in Charleston, South Carolina during Tony's tenure there at Kahal Kadosh Beth Elohim. She takes delight in their three wonderful daughters and sons-in-law and in their eight perfect grandchildren.

11

A RABBI'S CHILD INTERMARRIES: WHEN THE PERSONAL AND COMMUNAL INTERSECT

SHERRY ISRAEL

BECAUSE DICK WAS A HILLEL RABBI, NOT A CONGREGATIONAL RABBI, I suspect my experiences as a rabbinic spouse have been different from the majority of others who married rabbis.

We spent our first two years as a couple at UCLA, where Dick was the associate Hillel Director and I started graduate school to study social psychology. Then we moved to New Haven, where he was Hillel Director at Yale for twelve years. Our four children were all born there. I finished my Ph.D., worked part time and sporadically until our youngest was in school, and fed Shabbat dinners to lots of Yale undergraduates (among other ways of supporting Dick's work). We were not in the public eye the way so many congregational rabbis' families were. If anything, our children enjoyed the company of a slew of young quasi-uncles (Yale was not yet coed), who were happy to be around a family that stood in for the ones they had left at home.

My peers were other academics, our best friends other Hillel directors and their wives (along with the parents of the kids ours went to school with, but that was later). Dick's professional rabbinical gatherings were the annual Hillel Directors' conferences, where we socialized with other Hillel folks. This remained true even after he became the regional Hillel Director for Metro Boston and we left New Haven for Newton, Massachusetts. The CCAR conventions still mostly didn't address his professional concerns, so he didn't attend, and I didn't meet the wives who got to know each other there. I look forward to reading what they have written for this collection.

When our children were old enough to begin dating, my husband Dick, *z"l*, made his position very clear: it was very important to him that they marry Jews – so much so that if any of them intermarried, he told them that he would not attend their weddings. I let them know that it also mattered to me that they lead committed Jewish lives and have Jewish families, but I didn't talk about what I'd do if they chose otherwise; to be honest, I didn't know.

Both our daughters married in their twenties and both married Jews in joyous Jewish weddings: one son-in-law a Jew-by-birth and one a Jew-by-choice. Our sons went through their twenties unmarried, like so many others of their generation. The elder, by this time in his mid-thirties and working in New York, had resumed dating a woman he had first met when they had worked together in Boston. She was also now in NY, finishing a Ph.D., and they were getting serious. She wasn't Jewish.

I had dinner with him one evening when I'd gone into New York for my work and we talked about it. Our conversation was frank but warm. While he was clear that he intended to have a Jewish home and raise Jewish children, I challenged him. "But how can you do that? Don't you hear the contradiction?" His response: "I know, Mom. It would have been easier if I had fallen in love with a Jewish woman, but I didn't. She is right for me. She knows how I feel. We'll make it work. I'll just have to be a single Jewish parent."

I came away from the conversation full of respect and relief that they had been talking about their religious differences and future family plans and almost convinced that he would be able to do what he said he intended. I now knew what I would do if one of our children were to marry a non-Jew: I would accept his choice, love his chosen as another member of our family, and support them as much as I could in creating a Jewish home.

They made it official soon after. But Dick's feelings had not changed. I wrote in my journal entry for the day, "March 27, 1999. David and Pamela called to announce their engagement. Dick digs in." They set a wedding date for December 19th of that year.

Pamela's parents lived in Boston. The kids said they would get us together to meet the next time they came back to Boston. We didn't want to wait that long, so we invited Pamela's parents over for tea and conversation. Given what David had told us about his future in-laws, we expected to get along, and to like them, and indeed we did. Along with our tea and cookies, we were able to have a very open conversation about our children's inter-religious choices and I learned the first of many important lessons: the non-Jewish family in an interfaith marriage may be as unhappy/upset/concerned about their child's choice of a mate from a different religious tradition as we are as Jewish parents. While they do not usually share our Jewish preoccupation with numerical survival, they can anticipate all the other issues – grandchildren who will not share their religion, life-cycle celebrations that will not be those of their tradition – as involving great personal loss, just as we would if the tables were turned. If the Jewish family is lucky, as ours was, the soon-to-be *machatunim* (in-laws) would also have resolved to love our child as a member of their family and to support the couple's life decisions, and also to approach all the differences ahead with good will and positive curiosity.

But none of this made Dick feel any better. We did not throw an engagement party for David and Pamela. He loved both of them personally, but he felt, as he put it, that he could not joyously share the fact of their engagement with our community of friends.

Dick was a very complex person. For one thing, who he was as a person and who he was as a rabbi were inextricably entwined. This was both one of the most inspiring and beautiful and one of the most difficult things about him. Being a rabbi was a calling for him. Helping the Jewish people survive and thrive was not just his job; it was what he cared about totally. The downside of this dedicated position was that when his job came into conflict with more personal matters, the latter often had to give. (I think it's a situation many rabbinic spouses and family members have experienced.). And so, too, here: no matter how much he loved David and respected Pamela personally – and he did both, with no reservations – in his role as rabbi, he could not be joyous when any Jew chose to marry outside the Jewish tradition. And so he could not share David's joy at finding the woman he wanted to marry and share his life with.

Dick's professional reservations were compounded by some personal considerations as well. He was always a Jewish boundary crosser. Ordained at HUC-JIR, he had membership by right in the CCAR as soon as he graduated, but he also applied for and received membership in the Rabbinical Assembly as soon as he went to work for Hillel, work he chose in part because it allowed him to work across all the "denominational" boundaries and beyond. He applied to the Orthodox Rabbinical Council of American, too, but they demanded exclusive allegiance even back in the late 1950s, so he never did join the RCA. Here in our community, his (and my) Jewish pluralism continued. We were founding members of the non-affiliated traditional-egalitarian Newton Centre Minyan, and also participants in the life of Shaarei Tefilla, a modern Orthodox synagogue in the neighborhood.

At Shaarei Tefilla, as at Orthodox congregations in general, members' children do not intermarry, or if they do, there is so much shame about it, a suggestion that perhaps the parents had done something wrong, or not done enough of the right things, that people don't admit to it. So, too, for Dick: he could not invite our Shaarei

Tefilla friends to an engagement party, because he was personally, not just professionally, ashamed that his child had made this choice. In fact, he could not even bring himself to tell Shaarei Tefilla people about it.

Here, too, I made a different choice. I knew we were not the only family in these circumstances. I think it is healthier, both personally and for the Jewish future, to be open about what is going on. So I told our Shaarei Tefilla friends of David and Pamela's engagement, along with everyone else I shared the news with. In some ways, I suppose I was helping Dick in a co-dependent way: since he knew I was telling our friends, he didn't have to, and was spared facing the full impact of his choices.

David and Pamela began to plan their wedding. It would be the wedding Pamela had always wanted, at a downtown Boston hotel, but with a non-denominational ceremony they created themselves, led by two sets of friends. (One is not required to have a clergy or otherwise officially led ceremony in Massachusetts.) In deference to both Dick's and some of our friends' sensibilities, we would invite only a very small circle of intimate friends. But it turned out that Dick was still committed to what he had been telling our children all those years – that if they were marrying a non-Jew, he would not attend the wedding.

Dick and I shared most basic values, including religious ones, though we differed on a number of particulars. Normally, we respected and supported each other's differences, including those regarding religious decisions. Dick was a very principled person, again an admirable trait, made even more so in a person who had his eloquence and ability to articulate his principles. But another word for "principled" is stubborn. Of course, so am I, when it seems called for. This time, I thought he was making a terrible mistake, and I would not leave him alone.

From the beginning, I experienced what was happening to us as a classic Kolhberg-Gilligan conflict. For those who aren't used to this psychological jargon: Lawrence Kohlberg did a set of classic studies on moral reasoning that led him to posit a continuum of moral development along a scale whose summit was reasoning based on abstract moral principles. For example, if a person was asked whether a man who could not afford the medicine for his mortally ill wife was justified in stealing it in order to save her life, Kohlberg saw those who invoked abstract principles about the value of life above the rules of ownership, for example, as making the most mature moral judgments. Subsequently, Carol Gilligan noted that some people, most often women, were using different principles, based on human relationships, to reach equally mature moral positions. So, too, with Dick and me. He was arguing that he should make his decision about attending the wedding based on his principled position about intermarriage. I argued that such a decision would irrevocably damage his relationship with Pamela – that he could say staying home from the wedding had nothing to do with her personally, but how could she not experience it as personal?

In fact, there are multiple conflicting principles in Jewish tradition. The sages, at times, counseled even more drastic counter-normative activity than attending intermarriage ceremonies, *mip'nei darkhei shalom* (for the sake of peace) – a phrase that suggests to me an understanding that in a conflict between principle and relationships, there are times when the latter should prevail – whether for pragmatic or Gilligan-ish reasons doesn't matter here. We talked a lot; some days, it seemed, about nothing else. We visited with friends with whom he was willing to let me open the same conversation. Finally, since Dick himself had written that any religion that does not make its practitioners better human beings should be suspect, he was able to hear my concerns.

I think something else was also going on, although I don't think I spoke of it with Dick at the time. As I suggested earlier, it is sometimes hard for rabbis to separate their professional and personal commitments. It is essential for rabbis to be aware of this dynamic.

But it is equally essential for them not to confuse the persona that evokes these projections with their own actual selves. That rabbinic persona was not the whole of the man I married, although I knew how great a part it was of his life as he lived it; nor was it the whole of our children's father. I think Dick was having a hard time making the distinction, and it was compromising his ability to be a good father (and father-in-law to be). I mention it here because I know how hard it is for rabbis to resist getting caught in this dynamic. Another reason, beyond the claims of parenthood, that it is essential for rabbis to be able to resist it, is that part of what they are modeling, part of what people are always watching in their rabbis, whether we want them to or not, is how to have loving Jewish families. In this regard, how one responds to intermarriage is just (!) another living out of family patterns.

Besides these three key frames of self, family, community, Dick had one more reference group to contend with: his rabbinic colleagues, in the form of the official policies of the movements. I assumed that in late 1999 other Reform and Reconstructionist colleagues had already faced the issue of a child intermarrying; if that were the case, we did not know who they were. No one was talking about it.

Apparently, this hasn't changed much. Silence is still the norm. The Conservative movement's official position in 1999 was that not only could its members not officiate at an interfaith wedding, they could not even attend one, not even for a family member. This position has not changed. I asked around discretely among some Conservative rabbinic friends at the time and learned that there were Rabbinical Assembly members who had attended interfaith weddings of close family members – a brother, a cousin – but "don't ask, don't tell" was the going practice. On hearing this, Dick was still certain that he must be the first RA member to have a child intermarrying, so his shame, his sense of failure, was compounded. I believe official policies that encourage people to hide their important personal truths serve neither those individuals nor *klal Yisrael* (the Jewish people) well. We cannot diagnose our Jewish condition and devise effective strategies for intervention if the very people who will need to be most involved in implementing those strategies have to keep their own personal involvements secret.

Eventually, Dick agreed. He would be at the wedding.

He had not changed what he believed as a rabbi, but he was able to realize that if he didn't attend, the fact of his absence would overshadow David and Pamela's place at the center of everyone's attention, and he didn't want that to happen.

However, as it turned out, he was not there, but not by his choice. He was hit by a car as he returned from his daily run on the morning of the wedding. Another family member accompanied him to the emergency room as the rest of us dressed for the wedding. Word came to us that although he was terribly bruised, nothing was broken; he would be fine, and he wanted us all to go on to the wedding. We went. We even danced. One physician friend who was at the wedding kept in touch with the ER and gave me bulletins every fifteen minutes to reassure me and enable me to be present to David and Pamela and all the others there to celebrate.

Later, when some of us were visiting Dick in his hospital bed, he cracked, in his inimitable way, "Well, I didn't want to go to the wedding, but the *kadosh barukh hu* sure plays rough."

All the while I was urging Dick to change his mind, to back off from his earlier decision and declaration, what I was thinking about was how our son and new daughter-in-law would feel if he didn't attend.

But I think there are also wider communal considerations that are worth bringing into the picture. So, allow me please to change perspectives from wife and mother to observer of the American Jewish scene. Here, the issues become those of Jewish identity and Jewish continuity, so important to all of us and, perhaps especially, to rabbis who serve as exemplars in the public sphere.

First of all, we should note that most Jews in America are not Orthodox. Most of us do not live in sequestered communities. Our children go to school and college with non-Jews and do not marry until relatively late, some in their late twenties, or more often in their thirties. Their social and work lives are lived in multi-cultural surroundings. Under these conditions, it is safe to say that some amount of intermarriage is not only possible, it is inevitable. But also because of these same conditions, intermarriage in our day does not mean turning one's back on the Jewish people, as it once did. In twenty-first century America, ethnic and religious identities are no longer seen as ascriptive, as given at birth and then imprinted forever. They have become matters of individual choice. Additionally, couples now assume that each one can maintain his or her identity as an individual even if married to someone who has made a different choice.

The evidence is very convincing. Intermarriage does not reflect a rejection of Jewish commitments; rather, it is an acceptance of American norms. If this is so, preaching against intermarriage may make rabbis feel better, but it's not likely to impact the behavior of the next generation. Assuming we oppose intermarriage because we want to support Jewish continuity and to increase the odds that our children's offspring will be Jews, the best thing we can do, I believe, is to make our children so deeply Jewish in both identity and understanding that they will make Jewish homes no matter whom they marry. This means giving them a thorough Jewish education and the experience of deeply lived Judaism in our homes and communities. It doesn't guarantee anything. Nothing does in life. But it ups the odds.

I had come to this conclusion and was teaching it to my students well before my own sons both became living examples of my academic conclusions. I confess that my academic knowledge did not make it personally easier to be comfortable with my sons' choices initially, but it did give me language to help me understand what was happening.

I could see that Dick and I had not, in fact, failed as Jewish parents. Our sons have intermarried, but they remain committed to living Jewish lives and having Jewish families. They are continuing to be links in the chain of Jewish life.

Second, because we know that Jewishness happens not just inside people's heads, but even more in communities, if we want Jews to continue to choose to live Jewish lives, it is imperative that we make our communities, families, and institutions welcoming to them. This is as true for in-married as for intermarried couples. Intermarriage is an inevitable by-product of what our grandparents dreamed of when they came to these golden shores: that their offspring would make it in America and be fully integrated into American life. Their dreams have come true, and intermarriage is the other side of the coin of the success of their dream.

I happen to think there is also a good traditional framework for such a position: the distinction between decisions made before something has happened, and what applies after the fact. Rabbis can believe that it is easier to raise Jewish children in a home in which both parents, and both sets of extended families, are Jews (although, to be sure, this depends a lot on the families' Jewish feelings and commitments) and so argue for in-marriage, and can continue on principle to decline to officiate at an intermarriage as if it were a Jewish marriage. But once the deed is done, and we are presented with the fact of an intermarried couple, if they show any signs of wanting to be part of our Jewish communities and institutions, we must encourage, support, and welcome them. Every movement and institution will have to work out its own solutions to the boundary issues this presents, but there are enough examples of ways to do this with integrity that anyone who is of good heart and mind can work through the details.

Pamela and David are happily married. Their first child, a son, had *milah l'shem gerut* (a circumcision as the first step in halakhic conversion), and when he was old enough, David brought him to the mikvah to complete the process. At the circumcision, my joy was tempered by empathy for my machatunim (in-laws), who came to celebrate with the family, but for whom the fact that their first grandchild was not going to be baptized was not easy. Our second son, Joshua, is now also married, and his wonderful wife, Mary Anne, who is not Jewish, has agreed to raise their children as Jews and support Joshua in doing so. Their first son, named after Dick, has also had milah and mikvah. Since I first wrote this essay, in early 2005, each family has been blessed with a second son.

We are all sad that Dick never got to meet these grandchildren. I'd like to believe that he would have continued to soften his principled stand and come to feel the love and pride I do as I watch our sons being loving Jewish fathers and husbands and enjoy the goodness and accomplishments of our daughters-in-law. But to tell the truth, I'm not sure.

Excerpted and adapted from the CCAR Journal: A Reform Jewish Quarterly, LIII, 2, Spring 2006, pp 82-90. Rabbi Richard J. Israel, z"l, was ordained by HUC-JIR in 1957.

Dr. Sherry Israel is a social psychologist. In her last full-time position, she was an associate professor at Hornstein: the Jewish Professional Leadership Program at Brandeis University. She retired in 2007. This essay was originally written in March 2005, revised March 2006 and adapted for publication here in 2018.

12

A RABBINIC LINEAGE

MARIANNE C. DREYFUS

GROWING UP AS THE GRANDDAUGHTER AND GREAT GRANDDAUGHTER OF rabbis, I had an early exposure to Judaism, though not necessarily direct insights into the life of a rabbi and his wife.

Living in Berlin in my early years (until 1939), my parents and I spent many Friday evenings in the apartment of my maternal grandparents, Rabbi Leo and Natalie Baeck. At that time, before Shabbat dinner, my grandfather used the opportunity to teach me the elements of Hebrew and Judaism. On Shabbat morning, we often went to synagogue for services to hear my grandfather preach. I sat in the front row of the women's gallery with my mother and grandmother. I remember enjoying the organ music and choir, but not necessarily the sermon.

After I was sent to London from Berlin in January 1939 on a kindertransport, everything changed. I lived with Rabbi and Mrs. Israel Mattuck, who were wonderful. They arranged for me to attend a small boarding school. I was the only German Jewish girl in the school. A teacher from the Liberal Synagogue in London came once a week to teach me Jewish subjects and give me homework. Later that year, when the war started, the school was evacuated to Wales, and my religious instruction continued by correspondence. Fortunately, my parents immigrated to London in April of that year and I could visit them during school vacations. The Liberal Synagogue arranged a Confirmation service for several of us during spring vacation in 1941, shortly after part of the building suffered severe bomb damage.

After graduation from secondary school, I attended London University to study chemistry. I was also involved in the youth group activities of the synagogue which my parents had joined. In 1945, Leo Baeck came to live with us, after surviving the Terezín concentration camp. I had finished my Bachelor of Science degree and was working as a research chemist.

A few years later, Leo Baeck was asked to go to Hebrew Union College in Cincinnati to teach for a few months. By then, I had completed my MSc degree at the university and was looking for another job. However, my family asked me to delay my search so that I could accompany my grandfather to the USA. We had a suite in the college dormitory, where many of the rabbinic and doctoral students were living. It was at that time that I met, among others, Rabbi A. Stanley Dreyfus, who was teaching liturgy, working on his Ph.D. and serving a small congregation on weekends. There were no spouses at the College, but I got to know the wives of some of the faculty members. I helped out in the office and also attended some courses at the University of Cincinnati but returned to London with my grandfather after his teaching assignment was completed.

After another visit the following year, Stanley and I decided to get married. We were married in London in 1950 because I only had a visitor visa for the United States. A few months later, I received an immigration visa and was able to join Stanley, who had accepted a position at East Liverpool, Ohio.

Although I may have known something about a rabbinic household, I had not given any thought to the duties of a rabbinic spouse. My grandmother took care of their home and worried about her husband and all that was going on in the 1930s in Berlin. Moving from London, England to East Liverpool, Ohio was quite an adjustment for me. This was a congregation of forty families, which was certainly different from the London congregation I had known.

While living in East Liverpool, we also commuted to Beaver Falls, Pennsylvania every other week. I was received warmly and met some wonderful people.

After a year, we moved to a larger congregation in Terre Haute, Indiana. I did not look for a job in chemistry as our older son was born there and I was glad to stay at home. I participated in the congregation, but never felt stressed because I was the rabbi's wife. A change took place in 1953, when Stanley was called into the Army chaplaincy and was sent to Kaiserslauten, Germany. The congregation gave him a leave of absence for two years and our son and I joined him. There were only a few Jewish couples, but we banded together and entertained many GIs, cooking and baking for Shabbat and festivals. We made longtime friends. After a year, we moved to Galveston, Texas. Our younger son was born there. I was involved in the congregation, did some teaching and helped at the temple pre-school, which was founded at that time.

Moving with both of our sons in 1965 to the Union Temple, a large congregation in Brooklyn, was another big change. Brooklyn seemed very impersonal after Texas. It was more difficult to have close friends in the congregation. We never had family living close by. However, it gave us the opportunity to meet other rabbis and their spouses in the city. We even had our own "Brooklyn Reform Rabbis Group," which included the spouses. I was involved with the temple and its activities. I investigated some chemistry positions, but as I had not kept up with advances in the field and did not want to go back to college, I did not pursue professional work. As Stanley was also teaching part time at the New York School of HUC-JIR, I was often involved with the students there.

When Stanley left the congregation to become Placement Director for the CCAR, we continued to live in Brooklyn. I met many rabbinic spouses during our visits to regional CCAR meetings. At one time we had regional spouse support groups. We attended the first get-together of what later became NAORRR in 1984 and have regularly attended until it became too hard for me to do so.

After Stanley's death in 2008, I moved to a retirement community in Chicago. Now I am just a member of the local Reform congregation.

Finally, I should mention that I have a son who is a physician and a grandson who is a physicist. Both of them are married to rabbis, each of whom has a fulltime rabbinic position. Their stories will be different.

Rabbi Dr. Stanley Dreyfus was ordained in 1946 at the Cincinnati campus of HUC.

13

OUTSIDE AND INSIDE

SIMONE LOTVEN SOFIAN

IT IS DIFFICULT TO WRITE ABOUT ONE'S LIFE, AND ESPECIALLY ONE'S LIFE as the wife of a rabbi, and not get into clichés: "It's all about making choices," "You have to be true to yourself," and even the well-worn, "I'm the spouse of the rabbi, not the rebbetzin." Reflecting upon the trajectory of these years, first engaged and then married to a rabbinic student who became a congregational rabbi, I have come to realize that the circumstances and time frame of my formative years have had a lasting impact on how I have navigated through this role.

I was born in the Ozarks – in Springfield, Missouri to be precise – the land of tall, taller and tallest and blond, blonder and blondest, where the vast majority of the population have been American "forever." My parents were immigrants, my mother from France and my father from what is now Belarus. My father was five foot two inches tall and my mother at her tallest was four feet eight-and-one-half inches. Although my father had dirty blond hair and bright blue eyes, I take after my mother's side with dark hair and eyes and obviously was the shortest person in my class. I did not speak much English until my mother decided to send me to preschool as I was turning three, since all I heard at home was Yiddish and French.

Early on, I realized that I was just different: a Jew in a town where the Assemblies of God has its headquarters, and not just a Jew, but one whose family kept kosher with the closest kosher meat four hours away. Because I taught myself to read when I was about four, my father decided to teach me to read Hebrew when I was five, much to the consternation of my first-grade teacher. She did not quite know what to do with a pupil who already knew how to read and who proudly informed her she could do so in Hebrew too. Early on, I realized that I lived in a multiplicity of different worlds and had to figure out when to conform – and when and how not to.

In 1951, the year I was born, Springfield was a segregated town with segregated schools and, although there were no signs for drinking fountains or bathrooms, I don't remember seeing African American families at the public swimming pools, restaurants or hotels. The vast societal changes that began with *Brown vs the Topeka Board of Education* only underscored the differences between my family and most of the rest of the town. My parents cheered the changes that *Brown* and the later civil rights laws forced upon Springfield, and my mother openly opposed the Vietnam War as early as 1966. By my early teens, I understood that I needed to leave my conservative – I would call reactionary – hometown as soon as possible and never look back. I tell stories about growing up there, but there is no hint of nostalgia.

I have to thank Springfield for one thing – my violin. The Springfield public schools had a robust music program. At the beginning of third grade I brought home a note saying I had excelled at a music test and should play an instrument. Being good Jewish parents, my father and mother promptly bought me a pawn shop three-quarter size violin, bow and case complete with rosin for the sum of twenty-five dollars. By the time I was in high school, I was playing in three orchestras: my high school orchestra, the Youth Symphony and the Springfield Symphony Orchestra. I was playing and practicing an average of three to four hours a day and loving it. But above all, the violin was my ticket out because I received a full scholarship and a work-study stipend from the University of Missouri.

Those years both as an undergrad and in graduate school gave shape to my approach to my Jewish identity and not simply because I dated and then married a future rabbi. The university allowed me to explore and revel in the rigors of intellectual and critical thought as I continued to play the violin. It opened up the world to me. It was truly the gateway that allowed me to choose to pursue an academic path rather than become a professional musician, as it gave me the tools to shape the various components of my life.

My world consists of various social, professional and religious circles which are often separate, sometimes bump against each other and sometimes intersect. The people with whom I have worked and interacted, who often have had little or no connection to me as the rabbi's spouse, gave me the luxury of distance and the opportunity to analyze my Jewish identity and my role as rabbi's spouse. Through these circles, I have been able to find religious sustenance even in the most secular of activities. The rigors of practicing and performance as part of an ensemble, my professional colleagues, preparing and teaching classes, academic research and the interaction with my students gave me insights that are not overtly connected to my Jewish circle. Growing up feeling apart, feeling different, has allowed me to stand back from these circles and analyze what I am doing and how much I want to be a part of each of them.

I have come to understand that I belong in a synagogue. I like formal religion and find meaning in organized prayer and ritual practice. Beyond attending services and performing mitzvot, I actively pursue Jewish text; I continue to learn Torah in the largest sense. Studying liturgy, analyzing the Hebrew, and delving into Jewish sources gives me the tools and opportunity to open myself to perceiving holiness in the universe, and to finding avenues to communicate with God. I find these opportunities in prayer, but it also occurs in *hevruta*, learning Talmud, Rashi and Tosafot, studying Jewish philosophy and exploring Jewish feminist thought.

These opportunities to stand back and analyze my Jewish world and my role as rabbi's spouse have also led me to embrace certain aspects of being a rebbetzin. I have come to a personal understanding of the term and have embraced it by working in the kitchen. Like most things I do, cooking for me is a discipline which I study, analyze and practice. Through the synagogue kitchen, community is created that radiates throughout the synagogue. An example is the communal second night seder. I started to help organize and cook the synagogue's second seder in Lancaster, Pennsylvania in the1980s. It grew from seventy-five to eighty people in Lancaster, to about 120 in Chicago, and finally to more than 140 in Dayton, Ohio. I did not organize and cook a seder meal for 140 (obviously, with a whole crew of volunteers) because that is what a rebbetzin is supposed to do. As far as I am concerned, that role was outdated fifty years ago. I did it because community is created in the kitchen. We brought a group of individuals together who forged bonds, participated in significant ritual and helped foster the future of the Jewish community. The seder's profits provided scholarships to URJ camps. Three hundred matzo balls did not just satisfy the participants; their creation helped nourish and give meaning to my religious soul.

I am a religious Jew, but I must admit that I am not terribly spiritual, at least not in the way the word is generally used. The term spirituality is meaningless for me, some sort of nebulous aura that I cannot seem to either define or hold onto. Even when I have sought out new challenges and encountered inspiring experiences, I tend to analyze them afterward, separating myself from them to gain a deeper understanding and perhaps a more sustainable integration of them into my life. Perhaps the biggest challenge was joining the women's Hevra Kadisha in Lancaster, Pennsylvania. When I joined, I was deeply engrossed in completing my dissertation in medieval French literature. Death is everywhere in the medieval world and in medieval literature. I realized that death was not real to me, but rather just a topic of intellectual discussion. Washing bodies in the Hevra Kadisha caused me to confront the reality of death but I also gained new insights into the role of mitzvah in shaping a Jewish life. I studied Jewish sources on death and mourning rituals and developed personal criteria, a kind of meta-*halakhah* through whose lens I decide the relevance of any mitzvah without dividing the mitzvot into "ethical" and "ritual" categories. These principles continue to guide me as a religious Reform Jew.

As it was difficult not to begin with clichés, it is also difficult not to end with them. Therefore, to close I must simply say that writing this essay has been challenging and rewarding, and for this I am grateful.

Simone Lotven Sofian and her husband David made aliyah upon retirement in 2015 and live in Modi'in. She received her Ph.D. in French from the University of Cincinnati with a minor in classical and medieval Hebrew. Simone and David enjoy being "just" synagogue members; they are active in Kehillat YOZMA in Modi'in. They come back to the United State for the fall hagim and Pesaḥ to be with their children, Joshua (Samara) Sofian, Nehama (Chad) Miller and Aaron (Abigail) Sofian and their grandchildren, Ilana, Reagan, Meira, Nadav, Ziva, Orly, Isabella, Levi. and the newest addition, Finneus Adir. David M. Sofian was ordained in Cincinnati in 1977.

14

REMEMBERING ME

JOAN MAG KARFF

A NOTE FROM THE EDITOR:

IN REVIEWING AND EDITING THE PIECES SUBMITTED FOR OUR SPOUSE book, I had the privilege of reading the beautiful words Joan Mag Karff wrote in September 2008 for her family after she was diagnosed with ovarian cancer. *Remembering Me* is sixty-nine pages long. It is both very personal and wonderfully evocative of a life beautifully, energetically, enthusiastically, creatively and bravely led.

I had met Joan at CCAR conferences and NAORRR conventions over the years, but we really didn't know each other. I got to know her through what she wrote – and discovered that not only were we both deeply involved in modern dance (she, much more accomplished than I), but we had both been on the same Machon Kayitz trip to Israel in the summer of 1958 and quite probably on the same kibbutz. I was an entering freshman at the time and Joan had just graduated from college, so our social contact was limited although we quite possibly choreographed and certainly danced together in some of the shipboard dance presentations as we made our way across the Atlantic on board a Zim Lines ship from New York to Haifa. Knowing this made choosing how best to show her through excerpts of her writing all the more important a task for me.

For the sake of continuity, I have tried to maintain the flow of her narrative, occasionally joining sentences that are nonconsecutive in the original. Joan's book talks about her family and her upbringing; about her brilliant career in dance; about her life with and love for Sam Karff, "my elegant, smart, kind husband." I have focused on her evolving Jewish consciousness and her role as she chose to live it as the wife of a congregational rabbi.

-Naomi Patz

THOUGHTS ON A LIFE HAPPILY AND, HOPEFULLY, USEFULLY LIVED...

I WAS BORN JULY 30, 1936 IN THE MIDSIZE TOWN OF NEW BRITAIN, Connecticut. New Britain from the 1920s through the 1960s was a small but dynamic community. When I arrived on the scene in 1936, it was a thriving town. My grandfather, Nathan Elias Mag, who had come penniless from Eastern Europe and spent his early years selling bits of clothing throughout New England, settled there permanently, opening a small store on Main Street to sell men's shirts and ties. As the store prospered, they began to sell suits and sports jackets, finally becoming the most elegant men's wear store in central Connecticut.

At a very young age, probably only three, I started dancing lessons. I took tap and immediately knew that moving to music was something special for me. I was a fish in water. I loved the feeling of giving my body instructions and having it respond.

Being Jewish in a Catholic neighborhood made you feel different. I knew we didn't get dressed up to pray at St. Francis every Sunday morning. We didn't recite the "Hail Mary" or use rosary beads. We did, in our way, try to share in their major holidays. We hung our stockings at the fireplace Christmas Eve and we celebrated this "American" holiday with gifts and a family dinner. On Easter, we boiled eggs and dyed them pretty colors. Then they were hidden around the house for the children to find. Yet we knew we were Jews. I just had no idea what that meant.

My father's family was the first generation of Polish Jews to come to America. They would have been more comfortable passing on Jewish traditions to their four sons but only one retained a Jewish lifestyle. My mother's maternal family had been Jewish-American citizens since the Civil War. My mother was very proud of her long American history and not so subtly imparted to me the feeling that German Jews were far superior to their Eastern European Jewish brethren. Saying *oy vey* was as much a sin in our household as uttering a swear word. So how did this very smart, well-read, musical gal marry the man who became my father? Because he was sweet and funny and had a good family business. Because he went to Yale and she could only dream of college because she was poor. Yet her worldview and her views of Jewishness and Judaism predominated. Her love of the intellectual and artistic, which she associated with the best of German pre-Nazi life, was coupled with a decidedly leftwing political stance. According to the 1930s liberal philosophy, the brotherhood of all mankind supersedes the divisive particularities of individual religions and ethnic divides. Being attached to ancient Jewish holidays, Jewish foods, Jewish life cycle events kept one from fully participating in either the American dream or in the wider idealistic goal of universal brotherhood.

I knew that being Jewish involved Sunday afternoon trips to New Britain's north side, where several Jewish-owned delis sold rye bread, hot dogs, pastrami and dill pickles we could get right from the barrel. I do not recall a single Jewish holiday that enriched my life. There were no markings of Shabbat, no Passover seder and no Hanukkah. I don't remember going to a High Holy Day service. When I was nine, probably at Daddy's insistence – certainly not my mother's – the cantor of the Conservative synagogue came weekly to our home to teach me the Hebrew alphabet. I have never been able to initiate the reading of Hebrew text, but if it is read aloud from the pulpit, I can follow along.

In November 1947, my father sat riveted to the radio listening to the United Nations cast its vote on a partition which would establish the Jewish State alongside a Palestinian state. I sat at his feet; somehow, I knew this was a momentous event for the Jewish people. As each country voted "yes" or "no" and the votes were tallied, my father became more and more emotional. By now, the world was aware of the huge devastation the Jews suffered at the hands of the Nazis. Miraculously, survivors began making their way to *eretz Yisrael.*

By junior high school, my social life was confined to interactions with New Britain's other Jewish kids. What we wore became more important, and who liked whom was the chief subject of discussion. Older Jewish boys from the surrounding neighborhoods would often come cruising the westside streets of town in their dad's cars, armed with the address of a cute Jewish girl they had met at the beach or at a party.

The summer following my junior year in high school, I enrolled in an intense modern dance program at Connecticut College School of Dance in New London. This was the summer home of the best of the New York dance companies, and I was thrilled to take Martha Graham and Jose Limon technique taught by the masters themselves. Dance for me was never just steps; it was story. And the desire to tell stories through nonverbal communication gripped me for a lifetime.

In my senior year I applied to Mt. Holyoke College. As much as I felt uncomfortable at Northfield High School in New Britain, an all-girls' school with puritanical rigidity, I fit right in at Mt. Holyoke, which also was women-only but with far fewer rules and restrictions. The number of Jewish girls at Mt. Holyoke was small but it didn't take us long to identify each other. Our bonding as Jewish girls was felt necessary to maintain our sense of distinction amidst the overwhelming majority of Gentiles, and, more importantly, we bonded together to establish a dating network with friends, brothers and cousins at all the neighboring men's colleges. We took this job very seriously and, as a result, the Jewish girls had the most active social life.

My most amusing romantic encounter my senior year was with the assistant rabbi at Temple Beth Israel in Hartford. We had been fixed up and we went out more than a few times when I was back home from school. That is, we went dancing; he, tall and lithe, could have been another Fred Astaire. And I loved to dance. But there was no way on earth I could ever love him, so at the end of the year I brashly told him, "This has been a great year, but I could never marry a rabbi!"

When I returned to Mt. Holyoke in the fall of my senior year, I was told by the Sociology Department chair that I qualified for a degree with honor if I wrote an independent thesis in lieu of one of my five classes. I immediately accepted. I chose as my subject, *The History of the Kibbutz Movement in Israel.* Looking back, some fifty plus years later, I wonder why, with my assimilated background, I was curious about Israel. My only two memories of emotional connection to Israel were the UN vote on partition and the influence of Zionist youth leaders at my BBYO meetings. But somehow my interest in Jewish statehood and the idealistic concept of collective settlement was strong enough for me to want to spend the entire academic year learning as much as I could.

◆═◆

I graduated in May 1958 and left for Israel in early July, joining a group of mostly New York area Jewish kids. The New York kids were a revelation to me. I had never before met Jewish kids who had Hebrew names, spoke the language fluently, lived devotedly by Jewish time, and felt a spiritual connection to the land of Israel. And they had never met a Jew like me – who was educated at Christian schools, celebrated Christmas and had only a vague notion of being Jewish. "You must at least have a Hebrew name," my new friends told me, and I decided to be Shoshana for the rest of the summer. Our group, our Machon Kayitz summer program, was housed in a large teachers' college in Beit HaKerem. The school was not intended as a dormitory, so we slept in classrooms on hard mattresses with no pillows. As I recall, toilets were scarce and often unusable. The food was primitive and there was no sanitary way to wash our dishes. But it was worth it. Each foray into the magical city of Jerusalem evoked awe and pride.

We left Beit HaKerem for a long stay at a kibbutz in the Upper Galilee. This was of great interest to me, for I was to see all that I had read about come alive. Everything was done in common. No one had their own personal items. Work was assigned, income shared, policy voted on at communal meetings and, most uniquely, all children lived in the "children's house." Although at first I was assigned to pick apples, word somehow got out that I was a dancer and the managers at the kibbutz asked if I would work in the children's house and teach dance.

◆═◆

I returned to Connecticut both elated and exhausted. My trip to Israel filled me with pride. It was very clear to me that the rebirth of the State of Israel was a major milestone in the life of my people, and I pondered what it would be like to live there and be part of this monumental undertaking.

Several weeks later, I had moved to Hempstead, Long Island to become the dance instructor at Hofstra College. One weekend toward the end of October, I came back to New Britain to see my parents. It was the weekend of the yahrzeit of my grandmother. Everyone wanted to attend services at Beth Israel in Hartford, so I went too. The senior rabbi, Abe Feldman, was away, and the new assistant rabbi, twenty-seven-year old Sam Karff, was giving the sermon.

I confess that part of my reason for wanting to join my family at this service was the fact that local gossip had begun to sing his praises: "handsome," "brilliant," and "a great guy," were adjectives I heard from my parents' Hartford friends. And single. I had to check him out. His sermons were different from what I had expected. For Sam Karff, the essence of Judaism was both spiritual and covenantal. A Jew's bond with the God of Abraham was enriched by ancient texts but was as current as one's morning prayers. The depth of this meaningfully theistic approach to Judaism was entirely new to me. What I had experienced in Israel was ethnic pride, leftwing socialism and the miracle of Zionism, but there had been no God-talk in the language of nation-building. As my relatives and I went through the receiving line at Beth El's doorway, I smiled my prettiest smile at this handsome, intriguing rabbi and coyly said, "Good Shabbos, sir."

That was October. I returned to Long Island and heard nothing from Sam Karff until I was back in New Britain for Christmas break. He called to see if I would have dinner with him on December 30th. "Wonder who he is dating New Year's Eve?" I asked myself.

The night of December 30th, we drove to dinner at a town about half an hour away. My date lit up a cigarette and ordered us drinks. "Cool," I thought. "Not a square at all." For an appetizer he ordered a shrimp cocktail and I sighed audibly as I rejoiced over the fact that this most eligible bachelor did not keep kosher. Conversation between us was easy and far-ranging, but I was struck by the fact that we had extremely different backgrounds. My fourth generation, very American mindset was bolstered by upper middle-class advantages and a boarding school ethos. I knew few Jews who took their religion or their ethnicity seriously. Mostly, my life was about taking advantage of American values and an American lifestyle. If this at times closely resembled living in a Protestant household, well, that was the price of assimilation.

Sam's parents were proud Israelis who had settled in Philadelphia in the 1920s to do better economically. But they never did better themselves economically. Sam's father became the principal of a Jewish day school, and his mother taught Hebrew to afternoon classes of mostly uninterested young Jewish children. They were American citizens, but their entire ambiance was Jewish. They read Hebrew newspapers, had Hebrew-speaking friends, sought out only current event items that related to the plight of Jews, and never ventured far from their circle of Jews and Jewishness.

Sam came from this world, but it didn't take him long to realize there were other worlds out there, and that he should spend his life devouring knowledge on all fronts – with an intellectual curiosity that was both remarkable and amazing.

I remember thinking after that first date that this was a grownup, a man comfortable in his own skin, a whole person, a true mensch.

That winter we had exactly four more dates. Our fifth date was on a cold, snowy New England day. We had a romantic dinner at a beautiful restaurant. Driving back to my grandma's house, where I was going to spend the night, my sweet rabbi said quite tentatively, "I think I am falling in love with you." And my response changed his life forever. "That's wonderful," I said. "Me, too. I absolutely want a June wedding!" And before Sam Karff could ponder his fate, we had arrived at Nannie's. I bolted upstairs, woke the shocked lady out of bed and announced gleefully, "I'm getting married!" Sam could not possibly get out of this now.

◆═◆

Finding myself "the rabbi's wife" at twenty-two was a huge adjustment. Much of the leadership at Beth Israel were folks in their sixties and seventies, and suddenly I was socializing with people old enough to be my grandparents. Free time was now a prized possession. Abe Feldman liked to stay at Saturday bar mitzvah parties until three in the afternoon and Sam, not wanting to seem rude, felt we had to stay too. I soon made it known that I could not handle that; we needed more time to just be together, away from a well-meaning but overbearing congregation.

In December of that year, I became pregnant, and shortly after, we left Hartford so Sam could have his own pulpit in Flint, Michigan. The congregation owned a very adequate house that seemed quite roomy after our small, two-bedroom apartment.

We became involved with a new congregation and a new baby almost simultaneously. The morning my labor pains began, we received word that the patriarch of the Reform Jewish community had died, and Sam wrote his eulogy in between contractions. Rachel Lee (Rachelli – "Rachel is mine") was delivered at 3:00 a.m. At 9:00, Sam left for the funeral in Flint and the burial in Detroit. He got back to the hospital looking much more exhausted than his now-rested wife.

The majority of my two years in Flint was spent learning how to be a mother and caring for two babies fourteen months apart. Those years in Flint, however, were very stressful for Sam. He needed to get used to being a husband and then, very quickly, being a father, and at the same time establishing his relationship to a new congregation. And this congregation, he instinctively knew, was not the place that could bring him fulfillment. Preparing masterful sermons for a Friday night group of about thirty-five faithful attendees didn't work. Sam needed to be in a large congregation in a big city and he needed to know that his gifts were making a decided impact. His spirits sank and he was wise enough to seek counsel from a kind and insightful therapist.

I remember that at one oneg Shabbat following services, an elderly gentleman came up to me and said, "I hope you enjoy your stay here." It occurred to me then that the congregation did not expect Sam Karff to be there a long time. They immediately recognized his superior talent as a rabbi, teacher and leader. They knew he was destined for bigger things, and that happened very quickly.

In the winter of 1962, Sam was working on his doctoral dissertation for HUC-JIR when he got a call from Dr. Louis Mann of Chicago Sinai Congregation, who was looking for a successor. In a pompous tone, he said that Sam was at the top of everyone's list at the college and, with Sam's permission, he wanted to send two of Sinai's board members to hear Sam preach next Friday night. Sam, knowing of Sinai's esteemed role in the history of classical Reform Judaism, immediately agreed.

It didn't take Sinai long to offer Sam the position. Sinai had a long, highly respected place in the development of a very specific, left wing, truly American expression of Judaism. Very little Hebrew was used in the service, the music contained mostly English hymns that sounded extraordinarily close to the music of the church and the main service was on Sunday morning.

Sam was not a classical Reform Jew. He knew that one of his tasks at Sinai would be to move the congregation slowly back to the center. He knew that he would do this over time and would accomplish his goals by "standing on the shoulders" of the great leaders of Sinai's past. First, he needed to establish a solid relationship with his new congregation, and he was amazingly adept at this. We seemed to have a mission during the 1960s to make Sinai as progressive and dynamic as it had been in its heyday. And we did very well for over ten years. Sinai had always been a preaching congregation. Emil S. Hirsch and Louis Mann were nationally known orators who succeeded in making Judaism relevant to their generation. Sam Karff continued that tradition of insightful and stirring sermons. The focus of the Sunday morning service was the sermon, and hundreds would come to hear Sam speak. This was a perfect matching of congregation and rabbi.

Slowly, with a wise understanding of his classical Reform constituents, Sam introduced more Hebrew, had thirteen-year-olds study to read Torah, and explained the reasons why Jewish life was now reclaiming aspects of itself once thought outdated.

The Sinai years for us were almost a "Camelot" experience. We loved Chicago... and besides our precious coterie of close friends, we were constantly being hosted by the charming elder statesmen of Sinai loyalists.

Once back in a metropolitan area, I immediately sought out the modern dance community. These were the early years of "women's lib," and the impact of this powerful movement was not lost on me. I knew deep down that I needed to participate in society in a way that would utilize my particular talents and interests. When our youngest turned three, I applied for and got a part-time job teaching dance education at a small downtown college.

◆═◆

The responsibilities of overseeing Chicago Sinai Congregation probably took ninety percent of Sam's time, and the social life which flowed from Sam's position involved me as well. For Sam, in addition to working diligently on the Sunday sermon, there were teaching projects, life cycle events and constant meetings. Luckily, to keep our marriage and family life intact, we discovered a charming lakefront summer community that we came to feel was part of our souls.

Why, then, did we move to Houston? We adored Chicago, cherished our friends, and were part of one of American Jewry's historic congregations. But a rich history isn't always sustained. Times change, neighborhoods change, institutions change. And so it was with Sinai. Vital young families opted for Highland Park instead of Hyde Park. They wanted good public schools and single-family homes. They didn't want their kids to be afraid to explore their neighborhoods. They looked with trepidation at an encroaching inner-city population and feared that it would bring urban blight and decay. Hyde Park families with grown kids moved into the fashionable apartments of the near north side.

The enrollment in Sinai's Sunday school began to drop in noticeable numbers by the 1970s, and it seemed as if Sam was forever doing funerals for the old guard. We wanted a congregation where children, parents and grandparents were all active members. We sought an urban congregation which was dynamic and growing. Many congregations wanted Sam, but either the timing or other particulars were not right. Houston, Texas seemed very right. Houston's Jewish life centered in Meyerland with an active Jewish community center, Federation, senior housing and lots of Jewish families in close proximity. Beth Israel, the oldest synagogue in Texas, was there. In 1974, we decided to make this very big change in our lives. Sam was to succeed Hyman Judah Schachtel, who had been rabbi at Beth Israel for thirty-five years. The move was scheduled for the spring of 1975. It was very hard to leave Sinai.

We were welcomed in Houston with its legendary southern hospitality. Everyone was gracious and kind. I remember receiving scores of gifts, plants, fresh flowers, homemade cookie and delicious pastries which arrived daily. I dutifully made a list of each present and who sent it so I could write a thank you note. One Friday night, after services, a woman introduced herself and I recalled her name as the sender of one of those thoughtful gifts. "Thank you so much, Mrs. So-and-So!" I immediately exclaimed. "We ate every bit of it." When we got home, I checked the list and discovered that Mrs. So-and-So had sent a plant!

Beth Israel at the time of our arrival was in the process of turning the mantel of congregational leadership over to a bright young group of people in their early forties. We were delighted to have this group, just our age, become the driving engine of the temple.

The seven years that I had spent teaching in Chicago made me realize I wanted to continue teaching dance on the college level in Houston. I did not define myself as the rebbetzin. I had long ago learned I functioned best as an individual rather than as a member of a group. A Mt. Holyoke sociology textbook once introduced me to the concept of "inner direction" as opposed to "other direction." I have felt most comfortable in life making decisions and planning activities on my own rather than as a member of a group. I applied to the renowned Rice University to see if they would hire me to teach modern dance, and I was hired immediately. In Chicago, I had arranged for one of the local choreographers I knew to create a Hanukkah Dance Service. The service used Debbie Friedman music and it was a huge success. Now I had the chance to duplicate that experience in Houston. I hired six well-trained dancers who would perform for a small stipend. I spent about a month on my own choreographing the dances to Debbie Friedman's very rhythmical songs. The choreography, which consisted of about ten three-minute dances, was interspersed with the traditional Friday night service and the dancers had to spend quite a bit of time memorizing the cues the rabbi spoke to know when to begin a new segment. It took a lot of time and energy to make it perfect and to adjust to dancing on two levels of steps and the altar as well. But it worked. We had a High Holy Day size crowd and it was a very innovative and exciting way to celebrate Hanukkah.

In 1976, I was asked to do some choreography at the Jewish Community Center. Knowing that the Center had a large, well-constructed dance studio, I told the head of the JCC Theater Department that I would be more than happy to do the choreography if I could use the studio from noon to 3:00 p.m. three days a week. I didn't leave that space for twenty-four years.

New Dance Group was formally incorporated in 1979. The ensuing years were, for me, greatly focused on creating an interesting and innovative dance company with the best dancers I could find. My days for almost twenty-five years were built around the demands of the dance group. Mornings, I would spend going over my choreography so I could teach it smoothly. Three afternoons a week there were rehearsals. And there was always fundraising, costume design, publicity issues and innumerable details to engage me. Choreography, rehearsals and performances were challenging and creative endeavors. But there was a great deal of anxiety and often harsh difficulty in producing these concerts. Money was very hard to come by. Grant writing was laborious and often fruitless. At 3:00 each afternoon I headed home, for it was important for me to be there when the girls got there.

Sam's Beth Israel life was very full. In addition to preaching and teaching, there were always meetings, life cycle events and temple-related social life. I was always at Friday night services, and, having spent my days involved in my own world, I never then resented joining him in his. Quite the contrary, I usually found it very refreshing to think of something besides dance combinations at the end of the day. And, more importantly, if I was at services, I was able to share the experience with the husband I so admired and loved.

Many rabbis' wives in today's two-career households never appear at temple events, and I'm certain their marriages are impaired without the wives participating in any way in their husband's professional lives.

For years, I had been reluctant to travel, and sometimes insisted that Sam and I fly on separate planes when the girls were young. Sam had taken several temple groups to Israel, but I was never comfortable leaving little children and I never went along. In 1970, when the girls were ten, eight and five, we worked out an Israel trip that would be right for our family and we set off for our own adventure. I was to take many more trips to Israel accompanying Sam as the leader of temple groups. Each group we took felt a deep sense of spirituality at the Western Wall, and they felt pride in the triumphs of agriculture, medicine, culture and modern technology that this new and small country was able to create. We knew that our Texas Jews could never imagine themselves living in Israel but, after spending time there, they came to realize why this corner of the earth was a necessary haven for their post-Holocaust brethren.

Later, we traveled a great deal. The most relevant of all our trips was certainly a ten-day cruise in honor of our fortieth wedding anniversary. We sailed from Barcelona to Cadiz, got a glimpse of Lisbon, disembarked in Brest, France and on to Cork, in Ireland. But by far the most fascinating part of the cruise was the daylong trip to Normandy to the site of the World War II invasion. I loved the newness of travel, exploring other older cultures and meeting people whose life experience differed from mine.

But I was always happy to return home. In truth, my ties to our three wonderful daughters and, later, to their families, were always central to my life. Always being there for them was part of my psyche. Even today, something pulls me homeward at 3:00 p.m. My daughters' triumphs were my triumphs, their pain my pain. I took great delight in fashioning holidays that were fun and memorable. I very consciously recreated our family Hanukkah to look suspiciously like the Christmas I had known and delighted in as a child. What I loved about this non-Jewish holiday was the magical ability to transform an ordinary living room into a place piled high with beautifully wrapped gifts. To add to the spectacular moment of our Hanukkah, I implored a local Chicago carpenter to build us a three-foot high menorah big enough to house colorful dinner-size candles. I learned how to make potato latkes, for years grating huge numbers of potatoes by hand.

My extraordinary husband and wonderful family have sustained me when life has delivered its inevitable blows. Six months after my mother died, Sam and I were dealt another grave misfortune. During a severe January thunderstorm, our house was struck by lightning and burned to the ground. Half of the 1400 books in Sam's study were destroyed; the remaining half had to be treated for smoke damage. All my clothes were incinerated. All the furniture and display pieces in the living room, dining room and family room were charred beyond use. And worst of all, the old family albums housed on the second floor were completely gone. I suffered post-traumatic stress syndrome, feeling completely vulnerable and intensely dislocated.

◆═◆

By 2001, I knew I had to make a dramatic shift in my life. I was almost sixty-five. I needed a new focus. I sat down one day and drew up a mentoring program for minority high school seniors that would encompass everything my mother had passed on to me: a great love of books, a passion for the arts, a commitment to social justice and a deep respect for education. I named my project *Women on the Way UP*. Six months after I formally ended New Dance Group, I met my first group of students at Lamar. The school had gotten recommendations from teachers to find girls who were motivated and serious about their futures. The economic need was determined by whether or not they had signed up for the free school lunches. I interviewed thirty-five and chose ten. I try very hard to keep up with the seventy girls who have now gone through the program. I follow the education and career choices of "my" girls. Almost all of them have remained motivated and determined.

It has been extraordinarily important to me to have creative and independent outlets in my life. Using my skills as a choreographer and mentor gave my life purpose and meaning. But being married to Sam Karff and sharing in his activities and accomplishments has been equally wonderful. "Living by Jewish time" means the beauty of the weekly Shabbat dinner, attending services, watching the delight of children and later grandchildren at our family Hanukkah and enjoying the magic of a visually appealing Passover seder.

And listening to Sam Karff's sermons every week gave me a chance to kvell at the mastery of that now almost-defunct part of the Jewish service. Sam's sermons were well-researched and grounded in both Jewish and general knowledge. Moral dilemmas were treated in a thoughtful and nuanced way. Sam always recognized the complexity of life and his sermons reflected and respected opposing points of view. To be a rabbi in the highest sense of the word, one must combine true scholarship with a genuine love of people. I watched Sam excel at both, and his dedication to continued learning and service to others gave my own life great richness.

But the truest sense of a man's worth lies not in erudition or even in "knowing the heart of the stranger," but in how that man treats his own family. For almost fifty years, our daughters and I have been able to count on the unfailing love, devotion and counsel of Sam Karff.

"It is easy to love when all goes well," is part of one of Sam's wedding sermons. "But," it continues, "love is truly tested when dark clouds dim our vision." The Karffs have had their share of dark clouds. Our house burning down, the loss of our parents, the discovery of cancer, first with our youngest daughter Liz, at age thirty-three, and then twice with me.

As I write this, I am gaining strength after a long and arduous surgery for ovarian cancer. That surgery, and the chemo treatments that followed, left me in pain, very weak, and for the first eight weeks, very down. But I have not been on this journey alone. Caring daughters and grandchildren have all been wonderful. And Sam's support has been a true blessing. For almost three months he did household chores, ran errands, sat through innumerable doctors' appointments and held me tight through long periods of despair. To be told how beautiful you are when your three remaining hairs stick straight up from your balding scalp is both very funny and very encouraging. To hear your husband say on the phone, "We have chemo tomorrow," is to know that "we" are an inseparable team. To have such a marriage is a gift that has blessed my life.

So now, after seventy-two years of living, what do I hope to impart to my beloved family? Most important of all, treat those closest to you with respect and love. Do not use words of anger which you will regret in the morning. Nurture the love of your parents, siblings, spouses and children. Be sure that your intimate relationships are built on solid friendships and very tangible affection. Don't be afraid to admit vulnerability or defeat. For in the end, love is the sustaining force of a life. Kindness and helpfulness and mutual respect are the ingredients that make that love last. Love is the greatest blessing. It should be the cornerstone of your life at home, and it will prove to be your strength as you go forth to meet the world with intellectual curiosity, with a desire to serve others, and with the ultimate goal of establishing a life of meaning.

Joan's husband, Rabbi Samuel Karff, was ordained in Cincinnati in 1956. Joan died in 2016.

15

WHEN YOU ARE A RABBINIC SPOUSE

JEANNE DANZIGER

PICTURE THIS INTRODUCTION TO "RABBINIC SPOUSEHOOD": I AM A recently married, barely twenty-year old college junior. I'm fresh out of living the "typical dorm life with a roommate" scene, whose meals have all been eaten thanks to the associated dorm cafeteria. I'm attempting to cook for my new husband while taking eighteen credits a semester to be able to graduate on time. Harry and I are out with friends for coffee. Spotting me, a woman approaches and says, "You really need to talk to the temple kitchen staff! The coffee at our oneg Shabbat has been so bitter lately!"

Note: I'd never even attempted making coffee and am the very lucky recipient of the wonderful brew which Harry brings me every morning in bed.

Not wishing to offend this person and rarely at a loss for words, I nonetheless stammer. "Gee, I don't know anything about making coffee and wouldn't even know what to say or how to approach the kitchen staff!" And I'd thought being married to a rabbi was going to be like being married to any other professional!

Further note: Writing this more than fifty-one (really?!) years later, I'm still tickled because Harry had to show me how to make coffee before he left recently to speak out of town.

MY ISRAELI SECURITY SAGA:

After Harry and I co-led a congregational Israel trip, our group is going through security before departing Ben Gurion International Airport. Everyone except the two of us is proceeding quickly through with little questioning and no suitcases opened. We, the group's leaders, are directed to the adjoining check line. Our tour agent proudly announces to the security person, "This is our rabbi and his wife!" What? Harry is the group's rabbi and I am the rabbinic spouse? Harry doesn't have payes, and he isn't wearing a kippah or tzitzit, and I'm wearing pants and no sheitl! After many questions about our expenses, purpose, and itinerary, Harry and I are directed to open our suitcases. His suitcase looks innocent, but mine proves exasperating. Why? A plethora of olive wood crosses, rosaries, and other religious objects spill out. This agent looks at the Christian objects, looks at me, shakes her head, closes my suitcase, and sends me on. American meshuganah! What I didn't bother to tell her (and in case you are wondering), I worked at MIFA, Metropolitan Interfaith Association – a faith-based network founded to address critical community needs. I was the Marketing Manager of the Memphis/Mid South Food Bank. My co-workers were very diverse and practiced many religious traditions. I was bringing the gifts for them.

ME AS A RABBINIC SPOUSE:

Since Temple Israel is very large, with 1500+ families, I always hope members will feel connected, part of a congregational family. Being the outgoing person I am, I am both kidded and appreciated for keeping up with members' families and happenings. I'm known for "working the room." We all joke, retired or not, about the congregant who stops at our table while we're dining out. We're offended if he doesn't stop to greet us but resentful if he visits too long! I'm often accused of asking the leading questions that cost us another fifteen minutes. But I ask...and detain...and get kidded! I guess the visitors notice that my questions cost them another fifteen minutes too!

I love this touching story of our Temple's MAZON and Food Bank High Holiday Food Drive. Many members respond to the call and remind others to contribute money or food at a phone-a-thon I organize at a local realtor's office. On this particular occasion, one mom brings her six-year old daughter with her. Kelly, the child, takes membership lists and also begins calling members. She's adorable and very effective. When we're ready to leave, Kelly insists she's not finished and is taking more names home to call! I may feel good about our synagogue's tzedakah, but she lives it. Now, *that's* a mitzvah!

My absolute favorite rabbinic spouse story comes during a regional sisterhood convention in Memphis. I excuse myself during a break to go to the restroom and am stopped in the adjoining lounge. A visiting woman with gray/blue hair asks me, "Do you know what you have to do to be a good rabbi's wife?" I am prepared to hear the long litany of my duties to the congregation. The visitor announces gleefully, "You have to sleep with the rabbi and keep him happy!" For once, I'm speechless and dissolve in a puddle of tears of laughter as she, without another word, returns to the meeting!

My picture as part of a close-up crowd photograph hangs in the National Civil Rights Museum in Memphis. It reflects the horror felt community-wide when a determined killer caught up with Dr. Martin Luther King in our city and shot him. I was with friends at an outdoor prayer service in a football stadium memorializing Dr. King. Harry was not in the stands with us because he was down on the field of the stadium preparing to speak and pray with all of us heartbroken mourners.

We'd just learned we were expecting our first child.

The service brought healing to a shocked, fractured community. After all, we Memphians had peacefully and successfully integrated our schools, library, zoo, and restaurants – though equitable city labor salaries remained to be negotiated. A successful Irish American executive seated next to Harry spoke before him. Addressing his family's immigration, education, and determination, he admonished African Americans to "pull themselves up by their bootstraps as well!" There was a universal gasp! I held my breath then – and now, just thinking about it –realizing that if anyone had a rifle, shot him, and missed, our baby would lose his father and I, my love. Thank God it was 1968 and not the present when guns are more universally carried. No shots were fired that day, and I am honored to be in the photo.

"The mayor's office is calling for you, Jeanne," said my co-worker. "We want to better represent Memphis's diversity by displaying Hanukkah decorations as well as Christmas decorations on main streets during the holiday season," the mayor's assistant explained. "We thought you could give us some simple Hanukkah symbols to replicate vertically and hang on streetlights." Our synagogue educator and I found suitable designs for menorahs and dreidels to recommend. The decorations were made, hung, and we still hear from surprised visitors how really lovely they find it – especially in the heart of the Bible Belt.

A bit more insight into our city: I go to a women's candidates' forum in the clubhouse/ party room of a usually-gated, mixed ethnic and religious community. A convener of the event has her spouse manning the gates because, according to HOA rules, gates can only be open for a shiva!

Both Congressmen from our Memphis metropolitan area – one a Democrat and the other a Republican – are members of Temple Israel. And to think many folks have no idea that Jews live in Memphis!

WONDERFUL TIMES:

In recent years, Harry has served as visiting rabbi at Adath Israel in Cleveland, Mississippi, on the famed Blues Trail, home to the new Grammy Museum, fourth site for Teach for America, Delta State University and city of mixed schools and jobs – right in the heart of the Delta. A few years ago, the state of Mississippi honored our synagogue with a designated historical marker. Even more heartwarming is the warmth of the congregation and worshipers who join us on Shabbat. Citizens from all parts of the community inquire when we're coming and arrive with cooked dishes to add to our delicious and dangerously tempting buffet after services. Yes, visitors join us because they enjoy hearing and learning from Harry. Yes, they enjoy the fellowship and dinner, but – I'm convinced – they come to support their Jewish friends and to keep this now-small synagogue viable. What a treasure!

As you can perhaps tell from my essay, I react positively to whatever happens. My celebration of life stems from my parents' optimistic outlook after they and my sister survived the Holocaust and immigrated to the United States in 1942. As a second-generation survivor, I view our vibrant family as a personal victory over Hitler. After Rabbi Stephen Wise's Belgian assistant secured visas for my family, they overcame the loss of their Brussels home, their time in hiding in southern France, and then the Nazi strafing of the civilians who drove through Fascist Spain to board their ship in Lisbon. The ship on which they were supposed to sail was torpedoed in the Atlantic, but they had been reassigned to a different ship.

Later, my father pinpointed sites of Nazi armament factories for the Allies to bomb. Before the war, he'd visited those plants as an officer of a Swedish roller bearing manufacturer.

I am an educator with an M.A in history who has taught high school history as well as preschool in Memphis, Tennessee. Between teaching stints, I served as Director of the Job Bank, then Marketing Manager of the Memphis/Mid South Food Bank at MIFA – Metropolitan Interfaith Association – to help address critical community needs following the assassination of Dr. Martin Luther King. My remuneration has truly been "coins of the heart," some pay and much pleasure! I take great joy in my family, community, synagogues, education, music, theater, literature, and the outdoors. I am married to my "best friend who spends the night," Harry K. Danziger, who was ordained at HUC-JIR in Cincinnati in 1964. We are the blessed parents of Rona and Jeff, Shara and David, and Rabbis Lindsey and Michael, and grandparents of Caroline, Madeline and Nathaniel as well as Benjamin, Aviva and Noa.

16

RABBI'S WIFE, LOVING PARTNER, HELPMATE: TEEN DREAMS FULFILLED

PAT BLOOM

ALTHOUGH I DIDN'T KNOW IT UNTIL LONG YEARS LATER, MY JOURNEY began when I was in the eighth grade. It was the year that culminated in Confirmation, a major ceremony for a major milestone in my congregation, Rockdale Temple in Cincinnati, a citadel of classical Reform. Before being confirmed, we confirmands were required to attend a substantial number of Saturday morning services and write a brief summary of the sermon. Cruel and unusual punishment. I was excruciatingly bored. But along the way something else was happening. I began to feel uplifted by the beauty and poetry of the Union Prayerbook and even more by the high and lofty language of what we then called The Holy Scriptures, a translation modeled on the King James Version dear to Protestants. Since I had to read those texts week after week, they seeped into my consciousness and became part of my experience of Judaism. I hated having to be there, but I feasted on the language.

It was the Age of Social Justice, which was the theme of most of the sermons. Judaism taught us morality, justice, mercy, caring for others and all the wisdom of the Prophets. Those teachings lifted me up out of the ordinary and showed me a God who asked us to make the world better. Bored though I was, I still somehow soaked up the message.

During this same year my rabbi, Victor Reichert, described in several poignant sermons the life and tragic death of Regina Jonas, the first woman ordained as a rabbi. She studied at the Hochschule fur die Wissenschaft des Judentums in Berlin and graduated in 1930, but was denied ordination. She was finally ordained as a rabbi five years later. Unable to find work as a pulpit rabbi, she served as a chaplain for various Jewish social agencies and taught classes in Jewish subjects. In November 1942, she was sent to Theresienstadt where she continued to work as a rabbi, helping to persuade inmates not to commit suicide and meeting the incoming trains to help new arrivals cope with shock and disorientation. Two years later, in 1944, she was deported to Auschwitz, and, soon after arriving, she was murdered. Her death was a terrible loss to the entire world of liberal Judaism around the world.

I heard the reverence with which he described her life and the significance he ascribed to it. Her story penetrated my heart and kindled a little fire there. I began to imagine the possibility that someday I might be able to be the next woman rabbi. I said nothing and did nothing, but the little flame quietly burned.

In the summers before my junior and senior years in high school, 1949 and 1950, I attended two of the very early NFTY Leadership Institutes. I floated in euphoria, both times. There I met HUC-JIR students who were fun to be with and to laugh with, wore shorts(!), and at the same time were intensely devoted to Judaism. I had a few crushes. Together we studied, planned and executed projects, sang and sang and sang, did Israeli dancing, and sat enthralled around a late night campfire while Rabbi Abraham Cronbach, dressed in a suit, dress shirt and tie, recited dramatically the passage from Isaiah which begins "In the year that King Uzziah died...." Shabbat worship was like nothing I had ever experienced. After the austerity of Rockdale, here we were at the shore of the lake, under the blue sky, feeling the beauty of God's creation and giving praise to the God who made it.

The two NFTY Institutes were life-changing experiences for me. I cherish the memories I have of those days and feel their influence on my life even now, after all these years.

In November of my senior year in high school, I was invited, together with my three classmates in the Rockdale Temple high school program, to attend Shabbat morning services at HUC-JIR and stay for lunch. At the table with us, in addition to our instructor, were three rabbinical students, two of whom have completely disappeared from my memory, and one, very young, very shy student who brought his Southern accent with him from Georgia. His name was Irving Bloom. I liked him very much but in a quiet and private way, without drama, without fireworks, just with a feeling that was warm and good. I was seventeen and he was almost nineteen, a sophomore at the University of Cincinnati and in the HUC-JIR pre-rabbinic program.

Soon after that day, he called me for a date. One date led to another, and we continued to date for the rest of my senior year in high school. He remained in Cincinnati over the summer, taking courses at UC, and we spent the summer together, joyful, exuberant, laughing and starting to fall in love... And then I left Cincinnati to go to college.

During those four years, Irving and I were lonely for each other, seeing each other only at winter break and during the summer. Letters did not suffice. We really had not had enough time to build our relationship in depth, yet we knew with great certainty that we wanted to marry and to walk into the future together. The fact that he was preparing to devote his life to the rabbinate brought forward my submerged dream and allowed me to envision a new kind of life in which I could be at his side, participating in his rabbinic life. I wanted to marry him because I loved him for himself and for everything he was. And I also wanted to marry the rabbi.

We got married in the summer after I graduated from college and, after a brief honeymoon, went to Cincinnati, where Irving still had one more semester at HUC-JIR. It was the first time we had ever spent such a long time together, and when we first began to build our marriage. At the end of the fall semester we moved to Charleroi, Pennsylvania, which was then his bi-weekly pulpit, and stayed there till the end of the school year. It was a pleasant interlude and provided us with more time to grow together. The climax of that year was ordination at Plum Street Temple, one of the great thrills of our lives.

Irving's first "job" after ordination was to join the U. S. Air Force as a chaplain. He was sent to Germany, certainly not a place he would have chosen, but it turned out well. I joined him there after a short waiting period, and we enjoyed his two-year stint which involved driving in his own car, with permission to take me along, on assignment to visit a dozen or more bases in Germany and France to provide Jewish chaplaincy services, as well as to be the Jewish chaplain at our home base, Ramstein Air Force Base. It was a great assignment that gave us ample opportunity to travel and to become familiar with that part of Europe, which we could not have done any other way. Toward the end of his tour of duty, two important milestones occurred. I became pregnant, a thrill for both of us, and Irving accepted a position as assistant rabbi at Temple Sinai of New Orleans.

We moved to New Orleans in the overpowering heat of mid-summer, with me in my fourth month of pregnancy. There, we began our lives in the congregational rabbinate, which became our core for the next thirty-nine years (not counting an extended coda). The senior rabbi was Julian Feibelman; his wife was MaryAnna. They were both lifelong Southerners going back generations, she from old German-Jewish aristocracy in New Orleans, and he from a longtime Jewish family in Vicksburg, Mississippi. They were warm, gracious and embracing, and did everything they could to help us integrate into New Orleans, which was a world of its own, very different from anything either of us had ever known, a society not easy to get to understand. We were young, unsophisticated and not worldly-wise, and so as time went by the relationship became somewhat paternalistic. We were always treated with great respect, Irving as a colleague by Julian, and I as some form of "colleague" of MaryAnna's. Yet they also took on the role of mentors and guides, helping us "young kids" to learn the ropes. For me, this was a welcome training program. MaryAnna was always diplomatic and socially skilled in public. In private, and with deadpan humor, she was sometimes less discreet. When we first came to New Orleans, I was terrified about being able to do and say the right things, and I gladly learned from her and gained considerably in poise and confidence. In the beginning, I was taken out to lunch many times and I admit to enjoying the glamour of it all, but I knew full well that it was not about me; it was about the "Wife of the New Young Rabbi." The glamour wore off as I began to attend many activities at the temple. The title "rebbetzin" was completely unheard of in that historic old classical congregation, but the effect was quite the same. I thought I was "me," and they knew that I was the "Wife of the New Young Rabbi."

Despite the absence of title, now for the first time I was really a rebbetzin. I had an identity as such and a role to fill. There were expectations of me in terms of my presence at events, including all religious services, participation in general in temple activities, and careful attention to propriety and proper decorum in my daily life. I remember that I had to dress properly, i.e. wearing a dress, to go to the supermarket. But the expectations were reasonable, and basically life was good. Our relationship with Julian and MaryAnna was warm and encouraging, and I think we were well thought of by the congregation. But by far the best of all was that in December of our first year in New Orleans, Baby Jonathan Charles Bloom arrived and utterly focused my life. I did not have a very demanding schedule and so had ample time to be with Jonathan, to play with him and listen to the sounds he made, and to immerse myself in motherhood. And, in June of our second year, once again I became pregnant.

Time passed quickly, and soon our two-year tenure in New Orleans drew to a close and we moved eastward about 150 miles along US Hwy 90 to Mobile, Alabama. I was carrying Baby Number Two. The temperature was in the '90s as we moved into a different culture, a different world, a different life. Our years in Mobile were to become among the most meaningful periods of our lives, but I didn't know that then. All I knew then was that I was a stranger in a strange land.

Now, for the first time, Irving was the captain of the ship and I the first mate. It was exciting. We were eager to immerse ourselves in the life of the congregation, *our* congregation. I loved hearing him share with me the activities of his day, and at least to a small extent I was able to be part of his activities. We were very warmly received, I would even say embraced, and the leadership of the congregation gradually became our dear friends. Some of those friendships continue to this day. But as things unfolded, it became clear that there were also individuals who strongly disagreed with some of Irving's comments from the pulpit. I thought his words were measured, reasonable and based on the Jewish values we had learned all our lives, but deep in my secret heart of hearts I wished he could have spoken out more strongly. I knew perfectly well why he didn't.

We came to Mobile in 1960, a time when Mobile, like the rest of the south, was smothered under a heavy blanket of deeply entrenched and pervasive segregation. Of course, I knew that there was segregation in Cincinnati as well as in the rest of the country, but I had never experienced anything remotely like what I saw in Mobile. There were signs everywhere indicating who could or could not go here or there. I was ferociously angry and more than a little frightened. Our congregants were lovely people, refined, educated and caring about others, as were the non-Jewish Mobilians we came to know. Yet there was a dark underside to the city, and I could not reconcile those two realities, nor could I say or do anything.

I immersed myself in temple activities, where I felt comfortable, and little by little Irving and I began to develop relationships, some of which were real friendships. There were congregants who would have liked Irving to say less about civil rights, and I worried about those people, but the congregation believed strongly in freedom of the pulpit.

In December of our first year there, Baby Number Two, Judith Anne Bloom, arrived on the scene, and my days became more and more occupied with Jonathan and Judy. We had fun, we played, we sang songs. We were a happy young family.

The years rolled by, and along the way things began to change – in our lives, in our city, and in our country. The civil rights movement was taking place all around us, and by the mid-1960s we could begin to see changes in Mobile, no less significant for being small ones. I was a board member of the League of Women Voters when we became the first women's organization to invite black women to membership. This was a monumental accomplishment, since it involved having the meetings in our homes, with coffee and pastries before the meeting, and thus there was a social element. Later I was heavily involved in WICS, Women In Community Service, an interfaith, inter-racial group delegated by the Federal Government to recruit, screen and process applications from young women seeking to enter the Job Corps. I learned much from the other women – about themselves and their lives, and about our city, and I value those days highly.

Gradually I began to feel at home. Judy and Jonathan went to pre-school and then to elementary school, and as they made friends, I became friends with the mothers of their friends. Our children were growing up and, as I look back, I realize that Mobile was the place where Irving and I were also growing up. Relationships within the congregation were good. Irving felt that things were going well. I felt that I was contributing to his work in many small ways and sharing it with him. And I began, slowly, an inch at a time, to look below the surface and gain some understanding of the society we were part of, to see its culture and its history. I learned that I could be friends with, respect, and even admire some of those with whom I strongly disagreed. It was a hard lesson for me, but as time passed, I got there. And although I was still, as always, the rebbetzin, I felt that in Mobile I was more and more recognized for myself.

There have been countless times over the years when I have been especially proud of Irving, but there is one event which took place in Mobile that stands at the very top of the list. In the spring of 1965, a Unitarian minister, Rev. James Reeb, was beaten to death in Selma, Alabama for civil rights activity. Shortly after that, the black community organized a memorial service to be held in a local black church, and Irving was asked to give a Bible reading and then speak. There was no question in my mind that I would decide to go: to show my support for him, and also to make my own statement just by being there. We arrived at a church that was crammed full, the men in suits and the women dressed up and wearing hats. There were very few white people. I remember the mayor, an outstanding example of openness and good communication with the black community, a white Protestant minister, and maybe one or two others. We sang, we prayed, Irving read and then spoke. While he spoke, the congregation responded, as is their custom, with a chorus of shouted affirmation whenever he said something they liked. He got quite a few of those. I was given a seat toward the back, squeezed into a crowded pew in a crowded church. At the end we all linked hands, with our hands crossed in front of us, and sang "We Shall Overcome," which I sang with a lump in my throat and tears streaming down my face. The women on either side of me had tears to match my own.

After the service, nothing happened. All was calm. No demonstrations, no bombs or even threats, no graffiti. I was greatly relieved. Before and during the service I had held two emotions: a great welling up of pride in Irving and love for him, and a serious amount of fear. It would have been quite easy for a carful of white punks to drive past the church and throw a Molotov cocktail in through the open door. We had received telephone threats through the years, and we were aware that one of the leading bombers, the man who bombed the temple in Jackson, Mississippi, lived in Mobile, not far from our synagogue. But we went home uneventfully and safely.

Life went on. In 1972, after twelve years in Mobile, Irving began to think that he wanted to move upward to a larger congregation to advance his career. He started the process, and in 1973 he chose Temple Israel in Dayton, Ohio, and we prepared to move, this time with Jonathan and Judy, now fourteen and twelve years old, but *no* Baby Number Three coming along.

Temple Israel opened a new chapter for us. The city was much larger, as was the Jewish community, and the temple was five or six times the size of our temple in Mobile. The new temple had a full-time executive director, a full-time educational director and a complete staff. The professional choir, supplemented by temple volunteers, was directed by Paul Katz, the founding conductor of the Dayton Philharmonic Orchestra. Wow! As Dorothy said to Toto, this certainly didn't look like Kansas anymore – or Mobile either. Irving's career opportunities were far greater. He gradually became involved in interfaith and interracial activities, and when the Dayton school system was preparing to integrate on a system-wide basis, Irving was asked to be part of the Citizens' Advisory Committee, something he had done years earlier in Mobile.

Proximity to Cincinnati, an hour away, meant proximity to HUC-JIR, a great joy to Irving. He was, at various times, the College chaplain, the president of the HUC-JIR Alumni Association, a member of the Admissions Committee, and held several other posts. The temple also benefited by our being able to have several student interns during the years. I enjoyed the opportunity to take the course on Jewish liturgy, taught by the esteemed musicologist Dr. Eric Werner.

While Irving was immersed in temple, I was carving out a new part of my life, taking music theory courses at the local university, Wright State. I loved it. I had wanted to pursue this study for many years, and now I had the perfect opportunity. I was delighted with my student life. Only later did that classwork enable me to fulfill a lifelong ambition and bring a major benefit to the temple.

Paul Katz, our choir director, was a very fine musician. Sadly, as he became older, his health declined. He had more and more difficulty climbing an extremely long flight of stairs to the choir loft, and the temple kept oxygen on hand in case he should need it. But none of that was acknowledged openly, and it was clear that he would stay until his body simply would not carry him up the stairs anymore. Irving realized all this and was extremely concerned. What if he keeled over during a service, especially for the High Holy Days?? Irving and I talked about it and came up with a plan. I began sitting at Paul's feet while he stood on a raised platform, keeping him on the right page in his music notebook and being ready to jump in if it ever became necessary. I will be forever grateful that there was never an emergency and I never had to do that. But I was ready, and Mother Nature finally took over. When Paul had to relinquish his post, I simply stepped in – unappointed, unelected, unauditioned – and unpaid. Supposedly I would be a temporary fill-in, but life takes funny turns, and temporary became permanent. The temple board never gave thought to any part of this situation and so we just rocked along. It was one of the most fulfilling periods of my life, giving me a venue to use my skills as a conductor and my knowledge of the music and the texts, to speak the language of music as a way to express my Judaism. Yes, it was about the music, but it was also about another way to worship. And I, who am beset by self-doubt and anxieties, never, ever experienced them in this role. I was totally sure I knew every bit of this music – where louder, where softer, where to breathe, where not to breathe, and how to express what it meant.

Meanwhile, Irving and the temple leadership embarked on an exciting venture, a new building for the congregation. As demographics changed and the members of the Jewish community were moving in ever-increasing numbers to the opposite side of greater Dayton, it was clear that we had to move too. At first, we tried a small branch in the newer area, but it was never really a success, and so Temple Israel embarked on building its new home. It was a long-term project, stretching out over three or four years, from raising funds to hiring an architect, to deciding on a site, to discussing how the building would be used; many decisions large and small. When the new building was completed, we moved in. I will never forget the procession walking from the old building to the new, carrying the Torah scrolls to their new home. It was a fitting capstone to Irving's career. After the move, he stayed for another two years to enjoy the new building, and then retired.

We moved to Fairhope, Alabama, across Mobile Bay from Mobile, and into a new house which I designed. We reunited with many old friends but resisted the temptation to try to reconstruct the past. I started a volunteer choir at our old temple, and I'm happy to say that it still continues. Irving embarked on a nostalgia trip in the early 2000s, driving once a month to Anniston, Alabama, his bi-weekly from 1953 to 1955. He and I both love it. The congregation is extremely small and not likely to survive long-term, but they won't quit before they have to, and meanwhile they keep on keeping on. They appreciate us and we them. He retired in June 2018, and although we knew it was time to say goodbye, we did so with more than a few weepy eyes and clearing of lumps from throats.

It's been a long journey. Reflecting on those years, I feel that we have had a good life together – loving, caring, striving together. When I look back, I feel comfortable, and proud of us.

Irving was ordained in 1956 in Cincinnati. In 2007, we moved from Fairhope to Atlanta to be near our daughter, Judy, and her family. Our son, Jon, and his family live in Columbus, Ohio, and we see them as often as we can. Irving and I live in a large retirement community with many activities. Once a month we have a DVD of an opera from the Met, La Scala, or another of the leading opera companies shown here for all interested residents. I write some of the program notes and short bios of the singers to be handed out at the door. Besides that, I am trying to repair the world one person at a time by serving as a Stephen Minister. Stephen Ministers are trained volunteer caregivers who provide emotional support and encouragement to people who are dealing with personal issues and ask for help.

17

CONFESSIONS OF A MALE RABBINIC SPOUSE

DR. JERRY GOLDEN

PRE-SPOUSEHOOD

THERE ARE MANY ANECDOTES RELATED TO THIS PERIOD WHICH SHOULD not be shared in a public forum. There was, however, one occurrence that remains fixed in my mind. We had not yet been married, but decided that the logistics of parking at the High Holy Day services at Temple Israel, Memphis, were such that I would drop Connie off for each early service and would then return for the late service and use her parking space. On Rosh Hashanah, when I went to park, I was accosted by the president of the congregation. He was irate that someone had the impudence to try to park in a designated rabbinic space. The situation was quickly resolved when he recognized me. He told me that he knew that people would go to great lengths to get a good parking space, but that getting engaged to the rabbi was something beyond what he had ever seen! My impudence did not go unpunished, however, as during the service, a large horse chestnut fell on my car, denting the hood.

SPOUSE OF A WORKING RABBI

It was clear from the start that neither of the two congregations at which Connie worked full-time had any expectations I would play what would be considered a traditional spousal role in congregational life. I did attend Shabbat services regularly, and served on the board of Temple Israel, by my choice. Connie and I decided together if it would be appropriate for me to attend a particular life-cycle event or social function. If we decided I should, I did, as long as my own rather heavy travel schedule allowed.

After her time at Temple Israel, Connie did monthly Shabbat visits at congregations in Blytheville, Arkansas, and Meridian, Mississippi. She also officiated at any life-cycle occasions at both temples. With the pressure of the time she spent on the road, after six years I saw clearly that a two-career move would be desirable if the details could be worked out. I told her to look for a job, with the only constraint being that it needed to be in a city with a medical school, as I was certain I could find a position almost anywhere. The details are somewhat convoluted, but we moved to Philadelphia, where I became a vice-president at the National Board of Medical Examiners, and she soon became associate rabbi at Old York Road Temple – Beth Am.

When Connie was in her new position, I had more control over my schedule than she did over hers, which gave me the opportunity to meet her for a quick dinner or to bring take-out food to her office at the temple during her brief time between the day's work and evening activities. This allowed us to have dinner together almost every night, which was time together that we otherwise would have missed.

Early in our marriage, we both attended Connie's CCAR conventions. At one, I found time and space to hold a meeting of the male rabbinic spouses who were attending; there were six of us, all in various professions. At that time, one group member was taking two years off to be the primary child-care person and house-husband so his wife's career could advance, but all the others were working full-time. We found that my status in the congregation was not unique and that none of us had felt pressure to attend services, serve on committees, join the men's club or participate in any way that did not meet our own personal interests. In addition, all the members of the group agreed that the need to attend social functions had been worked out together with their spouses. Our conclusion was that the members of each congregation viewed us as professionals who were married to their rabbi, but they never thought that they were "getting two for one" to serve the congregation. Because there were no demands made on us, we were all comfortable with our positions and there was nothing further to discuss!

Actually, Henry Jacobs Camp did get "two for one." During each of the eight years we were in Memphis, we spent a week there, Connie as the rabbi-in-residence, and I as the doctor-in-residence. We cared for the campers, body and soul.

RETIREMENT AND NAORRR

Connie was the first woman rabbi to retire, so we were an unexpected couple at our first NAORRR convention. A few of the rabbis had already known Connie, and either had known me or understood who I was. Most of the attendees, however, did not know either of us; therefore, given my gender and my beard, the obvious conclusion was that I was the rabbi. So, why had they never seen me before? Had I been a prison chaplain in North Dakota? Had I served the Dunedin Jewish Congregation in New Zealand? Had I been a Jewish missionary in the Democratic Republic of Congo? The confusion was dispelled when we were introduced at the first plenary session but, even today, I sometimes am asked where I served. Old stereotypes die hard.

Connie and I now live in Norfolk, Virginia and have recently moved into independent living at a continuing care life community. I am long retired, but very active in volunteer activities. Connie leads weekly erev Shabbat services and teaches classes at our new home, and I remain a congregant. One of my two daughters lives nearby. Our lives are busy, and we still enjoy taking cruises, some as long as forty-four days; we have visited close to 100 countries. Connie was ordained in 1984 at the New York campus of HUC-JIR. I was a widower when we married in 1986.

18

A MULTI-GENERATIONAL ACCOUNT

EUDICE GOLDMAN LORGE
GRETA LEE LORGE SPLANSKY

Notes on rabbinic spouses' experiences from a series of interviews with the late Eudice Goldman Lorge by her daughter, Greta Lee Lorge Splansky. Greta Lee, who is also a rabbi's wife, wrote down her mother's stories and added her own personal perspective as well as brief mention of two other generations of rabbinic spouses in the family.

EUDICE GOLDMAN LORGE

PERSONAL HISTORY PRIOR TO MARRIAGE

Eudice Lorge was born in New York City and raised from six months of age in Cincinnati. Her parents were Sue Rose Kaufman and Albert Goldman, and her younger siblings were Elmer Goldman and Miriam G. Bernstein.

UPBRINGING

The family belonged to Congregation Adath Israel. Eudice attended Avondale Public School and went six days a week after school to Talmud Torah, Habonim and other Jewish activities; she graduated University of Cincinnati with a B.A.in education, taking additional courses in Jewish studies at Hebrew Union College. Eudice also became a member of Delta Phi Epsilon Sorority at UC. Her family was very much involved in Zionist and Hebrew culture activities. When Eudice was eleven years old, her mother hosted Golda Meyerson (Meir) at a Habonim youth luncheon in their home. Albert and Sue Goldman were leaders in the very strong Cincinnati Zionist and Hebrew culture communities. Ernst was the youth leader of the high school Habonim chapter, of which Eudice was a member. Later, Eudice was the organizer of Habonim groups on the UC campus.

PERSONAL HISTORY OF ERNST MORDECHAI LORGE PRIOR TO ORDINATION AND MARRIAGE

Ernst Lorge was born in 1916 in Mainz, Germany, the son of Hedwig Steinweg and Rabbi Maurice Meir Lorge, Ph.D. His older sibling was Dr. Heinz Joseph Lorge. Ernst enjoyed a large extended family of aunts, uncles and cousins. The earlier generations came to Germany in the seventeenth century; according to family tradition, they came from Spain. After graduating as valedictorian from the Jewish Gymnasium in Frankfort, Ernst worked one year as a laborer in a tannery in Germany. He came to the United States in 1936 at age nineteen on an international scholarship that brought him to Cincinnati, Ohio to attend UC and HUC. He was preceded here by his uncle, Dr. Paul Steinweg, in 1932, and by his brother, Dr. Heinz Lorge, in 1934. After Kristallnacht, Ernst and Heinz managed to bring their parents to Cincinnati on a special visa in 1939. His father was officially hired as a rabbi by the Norwood synagogue in Cincinnati to satisfy the terms of the United States visa. Through the kindness of the synagogue, Ernst's immediate family all made it safely to the States.

FIRST-PERSON ACCOUNT FROM EUDICE LORGE, DICTATED TO AND EDITED BY GRETA LEE SPLANSKY

Ernst and I met and went out socially while I was in high school. He was also my Habonim youth leader. We really started dating when I was a college student at UC and HUC. We announced our engagement at a Delta Phi Epsilon sorority formal dance in the Hall of Mirrors at the Netherland Plaza Hotel. We were married in the HUC chapel on June 7, 1943, the day after Ernst was ordained. My father-in-law, Rabbi Maurice Lorge, officiated. After a honeymoon trip to see family in New York City, we spent the summer as camp counselors at Camp Nahilu in New York.

TALLAHASSEE, FLORIDA

At the end of the summer, Ernst and I moved to Tallahassee Florida, where he had his first congregation at Temple Israel and was also the Hillel director for Florida State College for Women (later, Florida State University). I was very young, only twenty-one years old, when we arrived in Tallahassee. I was not sure what was expected of me as the rabbi's wife. We lived in a nice house, furnished and owned by the congregation, next door to the temple. Some women of the congregation were friendly and helped us get settled. They even stocked the kitchen with groceries. But they were much older than I, so at first, I felt lonely, missing family and friends and my activities in Cincinnati. I was also frustrated because I didn't know what to do as the rabbi's wife. I learned to cook for the first time and invited girls from Hillel to Shabbat dinners on Friday nights. My first attempt to make a fancy lemon crème pie with meringue topping for dessert was a disaster. Eventually, I mastered the skill, which was a big deal for me. Months later, my husband told me he didn't much care for lemon crème pie. We had a pecan tree in our backyard. Desserts with pecans made according to local recipes were more successful.

WORLD WAR II YEARS

During this time, Ernst enlisted in the United States Army, as did most of the young men in our family. His goal was to serve as a chaplain. On March 20, 1943, on the morning of erev Purim, our first child was born at the Johnson Sanatorium, in Tallahassee. She was named Greta Lee in memory of my maternal grandmother, Golda Leah. My mother came to Tallahassee to help care for the baby. Women from the congregation were also helpful. Soon after, Ernst was inducted into the Army. His basic training was at Camp Shelby, in Hattiesburg, Mississippi. It was very difficult to live there with a baby during wartime. We reached out to Jewish soldiers who were lonely away from home for the first time and invited them to dinners.

After that, Ernst went for chaplain training at Harvard. I returned with my baby to my parents' home in Cincinnati. I was relieved to have the help and support of my family in caring for the baby. Ernst's departure to Germany with the Fifth Army, 69th Division, was in the fall of 1943. The terrible news from Europe was on the minds of the Jewish community all the time. Ernst served as chaplain for three years. During that time, letter writing was the only contact between the service men and women and home. (Many of those letters remain with us as a record of the time.) The separation was very hard, both on those overseas and on those at home.

Ernst stayed in Europe with the Army for one extra year after the war ended to help the survivors of the concentration camps make contacts with their relatives wherever they might be, and to help them move to the west rather than east to Russia, to the extent possible. He was offered a promotion to the rank of major if he would stay in Germany with the US Army, but by then, we had been apart for three years and our child did not really know her dad. Ernst declined the offer and returned home, although he remained in the Army Reserves.

We went back to Tallahassee in 1946. This time it was easier for me because, as a mother myself, I had more in common with the younger women of the congregation. The small southern congregation was very good to us. However, in 1947, we decided we needed to move back north. Ernst accepted the position of assistant rabbi to Rabbi S. Felix Mendelsohn, at Temple Beth Israel in the Albany Park neighborhood of Chicago. The Tallahassee congregation bought a car for us, but my father, Albert, a very generous and ethical businessman, insisted on reimbursing the congregation for it.

CHICAGO

Ernst spent the rest of his long rabbinic career at Temple Beth Israel in Chicago. On June 16, 1947, our daughter, Sue Ellen, was born, named in memory of my mother Sue and Ernst's mother, Hedwig, both of whom had passed away during the 1940s.

It was again a hard time for me personally, and it took some time to get accustomed to big city life. Housing after the war was in short supply. We first lived in a furnished apartment that was dark and very old fashioned. It still had an ice box instead of a refrigerator. After six months, we were able to move into a new co-op, thanks to the GI bill.

Ernst and Rabbi Mendelsohn enjoyed a very good relationship. His wife, Nan Mendelsohn, had Cincinnati roots and took me under her wing. We also became good friends with their son, Herzl Mendelsohn. Since we had no extended family in Chicago, the Mendelsohns and a few other temple families became like extended family. Ernst worked hard and the congregation grew, as did the Jewish population in Budlong Woods, the area north of the temple, where new homes were being built rapidly. Ernst was especially involved in religious school programming, youth work and young couples programming. We made many friends and had happy times within the temple activities. I became involved in sisterhood programming and supported the social events. We moved to a new house in Budlong Woods. On March 19, 1953, our son, Michael Maurice Lorge, was born. He was named in memory of Ernst's father.

During the Korean War, Ernst was called up from the Army Reserves. An arrangement was made for him to spend the weekdays stationed at Fort Sheridan, outside of Chicago, where he counseled soldiers, with leave to serve the congregation as rabbi on the weekends. During that period, I helped by tutoring the bar mitzvah students after school with their Hebrew Torah portions. We attended the parties that celebrated the bar mitzvahs, weddings and confirmations, as well as informal temple picnics, barbecues and fundraising events. We started an annual practice of inviting the whole congregation to our home for an open house on the Sunday afternoon of Sukkot. In the style of the day, we made the party as festive and as elegant as possible, both inside the house and in the sukkah outside. No matter how busy we were, we always sat down as a family for a traditional Shabbat dinner on Friday evening. Ernst was able to enjoy the family time, even though he needed to get to temple by 7:30 in time for the 8:00 p.m. service. Friday night services were the main adult service, with a formal sermon, beautiful choir and organ music, and a Torah service – often with bar mitzvah readers, followed by a lovely oneg Shabbat social time. Dressing for all these occasions was important, especially for the women. One needed the right outfit.

During this time, long before cell phones, we had an extension to the temple telephone installed in our home. This afforded us an extra hour in the morning so Ernst could take urgent calls without being in the office. This hour made up for the many evening meetings and busy weekend schedules that kept him from home. Often, if he had already left for the office, I took the calls and did the best I could to provide information, sympathy and counseling "first aid" to people in need until they could reach the rabbi at the temple.

UNION INSTITUTE AT OCONOMOWOC, WISCONSIN AND CONGREGATIONAL TRIPS TO ISRAEL

In the early 1950s, Ernst and a few of his Chicago rabbinic colleagues were able to start a summer Jewish study program for college students, and NFTY programs that rather quickly grew to be a full summer camp for Jewish youth. In the early years, the rabbis' wives helped in many ways, from scrubbing the old facilities to running programs and supporting the young counselors with advice and bagels. The camp turned out to be a wonderful way to enrich the Jewish studies of the kids who were in the afternoon Hebrew schools of the Chicago congregations, and to develop young Jewish leadership among the counselors and rabbinical school students. It also was a way for the rabbis and their wives to have time together to become closer friends, and enjoy friendships that have lasted a lifetime.

In the summer of 1958, Ernst and I made our first trip to Israel. He reconnected with cousins, and we both saw the land that was the fulfillment of our dreams as young Zionists in Habonim. By the end of the 1950s, we invited congregants to join us on organized trips to Israel. Just as the camp in Oconomowoc enriched the Jewish experience of the youth, the temple trips to Israel greatly enriched the Jewish experience of the adults. We can't count how many trips we made, but at least once every two years and sometimes more often, each time taking twenty-five to thirty people along. And, of course, there were lots of happy times on these trips, friendships were strengthened, and the temple community was energized by the new relationships.

MY CAREERS

Although I had graduated with a degree in education from the University of Cincinnati, I did not have an opportunity to do student teaching or be certified as a public-school teacher after college. So, I went back to school in the later 1950s to take some required courses and be certified to teach in the Chicago public school system. I worked as a primary grade substitute teacher, sometimes for just a few days a week and, occasionally, for extended times with a single class.

After I had taught for several years, another opportunity arose. The Vega travel agency that had arranged our tours to Israel invited me to join the company as a specialist in Israel and European group tours. I accepted this invitation and learned about the travel business on the job. After a number of years there, I resigned from the downtown company, which had necessitated a long commute, and started my own travel business from our home. The nature of the business allowed me to make my own schedule, with time to stay involved in temple activities and to travel with Ernst and the children.

LATER YEARS

In the 1950s and '60s, Ernst became increasingly involved in the civil rights movement, both locally in Chicago and on a national level. Sometimes, we received vicious, frightening telephone calls in the middle of the night from neo-Nazi groups opposed to the civil rights movement. Ernst's experience in Germany made him resolute to work for equality in the United States. I found the calls very upsetting.

In response to the changing demography of the Jewish population, Temple Beth Israel moved north from Chicago to Skokie, Illinois. The first part of the move involved just the Hebrew school to the "branch." Eventually, the temple complex in Chicago was sold to a Korean church, and the temple moved entirely to Dempster Road in Skokie. During the following years, the temple hired a series of assistant rabbis. Rabbi Michael Weinberg became the successor as senior rabbi of the congregation when Ernst retired. Ernst enjoyed a very good relationship with Michael, both before and after retirement. Michael Weinberg was a close friend of our son, Michael. Our daughter Sue worked closely with Jodi Weinberg at the Schechter

Day School in Skokie, as did our daughter-in-law, Susie Fox Lorge. Temple services here changed to a more informal style, as they did around the country. The spirit of a friendly Jewish community and an interest in Jewish education, in the camp in Oconomowoc (now Olin-Sang-Ruby) and in Israel, remained strong.

By the 1980s all three of our children were married and we had ten grandchildren. Growing up in the temple and attending services and summer camp provided them with a deep understanding of organized Jewish life. My son, Michael, is a leader in Temple Beth Israel and serves on the national boards of the URJ, HUC-JIR and OSRUI summer camp. Two of my grandchildren, Yael Splansky and Ari Lorge, became rabbis, ordained by HUC-JIR.

In February 1990, Ernst passed away. His yahrzeit is observed, along with that of Rabbi Mendelsohn, with a guest lecture at the synagogue every year. Tragically, in 2003, my daughter, Sue Ellen, died in a house fire. The loss of both of them is more than I can express.

Later in 1990, I moved from our home in Chicago to a townhouse in Highland Park, Illinois, where I lived for twenty years. It was the first time I have ever lived alone. I kept my travel business active for many years, but eventually closed the business and, in 2013, moved to a condominium in Skokie, closer to my son and his family and to my temple friends. The friends I have made over the years in Chicago among congregational members, Zionist circles, and especially among the rabbinic families have continued to be very important to me. My children and grandchildren are my support and delight.

Eudice Goldman Lorge, born September 4, 1921, was the wife of Rabbi Ernst M. Lorge, who was ordained in Cincinnati on June 6, 1942. They were married the next day. Ernst Lorge died on February 24, 1990. Eudice died April 9, 2019, at the age of 97.

GRETA LEE LORGE SPLANSKY

Don and I met at Olin-Sang in Oconomowoc in 1959. In the summer of 1960, we each went to Israel, I on a tour for high school graduates organized by the Hebrew Culture Society, and he for a junior year at Hebrew University. By chance, our groups sailed together on the S.S. Zion from Brooklyn, New York, to Haifa, a ten-day trip. We started dating long distance the next year when he returned to Columbia and I was a sophomore at the University of Michigan in Ann Arbor. We married in December of 1963, after my graduation. We lived in Bergenfield, New Jersey, near the George Washington Bridge. I taught general science at the Yavneh Day School in Paterson, New Jersey. We spent the 1965-66 academic year at HUC-JIR in Jerusalem, a wonderful experience with great teachers and friends.

There are many similarities and, of course, differences between my experiences as a rebbetzin and my mom's. My big advantage was having grown up in a rabbi's home and congregation. I did know rather well what to expect. I felt at home in the temple. I had learned to enjoy the community but to understand the limits of congregational relationships. Also, I was very lucky. Don's first two congregations were in Cincinnati, where I had family – aunts, uncles, cousins, dear family friends – and also the HUC-JIR community. We were only a five-hour drive from our immediate families in Chicago, so I did not have the sense of isolation or complete dependence on congregants that some rabbis' wives experience. Our daughter, Karen, was born seven months before we moved to Cincinnati. My first concern at that time was taking care of the baby.

Don is always a gentleman, and therefore got along very well with the three senior rabbis in his early Cincinnati career, Rabbis David Hachen and Harold Hahn, at Rockdale Temple, and Stanley Brav, whom Don succeeded at Temple Sholom. In that way, his experience was similar to my dad's. When the rabbis in a congregation are respectful of each other and there is so much work to be done, there is no need for competitiveness or conflict. Instead, there can be collaboration and affection. Our friendships with those rabbinic families stemmed from the rabbis' basic good relationships. During our sixteen years in Cincinnati, Don earned a Ph.D. in Targum, taught homiletics and served on the HUC-JIR admissions committee.

I enjoyed temple life. I have a more reserved personality than my mom, and did not have quite the social impact on the community that she often had. My contributions were as an amateur in the arts, designing Torah mantles and organizing a needlepoint club to produce them, participating in sisterhood and school programs, making scripts and sets and directing temple plays. Our daughter, Yael, and son, Joshua, were born while we were in Cincinnati. I took graduate courses in biology and chemistry to keep up with the fast-moving field of my undergraduate work at the University of Michigan. I worked part time in the University of Cincinnati allergy research lab of my uncle, Dr. Leonard Bernstein. Then I undertook a master's program in biostatistics and epidemiology at UC, which I completed just at the time Don accepted a position as successor to Rabbi Alfred Friedman, at Temple Beth Am in Framingham, Massachusetts. This degree was fortuitous because it led to a position at the Framingham Heart Study, first part-time, while our children were still in school, and then to more responsibility. I continue to work there for the past thirty years.

Like my parents, Don and I have been involved with the Reform Jewish camps in Oconomowoc, Wisconsin; Zionsville, Indiana; Torah Corps in Littleton, New Hampshire and at Eisner in Great Barrington, Massachusetts. We also led many congregational trips to Israel.

◆═◆

A few words on my view of rabbinic and spouse pro bono work within a congregation: Every rabbi's spouse knows that the job for the rabbi is far more than forty hours per week. I clocked Don's peak time at ninety hours in the busiest years, and more typically around eighty hours a week, including phone calls at home at all hours. Many people in other professions and businesses today put similar hours into their careers. There have been a lot of complaints about such a burden on the rabbi and on his/her family. In response to these complaints, it helps to understand that many rabbis feel a need to practice what they preach. If they are instructing congregants to volunteer in the Jewish community, to give generously to tzedakah, to follow the commandments to care for others without measure, these rabbis lead by example. If children see their parents sincerely caring for the congregation with positive feelings, including love for Judaism and the Jewish people, the children will understand and be enriched by the models, rather than feeling cheated. A congregation should not – and today usually does not – dictate what contributions the rabbi's spouse should make to the temple. But the spouse will feel more a part of the endeavor if, somehow, s/he finds ways to contribute, as do the other members of these communities of volunteers.

Please note that rabbis are almost always excused from temple dues, auxiliary dues, temple dinner costs, and religious school tuition. Over many years, such fees represent a large financial commitment made by temple members and their families. In many congregations, the rabbi's salary is often equal to the median of congregants' incomes. It is important to the happiness of the entire rabbinic family that the spouse does not become embittered by the demands of the rabbi's vocation. There is a whole lore about the suffering of clergy spouses, going back generations to the time when ministers and rabbis were indeed almost as poor as church mice, and perhaps isolated as the only college-educated individuals in small rural towns. There are still such cases, and some clergy do have very difficult lives. Certainly, they need the support of their colleagues and their conferences. But such sad situations should not be understood as the norm or the common underlying relationship among rabbi, spouse and congregation today. To adopt such a view could create a self-fulfilling prophecy and sour the potential for a very energizing and expansive experience for the entire rabbinic family.

The balance of family life, temple life and professional work has been very satisfying for me and my family. Having a sense of service to the Jewish community, and finding a way to express it that fits with one's own personality, is perhaps the key to being comfortable, stimulated, happy and fulfilled in the role of rabbi's spouse.

Two other generations in my family include spouses of rabbis. My grandmother, Hedwig Steinweg Lorge, did not want to be involved in any congregational life in Germany. She and my grandfather solved the problem by his going into teaching in Mainz, rather than serving a congregation. He did, however, conduct services and preach at the liberal congregation in Mainz for the major holidays and festivals when extra services were scheduled. It was this position that qualified them to come to the States in 1939, on a special quota for ministers with congregations in the United States that needed them. We are very grateful to the congregation in the Norwood neighborhood of Cincinnati for creating the position that rescued them while there was still a chance.

My son-in-law, Adam Sol, married our second daughter, Rabbi Yael Splansky. Adam is a published writer and poet who teaches writing at the University of Toronto. I will leave the telling of his stories to him. I will only mention that he is active at Holy Blossom Temple, especially in the areas of Purim plays and Shabbat evening musical ensembles, as well as in the social life of the congregation. So even in this millennium there can be found meaningful ways for rabbinic spouses to contribute to the strength of their synagogue and community.

Above all else, we rabbinic four spouses have each found ways to help our children find their own places in the life of the synagogue and the broader Jewish community, while they were growing up and into adulthood.

Hazak, hazak, v'nithazeik.

Greta Lee Lorge Splansky, born on March 20, 1943, was married on December 29, 1963 to Donald M. Splansky. Greta Lee graduated with a B.A, in biology from the University of Michigan and earned an M.A in epidemiology at the University of Cincinnati in 1984. Donald M. Splansky grew up in Berwyn, Illinois, was president of the Chicago Federation of Temple Youth and worked as a kitchen boy, counselor, and finally unit head of Chalutzim at Olin-Sang. He graduated from Columbia College, after spending his junior year at Hebrew University. He was ordained at HUC-JIR in New York in 1968.

19

A Hillel Way of Life as a Hillel Rabbi's Wife

MARCIE SCHOENBERG LEE

WILD RIDE

THE THRILL OF CENTRIFUGAL FORCE PULLING US ALL TOGETHER AS OUR roller coaster car took a huge curve is what Hillel conferences and meetings once felt like. We were Reform, Conservative, Reconstructionist, and Orthodox rabbis and Jewish communal service professionals studying text together, cozily packed into a room that became that awesome roller coaster car we were happy to ride in, laughing and screaming together.

We purposely made our religious differences invisible to ourselves and our students, keenly aware and proud that we were the only Jewish organization in America with staff who trained in and belonged to all movements in Judaism and who routinely sat around tables studying Torah together. We purposefully modeled and thrived on pluralism before its time. Our diversity was designed to allow all students to see themselves welcome at Hillel, whether or not they actually participated.

We understood, above all else, that for students to simply know a full-time rabbi was present at Hillel was itself a Hillel program, perhaps the most important one, even though we couldn't list it on a program report and dutifully tout its attendance numbers. There was no such thing as bringing in a rabbi "for the religious piece" of Hillel programming because rabbis were there for both the piety and the partying. Back then, I was the program director of Hillel at UCLA.

Then, the roller coaster was closed for repairs it didn't even need, and it never reopened.

BACK TO BERKELEY IN THE SIXTIES

The first week of college, I fell in love with a Jewish guy in my freshman English class at the University of California, Berkeley. He dumped me in our senior year. My heart was broken. But that heart had been nurtured by Berkeley's Radical Jewish Union. The RJU was a community instrumental in the creation of Jewish Studies courses and departments at American universities and had a lasting impact on Jewish life through its activists who spent their lives as diverse community professionals serving the Jewish people around the world. In 2012, in a fascinating turn of events, the Radical Jewish Union at Berkeley – including my participation in it – became the subject of a doctoral dissertation by Elizabeth Imhof.

I traveled to Israel twice during college and was invited by an Israel Defense Forces Nahal Unit on a kibbutz where I worked one summer, to live with them for a month. At the end of that stay, I desperately wanted to remain in Israel and join the army but my dear parents would never have understood. More importantly, I did not know how to ask or how to tell them, so I returned to Berkeley and never spoke of it again, even to my own children.

LUNCH WITH MY MOTHER

I left college with no employment prospects and moved home to Los Angeles. While I was dining across the street from UCLA with my mother one day, she saw an old friend and asked her, "Do you know of any jobs for Marcie?"

"Well," she said, "I am about to leave my job at Hillel, just down the street."

I, who was active during college in an alternative to Hillel, went to work for Hillel from 1972-1976. Along the way, I met a fabulous Hillel rabbi, Barton Lee, at one of those great conferences, and experienced a thrill rather different from that of the roller coaster ride. I went from working for Hillel to marrying it.

LAST ONE OUT, CLOSE THE DOOR

We designed our home to be a Hillel satellite, choosing a neighborhood far enough from campus to give us space from "work," but close enough for any student to get there by car, bike or on foot. Students were welcome most anytime, were trusted and consequently trustworthy, and occasionally outlasted us in our own home into the wee hours of the next morning. They knew that the last one out closed and locked the door. By then a graduate of the HUC-JIR School of Jewish Communal Service and a clinical social worker, I taught and lectured part time so I could serve Hillel students alongside a rabbi all students deserve and, eventually, also be a (mostly) stay-at-home mom. Now, with our children grown, I proudly work for one of those American universities with a Jewish Studies program, happily serving Arizona State University students, staff and faculty as I had served Hillel students as a Hillel wife.

MY MOTHER'S GIFT

I inherited from my mother glee at finding, wrapping and giving the perfect gift to each family member and friend. My gift to Hillel students over the years was always introducing newcomers so that everyone knew each other. It was never true for more than five minutes that a student could say, "I don't know anyone here," or ever come away from any Hillel event saying, "I didn't meet anyone."

Not everyone returned, but no one felt turned away.

ONE STEP REMOVED

When you work for constituents who don't pay your salary, it is easier to be Nathan to King David. We could risk challenging students to grow in ways we might not challenge congregants in a synagogue or members of day school or summer camp boards. The Hillel structure was a treasured element of relationship integrity. It not only freed us, but also allowed students to listen and respond to the compassionate constructive criticism mandated by Judaism with minimal risk that they would turn their energy for personal change into a knee jerk attempt to get the rabbi fired. There was a special space for a cooling off period if students heard things they weren't ready to hear from their rabbi, and also for those times when the rabbi and/or his wife needed to hear valued criticism from students. There was more freedom to be candid partners, all developing our best selves.

HAIR COLOR

Many years ago, when Barton's hair was brown, he asked me, "Do you think students will still relate to me when my hair turns gray?" They joyously related to him when his hair turned gray and then when it turned white. Students want to talk to and come to know rabbis whose hair color doesn't matter but whose emotional availability and transmission of the glory of Judaism do.

I HOPE I LIVE LONG ENOUGH

I want to see the retired rabbis of NAORRR fire up the roller coasters that have been sitting idle for so long by generating proposals to Hillel for full-time paid and/or volunteer rabbinic presence on campuses. Because there are now so few full-time rabbis on most university campuses, Hillel has become the de facto longtime membership chair for Chabad. Chabad understands the importance of having rabbis available all the time and not just for "the religious piece." If some retired Reform rabbis can be that coverage, or part of a team of rabbis whom students delight in knowing during college – a time when students are exposed to and open to so much – the students who choose to be involved can experience pluralism and not just polarization in Jewish life as they grow through their college years. University staffs and faculties will once again, through their work with rabbis of different stripes, interact positively with their Jewish students and with the rabbis that serve their campuses. I want to live to see rabbis have thrilling roller coaster rides and take their Hillel students along with them.

THE ISRAELI ARMY

During her junior year abroad in Israel, our daughter Nira told us she had decided to become an Israeli soldier after college. She served with distinction as a Lone Soldier and an officer on the West Bank and at the Gaza border. When Barton and I finished pinning her lieutenant stripes onto her uniform during a promotion ceremony at her base, I turned to the other proud parents packing the room and, too emotional to attempt remarks in Hebrew, asked Nira to translate as I spoke.

She said, "My mom is standing beside a child who never knew that her mother wanted to be an Israeli soldier until I decided to become one." The noisy room, full of joyous Israeli parents fell absolutely silent. I heard my daughter's voice and my own, and I looked out and realized that this was the land that a life with Hillel had shown me.

Marcie Schoenberg Lee has a unique job at Arizona State University (ASU) where she is charged with joy promotion – creating new programs and avenues for supporting and celebrating students and staff. She graduated from the University of California, HUC-JIR, and the ASU School of Social Work. While being an integral part of

Hillel students' lives, she also developed and taught the course "Women in Judaism" at ASU for twenty-eight years and also taught "Human Sexual Behavior" and a course on basic Judaism. She is in her thirty-first year of teaching wildly diverse courses for the Bureau of Jewish Education, has lectured widely in her hometown and around the country, and developed and taught a Jewish sex education curriculum. Her long-held, passionate, and typically ignored insistence that Jewish views of sexuality ought to be taught and made a foundation of every Jewish institution was finally published as an essay entitled "The Magic of Sex-in-Text Education" in The Sacred Encounter. When not at home in Tempe, she is likely in Bosnia Herzegovina, her home away from home, where she teaches and works with Jewish, Christian, and Muslim community leaders, many of whom are the faces of the Reconciliation Movement after the Balkan War of the 1990s. For five years she had the honor of conducting Shabbat services for Aviv of Arizona, a wonderful community of LGBTQIA+ and straight Jews who celebrated a gay wedding just after Arizona legalized gay marriage. Marcie's husband, Rabbi Barton Lee, was ordained by HUC-JIR in Cincinnati in 1970 and served Arizona State University through Hillel for forty-two years.

20

MY SUPPORTIVE HUSBAND

JUDITH GAMORAN

IN 1955, WHEN I WAS A NEWLY-MINTED REBBETZIN AND MY HUSBAND was in his first congregational pulpit, the sisterhood planned a second seder in a hotel in a nearby resort area. My concern was, "Should I wear a hat?"

I asked my husband several times, "Dear, should I wear a hat?" "Darling, do you think I should wear a hat to the seder?" He finally responded, "Dear, anything you choose to do is right."

So I bought a simple hat of the pinch-it-to-your-scalp kind. And I wore it to the seder. To my great relief, almost all the other women were also wearing hats.

However, by the time the soup was being served, I was in pain from the darn hat. It really was pinching my scalp! Finally, I could bear it no longer. I removed my hat from my aching head and put it on the rug, under my chair. I kept my eyes on my bowl of soup; after all, I was new at the rebbetzin thing – and I did not wish to look up and find every other woman at the event staring straight at me.

To my intense surprise, thirty other hats had been removed from most of the sisterhood ladies' heads!

All I could think was, "Oh, my dear, sweet husband. You said that whatever I decided was right, and you were absolutely correct!"

◆═◆

We arrived on the prairie at about 10:00 p.m. on a September 1960 evening. In the darkness, my dear husband drove us – me, the two young children and himself – to our new home on the edge of a huge field of ripened corn... acres and acres of corn stalks. I could barely make out in the distance the faint lights of the brightened highway.

So, I thought, this is Illinois!

We put the boys (ages eighteen months and three-and-a-half years old) to sleep at once and went quickly to bed ourselves.

In the morning, around 9:00 a.m., a sisterhood woman rang the front doorbell. I went to meet her and invited her into our home. She was warm and talkative, and stayed only about twenty minutes.

As she was leaving, she asked, "Did you go to college?"

"Yes, I did," I responded.

"Oh, I went for a year, too," she answered. And continued, "Of course, the men have to go so they will get good jobs! But it really isn't necessary for the women to go."

And I thought to myself, "OMG, where am I really?"

Judith Gamoran lived the first ten years of her life in the university town of Norman, Oklahoma. She and her younger brother were the only Jewish children there. The family was secular. As a teen counselor in a Jewish summer camp, she met a sparkling blue-eyed fellow named Hillel. The rest is history, although we should add that Judith graduated from Oberlin College with an A.B. degree in liberal arts and looked forward to teaching French or Spanish in the coming years. Hillel Gamoran was ordained by HUC-JIR in New York in 1956.

21

CONGREGATION AND COMMUNITY

PHYLLIS SILVERMAN

MY ROLE AS A RABBI'S WIFE HAS MADE MY LIFE VERY INTERESTING AND fruitful and challenging.

My values developed as an Orthodox Jew growing up in Borough Park, Brooklyn. I never heard my parents say a bad word about anyone. My mother always said you must deny yourself and give charity. When I fell in love with a Reform rabbinic student, my parents did not object. They valued Martin's knowledge.

My background increased my desire to help realize Martin's goal to enhance Judaism, and especially Reform Judaism, and to keep it alive and flourishing.

I attended ninety-nine percent of Friday evening and Saturday morning services, even during the period when I raised three children and, for many years, taught full-time.

In Monroe, Louisiana, Martin's first pulpit, I did community work and served as one of the chairpersons organizing cultural events for the congregation.

In Chicago, I taught Sunday school as a volunteer.

When we lived in Albany, New York, where Martin served for the majority of his career, I was a substitute teacher in the religious school and in the Hebrew program. And when Beth

Emeth had its first adult bar and bat mitzvah classes, I taught the group to read Hebrew.

I served as sisterhood president, as well. I also introduced a donor event to Beth Emeth's sisterhood. It started as a luncheon and for years now, has been a dinner. I also successfully introduced the practice of having the oneg Shabbat underwritten by members of the congregation, or by their families in honor of a life-cycle event.

In the early 1980s, I helped Martin and Bishop Howard Hubbard lead a Jewish/Catholic trip to Rome and Israel. It was one of the first such joint sponsorship in the United States.

Martin was the first rabbi to serve as president of the Albany Jewish community federation. It was in Albany that I, too, got involved in federation, ultimately becoming head of the annual fundraising campaign and winning awards for leadership. I was also a member of the Women's Division board and then the head of Women's Division. To this day, I am honored to continue my involvement in fundraising as well as serving on the board of Women's Philanthropy and on the board of the federation campaign.

For many years, I have been very involved in Jewish/Catholic dialogue and have been one of the dialogue's chairpeople for the past ten years. Martin and I were involved with the Muslim community, as well. I also volunteered at the local soup kitchen.

I am proud of my family, and of what I have accomplished for our congregation and the Jewish community.

Phyllis Silverman is a graduate of Brooklyn College, where she majored in elementary education. Over the years, she took many additional graduate courses. Phyllis is the mother of Sara, Amy and Ethan, the grandmother of four, and the great-grandmother of five. Rabbi Martin Silverman, z"l, was ordained in Cincinnati in 1953; he died in 2004.

22

UNANTICIPATED BLESSINGS AND JOYS: MY LIFE AS A RABBI'S WIFE

LYNN C. STAHL

A FEW PEOPLE IN MY LIFE HAVE ASKED ME HOW I HAD PREPARED TO be married to a rabbi. I always responded with, "Never did I – who was raised in Ishpeming, Michigan, in the boondocks of the state's Upper Peninsula – expect to be a rabbi's wife." I had never interacted with a "rebbetzin," since the only rabbis I knew were students at HUC-JIR in Cincinnati. Once a month, they made the arduous trek to the Upper Peninsula to serve our little thirty-family Temple Beth Sholom, whose membership included Jews within a fifty-mile radius of Ishpeming.

Nonetheless, in 1965, when I returned from my graduation from the University of Michigan, I met the raved-about Sam Stahl. He had been the monthly rabbinical student that my parents had described to me all year. They felt certain that my roommate/sorority sister, who spoke fluent Hebrew and was tapped to Phi Beta Kappa in her junior year, would be an ideal woman for Sam to meet. Previously, I had been fixed up with rabbinical students and concluded that this would not be the profession to which I would like to attach myself for life.

So, when Sam and I were alone together in my family's living room, I had no agenda other than just checking out my roommate's future date. But by the end of that weekend, during his last visit to Ishpeming, it was obvious that we were interested in far more than just a friendship. Fourteen months later, after I had completed my M.A. from Stanford in speech pathology, we were the first couple to be married in our little temple in Ishpeming.

Now, almost fifty-two years later, I can look back on our initial attraction and believe it truly was meant to be, *bashert*. No matter what marital challenges we have confronted, we have always been buoyed by the underlying confidence that we would make things work out. Once, during one of our arguments, one of our then-little daughters ran in and asked, "Are you getting a divorce?" This was a sad question for a young child to ask, since I didn't even know the word "divorce" until I was much older. In any case, we both laughed and were able to assure her that we were just disagreeing and would certainly resolve our problem. It is Sam's sense of humor that has so frequently broken the tension and enabled us to move on.

When I review these past fifty years, I do believe that there is definitely a divine element in our life's choices. I happen to be lucky to be a Leo, in astrological terms. I love people and am grateful that I can connect with all kinds of people during their most vulnerable, as well as their happiest, moments. There seems to be an automatic trust that people afford me just because I am married to a rabbi. Thus, I have an instant entry into their lives. I have loved this aspect of being the rabbi's wife.

We were married on August 28, 1966, shortly before Sam's last year at HUC-JIR. He was one of only four classmates who weren't married by the end of their fourth year. So, I became the new spouse of the "Wives' Club," and we instantly were embraced by many of his HUC-JIR single and married friends. Because Sam had an incredibly busy senior year, between taking classes, teaching undergrads (including Sally Priesand), studying for his comps, writing his senior thesis, preparing his senior sermon and going to his bi-weekly, we did not spend a great deal of time together during our first year of marriage. In retrospect, I realize that his frenetic schedule ultimately served me well in preparing me to build a life of my own. Although I held a full-time position as a speech pathologist at the Cincinnati Speech and Hearing Center, I was relatively free in the evenings. On many nights, I arranged to meet other spouses or friends that I made in Cincinnati so I could be fulfilled without expecting to be with Sam. However, I treasured the times that he and I shared together.

Sam's student congregation during his senior year was Temple Emanuel in Mansfield, Ohio. Often, I rode the bus there on Friday night, after I had finished work. We did have long car rides back from Mansfield every other week. At those precious times, we could reflect on our current concerns. The student congregation didn't really offer me much of an opportunity to begin my rebbetzin training, other than visiting some shut-in's and making a couple of condolence calls with Sam.

I vividly remember walking out of the house of a mourning widow and feeling as if we had flunked "Sympathy Call" that day. I had persisted in my nervous jabbering. Sam had said very little, except, "I know how you feel." Later, we both understood that articulating these words is both inappropriate and off-putting. Thankfully, we have learned a great deal since that botched visit, and both of us are far better listeners. We now try to worry less about what we say and more about being present with the suffering person.

Sam's rabbinical ordination in June 1967 made a powerful impact on us. It occurred just two days before the Six-Day War erupted in Israel. Shortly thereafter, Sam was required to attend Army chaplaincy school at Ft. Hamilton, which is at the southern tip of Brooklyn, New York. His assignment provided an opportunity for us to spend our weekends exploring New York City and its environs.

I secured a frivolous job as the assistant personal shopper at

Bonwit Teller, in Manhattan, a store similar to Saks Fifth Avenue. This newest career was totally different from my previous ones as a camp counselor and as a speech pathologist. My time at Bonwit Teller possibly did help my future as a rabbi's spouse in one respect. I learned to deal with some very entitled customers whose demands were frankly astounding to this then-twenty-three-year old, naïve, small-town girl.

After Sam completed his ten-week stint at Ft. Hamilton, he was assigned to Ft. Belvoir, Virginia, which had the country's largest Jewish military congregation. He was responsible for the religious needs of all Jewish military personnel in the greater Washington area. I was working full-time as a speech and hearing therapist at D.C. General Hospital. During that period, I saw my "rabbi's spouse" role as that of attending every Friday night service and entertaining many of the congregants in our apartment.

Candidly, I must add that our social life during our time in the greater Washington, D.C. area was unfulfilling. At most parties, we felt as if we were being judged on our professional status rather than our personal qualities. We had too many vapid nights when we were grateful to cling to each other for emotional nourishment.

Because Sam was a strident, outspoken opponent of our government's military involvement in Vietnam, our time in Ft. Belvoir lasted only eight months. He made the grievous mistake of sending an ardent appeal to the leaders of the CCAR on official government stationery to end the chaplaincy requirement for graduating HUC-JIR seniors. He believed that serving in the chaplaincy implied an endorsement of our country's involvement in Vietnam.

As a result, he was punished and reassigned to Seoul, South Korea. I was lucky enough to secure a job with the Department of Defense system to be the first speech therapist in the U.S. Army's elementary school system in Korea. This position afforded me the rights to housing, which, combined with Sam's housing allowance, enabled us to live in a little apartment in a building with other army officer/teacher couples. What his military superiors intended as a curse became a blessing. We enjoyed a stellar adventure that year in the Far East. We savored the unique cultural offerings of Asia and were able to visit Japan, Taiwan, Hong Kong, Singapore, Malaysia, and Thailand. However, I never had the sense that my being married to a "captain chaplain" was any different from our friends whose husbands were "captain doctors" or "major attorneys."

In 1969, upon our return from Korea, Sam was invited to serve the historic Temple B'nai Israel (The Henry Cohen Memorial), in Galveston, Texas. We lived a short distance from the Gulf of Mexico, with its long stretches of beaches. I suddenly saw the mantle of a rabbi's wife in striking technicolor. I remember donning a hat and putting on gloves in the ninety-five-degree heat just before we walked into each Shabbat service.

We soon happily discovered that Galveston was, in many ways, a laid-back community. One day, during that first excruciatingly hot summer, I rushed into the local fish market to buy something for dinner. I was dressed in my bathing suit, flip-flops and a cover-up. Of course, I bumped into one of the "*grand dame*" congregants and immediately apologized for wearing attire not befitting a rabbinical spouse. She assured me that she was happier for me to have "sand between my toes" (a favorite expression of native Galvestonians) than to worry about the way I appeared.

I worked diligently at learning people's names, as I had done while I was rush chairman of my sorority at the University of Michigan. It had become obvious to me that my remembering someone's name was vitally important to our relationship with that individual. Fortunately, both Sam and I could recall names easily. As I have aged, I wish that I still retained that ability.

Our congregation owned a "rabbinage." At age twenty-six, I felt as if I were moving into my parents' home. It was far too grand for our needs at that time. It featured an immense living room and three sizable bedrooms, as well as two and a half baths, a full dining room, family room and large kitchen. Though our home was rent-free, we were responsible for the exorbitant cost of the utilities. An excessive amount of air-conditioning was needed to cool a home comfortably in South Texas, with its high humidity.

Every time our toilet or a pipe was not working, or something went awry with the electrical system, our temple's house committee chair had to come to our home, assess the situation, and then find the appropriate solution. Often the person our temple board hired to fix the problem was the one who had submitted the lowest bid, and all too often we found the work unsatisfactory. Because of Galveston's tropical climate, with its salt air, our house and garage desperately needed repainting almost every year. The "expert" painter who was hired arrived on a bicycle, with a can of paint on each handlebar, no drop cloths, and with the ladder slung over his shoulder. He began to repaint the detached garage from the bottom up. Thus, by the time he was painting the top of the garage, the new paint was dripping down on the lower boards!! What a "lovely" look!

Every year, we hosted a Rosh Hashanah open house for our entire congregation, which numbered approximately 175 families. I did the bulk of the baking and preparations and accepted very few offers of help with the food. My self-imposed "martyr" role somehow seemed to be reinforced by doing the yeoman's work. Nonetheless, we received scores of accolades and created a very accepting, supportive congregation. Little did I realize how ephemeral such flattering recognition ultimately is in life. However, I was still very young and unseasoned.

The first two years we were there, I worked as a speech pathologist at a school for children with cerebral palsy. This position offered me a marvelous avenue to establish myself as a professional. Although I felt compelled to join Sam on shut-in visits on the weekends, I did not make hospital visits with him nor attend every funeral at which he officiated, which several rabbis' wives were doing at that time.

One of the very first Jewish community social events we attended in Galveston was a B'nai B'rith dance. We were not there for more than twenty minutes when a temple member rushed up to Sam and said, "Rabbi, can I speak to you for a moment?" Seventy-five minutes later (I am not exaggerating), Sam emerged! I had tried to entertain myself during this agonizing time with people I had met only briefly. I even pretended that I didn't mind not dancing, since no one had asked me to dance anyway. However, I can tell you that evening has had an impact on us until this day. Boundaries are important, and Sam has had to learn how to say, "Now is not an ideal time...Can you call me at my office?"

My role in sisterhood was complicated. I attended almost every meeting, while cringing during the endless hours of haggling over the budget. After many of the sisterhood meetings, I fled into Sam's office in tears. I felt miserable about having to sit through the ponderous and seemingly trivial discussions. I absolutely did not enjoy this aspect of my "rabbi's spouse" role! However, I presented a few programs that were synchronized with my interests. One year I even volunteered to bake 140 *dozen* schnecken, using my grandmother's *very involved* little sweet roll recipe, for a Jewish food festival that was our annual sisterhood's fundraiser.

I knew that, because of some prior physiological issues, I most likely would not be able to birth my own children. When we decided to marry, Sam was totally accepting of our pursuing adoption. However, I thought it was not safe or prudent to share this information with anyone at that time. Therefore, we kept this whole process secretive until our older daughter, Heather, arrived in the fall of 1971. With her adoption, an enormous number of congregants and others in the Jewish and general communities of Galveston showered us with gifts. Then, two-and-a-half years later, we adopted Alisa, who again was generously welcomed into the community.

During our seven years in Galveston, I was leery of forming any close friendships within our congregation. This choice was really a denial of who I am, because I thrive when I can enjoy the intimacy of close friendships. Happily, as life unfolded, its lessons taught me that I, in fact, could establish safe relationships with trustworthy people, even within the congregation. That insight has been lifesaving for me.

While in Galveston, Sam was working on his Doctor of Hebrew Letters degree, studying for his comps and writing a dissertation. Fortunately, I was able to find more than enough to do with our two children as well as in the League of Women Voters. In addition, in the mid-1970s, Sam and I became rabbinical team leaders for Jewish Marriage Encounter. This role provided me with a purpose and a passion that met my deepest emotional needs at that time. It was ideal both for enhancing our own marriage and nourishing my introspective nature. At the same time, it enabled me to feel as if I were giving back in a manner that grew my strengths.

When we finally decided to move to San Antonio in 1976, for Sam to become senior rabbi of Temple Beth-El, I really worried about hurting any of our congregants' feelings because of our departure. In reaction to my insecurity, I literally wrote about 175 individually worded letters. I informed each family that as much as we had valued our seven years at Temple B'nai Israel, we felt it would be wise for us to move to a larger congregation.

We received a wide variety of responses. One active member of the congregation wrote to pour out her heart. She revealed that, before we arrived, she had promised herself that she would never allow herself to be vulnerable to new relationships, for fear they would abandon her. She had failed to fulfill that vow. Now, even though she had fully embraced us, we were, in her mind, rejecting her. This response was tough for both of us. Whose issue was this? Hers? Ours? How much power do we really have?

Thankfully, with numerous hours of therapy after coming to San Antonio, I was able to see that these kinds of issues were not about me. How bereft my life would be without the superb counseling I have received since 1980.

Moving to a large metropolitan area like San Antonio, after having been raised in a town of 8,000 people, was thrilling for me. Unlike our time in Galveston, I no longer had to drive an hour or more into Houston for a haircut, theater, lecture or social event. Sometimes, I had traveled to and from Houston twice in one day. The San Antonio community greeted us with open arms and we immediately felt at home in our first personally-owned home. We loved being able to make it totally ours.

When Sam was installed seven months after our arrival, we wanted to invite the entire (then 875 families) congregation to our home to try to reciprocate their warm, generous welcome. I did all the baking and preparation, although I did allow some of my friends to help me that day. Getting all those people in and out of our home, in two shifts, was so daunting that never again did I attempt such a stupid, ill-advised task. No one complained, but I can't fathom what they were thinking when they had to leave their cars in a church parking lot about half a mile away, take a shuttle to our home, and then push through the crowds once they arrived inside.

Unlike Galveston, where I had followed a rabbi's spouse whom many congregants considered distant and unavailable, in San Antonio there was Helen Jacobson, the "Eleanor Roosevelt of the rabbinate." She was incredibly involved with every aspect of her husband, David's rabbinate. She not only accompanied him on all hospital visits, she also attended every funeral at which he officiated. In addition, Helen was a respected leader, in her own right, of a myriad of Jewish and general causes locally and nationally.

During our first year, we went to a dinner at which she was the honoree. As I sat listening to her lengthy list of honors and the organizations to which she had given her boundless dedication, I sank further and further into my seat.

When we drove home and I shared my feelings of inferiority

with Sam, he reminded me of the Hasidic story: "When Rabbi Zusya dies, God will not ask him, 'Why were you not more like Moses?' Rather God will ask, 'Why were you not the best Zusya you could have been?'" I resolved to try to be the best Lynn Stahl and not compare myself to this phenomenal rabbi's spouse who gave unstintingly of her multitude of talents, energy and intellect. That was a vital lesson for me on many levels at that time, while I was still in my early thirties.

In our new community of San Antonio, I was deliberately slow in developing close relationships right at the beginning since I knew that it is far easier to form a friendship than to sever it. Consequently, since I initially proceeded with caution, my closest friends today, who mainly are temple members, are people whom I can fully trust. Only on thorny temple issues did I not share my most intimate feelings with these special friends. Thankfully, I had Sam for those discussions.

As the years have gone by, we have formed more and more "safe" friendships. Now, having been retired sixteen years, we are incredibly grateful for the support we have enjoyed in San Antonio. I have always believed that we would live out our days here; we have already arranged for our burial plots in our temple cemetery.

San Antonio was a comfortable place in which to raise our daughters. Sam tried to be home for dinner every night, although many of those nights he had to return to temple for a meeting. He was inordinately busy over the years when the girls were growing up. Not only was he overseeing a growing congregation, but he also served as president of the Kallah of Texas Rabbis and the Southwest Association of Reform Rabbis. For six years, he was editor of the Journal of Reform Judaism (now the CCAR Journal) and held a wide variety of other organizational commitments.

During the first decade or so, Sam confronted a very controlling temple board. Its members were largely politically reactionary assimilated Jews. They had little interest in the religious or programmatic life of the congregation. Their main goal was to maintain a balanced budget without raising membership dues. As a result, they were tight-fisted in allocating funds for important temple needs. Sam frequently felt incredibly frustrated by his lay leaders, some of whom even considered themselves our good personal friends.

I could not discuss those challenges with any of my closest friends, who were temple members. I often urged Sam to call either Rabbi Jack Stern or Rabbi Sam Karff, who served as effective counselors for both of us. Whenever my Sam would talk about applying for another congregation, I would say to him, "Happiness is changing one set of problems for another! Are you sure you are ready to throw in the towel?" Thankfully, he did persevere, so that after fourteen years and many struggles, he – at long last – shaped a board that reflected his values and ideals.

I would say that one of my biggest weekly challenges in those early years was finding responsible babysitters for Friday and, sometimes, Saturday nights. We tried to go to many of the bar/bat mitzvah parties, especially of those families who did not seem to have a lot of friends in the congregation. Frequently when we were at a party or a wedding, we knew almost no one except the families who were hosting the event. I cherished those times since it gave Sam and me a few hours to connect with one another, in a happy setting.

One of the major perks of being a rabbi's spouse is that I often gained entry into families' lives when no one other than family members was included. How many small golden anniversary dinners did we attend where we were privy to precious family's stories and shared experiences? How many times did I, as Sam's spouse, get a bird's eye view of the way a family was coping with a loved one's terrible illness or death? These opportunities offered me valuable insights in dealing with life's slings and arrows.

I became more and more involved with my own volunteer work as our girls were getting older. Yet I knew that I needed somehow to find an outlet for my skills other than serving as an art museum docent, a symphony representative in the schools, the chairperson of our Jewish Federation drive, room mother in school, etc. Eventually, because of an ongoing struggle with an eating disorder and feelings of inadequacy as a mother, I decided to work with a psychotherapist. These sessions were incredibly well-timed and have served me so well over all these decades. At my first visit, my therapist urged me to take a respite from all my volunteer positions. After finally trusting her enough and making the leap into "nothing-but-mothering-and wife-ing," I began working on my inner self. Ironically, shortly after I pulled out of all of my volunteer activities, I was named "Volunteer of the Year" by our local newspaper! That certainly was fodder for the therapist!

Serendipitously, I soon was offered a position at Jewish Family Service as the Family Life Education Coordinator. Nothing could have been more perfectly suited to my interests and passions. Sam was incredibly supportive of my taking this part-time job. In that position, life-transforming horizons opened up for me. I developed different varieties of workshops dealing with everything from eating disorders to stress management to marriage enrichment. I led support groups for adoptive parents, those suffering grief and loss, parents of lesbian and gay people, cancer challenges, and many more over my more than two decades at JFS.

For several years, I worked with the parents of the consecrants at temple to explore the challenges they would be facing during the time their little kindergarteners were enrolled in our religious school. I also led a workshop for bar/bat mitzvah candidates and their parents to sensitize them to the emotional facets of bar and bat mitzvah.

The cancer groups that I was able to launch were eerily timed, for how could I know that eventually my sister would be diagnosed with breast cancer in the late 1980s? Much later, Sam underwent surgery for prostate and then bladder cancer; Alisa developed breast cancer, and Heather, kidney cancer. My ability to deal with these issues has definitely been enriched by my earlier work with the bi-weekly cancer groups that I led.

So many of my magnificent life's experiences have been a result of my being married, not only to Sam Stahl (my obvious soul mate of fifty-two years), but to a rabbi. Together we have co-led two congregational trips to Israel as well as four interfaith trips with a local Baptist minister. I would never have been able to benefit from these trips were I not the spouse of the rabbi who was largely responsible for organizing them. Interacting with people on journeys to Israel enabled me to grow my soul in a short time in a way that I never would have envisioned.

I found so many more positive by-products from this role than I did any real drawbacks. Were there family Shabbat dinners at temple at which I felt as if I were Barbara Walters, interviewing some of the shy, taciturn congregants at our table? Of course. Were there planned family outings from which Sam had to withdraw at the last minute because of an emergency in the congregation? Of course. But, by and large, the rewards of being a rabbi's spouse have been incalculable.

When Sam chose early retirement in 2002, at age sixty-two, I wisely decided that I should segue out of my Jewish Family Service position. That same spring our older daughter, Heather, was married to Jeffrey Katz. Then a year and a half later, just as I had turned sixty, she gave birth to our first "grand jewel," Austin Katz. Because of our new flexible schedule, we had far more opportunities to live the envious life of "Saba" and "Leelee." During the summer of 2003, Sam was appointed the Theologian-in-Residence at Chautauqua Institution. In subsequent years, we have returned to Chautauqua for the entire season of nine weeks. Sam has served as Chautauqua's unofficial rabbi and has worked as an associate professor in its Department of Religion. I describe Chautauqua as an "adult brain and soul camp."

Our second grand jewel, Carli Katz, was born in 2005. Alisa

and Marco Cimmino, a native of Perugia, Italy, were married three years later. Since then, we have been blessed with four more grand jewels, Sabrina Cimmino, Liliana Katz, Charles Cimmino, and Kyra Katz.

Being the retired rabbi's spouse has fortunately left no void in my life. We have done this retirement "dance" together, shared our feelings, and by and large felt exceedingly comfortable in our greatly reduced role in our temple. Many times, when I hear about one of our former congregants going through a crisis or celebrating a joyous occasion, I will send a note, email or make a phone call in both of our names. We are still part of the community, and still very much care about these people who have been in our lives for the last forty-two years. An unexpected bonus of retirement is our being able to enjoy many more social evenings where Sam is free of worrying about preparing for a wedding or funeral the next day. We've become keenly aware that nurturing relationships with younger friends is wise insurance for keeping us current and helping us avoid the typical "organ recital" regarding one another's health! Our younger friends have been remarkably willing to get together with us and to share their own views and challenges at their specific life stages.

I realize that although Sam retired from the temple, he did not retire from the rabbinate, so he still performs an occasional life-cycle ceremony, delivers a sermon, and is invited as a scholar-in-residence. This is more than enough for both of us, and we have a pact that when the day comes that he is no longer on top of his game, I will be the first to tell him that he must fully retire, even from the rabbinate.

As I reflect upon my life as a rabbi's spouse, I am fully aware of how blessed I have been. I love connecting with people. I love the spirituality of religious services. I love learning about others from their sharing of their experiences with me. I love Jewish music of all kinds. This marriage that I somehow fell into seems to have been divinely ordained. I am, indeed, a most fortunate woman.

Thus, each morning, I can gratefully affirm the words of our prayer book: *Ashreinu, mah tov hel'keinu*, "Happy are we; how good is our portion in life."

Lynn Cohodas Stahl served as the Director of Family Life Education at Jewish Family Service of San Antonio for twenty-three years. She has been an active volunteer throughout her life, serving both the Jewish and general communities. She was the founding president of ThriveWell Cancer Foundation. Each summer at Chautauqua Institution, she co-chairs the Chautauqua Dialogues, which encourages shared ethical and civil discourse. Lynn is dedicated to creating a climate of openness and sensitivity to "the Other." She has recently focused on voter registration and volunteering for compassionate political candidates who are willing to work for the less fortunate in our country.

23

THE GLASS

SUSIE COOK

MY HUSBAND'S TRAJECTORY IN THE RABBINATE AFTER ORDINATION was different from that of his colleagues. They were either going to be military chaplains or entering congregational work. Julian had already accepted a position with the UAHC as a regional youth director and Director of the URJ camp in Zionsville, Indiana, even before his ordination in 1972.

We met at the University of Michigan, when I was seventeen and he, eighteen. Believe it or not, we really did meet at the big Hillel mixer that everyone attended (even if they never appeared at Hillel again). We were married about a month after graduation.

During our Michigan years, we were very involved in campus activities. We worked at making a big community small, both together and separately. I occasionally worked on Hillel projects. But it wasn't until I ran out of the expense allowance that my dad had allotted me for the year that I began teaching religious school at the synagogue in Ann Arbor to keep myself both solvent and involved in Jewish education.

In college, Julian was searching for potential career directions. One summer, we worked at the Union's camp in Oconomowoc, where I was part of the Hebrew-speaking camp and he was the athletics director. His immersion in the camp culture and connections with amazing rabbis led to his ultimate decision to attend HUC-JIR and become a rabbi/camp director.

When Julian entered rabbinical school, my Hebrew and text knowledge were much greater than his. I used to help him and his study group with their homework. Sally Priesand, the first woman Reform rabbi, was in his ordination class. I now see that, with a little encouragement, the rabbinate would have been a wonderful career choice for me, as well. But teaching became my passion.

During our years at HUC-JIR, an organized Wives' Club met periodically for social activities. For the most part, we had very little concept of what our congregational role would be. We were busy supporting our spouses or continuing our education or starting families. There were no spousal expectations at the time, and the move to congregational life proved to be a big shock for some.

Our years in Cincinnati were challenging and fun. We had a core of friends who socialized together and supported each other in many ways. We became a very special extended family. Throughout the years, we have maintained contact with these wonderful people and love to visit and celebrate simchas when we can.

I know there are spouses who did not share the rabbinical school years and are reluctant to attend our conventions because they don't have that backdrop of shared experiences. I think that those who do come find a wonderful *hevra* and are warmly welcomed.

While in Cincinnati, I refined one of my basic beliefs about partnership: no matter what career my husband chose, I would be a supportive spouse, just as I expected him to support me in my career. This seemed different from my perception of the rabbis' wives in the temple where I grew up (Cincinnati, Ohio). Each of those women had a job, and that job was to be an extension of her husband. They were perceived as a single unit with intertwining – if unequal – roles.

Fortunately for me and those who have followed us, the situation and expectations have gradually changed – partly due to the feminist movement and partly to the ordination of women. In addition, their husbands would likely not tolerate the role we accepted as a given. When my husband was ordained, women were very slowly coming into their own as individuals and developing professional lives independent of their husbands' careers. Of course, even today, there are still congregants who hold fixed expectations of what the rabbi's wife (never husband) should do: attend services and sisterhood meetings regularly, participate in temple holiday celebrations, etc.

My personal choice was to maintain my Jewish commitment. I was supportive of my rabbi, while building my career, raising the family and pursuing further education, all endeavors that he supported in return. I was not responsible for setting the table for the oneg or making sure that there was wine and challah on the bimah or toilet paper in the bathroom. The temple had not hired me.

For years, I've thought that some wives (and now, partners as well) would benefit from a course in how to be a rabbi's spouse, though I know that this role can vary tremendously, especially today. Being old fashioned in some ways, I believe a rabbinic spouse's appearance is important. For that matter, so is the rabbi's. Setting standards for elevating appropriate temple attire at services was something I thought I could help to model. I was once teaching adult Hebrew and one of the moms asked me for any suggestions on how to get her kids to services. Here's what I suggested:

On Monday, you say, "Hey kids, we're going to temple on Friday night." On Tuesday, you say, "Hey kids, we're going to temple on Friday night." On Wednesday and Thursday, you continue to mention it, not discuss it, just state it as a fact. Then, on Friday, you say, "We're having dinner at temple at six followed by services. Be downstairs, ready to go, at..."

The mom tried it, and it worked!

Her next question was, "How do I get them out of sweatpants for temple?" And we (the class and I) came up with some suggestions: establish one habit at a time, once a month, twice a month... Habits take repetition to form. I do understand that in today's world, it is acceptable in some places to wear jeans. Okay, I can go with that, but they should be nice jeans, clean shirts, hair combed. One way or another, people's attire when they attend services should reflect the holiness of the time and space.

I was the product of a mixed marriage. I was seven years-old when my mom and (step) dad married. He was then president of the Conservative synagogue and my mom was president of the sisterhood at Isaac M. Wise Temple. I went to Hebrew school twice a week at the Conservative synagogue and religious school every Sunday morning at the Reform temple (which, by the way, held high school classes at HUC-JIR). I was an avid Ramah camper and counselor, active in USY (United Synagogue Youth, the very popular youth program of Conservative Jewry), and also very involved in our Reform youth group, attending many NFTY conventions.

I loved and love being connected Jewishly. The things I've done as a rabbinic spouse are probably the same things that I would have done had my husband had another profession. We still would have had that strong Jewish link. I am fortunate to be part of a deeply involved Jewish family. My uncle was Nelson Glueck, rabbi, renowned archaeologist and president of HUC-JIR. My maternal grandfather's half-brother was the founder and president of Yeshiva University, Rabbi Bernard Revel. My brother, Jonathan Brown, is a retired Reform rabbi. My step-grandfather was an Orthodox cantor, and two of my father's brothers became Reform cantors. My mom, Sally Glueck Brown, served at HUC-JIR as the community relations liaison.

We worked hard instilling Judaism into our three children and are proud they are all involved in Jewish life and education today. Our eldest, Alan Cook, is a wonderful congregational rabbi. His wife, Jody Cook, is also a rabbi. They live in Champaign, Illinois. Their three children have been attending Friday night services since infancy. Our youngest – our daughter, Emily – recently received her doctorate in Jewish education from the Jewish Theological Seminary. And our middle child, Steven – the one who always seemed to have a stomachache in the middle of Friday night services – is a restauranteur and cookbook author, with an emphasis on Israeli cuisine. Steven's flagship restaurant, *Zahav*, which he co-owns with James Beard chef, Michael Solomonov, is one of the "must eat" places in Philadelphia. His eponymous cookbook, *Zahav*, won the James Beard cookbook of the year in 2017 and, for the third year in a row, was named outstanding restaurant at the 2019 James Beard Awards ceremony. In addition to several other restaurants there, he is also the owner of a unique restaurant in Philadelphia whose net proceeds go to help fund the Broad Street Coalition for the Homeless. He and his wife are the parents of four Jewish day school students. Of course, our grandchildren are all amazing individuals!

◆═◆

In 1971, when our son Alan was nine months old, my mom was murdered coming home from Sukkot services.

It was devastating. She was a remarkable individual. Divorced when my brother was born and then widowed twice, she was the rock of our family. She was one of nine children. Our home was the one where the troubled cousins came to live, where holidays were celebrated, where ideas and people were valued. She was the connector for the family. She was always learning, listening and teaching. I believe that my mom's tragic death was the worst thing that ever happened to me. Even a TIA at twenty-six and breast cancer at seventy are dwarfed by my mom's death. I believe she can see what our children and grandchildren have achieved. Our memories of her give us strength. My husband and mom were very close. Her death took place during the academic year of his ordination, and his professors were surprised that he was able to create his rabbinic thesis while supporting us emotionally.

With her loss, I changed. I became more assertive, a trait that became so important to my career and my life. In essence, I grew up. I understood that after working through this tragedy, I could deal with whatever was before me. This loss propelled me in many ways. First, I was motivated to be the best at what I encountered. I did not wait for life to happen; I made it happen.

I was also propelled to accept challenges. I took the Long Island Railroad, subway and bus to Brooklyn by myself to get my New York Teacher Certification. (For New Yorkers, that's no big deal, but for Midwesterners, it was a series of scary, intricate maneuvers.) I drove from Turner Falls, Massachusetts, through the tunnel to the Boston Airport, by myself (before cell phones). I became a mentor teacher. I relearned Excel, and took up weightlifting at seventy-three. Each time I did something like flying to Cincinnati for Founder's Day at HUC-JIR, by myself, forgetting my cell phone, renting a car and getting exactly where I needed to be – things that caused initial anxiety – gave and continue to give me a wonderful sense of satisfaction, accomplishment, and pride, because I did them.

I'm a very high energy, outgoing person. I know not everyone is. Some rabbinic spouses are introverts and are perceived by congregants to be aloof and unfriendly, when that is not the case at all. For introverts, it takes a tremendous amount of energy to be outgoing for long periods of time. I don't think any of my friends would call me an introvert. Growing up, I had seen my parents surround themselves with friends, entertain and celebrate holidays with a welcoming table graced with all kinds of people. Granted, they weren't a rabbinic couple, but they set a model for me in terms of creating friendships and making other people feel welcome.

I have always been involved in Jewish life, from serving on the Federation board to National Council of Jewish Women and Hadassah, religious school, etc. In my retirement, I continue to plan family education for the temple, work on our Family Promise Project of housing the homeless, chair a Mitzvah Day project, serve on the educator selection search committee and sit on the temple board's nominating committee. I also volunteer for Jewish Family Service by providing free lunches and books so needy children can get school lunches during the summer.

Teaching everywhere we lived gave me wonderful opportunities for growth. I taught for more than forty years in public, private and Jewish day schools. At the same time, I worked in religious schools as a Hebrew and Judaica teacher, assistant principal and professional developer. I was a clinical instructor at Florida International University and began my M.A. work there. I completed the degree at Queens College, when we moved to Long Island.

One of the highlights of my Denver experience was my training as a consultant for Responsive Classroom, sponsored by the Center for Responsive Schools. As a result of my training, I taught and continue to teach the elementary teachers in my Denver school, Graland Country Day School. That philosophy pervades the classroom and enhances school climate by linking social and emotional learning. I've also taught this program to community-wide religious school workshops, student teachers, and all first-year employees at my school. Since I retired, I continue teaching my adult courses and substitute frequently. Because all seven of our grandchildren live far from Denver, I love having the "kid" connection. I also love to tutor math!

Many of my rabbinic wife friends tell me that they have a lot of acquaintances, but not a lot of friends in the community. We have been very fortunate. We've had a core of close friends everywhere we've been. They have followed us around the country, and we visit whenever we can. We've only been burned twice with relationships that changed and became acrimonious, but even Dear Amy says that some friendships have a limited shelf life. I have always been very careful not to air dirty laundry. I've listened to friends' lives and shared hopes and dreams for our children... but our friends would never know if Julian and I had had an argument or were going through a rough patch, as many couples do. My involvement with people, the community and friends has been something I have worked at. In one community, although we had social friends, my walking buddy and confidante was a minister's wife.

My husband and I share a love of cooking. We often gather our friends together around food. We are creative together. We share the same ideas and values and enjoy the same activities, except when it comes to exercise. That has been my path to sanity when I need to counter stress. Many of my friendships have grown out of my involvement in various groups. I've always had walking groups, hamantaschen baking groups, book groups and an Israel group composed of fellow travelers who have gathered together every week for the past six years for walking and bimonthly for dinner. Other than not going out on Friday nights to Happy Hour with school friends or attending a public event on Shabbat or a Jewish holiday, I can't recall an incident when being a rabbinic spouse interfered with my life. When one of our sons was co-captain of his high school football team that only played on Friday nights, I was there. Apart from that, I went to Friday night services regularly.

In recent years, Saturday has been for *me* unless there is a bar or bat mitzvah I want to attend, or a Jewish holiday. I worked six days a week for most of my adult life. When we became empty nesters, Saturday became my day. My husband wasn't thrilled, but we worked it out. I always cook Shabbat dinner. Throughout our married life, we have never eaten out on a Friday night, unless it's been a dinner at temple or at the home of someone who celebrates Shabbat.

Some rabbis' wives are resentful or critical of the time the rabbinate takes from home life, or that schedules are often unpredictable. Our family learned to go with the flow, and, during one period when Julian had late-night commitments, we took a picnic dinner to my husband's office so that he could have dinner with the kids. It took a bit of extra effort? So what! I think that's what couples should do for their families, no matter what career paths they follow.

Julian spent four years doing camp work, after which his career path shifted, and he became Associate Rabbi and Educator at Temple

Sinai, a congregation in south Florida. What a great place to raise kids! We were there for fourteen years, including three years at Temple Beth Am in south Miami.

But when we were ready to move on, we discovered that finding pulpits was tricky. The willingness to perform intermarriages had become the litmus test for employment. It made job searches particularly challenging, because the tide in the Reform movement was changing. It was challenging to be on the cusp of being offered a position and then being asked that last question: "Do you perform intermarriages?" When Julian said that he did not... Supporting each other through disappointment became key to my role as a rabbinic spouse. Still, Julian moved from associate to senior rabbi in Michigan and New York, after which we ended up in Long Island for six trying years. Finally, we landed in Denver with our good friend, Rabbi Steven Foster. He saved us and provided a perfect place for Julian to conclude his full-time career.

We have traveled a somewhat uneven path, but we have walked it together.

Last January, my husband and I became Interim Vice-Presidents of NAORRR, the National Association of Retired Reform Rabbis. It's been a great "together" project. It pushes us to relearn old skills and acquire new ones, to build on the marvelous work of our predecessors, and to continue to grow the organization.

I'm the glass-half-full girl. I'm also blessed with a short memory. I've always loved being part of this great rabbinic spouse club. Life has had its ups-and-downs, but the glass is still there when I wake up each morning.

Susie Cook lives with her husband, Julian Cook (C '72) in Denver, Colorado. They have three adult children and seven grandchildren. She and her husband are currently co-executive directors of NAORRR, the National Association of Retired Reform Rabbis. She is the Family Educator at Temple Emanuel in Denver, a substitute teacher at the school from which she retired, a volunteer on a reading project with Jewish Family Services and chair of the food committee for the congregation's Family Promise, an organization that houses the homeless. She loves to attend plays and symphony, read, walk, exercise and spend time with her husband. She is clearly unsuccessful at retirement.

24

THE BLESSINGS OF A RABBINIC SPOUSE

JANE PERMAN

WHAT'S THE BEST PREPARATION FOR BEING A RABBINIC SPOUSE? FOR me, it was being born into a family that loved, valued and celebrated Jewish life. I have wonderful memories of a childhood filled with home and synagogue observances of Shabbat and holidays. Every Friday afternoon, my siblings and I were called in from play to say "Good Shabbos," to our grandparents. My grandfather blew the shofar at our synagogue in his white robe each year on the High Holy Days. My parents were regular contributors to Jewish charities and participated in Jewish organizations. There was no question that I would continue my Jewish education through Hebrew high school. I held leadership positions in Jewish youth groups and went to Jewish camps, including Camp Ramah, where learning Hebrew was intrinsic and fun! Love of Israel was basic to our family.

When people ask me how I met my husband, Jim Perman, I always smile and think how prescient it was that we met in high school in Buffalo, New York, at the Jewish Center. There was a social event for Jewish teenagers on a Saturday night that began with a havdalah ceremony. Guess who was reciting the havdalah blessings? I looked up at that handsome sixteen-year old fellow and decided we had to get to know each other. We did, and we dated during high school until Jim graduated in 1958. When he chose to attend college in a joint program at Columbia University and the Jewish Theological Seminary, I set my sights on Barnard College and was accepted there in 1960. We were married in 1963, at the end of my junior year at Barnard.

The next question people often ask is, "When did Jim know he wanted to become a rabbi and how did you feel about that?" He made that decision while studying as a religion major at Columbia. Because of our shared values and our love of Judaism, I thought it was a great choice for both of us. Something I don't usually share with many people (but I think it will make you smile) is that when we became engaged, I actually had visions of our singing Hebrew songs together in bed. (Remember, I was still a teenager.) Becoming the wife of a rabbi was something I welcomed, and that positive attitude has served me well over the course of Jim's career.

As for my own career aspirations, I grew up wanting to become a teacher. While Jim was in rabbinical school at HUC-JIR in Manhattan, I pursued a master's degree at Bank Street College of Education. I graduated in 1965 and then taught at PS 11 in the Chelsea neighborhood of New York City. When Jim was ordained in 1967, our life took a dramatic turn. Jewish chaplains were needed in order to meet the increased demand of the military draft during the Vietnam era. At that time, HUC-JIR expected all newly ordained rabbis who met the physical and other criteria to serve as chaplains. Almost as soon as the ordination ceremony in New York City was over, Jim was inducted as an officer in the United States Air Force, and we were on our way across the country to Travis Air Force Base in California.

Without any specific training, Jim became the leader of a congregation of young Jewish airmen, doctors, dentists, lawyers and other military personnel who were serving at Travis. We formed friendships with everyone in this group and also with the Christian clergy and their families. Our daughter, Debbie, was born at Travis AFB and our community, especially those who already had young children, became our parenting advisors.

With my "vast" teaching experience, I helped run a Hebrew school on the base. In addition to learning to be a mom for the first time, I began to coordinate Shabbat and holiday parties, including a huge seder for the entire community. That had always been my parents' or grandparents' job, and I remember studying the books about how to make a seder, what to cook and which symbols had to be on a seder plate. A big part of our life became our relationship with the young, single airmen. We invited them into our home for Shabbat dinners. Although Jim and I were just a few years older than they were, our home became their place to "land," and we were like parents to them. We loved them, advised them and comforted them.

One year after settling into our new life as an Air Force family at Travis Air Force Base, Jim received notice that he had been promoted, and we were being transferred to Ankara, Turkey! Can you imagine our surprise and dismay? Travis AFB, at least, had been across the same country where our families and friends all lived, but Turkey was on the other side of the world!! Fortunately, we were young and full of confidence. Since we flourished in our first military adventure, we faced this new assignment with enthusiasm – and just a bit of trepidation. The thirteen months that we spent in Turkey turned out to exceed all our expectations! Living in another country, albeit as members of the United States Air Force, was an eye-opening experience. We learned that, although the United States was admired in much of the world, not everyone held Americans in high esteem.

Ankara, the capital of Turkey, did not have a US Air Force base such as we had known in California. Instead, we lived in an upscale neighborhood among foreign diplomats (including some Israelis who were attached to the legation located there), affluent Turks and other United States military and Foreign Service personnel. We shopped for food and other basics at the American Base Exchange, but also at local markets in our neighborhood. I took Turkish language lessons with some of the other wives. For two dollars a day, we had the services of Nazla, a Turkish maid/nanny whom we inherited from the previous Jewish chaplain. We did not have a car, a television set or even a telephone, so we spent a lot of time socializing and talking to people face-to-face in each other's homes. Our news came with the *Stars and Stripes* newspaper and the week-old delivery of our *New York Times*. Considering all that was going on in the US and Vietnam during 1968-69, we were often quite out of the loop, but that didn't seem to matter so much as we were busy helping our unconventional congregation.

Once again, I ran a religious school for American children, some Israeli kids and even a few Turkish Jews. As at Travis, we reached out to the single Jewish airmen and I planned Shabbat, holiday and lifecycle celebrations. The Jewish personnel whom Jim now "shepherded" were not just the airmen and professionals serving in Ankara. He was also responsible for all the Jewish service people in other military and NATO sites in Turkey, Greece, Iran and Pakistan. He had to travel frequently to visit, advise and comfort. He conducted services and lifecycle events for United States personnel serving in those distant places. I accompanied him on some of those trips, even after I became pregnant with our second child. Our son, Danny, was born in an American hospital in Ankara towards the end of our military service. His birth certificate was issued by the American Embassy and he has a Turkish one, too.

One recreational visit we made during that year, 1968, was to Israel. Each week, the United States military sent a huge, empty C141 cargo plane to Israel, and it returned to Ankara filled with Israeli eggs. The eggs were destined to supply American military installations in Turkey, Greece and other parts of Europe. A small area at the back of the plane had space for a few passengers. We got permission to travel in that section to and from Tel Aviv. Riding in that cargo plane with our one-year old Debbie and a huge shipment of Israeli eggs is something I will never forget!

Two of us had entered the Air Force, but we returned to the

United States, in 1969, as a family of four. Parenting Debbie and Danny was always our greatest joy. A fortunate coincidence occurred when Jim and I chose to spend part of a summer back in the New York area as staff members at the (then) UAHC Kutz Camp. We met Rabbi Norman and Naomi Patz and their very young daughters, Debby and Aviva. Naomi and I discovered that we both were missing the existence of a baby record-keeping book that reflected the parenting needs of modern Reform Jews like us. And so we set to writing one together. *In the Beginning – The Jewish Baby Book* was published by the National Federation of Temple Sisterhoods and the Union of American Hebrew Congregations in 1983. Naomi and I were very proud of our accomplishment, but, in addition, the path to that publication cemented a lifelong friendship between the Patzes and the Permans.

At that same time, Jim was pleased to accept the position of Assistant Rabbi at Stephen Wise Free Synagogue in Manhattan. He served there for three years. Both of us were extremely lucky to have had the mentoring of Edward E. Klein, senior rabbi of SWFS and his centered, intelligent, dignified and gracious wife, Ruth Klein. Ruth modeled steady support for Ed, for her family and for the community. Observing her behavior taught me the importance of being present in the life of the congregation. That held me in good stead as a rebbetzin in the ensuing years when Jim had his own congregation in Mt. Vernon, New York, and then in Naples, Florida. Fortunately, the coincidental rise of the women's movement in the '60s and '70s brought me the balance I needed to be a dedicated rabbinic spouse, a mother and a career woman.

Jim was rabbi of the Free Synagogue of Westchester in Mt. Vernon, New York, from 1972 to 1993. When our children were both in school full-time, I returned to the work world. No longer interested in being an elementary school teacher, as our own children fulfilled that need, I sought other work options. At first, I became a licensed instructor of Parent Effectiveness Training and also taught Hebrew and religious school at Westchester Reform Temple in Scarsdale. I hadn't considered being a Jewish educator, because I thought that would make our life too insular. However, I realized that my values and skills were coming into alignment. Promoting Jewish education and Jewish life was what I really wanted to do. I became the Jewish Programming Director at the Mid-Westchester YM-YWHA in Scarsdale. My educational training and new skills later led me to a national position as Consultant on Jewish Educational Programming at the Jewish Community Centers Association (JCCA). I worked with JCC professionals and Jewish educators to enhance the Jewish educational effectiveness of all the JCCs in North America and to promote their relationship with Israel. With Dr. Egon Mayer of CCNY, I co-authored Extending the Reach of the Center: Preparing JCCs to Serve Jewish Interfaith Families in 1992. That same year, Enhancing the Jewish Ambiance of Your JCC: A Resource Guide, which I co-authored with Ellen Singer, was published.

In 1993, Jim accepted a position as senior rabbi of Temple Shalom in the rapidly growing community of Naples, Florida. In the twenty-five years that we have lived in Florida, I have been a contributor to the development of the congregation and the Jewish community by serving in many volunteer positions. I have conducted workshops in Jewish parenting and holiday celebrations, led and served on boards such as Jewish Family and Community Services, taught Hebrew and Jewish studies to adults and even served in a crisis for one year as religious school director. Together, Jim and I led six congregational trips to Israel, and in retirement, we have spent a month living in Jerusalem.

During all the years of Jim's rabbinate, I attended CCAR and NAORRR conventions, served on the NAORRR Board, and, at many of the meetings, led workshops or was on panels. When *The Spouse Connection* was established in 1984, I participated until it became an online discussion group in the late 1990s. Eventually, the need for it seemed to evaporate with the generational changes in the rabbinate.

While it functioned, *The Spouse Connection* described itself as a "support group for rabbinic spouses and partners." Its mission was to "foster meaningful connections between people who share similar experiences and concerns through their lives in rabbinic families." Often, I found it affirming to know that other spouses had experiences and concerns similar to mine. We found humor when we shared some of the comments that congregants made to us. At other times, I returned from those meetings upset that some spouses experienced such frustration with their roles. I hope that our gatherings lent them the support they needed. As for me, the friendships that I have made with spouses and rabbis have nourished me and strengthened my commitment to Jewish life.

I am grateful to my parents and grandparents for imbuing in me the love of Judaism that gave me my start. I am grateful to Jim, a dedicated, successful and talented rabbi, who has been my partner in life. I am grateful that we have been able to share, together with others, our strong commitment to family, friends, community, Israel, learning, values and the joy of living a Jewish life. And, yes, I am grateful to God for giving me the opportunity to live the blessings of a rabbinic spouse.

Jane Perman resides in Naples, Florida with her husband, Temple Shalom's Rabbi Emeritus, James H. Perman (HUC-JIR, NY, 1967). Jane received her B.A. from Barnard College in 1964 and a M.S. in Ed. from Bank Street College of Education in 1977. Jane currently serves on the Board of Directors of The Naples Senior Center at JFCS and, along with Jim, was a scholar on a Jewish Federation of Greater Naples Mission to Israel in the spring of 2018. The Permans enjoy a loving relationship with their children, Debbie (Marcelo) Brukman and Daniel (Sheva Tessler) Perman and their four grandchildren.

25

REFLECTIONS ON FIFTY YEARS IN ONE CONGREGATION

TERRY KROLOFF, PH.D.

IN 1966, AFTER TWO SHORT STINTS IN BOSTON AND ON LONG ISLAND, my husband, Charles Kroloff, and I moved to Westfield, New Jersey, where we have lived happily for over fifty years. We came with three small children. Our congregation, Temple Emanu-El, has grown from 400 families to a lively assemblage of 1,100. Our children, happily married, have remained in the area, and we are blessed with seven grandchildren.

But how did I fare as the wife of an extremely busy rabbi? At first, I taught Hebrew in a nearby Conservative congregation. Our children began their studies at Solomon Schechter Day School. Then I happened to read Betty Friedan's *Feminine Mystique*, and I felt as if lightning had struck. I knew this book was also about me and that I had to get started with my own career.

I enrolled in Drew University, and, seven years later, received my Ph.D. in English literature, with a dissertation on Jewish immigrant fiction. As my children were already in high school and heading to college and Chuck was hard at work at our temple, I felt ready to begin teaching in a college or university. But where? Since we obviously were not leaving our present locale, I began to teach as an adjunct instructor at various universities in our area.

IN THE BUSINESS WORLD

After quickly realizing that this route required a great deal of work for very little remuneration, I hit upon another idea that Chuck and I thought might work. Helped by our many contacts in the congregation, I began composing newsletters for corporations and non-profit organizations in our region and nationally. Of course, this was before the advent of online publications of every type.

For over twenty years, I greatly enjoyed getting acquainted with the world of business – working with printers and layout designers, as well as interviewing executives and employees of companies and leaders of Jewish organizations. My company, first called Newsletter Ink, and later, Corporate Press, often produced eight or ten newsletters simultaneously, some monthly, some quarterly.

IN THE CONGREGATION WITH FEMINISM

Meanwhile, just as the feminist movement was emerging, I discovered that I wanted to become more involved in aspects of congregational life. I was happy to offer a short course at temple on Jewish immigrant fiction, in which we read short stories about life in the United States during the 1920s and '30s by writers such as Saul Bellow and Bernard Malamud.

Also, at that time, I attended a thought-provoking course offered at temple by Rabbi Marjorie Yudkin, *z"l*, about women in the Bible. This course, plus the general feminist atmosphere, inspired a group of women at our synagogue, including me, to write a Shabbat evening service.

It was truly a labor of love. We worked on the service for a full year, changing the terminology in the prayer book (the small gray volume) including writing our own kabbalat Shabbat candle blessing.

A postcard went out to members to announce the special service we were planning, and that erev Shabbat, the sanctuary was packed. We conducted the entire service ourselves, sermon included.

OUR WOMEN'S STUDY CIRCLE

Our group of women involved in the service so enjoyed the experience, we decided to continue to study together. There were some ten to twelve of us, including three rabbis' wives and one daughter of a rabbi. One member of our group later became a rabbi.

Deciding to meet monthly, as other Jewish women's groups were doing at that time, we named our circle Kol Nashim. Of course, the double meaning of this name was, "voice of women," as well as "all women." We met in each other's homes once a month – a timing that also had feminist implications – and continued to meet for about fifteen years.

Each of us researched a topic and then chaired the monthly session. We discussed topics such as upcoming Jewish holidays, important women in the Hebrew Bible, and recent books on Jewish feminine topics. Some of the books were *Women Speak to God*; *Taking the Fruit*; *Jewish Women, Jewish Men*; and *Kol Isha.*

From the time we wrote our women's service, we had been concerned about the masculine language of the prayer book. As a result, we altered the language of the Avot prayer and had copies taped to the inside cover of the congregation's copies of *Gates of Prayer*. The phrase, *"avot v'imahot"* – "fathers and mothers," instead of only "fathers" – became a regular part of our Shabbat evening service for many years. We were pleased that all later editions of the movement's prayer book have had more inclusive language.

Our Kol Nashim group also helped organize and lead our temple's first women's seder, a tradition which continues until today. I was happy to take a leading role in the programs and projects of Kol Nashim.

LAUGHTER IN HIGH PLACES

One amusing incident occurred during the 1980s that my husband and I laugh about to this day.

The temple had been running a guest speaker series that had been quite successful. On one occasion, Abba Eban, former Israeli foreign minister, and ambassador to the United Nations as well as to the United States, was invited to speak. The event was widely publicized and many hundreds of people, members and non-members, gathered in our social hall.

The day, which was quite warm, arrived and so did Abba Eban, properly attired in a white shirt, jacket and tie. Unfortunately, B'nai B'rith was holding a prior meeting the same morning, also in our social hall. And that event was running way overtime. Eban, quite perturbed, literally hot under the collar, was pacing back and forth in the hallway as he waited to go onstage for his presentation.

Realizing that we had a small problem on our hands, I approached Eban and asked him to follow me. Chuck's study could provide the perfect sanctuary for Eban at this moment. I took the perspiring Eban upstairs, away from the crowd, seated him at Chuck's desk, and brought the poor man a cool drink of water. Eban sat down with a smile, loosened his tie, and relaxed. When he went on stage half-an-hour later, he gave his usual spellbinding talk.

HELP FOR THE SAD AND LONELY

Since Chuck's retirement, a friend and I have chaired quite an important, heart-warming committee at our synagogue titled Bikur Holim. Our volunteers visit members who are usually living alone; most are elderly. Sometimes he or she may be recovering from an illness or from the loss of a spouse. These are folks that are not up-and-about in the community and are in need of regular companionship. Even if a family member also lives in the area, all parties are always delighted with our regular visits.

After a short training period, our volunteers visit these members once a week, either in-person or on the phone, for about an hour. Because many people are quite private regarding their needs, the names of those whom we visit are confidential. Our volunteers usually continue their visits for years, often until the death of these shut-ins whom we call our "special friends."

We have received a most positive response for our Bikur Holim activities. One relative even called our visits the most important program at the temple. This is an over-statement, but we know that our activities have been very meaningful, both for our special friends and for our volunteers.

In retirement, I can truthfully say that my involvement with our synagogue and its members has been most rewarding and fulfilling. That feeling is probably mutual, as the temple recently staged a fundraising event in our honor which was attended by over 400 members and their families.

Terry Kroloff: B.A. Wellesley College, University of Cincinnati; Ph.D., Drew University, English Literature; three children and seven grandchildren. Current interests: reading (book club), fitness, religious life, Bikur Holim group, friends, family, New York City art scene. Her husband, Charles (Chuck), was ordained in 1960 in Cincinnati.

26

A CHALLENGING LIFE

SUELLEN WINER

AT THE AGE OF THIRTY-THREE, MY LIFE WAS SHATTERED. PAUL, THE love of my life, whom I had married at nineteen, had died after four and a half years fighting leukemia, leaving me alone with my eleven-year old daughter and nine-year old son. After watching Paul suffer through the last six months of his life, I felt relieved when he died.

My temple's previous rabbi had left two weeks before Paul died, and the new rabbi would not begin until two weeks later, so my close friend's rabbi officiated at Paul's funeral. As a temple of young families, the entire community surrounded me with support during shiva, joining in mourning the death of someone their own age.

When shiva was over, I felt a need to talk to someone other than my family and friends. One of my close friends happened to be the rabbi's secretary. I told her that I wanted to talk to the new rabbi, as soon as possible after he arrived. I felt that my children should talk to him, as well.

I had regular counseling sessions with the rabbi over the next few weeks. In our discussions, he urged that I respond to my tragedy by growing as a person and by focusing on what I wanted my life to become. He came to my house to visit with my children. Immediately after his first visit, my son told me how much he liked the rabbi and suggested that I should go out with him.

So attentive was the rabbi with phone calls and visits that my mother became suspicious.

After a few weeks, he said to me, "I should refer you to another rabbi."

"Why?" I asked.

To which he explained, "If I weren't your rabbi and you weren't my congregant, I would want to ask you out."

Without hesitation, I responded, "And I would want to accept."

In the months leading up to his death, Paul had insisted that I remarry, that our children needed a father and that I needed to move on with my life. Through tears, I insisted that I couldn't do that. But Paul was right, and I was lucky to have Mark come into my life.

Mark and I were married a year later, after Paul's unveiling. Over 500 people attended the Friday evening oneg Shabbat in honor of our upcoming marriage. Gene Borowitz officiated at our wedding the following Monday.

Outwardly, my transition from congregant to rebbetzin made no difference in my life. As my father commented, "Suellen was always a rebbetzin waiting for the right rabbi." From the time I was four years old, I went to shul with my father.

I was already on the sisterhood board but, as rebbetzin, I became ex officio. I now taught the course that I had taken in Basic Judaism. Indeed, becoming the rabbi's wife offered me wonderful opportunities to grow.

As much as I loved being the rabbi's wife, I also knew that I needed to find my own space. With Mark's encouragement, I went back to school and became a CPA. I learned how to balance my professional career, my role as rebbetzin and my passion for being a mother and grandmother.

Twenty years after becoming a rebbetzin, I had exactly what I wanted in my life. I had a wonderful position in an accounting firm. I was living and working a few minutes from my first two grandsons.

Then Mark became the senior rabbi of the West London

Synagogue of British Jews. His professional dreams were in reach. But moving to London for me meant giving up my dream job, and even worse, leaving my children and grandchildren an ocean away.

As exciting culturally and intellectually as London was, it was a different world for women of my generation. Few of my British female contemporaries were university educated or professionally employed. An old British joke suggests that when the world comes to an end, you should want to be in England, because everything comes to England at least ten years late. For a while, I tried to be a full-time rebbetzin, but it really didn't work for me.

Fortunately, I got a job as the internal auditor of an international money exchange company. Within my London office, my colleagues were a "United Nations" of the world. The company sent me on audits to Australia, Prague, and every place in between. Audits in Toronto or Omaha enabled me to spend a weekend with my grandchildren on the way back to London.

I remained involved in the synagogue as rebbetzin, but in different ways. Being the wife of the West London Synagogue Senior Rabbi opened doors to a world I could not otherwise have entered. On a couple of occasions, I met with the Queen. I learned how to curtsy and enjoyed my brief conversations with this woman who was my height. On other occasions, I met Pope John Paul II and spent an evening with Tony and Cherie Blair at 10 Downing Street. Cherie and I compared notes on the similarities between being a rebbetzin and being the wife of the Prime Minister.

My most fulfilling role in London was leading a Jewish-Muslim women's dialogue in Central London. Our women's dialogue became the foundation of such projects as the joint Break Fast for Yom Kippur and Ramadan, and for a Passover seder in Parliament at the House of Lords. Working and living in the center of the most Arab neighborhood of London for twelve-and-a-half years, I spent every day involved in doing tikkun olam by fostering the friendship and partnership of Muslims, Christians, and Jews.

Being a rebbetzin for the last forty-one years has often been challenging. But I have been able to do so many wonderful things, meet such extraordinary people, and become the person I am today.

I am a graduate of Hofstra University. I'm retired from my work as a CPA. Mark and I have four grandsons, ages twenty-three, twenty-one, fifteen, and twelve. Mark was ordained by HUC-JIR in New York in 1970.

27

How I Survived and Thrived as a Rebbetzin

HELEN WOLKOW

"HELEN, I DON'T CARE WHAT THEY SAY ABOUT YOU. I'VE ALWAYS LIKED you!"

And thus began, after about a year into my being a rebbetzin, my journey as a rabbi's wife.

But let me back way up. I was living out my mother's dream: having a child go to Hebrew School every afternoon, Monday through Thursday, and on Sunday. Walking all the way, of course. There were no carpools in those days. My sister refused to go, so the task fell to me. I was the first bat mitzvah in my Conservative shul. I didn't do much, but it was still a bat mitzvah, with schnapps and sponge cake afterwards.

And then someone suggested Camp Ramah in the Poconos. Eight weeks of Hebrew the entire day. I thought it was madness. But my mother promised I could come home if I didn't like it. Little did I know she really didn't mean it. I loved it and went back for four years. I wanted a change after that and was a counselor at Camp Lown in Maine in 1955, and then at Camp Tevya in New Hampshire the following year, where I met Leo Wolkow (HUC-JIR 1962).

Going to Camp Ramah changed the course of my life. It was one of – if not the – most influential experiences I had as a child and young adolescent. I was hooked. I knew I wanted to spend the rest of my life living a Jewish experience. As I grew older, I wanted to marry a rabbi or doctor. Not because my mother told me to marry a doctor or rabbi, but many, many years later, through much thought and introspection, I realized I wanted to *become* the rabbi or doctor. By the way, and I think Leo will agree, it never influenced my standing in the congregation. I was never the "interfering rebbetzin."

So why didn't I become a pioneer? And go on to become a rabbi or a doctor? I have always felt that we are products of our own personalities and genetics, as well as products of the timeframe into which we were born. And although I was somewhat independent and traveled to Europe (with a group) and Israel (on my own) when I was nineteen, I wasn't willing to buck convention entirely.

My mother told me what every Jewish mother told her daughter at that time: be a teacher. I earned a college degree in English literature and education at City College of New York, but I didn't really want to become a teacher. My father saw no need for a woman to have a college degree – after all, I would get married and my husband would take care of me!! And go away to college? Never! I was lucky to go to City College.

Once I started college, I went to my rabbi and asked if I could teach Hebrew and Sunday school. To my surprise, he said "yes." So, during my four years of college, that's what I did. After graduation, I went to work for Young Judaea, but eventually did teach for a while. Later, when we came to Chicago, I earned a master's degree in social work at the University of Chicago.

Why, when I went back to school in my late thirties, didn't I consider the rabbinate? There were some women rabbis by then. I did think about it but wasn't sure my household could sustain two rabbinic egos at that point. Once again, we are products of our time.

With all this background, you may be wondering what sort of

experience I had as a rebbetzin. It was a very rewarding one. I had good role models. On the beach of Olin Sang Ruby Union Institute, I learned from rabbis' wives Lotte Schaalman, Eudice Lorge, Roberta Schwartz and Libby Strauss about how to conduct myself as a proper rebbetzin. Some of their advice I heeded, and some I ignored. But I listened to it all. And I had a good friend, the wife of the local Conservative rabbi, with whom I shared stories, problems and advice. That was very helpful. Two other factors played into my successful "rebbetzinut": Leo was a successful rabbi, and we had a very nice congregation. We stayed in that congregation for the entire thirty-seven years of Leo's active rabbinate and still live in the community.

One piece of advice I heard quite a bit was, "Do not become friends with your congregants." Well, needless to say, both Leo and I did. And it always worked out very well – perhaps because we stayed with the congregation for such a long time. And we still are friends with those same people to this day. I know there are certain subjects that perhaps are not appropriate in these friendships, just as I know that there is an unspoken understanding between rabbinic couples which makes it very comfortable for us to be with each other. I also realized, after a while, that sometimes people consider it an "honor" to be friends with the rebbetzin. It rarely happened, but I do particularly remember one woman who I felt "used" me – but only that one.

Early on, I came to realize that certain doors opened to me that might not have done so otherwise. It was much easier to get in to see a doctor, lawyer, teacher, etc. Appointments became easier. Let's face it: deserved or not, there is (or at least was, and I like to believe there still is) a certain honor and respect given to me as the wife of the rabbi.

Our congregation was founded by German Jews, some of whom came in the late thirties and some who came after the war. So being very proper Jews and very respectful of the rabbi and his family, they always treated us with great respect. I remember that one woman was horrified that the rabbi walked the dog and changed diapers! Every *yontif* (Jewish festival), the congregation sent us flowers or candy. And when we visited one family, its patriarch kissed my hand and said, "Welcome to our home." I knew then we would stay at that congregation for a while. And when another man called me rebbetzin, he said it with such warmth that I never minded. I know some women of my generation do not care for the term, but it has never bothered me.

In the beginning years, I was busy having and caring for children and then later went back to school and then worked fulltime. And although it wasn't an issue, I was aware that some people – most of them ten years or so older than I – questioned the idea of the rebbetzin's working. It was usually not openly expressed, but it was there. Again, perhaps, time and context. Many of my friends went back to school or work a few years after I did. By the way, I always expected that, as part of a rabbinic family, I would have to work. Rabbis (at least then) were not known for their high salaries. And we had three children we would have to send to college.

As ours was a small and intimate congregation, I attended many lifecycle events. And I pretty much enjoyed them all (except for the very loud bar mitzvah and wedding bands). I certainly learned to be comfortable sitting anywhere with anyone. There was always that head table with someone's grandma or aunt... It was a valuable life lesson. I also did my share of sisterhood programs, which I enjoyed very much. But it was quite nice to have a life outside the rabbinate. To be just Helen, and not "the rabbi's wife." And it was fun to see people's surprise to learn I was a person all on my own.

And then there was the woman who just loved the rabbi and barely tolerated me! When I wrote a poem to be read at an affair, she told me I had read it well and she was sure the rabbi had written it. I was a little miffed. But one day I had the opportunity to drive her somewhere, and we chatted and chatted and chatted some more, so she got to know the "real" me and we became good friends after that.

An added benefit of my rebbetzin life was that I walked into a congregation of wonderful cooks and bakers. And I, who did not know how to boil water, (after all, I was a college student – living at home and working, so my mother did it all) learned how to cook and bake. And I found I loved it. And when I learned that our congregation's tradition at yontif was to have an open house (coffee and cake) at the rabbi's house, with everything, of course, baked by the rebbetzin, I went along with it. And to this day, I still love to cook and entertain.

There were always petty annoyances, such as the man who said, "I didn't see you at So and So's wedding or So and So's affair." Well, I said, "I didn't see you at So and So's bar mitzvah or So and So's funeral." Or the people who would call and ask for the rabbi, bypassing me. Sometimes I would say, "Oh, hello, Mr. (or Mrs.) Whomever." That usually got them to acknowledge me.

I never was really an organizational person, so I didn't become too involved in the running of the congregation or the sisterhood. But I did attend services, life-cycle events, and congregational celebrations. We became part of our congregational family. We mourned with them and we rejoiced with them. There were sad times and happy times, and I consider myself lucky to have been a part of it all. And we still are. Our congregants of those years and their children all seem to say, "The old days at Bnai Yehudah were the best of times." And I am very happy to have shared that and played a part in it.

Helen Sue Bartfeld was born and raised in the Washington Heights area of New York City. She attended George Washington High School and was graduated from City College of New York with a B.A.in Education and English Literature. She attended Camp Ramah in the Poconos (1950-54). In 1956, Helen, then a counselor at Camp Tevya, met Leo Wolkow (HUC-JIR, New York, 1962). In 1957, she went to Europe and Israel. In 1958, she married Leo, and together they led the Young Judaea Year-Course in 1959-60. After Leo's ordination, they spent a year in Washington, DC, and a year in Verdun, France, during Leo's chaplaincy. They moved to the Chicago area in 1964 and still reside there. In 1977, Helen received an M.A.in Social Work from the University of Chicago; she worked as a school social worker for twenty-two years. The Wolkows have three children: Lisa, Rachel and Jason. In her spare time, besides volunteer work (hospice, PADS, Selby Gardens), Helen likes to entertain, read, travel, garden, practice yoga and play ping pong.

28

THE EVOLUTION OF A RABBINIC SPOUSE

SUSAN REMSON

I WAS BORN ON THE SECOND TO LAST DAY OF DECEMBER, IN 1945, SO I have never been quite sure if I am the last of the war babies or the first of the baby boomers. According to Wikipedia, boomers are people born during the demographic post-World War II baby boom, approximately between the years 1946 and 1964, giving an age range between fifty-one and seventy as of 2016. I feel much more like a baby boomer than a war baby so that one word, approximately, covers me, although I still have a little bit of identity confusion.

In a way, the "*in-between-ness*," being between two generations, suits me. I often think of myself as a "cusp" person, one with each foot straddling an invisible line separating the new from the old, the past from the present. That position has influenced how I look at everything from fashion to food, music to marijuana and my relationship with the feminism of the 1960s and '70s.

Although I was raised in the 1950s by a single mom, I was not raised by someone who would have called herself a feminist. My mother was left a widow at thirty-six years old with two young children to raise on her own. She had a high school education but no marketable skills, so she worked long hours in retailing. Growing up, I never read *Sex and the Single Girl*, and I didn't know that in the early sixties, Helen Gurley Brown was encouraging women to become financially independent. Although I read Mary McCarthy's book *The Group*, several highly educated women from affluent backgrounds who strive for autonomy despite societal expectation of marriage and childbirth, I just thought it was a good story, and I didn't read Betty Freidan's book, *The Feminine Mystique* until I was in my fifties. But from the time I was very young, my mother told me that a woman had to be able to take care of herself and that I needed to go to college so that I didn't have to stand on my feet for long hours catering to the shopping public.

By the time I was twenty-three, I had a college education and a good job, had bought a new car, and nice clothes, and traveled a little. But that was also about the time I fell in love with a rabbinic student and agreed to marry him before he went off to spend a year studying in Israel. It was 1969. A year later, I might have gone with him without a marriage license. In 1969, I still thought it necessary to be married before living with someone.

Four years later, following one year in Israel and three years in New York City (where I also had a good job), we moved to Kenosha, Wisconsin, where Michael would be the rabbi of Beth Hillel Temple. And there began my life as a rabbi's wife. If I did not know before what that meant, I was going to learn.

The truth is, I didn't know what being a rabbi's wife would mean for me. I had little experience with rabbis or their wives. My family did belong to a congregation when I was young, and I went to Hebrew school. But my mother was not active in the congregation, and I have no memory of whether the rabbi even had a wife. Michael's family was active in their Conservative congregation and I remember hearing stories about their rebbetzin. Indeed, she was a rebbetzin in the full traditional meaning of the word, with all of its positive and negative connotations. She attended every service and was an active participant in all congregational events. She was knowledgeable Jewishly and respected in the community. She was instrumental in starting the local Hebrew day school. But I had the sense that while she was certainly respected, she was not very well-liked. I did not see her as a good role model. At HUC-JIR in New York, there were no classes on "how to be a rabbinic spouse." But even if there had been, by the late 1960s, when women's roles were changing, spouses would have been more likely to attend a consciousness-raising group than a class on how to be a good rabbi's wife. Women in the early 1970s were well-educated, and we had our own career goals. Many bristled at the title "rebbetzin," and its implications. It was an old-fashioned term, and although it was meant to be a term of respect and stature, it defined a role with which we were not comfortable.

Like other students, my husband had student pulpits. As a student at the New York campus of HUC-JIR, both of his congregations were in the greater New York area. The first was a bi-weekly in Suffolk County, Long Island, and the other, in his final year, was a weekly in Queens. In both congregations, we were treated well, but it was clear that Michael was only a student and not in a permanent position. People were kind and hospitable and tolerant of mistakes. We both enjoyed our weekends "playing" rabbi and rebbetzin, but we did not live in the community, and although those weekends were excellent learning tools for a rabbi, they taught me nothing about the role of the rabbi's wife.

Our move to Kenosha went smoothly, although the day of our move was my first introduction to rabbinic life. Michael's uncle had died a few weeks before ordination and Michael had officiated at the funeral ceremony, but there had been a gravediggers' strike in New York City and so no burial. The strike was settled the week we were to move, and as so many bodies needed to be buried, the family waited to be assigned a time. Lo and behold, it turned out to be the same time the movers were coming to pack up our two-room apartment and move our things to Wisconsin. So, I stayed behind with the movers while Michael buried his uncle. He came back to an emptied apartment and an already packed car, and off we went. Lesson number one on being rabbi's wife was learned.

We were warmly welcomed to our new home, a lovely two-story colonial, close to the temple, in a great neighborhood, with a backyard, a two-car garage and a screened-in back porch. The house was owned by the temple. The house chairman came to show me how to use the newly installed garbage disposal. I also heard about the disagreement that had taken place a few weeks earlier, between two board members, about where to buy the new washing machine for us. Welcome to living in a rabbinage.

About two weeks after our arrival, the phone rang.

"Mrs. Remson?" said a male voice.

"Yes, this is."

"Hi," he said, and told me his name. "I want to welcome you to Kenosha. Glad to have you here."

"Thank you. We're glad to be here." A few more minutes of small talk followed and then he asked a question.

"Can you do some typing for me?"

Wait. What? I did not know how to respond, but I didn't have to because he went on.

"The last rabbi's wife did typing for me and I wondered if you could type for me, too?"

I found my voice and said, "No. I do not type."

It was true. I didn't type. I had never learned. It was the days before computers and keyboards and I consciously had not learned to type because women who typed became secretaries and I was not going to be anyone's secretary. I had a BS in medical technology, and had done some post-graduate work, and I was not about to be someone's typist. More than that, though, the question took me aback because of the implicit expectation. Did the congregation and the community expect a "two for one" deal? Was that what rabbis' wives did? If it was, I wasn't going to be very good in my new position.

But it wasn't an omen and, in many ways, I jumped right into my new role. I went to services and attended congregational and community events. We hosted a Rosh Hashanah afternoon reception and I invited twenty people to a break-fast. I taught an adult Hebrew class. I chaired the adult Purim party. I went to sisterhood meetings and hosted Shabbat dinners. I made kneidlach with the other women for the community seder and I baked for the Hadassah brunch. I was a rebbetzin, after all.

Kenosha is a small city, and the congregation was, at that time, made up of about 100 families. Although the city is close to both Chicago and Milwaukee, it was not a suburb of either. (It still isn't, although the congregation's geographical borders now extend south, well into northern Illinois, and north into Racine County.) The congregation was founded in 1926, and its middle class, multigenerational congregants were – and still are – merchants and teachers, with a few lawyers and doctors. In a small congregation, and in a small community, there is a sense that each person needs to contribute to the congregation's well-being, and so my participation in congregational events had as much to do with the sense of responsibility to the temple as it did to my new role as the rabbi's wife.

But there were things I didn't do. We were in family-planning mode but did not yet have children, and I went back to work. I was working fulltime so I didn't go with the other rabbinic wives to the UAHC summer camp when my husband went. I showed up for Shabbat and left on Sunday afternoon. At home, I missed confirmation because in this congregation they held the service on the Sunday night closest to Shavuot rather than on the holiday itself, and I worked Sundays. The mother of one of the confirmands wrote me a letter critical of my absence. I did not respond by pointing out the congregation's unusual choice of dates, but I was hurt by the letter.

Then we had children. The congregation was extremely welcoming to our firstborn and then our second, but my new role made me reconsider my activities. I chose to continue working part-time, but not to teach Hebrew or adult education, and my involvement in the congregation became minimal. Babysitters were expensive, and my priorities had changed. One parent needed to be home with our little ones, and that one parent was most often me.

I also found that congregational involvement was becoming more complicated for me. Although we had congregant friends, I became aware that there was an overtone to those relationships. Conversation at social gatherings always circled around and back to congregational matters. People our own age didn't seem as relaxed when we were around, afraid to tell an off-color joke or say something we might think inappropriate. Even if Michael said, "Call me Michael," they called him "Rabbi," and the role made a difference. I found my friendships outside the congregation, and for me, they were more comfortable and natural. When my children were young, I began graduate school, which required me to commute to Milwaukee, an hour each way, a few times a week. I pulled away from the congregation even more, and I found I liked it better that way.

However, I should be clear about two things. One is that when I did things for the congregation, I did them willingly. Neither the members nor my husband ever asked me to do anything beyond what other congregants did. The fact is that, in small congregations, there is a strong awareness that everyone has to pitch in to help make things work, and I understood and respected that. And secondly, the congregation was always appreciative. And if people were critical, apart from that early letter complaining because I hadn't attended confirmation, I didn't hear it.

But I had begun to realize that congregational life was not for me. I have often wondered what my role would be in any congregation, or any organization, for that matter, if my husband were not the rabbi. I sometimes call myself "organizationally challenged." I am not by nature a joiner. I am not an extrovert. I like people, but I don't like crowds. I also don't like cocktail parties, committee meetings, and places where you need to respond to challenging questions in public. I have learned how to stand around at an oneg Shabbat and make small talk, but I have never really enjoyed it. I prefer a real one-on-

one conversation, about anything but the congregation.

We left Kenosha after ten years because the future of the congregation did not look good. The major industry in town had closed. Families were leaving the community, and enrollment in the religious school was shrinking. Jewish merchants and professionals did not encourage their children to come back home after college. Although we cared for the people and the community, Michael needed a greater challenge. There also would be few job opportunities for me once I finished graduate school. Our daughter was entering third grade, and our son, kindergarten, so it was a good time for a move.

An excellent opportunity presented itself, and Michael became the first full-time rabbi of a startup congregation in Naperville, Illinois, in the western suburbs of Chicago. It was clear from the beginning that this new congregation was going to be very different from our earlier one. It wasn't just that Naperville was a quickly growing suburb of a large city. The demographics and attitudes were different, too. The average age of the members was much younger, close to our own age, and with children the ages of our children. People were well-educated. They were scientists, doctors, lawyers and others with advanced degrees. Many worked for companies that had moved out from downtown into the suburbs. Many were in transition from one job to another, working for corporations that had transferred them from another suburb, or from another state, or they would probably be transferred again. Members did not have long-term ties to the community, and certainly no loyalty to this new, emerging congregation. Some had never belonged to a synagogue before. Many were converts or married to converts.

I was different when we moved to Naperville, too. I was the mother of two young children, and we had aging parents in two other states. I also went back to working full-time at a job that I loved, but that left me little time for congregational involvement. My husband's job was harder in many ways, too. For one thing, it was a larger congregation, and so there were more meetings, classes, and life cycle events. As a startup, there were many issues to iron out, which was not always easily done. There were frequent tensions between board members, and between the rabbi and the board. But it was also a great opportunity for him to mold a congregation, and he saw many rewards.

I kept my distance from the congregation. It wasn't just because of my career and family responsibilities that I shied away from making close friends there; I had come to see that there is always an invisible barrier in friendships with congregants. It wasn't personal. It wasn't that people didn't like me. But there was always a distance between us, and I had come to accept it. Fortunately, we had people outside the congregation – childhood friends, a few relatives, and colleagues nearby and we had a satisfying social life outside the congregation.

If congregants were critical of my distance from them, I did not hear it. If they expected more from me, I did not know, and if they had let me know, it wouldn't have mattered. I was secure in my decision, and I was not being pushed by my spouse to be anything more than I was. On the other hand, my children were scrutinized. People watched what they did and reported back to us. Life in the fishbowl was hard on them, and I am certain there are many stories they can tell about what it meant for them.

But it was not just my role as a rabbinic spouse that was changing. Rabbis and congregations were changing, too. Women were being ordained in increasing numbers, and male spouses became more common. Congregations assumed that men had professional lives of their own, and did not expect them to teach Sunday school, volunteer in the office, or attend sisterhood luncheons. In fact, with more women working full-time jobs, there were fewer sisterhood programs and luncheons and in many congregations, there weren't even sisterhoods anymore. Women were assuming leadership positions on temple boards and as temple presidents Women's roles all over were changing, and the old, accepted role of rebbetzin, at least in liberal congregations, was disappearing.

Today, with male and female spouses, gay and lesbian rabbis, gay marriage, dual careers, late marriages, and second careers, the rabbinate has changed greatly, and continues to change. There are no longer discussions at seminaries about what role the rabbinic spouse will play, if indeed there ever were. Today, such a discussion is more likely to be about whether it is acceptable for a spouse to be a non-Jew or not, or to practice a religion other than Judaism. Spousal concerns may be about finding suitable placement for two careers in proximity, or two pulpits, when both partners are rabbis. Some congregations even employ husband and wife rabbi teams. Congregations and rabbis, like all other aspects of our society, continue to evolve.

In the 1980s, after more women had entered the rabbinate, a male spouse was asked, "What do you call the husband of a female rabbi?" His answer? "Lucky." It was an excellent response to a silly question. But the truth is, no one really attempted to come up with a title for him because it was clear that his role would not be the same as that of the traditional rebbetzin. There would be no term for him other than husband, spouse or partner.

The rabbi's wife, whether she is called rebbetzin or not, is a gender-defined role that accompanies marriage to a male rabbi. It comes with privileges, obligations, and restrictions – and is rapidly disappearing, even in the Orthodox world (although more slowly there). The rabbinic spouse, or partner, is someone married to, or partnered with, a rabbi and may be male or female. She or he is the person who shares the rabbi's life. Beyond that, every rabbinic couple should be able to decide for themselves what that role will be. It needs to suit the couple, their family, and their personalities, and whatever the choice, it should be respected by the congregation.

These days, names and titles related to gender identification and marriage status are complicated, and not just for rabbis and their spouses. An advice columnist was recently asked how to address the same-sex partner of a married couple. Should a woman be called husband or wife? What about the designation hersbands? Or wusbands? The columnist suggested that the couple be asked how they would like to be introduced. She also suggested that couples should not be too sensitive or take misnomers too seriously. That sounds like good advice for rabbis and their partners, too. I will keep it in mind when I am considering my baby boomer credentials as well.

One of my favorite members of our Naperville congregation used to introduce me this way.

He would say, "This is – 'Please don't called me rebbetzin, call me Susan' – Remson."

That works for me.

THE OTHER END OF THE PHONE

I have changed the names of everyone I have written about here for the sake of their privacy and the sensitivity of the subjects.

Six a.m. Thursday morning. The phone is ringing. It can't be good news.

"Is the rabbi there?"

"No. I am sorry. No. He's out running."

"This is Marsha. Please tell him that Henry is dead. He didn't wake up this morning. He's dead."

"Oh, my God. I am so sorry. Of course. I will tell him as soon as he gets back. He will call you."

Henry was forty-one years old. He had not been sick.

Nine a.m. Labor Day. The phone is ringing. Not too early to be alarmed.

"Is Michael there? "

"He's in the shower."

"Please tell him that Bobby was killed in an accident last night. In Michigan."

"Oh, my God. I am so sorry. He will call you back right away."

Bobby was eighteen years old.

Seven p.m. Relaxing on the couch. Who should get up to get the ringing phone? It's my turn.

"Howard committed suicide. He's in the basement hanging from the rafters. Ben found him."

"Oh, my God. I am so sorry. I'll get Michael. He's right here."

Howard was thirty-five years old. Ben is ten years old.

I don't know what to say. I wasn't trained for this. I didn't know I signed on for this. But I respond, I hope in a kind, compassionate way.

I don't want to be the person at the other end of those difficult phone calls, yet it's what comes with being a rabbinic spouse, male or female, young or old, learned in things Jewish or not. It's true for those who are active in the congregation or passive, regularly attend services or just show up on holidays and for special events. We all find ourselves on occasion at the other end of the phone. While it is undoubtedly not one of the easier aspects of being the husband or wife of a rabbi, yet it must certainly be one of the more important ones. It's almost as important as being there for your spouse when he or she is shocked and saddened by these losses yet needs to be strong and professional.

It is true that there are other professions that have similar challenges – and rewards – as those of clergy families. Husbands and wives of police officers and fire fighters know that every time their spouses walk out the door to go to work their lives are on the line. Spouses of pediatric oncologists share the sorrow of children lost to cancer and other medical professionals face similar sadness. They also have long, unpredictable hours and unexpected interruptions when they need to respond to others, often regardless of what is happening in their own families.

And it is not only rabbis' families that are challenged to live their lives as normally as possible under public scrutiny. I certainly would never want to be married to the president of the United States! Maybe politicians, movie stars and music idols receive more than enough compensation for living in the public eye, but rabbis usually don't nor do they usually want to live such public lives.

Do the rewards of the rabbinate outweigh the difficulties? Maybe because it has been several years since my husband has had a fulltime congregational position and time provides me some perspective, I would now say yes. But my husband was a congregational rabbi for over thirty-five years, serving two congregations long-term (ten years and nineteen years) plus as interim rabbi in five congregations, and I have not forgotten how hard it can be to live in a rabbinic family. I am sure my two children, now adults, have not forgotten either.

To begin with, there are the long, irregular hours. Dad is working when other people have leisure time. Dad can't come to the basketball game on Thursday night because he has a board meeting. Dad can't make the Sports Awards Ceremony because he has to do a wedding. Plans for a family outing have to proceed without Dad because someone died and the family wants to have the funeral at that exact time. Priorities may come into question when it seems that other families come first, and often the non-rabbinic parent must do double duty at the expense of her or his own interests and needs. In our day, it was only dads who were rabbis, but today it is both moms and dads and I can only imagine what additional impact that has on family life.

Then there is life in the fishbowl of the congregation. Our children are watched more than others. They are expected to be mini-rabbis and do everything right and when they don't, it becomes public record. When three little boys are running around the temple, a little mischievous and perhaps even out of control, the one that everyone hears about is the rabbi's son. When the rabbi's daughter wants to play her flute in the pep band for Friday night basketball games, some question why she is not at Shabbat services. And it is not just congregants who put this pressure on our kids. We do, too. We put our children in the position of exemplars. They don't have a choice of whether they will belong to the temple's youth group, and there's no pizza and a movie for them on Friday nights. Our children are held up to a higher standard and when they do not meet it, their fall is heard louder than that of other children. Yet those same children are exposed to people and places that many other children never are. For every congregational critic, there is a kind surrogate grandparent who thinks the kids can do no wrong. There are the guests at the Shabbat table who introduce them to new ideas. There are summers at camp, trips to Israel and the awareness that Dad is known and respected in the community. Still, it is hard on a child to be an RK, and some handle it better than others.

A spouse may understand that the rabbi has a job to do but a ten-year old child doesn't always get it. They don't get much say in their parents' lifestyle, but a spouse is different. In many cases, by the time you marry, you know what career path your intended has chosen. Some couples even start out with a joint interest and commitment, but most of us didn't know what it would mean to be married to a rabbi. What I didn't know and certainly didn't understand until many years later, is that – at least for our generation – the rabbinate is not just a career path or a profession. It is a life and a way of living and extends into almost every aspect of family life, even into retirement.

A rabbinic spouse may choose to be active in the congregation or not, but regardless of the public role we choose for ourselves, there are the private moments of serving as a sounding board and providing support, consolation and comfort. We are there when the rabbi comes home after dealing with angry congregants, testy boards and myriad conflicts, both major and minor. We feel their frustration when their words fall on deaf ears. We see their pain after a difficult hospital visit or funeral and hear their tired sighs after multiple workdays without a break. We are there when bruised egos need soothing as well as when overly inflated ones need to be brought back to reality.

However, if we are lucky, the advantages of the position outweigh the disadvantages. If we are lucky, we see their joy and happiness and hear praises from grateful congregants. We are privileged to live with a certain status that comes with the position. We get to meet interesting people and be a part of their lives in a way that is not always possible in other jobs, and we, too, are living a life of meaning and commitment.

The rabbinate comes with pluses and minuses for both the rabbi and the family. But as we look around us, everyone's life is filled with both good times and bad times and life in the rabbinate is no different. The rabbi and spouse can choose to moan and groan about the long hours, bad pay, nasty congregants, vindictive boards and the like. But if we choose to see only the negative, we will become bitter and unhappy. If we choose to find the rewards, they are there – in life and in the rabbinate. As it says in Pirke Avot: *Happy are those who are satisfied with their lot.*

8 p.m. Wednesday night. The phone is ringing. I'm home alone.

"Is the rabbi there?"

"No, I'm sorry. He's at a meeting. He probably won't be back until late."

"Oh, okay. Well, I can call him back another time. I just called to thank him. He has been so kind to our family. Especially with Ben. You know, after Howard died, things have just been so bad. We've all had a tough time, but the rabbi has been there for us when we needed him and we really, really appreciate it."

This time I know what to say.

I say, "Thank you. Thank you for your call. It means a lot to both of us."

SUSAN REMSON

Susan Remson currently lives in Kenosha, Wisconsin where her husband Michael (New York 1973) began his career serving the Beth Hillel Temple for ten year. The following nineteen years were spent in Naperville IL. Michael also was an interim rabbi in five other congregations. The Remsons have two adult children and two grandchildren. After a career in clinical laboratory sciences, Susan now volunteers as an advocate for immigration rights and literacy and enjoys writing, knitting and visiting national parks.

29

I WOULDN'T TRADE IT FOR ANY OTHER EXPERIENCE!

JUDY TASK

BOTH ARNY AND I WERE BORN IN CHICAGO AND SPENT OUR FORMATIVE years there. We met at activities of the Chicago Federation of Temple Youth (CFTY). I had been dating his best friend and he was dating mine. We were a foursome for two years. Then Arny went off to HUC-JIR and I started at the University of Michigan. At Christmas break, the two couples split up and, that spring, Arny and I started dating.

His proposal was unique. It came in one of the daily air mail letters we exchanged. He wrote, "What do you think of the idea of being a rabbi's wife?" Of course, I said: "I DO!" when he called that evening. We thought we would get married in a year or so and, in the meantime, I would transfer to the University of Cincinnati. Arny was twenty-two at the time and I was nineteen. My parents said NO WAY would I go to Cincinnati unmarried. As a result, we married in September 1955, and I continued my education as he and I had planned.

Dr. Louis Mann, of Chicago Sinai Congregation, and Rabbi Jacob Weinstein, of KAM Temple, co-officiated at our wedding. During his remarks, Dr. Mann pronounced, in his booming oratorical voice, a pulpit style still very popular at the time, "When you marry a rabbi, you marry a congregation." Arny and his three attendants burst out laughing. I started blushing and had to elbow Arny in the ribs to quiet him down. Two of the three later became rabbis: Mark Shapiro and Richard Weiss. The third was my brother, Alan Wiener, who had been a holy terror in religious school. I am so proud that for years he has been an ardent supporter, former president of and major contributor to his congregation in Tarzana, California.

Right after we were married, we traveled to Arny's High Holy Day assignment in Ishpeming, Michigan. We had to take two trains each way, the Michigan part of which was an overnight sit-up. In Ishpeming, we were invited every night to congregants' homes for dinner. The mistake I made was to tell the first hostess, Lois Cohodas, that I loved her chicken dinner. We ate chicken for ten days straight! It was there that we met Lois and Bill's little daughter, Lynn, who later became the wife of Rabbi Sam Stahl. And we are still friends. What a small world!

We needed to earn money to meet expenses, so we both taught Sunday School at Wise Temple under a wonderful educator, Cele Singer. Living was cheap. We paid $80 a month rent at Swifton Village, where a number of other married rabbinical school couples lived. The big draw was that the Swifton management let us keep our apartments for half-rent when we went off to our summer jobs, usually at a Jewish camp. Tuition was ridiculously cheap at HUC-JIR and at the university, and our parents continued to pay it until we finished school. I graduated with a degree in education and taught fifth grade at Bond Hill School, which helped us live better.

The temple where I grew up did not have bar or bat mitzvah. All they taught us was to say the barekhu and shema, so I joined a group of wives who had similar backgrounds and we took Hebrew classes at HUC-JIR.

In the mid-1950s, fifth-year students at HUC-JIR had to take a semester on the "practical rabbinate." If you were married, your wife had to attend too. The classes were held in the evening at the home of Professor Sylvan Schwartzman. We joked about the class, but it really was a good preparation for what was to come.

But while we, as rabbis' wives, were at least more or less prepared for congregational life, our children were not. They were in their formative years and, in the small cities where we lived, they felt – as they told us later –as if they lived in a "fishbowl." They were certain the community would judge their behavior, which would reflect on their rabbi/father. Since Arny was often at meetings at night, I was the parent who helped them maneuver through those sometimes-difficult years. We sent Susan and Sherri to non-Jewish sleep-away camps to avoid their being overwhelmed by too much Jewish exposure, but it turned out that at the YMCA sailing camp where we sent them, half the kids in their cabins were Jewish. Go figure!

There were two embarrassing incidents I remember about my life in Arny's first solo congregation, which was in Newport News, Virginia. The Orthodox rabbi happened to meet Arny in the waiting room of the hospital where I was in labor with our first child. He asked, "If the baby is a boy, where is the bris (ritual circumcision) going to be?" Arny told him that there would be no formal bris and no mohel (ritual circumciser) either. He would say the prayers at the hospital, with the doctor doing the circumcision on the day before the baby and I left to go home (about four or five days after the birth, at that time). The rabbi said he didn't wish us any harm, but bad things could happen if a circumcision were not on the eighth day. What a message for a new mother to hear! As it happens, the baby was a girl, as are our other two children.

The other embarrassing moment came when a dear lady told me at an oneg Shabbat one night that I ought to smile more. I was mortified, but I have been conscious about smiling ever since, so she probably did me a favor!

I have always attended services, not because my husband is the rabbi, but because I want to. In those days, no one brought young children; we all had babysitters. However, when our oldest daughter, Susan, was about three, we decided I would bring her to services at our very prim and proper classical Reform congregation. We sat in the back row, and she was a perfect angel until Arny asked the congregation to rise for the shema. In a VERY loud voice, Susan proudly announced, "That's my daddy." Forget his sermon, *that* was the highlight of the evening!

In Newport News, our closest friends were twin sisters and their husbands. Their children became good friends with ours. We used to visit the family at their home on the York River to swim and ride horses. There was a sudden rainstorm on so many occasions, just as we entered their property, that they joked that we were a jinx! Both couples were as fine as they come. One day, one of the twins arrived unannounced at our house with a color television. We only had a little black-and-white set, so this was a major gift. She said she thought Arny was underpaid. (We thought so, too.)

In each of the four congregations Arny served, one or more older couples "adopted" us and became like grandparents to our children. When we left Newport News for a new position in Greensboro, North Carolina, I was pouring my heart out to our dear "adopted" mother and her twin sister (yes, another set of twins!). I was nervous about the move and about meeting the new people. She told me, "Don't let those fancy people scare you. They have to go to the bathroom every day, just like you and me." Our favorite story about her is that she honestly believed she could control the weather for special events – and maybe she could! Arny would tell her that there was an outdoor wedding or the like, and she would assure him that there would be no rain. And there never was!

Back in the early 1980s, I was teaching second grade in the religious school. One day, our fantastic principal wheeled in a cart with a weird-looking contraption on it. "What is this?" I asked. He told me it was called a computer, and, when he bought it, it came with some Jewish materials to help our teachers. "What do I do with it?" I wondered out loud. "Don't worry," said my second graders. "We will teach you." And they did.

In Greensboro, it was our custom to attend all wedding receptions, b'nei mitzvah parties, etc. One weekend, we had a Saturday bar mitzvah followed by a lovely prime rib luncheon at a popular restaurant. I loved prime rib and loved the meal. That night, Arny had a wedding, and afterwards they served a lovely prime rib dinner. The next day we went to a late brunch to celebrate someone's major birthday and what do you think they served? Yes, prime rib. Enough already!

In those long-ago days, relatively few spouses worked outside the house after the children started arriving. I too became a full-time homemaker and volunteer. In every congregation, I was expected to be an active congregant, but I did not want to be called rebbetzin, which was the custom in those days. If someone referred to me that way, I replied, "Please, I am just Judy Task."

Our whole family was under stress when contract renewal came up in Greensboro. Our youngest daughter, Laurie, who was in junior high school, was taunted and bullied by a Jewish classmate. The parents of the bully, who were quite critical of Arny, had discussed the situation in front of their children. The boy's exact words to Laurie were, "When are they having the meeting to fire your dad?" It was extremely painful for me to see this happen to our child.

My favorite rabbi's wife story happened when we moved to Alexandria, Louisiana. We had rented an apartment while we looked for a house, and put a lot of our things in storage. Nevertheless, we found that we had too many large cartons to keep in the apartment, so we asked the moving company to add them to the rest of our things in storage. They said they could not, as everything was sealed up. So, I called the house chair, who soon became my best friend, and asked if we could store the boxes at the temple. She said, "Of course," and told us to ask the maintenance man to put them in an unused outbuilding. That Friday morning, we loaded the boxes into our cars and went, as directed, to the kitchen entrance of the temple. A member of the congregation was in the kitchen. When we asked for the maintenance guy, she said angrily, "You can't have him. He's busy preparing the reception for the new rabbi." I said, "My husband IS the new rabbi and the house chairman suggested we do this." The lady reluctantly agreed to let us look for him. We got everything stowed away, and I left the building in tears. I thought to myself, "What kind of people are we getting involved with? Can we go back to Greensboro?" I found out later that she was the exception, not the rule.

In Greensboro, I served as sisterhood president and treasurer, and was an active member of ORT, the National Council of Jewish Women and Hadassah. I was a Girl Scout leader for six years, and active in every PTA. In Alexandria, I was the volunteer Jewish Federation treasurer for years. I was on boards concerned with mentally challenged adults, Planned Parenthood, cancer and civil rights. However, I always felt I was doing it as Judy, not as the rabbi's wife. Fortunately, nobody in the congregation ever objected to my many volunteer activities in the general community.

After Arny retired, I did something I had always wanted to do but felt it was inappropriate for an active rabbi's wife, which is: to get involved in politics. I am active in our newly formed chapter of Indivisible, a group of grass roots organizations that have sprung up all over the country since the beginning of the Trump presidency. Our goal is to promote social action through non-violent methods by participating in marches and rallies and by working toward restoring truth in government. We call or email our elected officials in Congress when pertinent issues arise. We register voters, knock on doors and make phone calls to get out the vote.

I also am currently a CASA (Court Appointed Special Advocate) for foster children.

Arny retired in 2009. We have remained in our home in

Alexandria and have had wonderful relationships with his successors. The only problem is that our children and their families live on the east and west coasts.

It has been a wonderful life, with an awesome and beloved husband, three fantastic daughters and five amazing grandchildren. I have made lasting friends in the congregations Arny served, and with the wives of rabbis whom I have met at conventions. I also remember with great sadness those wonderful friends who have died. May their memories be for a blessing to all. I would not trade being a rabbi's wife for any other lifetime experience.

I am Judy Task and my husband is Rabbi Emeritus Arnold S Task, ordained in Cincinnati in 1958. He is known to most as Arny. We have lived in Alexandria, Louisiana for twenty-nine years.

30

TWO STORIES

SHEILA KASDAN

I WAS ALWAYS TOLD "NO!"

THE WORD, "NO," ENTERED INTO MY VOCABULARY EVEN BEFORE I HIT the "terrible twos"! The very first "NO's" that I can remember were those offered by my parents when I was very young: "NO, don't touch!" "NO, don't touch the candy!" "NO, don't touch the vase!" "NO, don't touch that dirty toy!" "NO, don't play in the rainwater. You will become very sick!" "NO, don't pick that up!" "NO, don't cross the street by yourself!" So many "NO" obstacles were placed in front of me that I'm sure I resented them at times. Now, in looking back, I see that my parents were just watching out for their little girl and that their restrictions were really for my own welfare.

But, in truth, theirs were not the only "NOs" I had to deal with.

Peter and I belonged to the same congregation in New York: Beth Sholom People's Temple, in Bensonhurst, Brooklyn. Even though we lived in different sections of the borough, then the largest Jewish-populated city in the world, I, in Sea Gate, and he, in the Midwood section of Flatbush, and though each of us had to take two buses to get to our temple, that's where our families belonged, and that's where we learned to be Jewish. That's where Peter and I met as young teens and fell in love. When we were both in post-Confirmation class, our teacher, Mr. Lang, told our parents on "Back to School Night" that the only reason we came to class was to see each other, that neither of us "had any interest in Judaism." When people ask how long we've known each other, Peter always tells them, "I used to snap her training bra in temple!"

When I was in my late teens and "going steady" with Peter, who was then taking pre-rabbinic courses at HUC-JIR in New York, I asked the dean if I could audit a Hebrew class. I had taken Hebrew for my language requirement in high school and simply wanted to expand my abilities. His response was, "NO, a woman would be a very distracting presence to the all-male class!"

A few years later, our rabbi, during his one pre-marital counseling session with us, also offered a "NO!" when he suggested that I think twice before marrying a "rabbi-to-be." He cautioned, "Your life will never be the same. It will never be your own." But I loved being part of a temple family; I loved going to religious school and participating in services.

When Peter was the student rabbi at Temple Adas Israel in Owensboro, Kentucky, I was quite often able to accompany him and learn what it would be like to be a rebbetzin. Since most of the families were in the retail business and usually didn't enter the sanctuary until the service was just beginning, I was often the one invited to light the Shabbat candles. When I told the other HUC-JIR wives what I was doing, they seemed both surprised and horrified that not only was I accompanying Peter to his student congregation, but that I would also participate in the service. Their response was, "NO, don't continue to go. You'll need to be involved in a congregation for the rest of your life, once Peter becomes a rabbi."

When we arrived at Temple Israel in New Rochelle, New York, I was immediately asked to become a member of their sisterhood's board of trustees and to chair the YES Fund. How refreshing! When the senior rabbi's wife realized what had happened, she told me, in the strongest terms, "NO, do not ever become a sisterhood president. You can go up to vice-president, but nothing more!"

When Peter accepted the pulpit at Temple Emanu-El in Livingston, New Jersey, and was asked to speak about himself and our family to the Women's Club at their first meeting that fall, he told them about our two young daughters and our third child, sex unknown, on the way. When he began to speak about me, he said, "Please don't refer to Sheila as a rebbetzin; she is not a 'little old lady wearing a *sheitl*!' She is a modern woman, a person in her own right, not an attachment of her husband. She is Sheila Kasdan, a contemporary of yours."

It worked. They were a bit shocked, at first, but the message got through, loud and clear, and I became one of the "gang." I spent ten years working for the Women's Club at every conceivable task. I chaired most of the committees until, one day, the chair of the nominating committee called and asked me to become the next Women's Club president. In that moment, despite the advice I had been given in my first months as a rabbi's wife, the word "NO" never entered my mind. I was so honored that they thought of me, not as "the rabbi's wife," but as one of them. While president of the Women's Club, I was also involved with the National Federation of Temple Sisterhoods District #4. Again, I chaired various committees and eventually was asked to assume the presidency of the District. What an awesome privilege and honor it was to serve in that role, and to know that I was now responsible for more than forty sisterhoods! In that capacity, I was also asked to serve on the NFTS Board of Trustees, a gift and blessing that I shall always treasure.

While the word "NO" is surely part of everyone's vocabulary, and I know that my parents were just trying to teach me right from wrong when they said "NO," the truth is that the "NO's" directed at me as a young adult and, later, into my older adult life, took on a different connotation. While the childhood "NO's" may have been beneficial and surely were aimed at stopping me from hurting myself, those adult "NO's" – "You can't!" "You shouldn't!" – were coming from rabbis, as well as from many of my peers, and I was determined that they weren't going to stop me from achieving my goals. I am thankful that I was strong enough, and capable enough, to carry them out with a sense of human dignity, and always with a love of my Jewish roots and heritage. Life's success is, after all, what you make of it yourself, never what others wish to determine for you. As Hillel reminds us: "If I am not for myself, who will be for me? If I am only for myself, what kind of human being can I become? And, if not now, when?"

CESAR AND ME

With Peter's work in social justice and *tikkun olam* a priority for both of us, we had the privilege of entertaining many well-known leaders and dignitaries at our Shabbat dinner table and, every year, at our seder. We always surprised our family and friends by introducing them to a special guest. One year, it was the president of the United Farm Workers Union, Cesar Chavez.

Cesar was the dinner guest who became closest to us, like a member of our family. I first met Cesar in 1986, when Temple Emanu-El conferred on him its first Shofar Award for lifelong service to the community. Like most of the famous people Peter brought to Temple Emanu-El, Cesar and some of his senior staff were Shabbat dinner guests at our home prior to the service. Cesar and I hit it off that night and, over time, developed a unique and lasting friendship. Cesar became a frequent guest in our home, along with his daughter Lu, son-in-law Arturo Rodriguez, and their three children, Cesar's grandkids, Julia, Olivia and Artie Jr. There were many times when he was in our neck of the woods for a protest or high-level meeting and needed a place to rest, sometimes for a few hours, sometimes overnight. He knew he was always welcome at our house.

One Passover, Cesar was in town and graced our seder table. That night, thirty-five friends and members of our family attended our seder. They welcomed him with open arms and, surely, with some curiosity. I seated Cesar next to me. He was totally absorbed in the seder ritual and, at one point, I noticed that he was not just tasting the matzah; he was devouring it!

I turned to him and said, “Cesar, you’re going to be so sick tomorrow!”

His reply was, “I love matzah – there is always a box sitting on the shelf in our communal dining room at La Paz.” (La Paz is the United Farm Workers Union compound in Keene, California where Cesar lived; it is now a memorial site and center of the Chavez Foundation). Then he explained to me that, many years earlier, he had taken a trip to Israel to study its drip-irrigation technique for desert agriculture.

Although he was a Roman Catholic by birth and practice, he understood that his beliefs were based on Jewish values. In a letter he sent to Peter and me, shortly after the Rodriguez family moved to Kenilworth, New Jersey so that his son-in-law, Artie, could be closer to the northeast boycott area, Cesar wrote the following: “Please make sure to teach my children and grandchildren all about Jewish values. They are so important to one’s becoming a good human being!”

Cesar passed away on April 3, 1993, in San Luis, Arizona. It was a sudden and unexpected death. In November of that year, following the UAHC Biennial Convention in San Francisco and a meeting of the Social Action Commission, a small delegation from our Reform movement drove south to La Paz. There, we met his wife, Helen, his brothers and extended family, and his partner in the creation of the UFWU (United Farm Workers Union), Dolores Huerta. Standing together at Cesar’s grave, Peter led us in a memorial service that he had been asked to write. Following that service, we learned that Cesar’s son-in-law, Arturo, had just been elected the new president of the UFWU.

While the other members of the delegation left for home, Peter and I stayed for dinner and were invited to remain overnight. Our son, Andrew, had worked there as part of the Union’s communications department, and we knew, from his vivid descriptions, of the sparse living conditions available at the compound. We had dinner in the communal dining where we saw, on the shelf, Cesar's box of matzah! As a way of honoring us for our years-long hospitality and friendship, Artie and Lu insisted that we stay in their bedroom, while they bunked with their kids. It was an honor that took our breath away. We realized that night, that is what family does for family! To this day, the date of Cesar's death is part of our family's *yahrzeit* tradition; his name is called aloud in the four congregations where we are affiliated. Each time I hear his name read it evokes precious memories of our time together.

Rabbi Peter Kasdan was ordained by HUC-JIR on June 3, 1966, at the historic Wise Temple in Cincinnati.

31

SIXTY-FOUR YEARS OF MY LIFE

PHYLLIS KUDAN

REMEMBERING PHYLLIS KUDAN

MY WIFE, PHYLLIS, PLAYED A SIGNIFICANT ROLE IN SO MANY LIVES. AT her funeral, people spoke of her kindness, her spirit, and her genuine concern for others. To me, she was the perfect *ayshes hayil*, a true woman of valor as described in the book of Proverbs. Her contribution to each of our three congregations was beyond measure. And, of course, her role as wife and mother was her greatest achievement. We had sixty-four and a half years together. I only wish we had more.

Zikhronah l'vrakhah – her memory is an enduring blessing.

-Harold Kudan

◆═◆

I WAS BORN IN GOSHEN, NEW YORK IN JULY, 1933. HAROLD AND I WERE both graduated from Skidmore College and got married in 1954. We moved to Cincinnati, Ohio, where Harold entered HUC-JIR and I became a social worker for Hamilton County, Ohio.

During the next five years, we created a summer day camp program, called Kamp Karefree for girls and Hals Pals for boys. The camps continued for a few years after we left Cincinnati under the aegis of other rabbinical students. I also began graduate studies at the University of Cincinnati toward a master's degree in psychology.

Our first son was born in 1957. In 1959, after Harold's ordination, we moved to Bloomington, Illinois, for Harold's first pulpit. Two more sons were born during those years. I was asked to be a religious school teacher, to which I readily assented. I recall one congregant's scolding me for not calling the day after a dinner party. From that day on, I never forgot to call to express thanks. One day, we awoke to find that swastikas had been painted on our garage doors, as well on the doors of the temple. The culprit was never found, and the congregation restored our property, but we learned in the process that the neighborhood had been canvassed prior to our moving in to see if Jews were permitted to rent the house.

In 1962, we moved to Glencoe, where our fourth son completed the family. I continued course work for my M.A. at Illinois Institute of Technology, and, after I earned that degree, did further studies at Loyola University. Over the years, I pursued a career in education as a guidance counselor.

Our need for babysitters was urgent from the very beginning. Two organizations in the community had the perfect solution. They arranged housing for young women who became pregnant out of wedlock and were relocated to our community until their babies were born and placed for adoption. In order for the women to earn some money in a secure environment, they became live-in helpers to local families. The family was expected to pay $15 a week, provide transportation for doctor visits and make sure that they got to the hospital on the day of delivery. I was amused often to be the only female in the waiting room to await an infant's birth. I did this nine times over the course of the years we had pregnant women in our home. Some of them chose to remain with us for a period of a few months, even after they gave birth. They became a real part of our family. I found my training in psychology very useful at this time.

◆═◆

In 1972, Harold became the founding rabbi of Am Shalom, in Glencoe. He always credits me with being a major player in the formation of the congregation. He retired from Am Shalom in 2002. After Harold's retirement, we took many enjoyable and memorable cruises when Harold served as the ship's rabbi.

One of the other significant aspects of our marriage was our involvement in Jewish Marriage Encounter. It had started as part of a Catholic church program, called Catholic Marriage Encounter. Some Jewish couples attended the Catholic program and decided that a Jewish version of the program would be beneficial for Jewish couples. Harold and l were invited to attend a weekend session and then to become the rabbinic leaders. We were engaged in this project for at least five years. Marriage Encounter was designed to improve communication between husband and wife. Each program was held over forty-four hours in a nearby motel. It was billed as an opportunity for couples who loved one another to make their marriage better. The principal object was to learn how to share feelings, in addition to beliefs, opinions or views. One of my talks was about communication. I quoted a famous psychologist, who characterized conversation as chicken shit, horse shit and elephant shit. For some reason, this has been the talk most often remembered years later. Over the years, we have met couples who participated with us, and they continue to express their gratitude. Many of the couples later became active members of our congregation.

Another part of our rabbinate has been our interest in travel, especially after Harold's retirement. We have traveled all over the world (even Antarctica) on some wonderful ships, where we met exciting people and visited beautiful places. One amusing incident – now, but not at the time – happened early in this endeavor. We had been invited to be the rabbinic couple on the Queen Elizabeth II in its final voyage, before it was sold to Dubai to become a hotel. We arrived in Southampton, where the ship was to leave, first for twenty-one days via a transatlantic passage to the United States and Canada, and then around the British Isles. When we presented our credentials, we were told that there was no room on the ship for us, as it was completely booked. A frantic call to the agency in the United States assured us that we would get on board. Five minutes before the gangway was to be lifted, we were told to go aboard to our cabin. We entered the cabin, which seemed to have only a single bed. We were told to look up. Yes, there was a bunk bed. Gladly, we took it and fortunately had to stay there only for the six days of the Atlantic crossing. When we got to the United States, a full-size cabin was found for us. It was truly a wonderful experience. The ship had a full synagogue, which had been donated by the Wolfson family, of England. In every port, we were greeted with special festivities just for our ship, including a special concert in Liverpool.

It is now fifty-nine years since Harold's ordination. There are so many ways in which I have been enriched as a rabbi's wife over the years in the three congregations that we have served. It is especially gratifying when people express to me how my presence has made a difference in their lives. It has been a two-way street, because I, too, have been greatly enriched by them!

Rabbi Harold Kudan was ordained by HUC-JIR in Cincinnati in 1959. David, the eldest of the Kudan's four sons, was ordained as a rabbi at the same campus and has a congregation in Peabody, Massachusetts. He and his wife, Barbara Abrams Kudan, live in Cambridge. They have a daughter, Talia, and a son, Ariel. Barbara is a French professor at Suffolk University. Harold and Phyllis lived in Glencoe from 1962 to 2004, after which they moved to Northbrook, Illinois. Phyllis died in February 2019.

32

DOES THE PUNISHMENT FIT THE CRIME?

ADRIANNE SUNDHEIM

IN THE '60S, OUR FLORIDA CONGREGATION CHOSE AS THE SCHOLAR-IN-residence Rabbi Balfour Brickner, *z"l,* who addressed the country's participation in the Vietnam conflict. Several members who had different opinions resigned from the congregation.

In 1970 and 1971, the county in which we resided was put under court order to desegregate the public school system. Because of my former positions and involvement in the community, I was asked to be the chairperson of the elementary school division. This was a tough job, and, after a year or more of hard work, our plan was adopted and put into effect. Yes, it did involve busing. After several years, the results were promising! We appeared before the Civil Rights Commission of the United States, a member of which was Rabbi Murray Saltzman *z"l.* They came to Florida to hear our story and widely publicized it. I also appeared before the Social Action Commission of the (then) UAHC. Kivie Kaplan was the chair.

There were some members of my husband's congregation who were not pleased with the whole program, and with my participation in it. Our home was egged; we received much hate mail, and there were resignations from the congregation.

Sadly, with the change of administrations, several years later, the court order was lifted and de-facto segregation was again in place and still is.

During those same years, I was the chair of the Health Systems Agency, a government-funded organization whose job was to help to keep medical costs down by limiting the explosive expansion of unnecessary facilities. We denied a CON (Certificate of Need) for a project that was being financed by a doctor who happened to be a member of the congregation, because it was a duplication of services and not needed. He promptly resigned from the congregation.

I ask you, did the punishments fit the crime?

On a lighter note, once when a fancy car did not heed a YIELD sign and almost hit me, I lost my temper and displayed an obscene digital message to the driver. She was a member of our congregation, and her husband was a board member, but she laughed and did NOT leave the congregation.

Lighter still: Many years ago, both my husband and I were faculty members for a NFTY convention held at one of the UAHC camps. Next door to us were our friends (and congregants), both nationally known poets. The accommodations were satisfactory, but far from the NFTY Hilton. The walls must have been very thin. Sometime after returning home, I received a phone call from a mutual friend. She told me that one of our NFTY neighbors had just called her with the incredulous message: “Can you believe? Rabbis do it, too!”

My husband had a very beautiful singing voice and often chanted the cantorial music as well as reading the rabbinic parts of the service. One Shabbat, a visitor to our temple was seated directly behind me, and about halfway through the service, said to her companion in a pretty loud stage whisper, “The cantor has a lovely voice, but isn’t it disgusting that we came all this way and the rabbi isn’t here!”

Some years ago, while I was being numbed for a cataract operation, a very kind nurse kept telling me how pleased I would be by the results. It was

December and the spirit was moving her. "The Christmas tree will look so much greener and the decorations will seem so much redder," she assured me. At that moment, the (Jewish) surgeon walked into the room, overheard her and bellowed, "I doubt that. Mrs. Sundheim is the rabbi's wife!"

Adrianne Sundheim was born in 1935 and grew up in Philadelphia. She studied at Beaver College (now Acadia University), the University of Cincinnati, and Hebrew University in Jerusalem. She has taught teens and adults for sixty years in Tampa, Miami, and Winter Haven, Florida. She has done creative work for many organizations, including the National Conference of Christians and Jews. She has designed Bible curricula, been a group dynamics facilitator and served on the faculty of religious education workshops. Her articles and poetry have been published in Reform Judaism and Lilith magazines. She is the mother of three, grandmother of five and great-grandmother of two. Adrianne was married to Frank Sundheim, z"l, for sixty years. Frank was ordained by HUC-JIR in Cincinnati in 1958.

33

LIVING OUR SHARED VALUES

KAREN WALD COHEN

MY MOM TOLD ME THAT, WHEN I WAS A LITTLE GIRL, I SAID TO HER, "IF I ever get married" (at that time thinking it something I would never want), "I want to marry a man who is changing the world."

After years working on Broadway and at Lincoln Center, I became an international tour director for the American Jewish Congress. I traveled the world, did two years of refusenik missions into the then-Soviet Union, and accompanied Elie Wiesel there. One day, while I was in Brazil leading a group of Jewish businessmen to Sao Paulo and Rio, I met a dynamic woman named Barbara Starr Wolf, who was an international art dealer. I spent several days with her, and before I departed, she asked me if I were married. I told her that there was no man in the world who would put up with my schedule, and that it didn't concern me at all.

With laughter in her eyes, she said, "There is one man who wouldn't mind your schedule and certainly lives by the same values as you do. His name is Rabbi Bruce M. Cohen, and he is going to be your husband!" I was very shocked. I had never thought about marrying at all, let alone marrying a rabbi!

Six months later, I took a wonderful woman to visit refuseniks. Her name was Rita Eisendrath. One night, when we were sitting together near the Kremlin, Rita told me straight out that she thought I should meet Rabbi Bruce Cohen and MARRY him! I laughed nervously and wondered: who is this man whom two women I respect think I should meet? Another question: Since he traveled as much as I did, was not only WHO he was, but WHERE?

A year went by, and I was hired by the World Union for Progressive Judaism to arrange a conference in Jerusalem. It was a huge event and Barbara and Rita both attended the meetings. They spotted me and told me that they had run into Bruce that morning and had asked him if he had a girlfriend or if he was married. He replied, “No, no woman would stand my schedule.” Both women assured him that they had met a girl with a suitcase and that she would be calling soon.

That very evening, one of the women called me at my hotel room. She told me that *THE RABBI* was in Jerusalem, too, and that we should meet. I told her it would be impossible, because I was off to another refusenik mission and, from there, I was going to Indonesia and Jakarta. Later that evening, Bruce Cohen called and asked if we could meet the next day. I told him about my schedule. We exchanged niceties, and that was it for another year, with no further communication between us.

A year later, Bruce was in New York and decided to give me a call. Fortunately, I was in New York at the same time. We decided to meet the next day, and I went to his office where he was working as the founder and director of Interns for Peace. For thirty-two years, he had been training ethnic groups that did not get along in their countries and also did peace work through community development. Instantly, I was taken with his passion for life and his commitment to bettering human society. He was extremely intelligent and compassionate, and had a love of Judaism as well as respect and tolerance for every creed, color and religion. He loved humanity. He could not rest while people starved in Somalia, were at war in Bosnia-Herzegovina or faced floods in New Orleans. I was stunned! I felt the same way! We talked for hours and hours. One statement I will never forget is when he said to me, "Karen, I am a Jew and I love Judaism, but I don't think HOW you pray is as important as how you treat your fellow human being." I knew, then, that THIS indeed was a rabbi I could marry.

Our children came just the way Bruce and I did: not in their birthday suits but rather, with a suitcase. We adopted Emil, a Jewish boy from Florida; Rimma Minnie, born in China; and Tarik and Iris, two teenagers from Bosnia. Our home was our sanctuary that grew larger and larger. Everyone was busy.

Then, after I had battled breast cancer for two years, we were shocked to discover that Bruce was ill. He battled sternum bone cancer for nearly a year and succumbed at home with all of us surrounding him. We lost the patriarch of our sanctuary on August 3, 2010. This dynamic man was suddenly quiet, and the world was less bright.

Even in death, Bruce was a true rabbi, a teacher. About a month before he died, he was in the hospital in great pain. After a visit with him, the children and I walked him back to his room. The rabbi who had "run" around the world was having trouble putting one foot in front of another. We were heartbroken. When we got to the door of his hospital room, Bruce asked us to hold hands and, in barely a whisper, told us that, "Life is a joy. It is not always fair, and this certainly isn't fair," but he expected us to take care of each other and then, "My legacy will be when all give back to humanity..." As I stood holding the hands of my children, I again thought about WHY I had married this spectacular rabbi and remarkable soul. This was a marriage made on earth, yet it seemed as if it had taken place in heaven. After we left the hospital, my son Emil said, "How many dying men would say 'life is a joy,' and be thinking of others...?"

We lost Bruce, but his vision, energy, values and passion live on in his family and the people he touched all over the world. Bruce told us, "people whom we love and lose live on in the good deeds that we do every day." My entire family tries to do good deeds. We are devoted to giving back to humanity.

AND SO LIFE GOES ON: CHAPLAIN, INTERN, REBBETZIN

It is not unusual for a staff member or visitor to the New York Presbyterian Hospital – Westchester Division to drive up the hill and see bearded, pious Jews in their black hats and long black coats on their way to visit a relative on the Four North Unit. I have had the privilege of working on Four North since it opened on September 14, 2009. The unit serves many Orthodox patients. I would like to tell you about the joys of that experience and also the difficulties I face every day in working with fellow Jews who believe that my Judaism is not quite "kosher." I try not to let my own beliefs and practices interfere with my work, and I am adamant that I do not try to "convert" the Orthodox Jews to my way of thinking. I see beauty in all cultures and diversities and try to maintain and teach respect and tolerance to everyone on the unit.

Until recently, many members of the ultra-Orthodox Jewish community would not admit to psychiatric challenges. For many in the Orthodox community, the idea of coming to an institution that is not Orthodox poses significant cultural and religious challenges. What about kosher food? Shabbat and other religious holidays? Or visitors who would need to be religiously and culturally accommodated? If an Orthodox patient is hospitalized in a totally unfamiliar and unrecognizable setting, there is very little chance for healing. Some enlightened members of the community determined to communicate with the administration of the hospital and prod them to help meet the needs of their Orthodox members. There must be no cause for an Orthodox patient who desperately needs help to say "no" for religious reasons. And the hospital agreed to meet the challenges.

When I heard about the birth of this particular unit, I was excited and felt blessed to have the opportunity to help build and guide it. I enjoyed the challenges, the learning and my association with the enlightened religious leaders of the various Orthodox communities who recognized that there was tremendous pain among their people that had to be addressed. This recognition, and the determination to do something about it, was very important, because in the *haredi* (ultraorthodox) community the rabbi is the teacher, the advisor, the "lawyer," the everything – only answering to *HaShem* (the Eternal One) is higher than answering to a rabbi – so it was only with rabbinic blessing that this unit could be born and these Orthodox patients treated. Rabbis do not have a special connection to God, but as they are considered the most scholarly and learned in the community, they are given so much respect that many members of their followers do not make ANY life decision without their advice.

In many ways, Four North – with its twenty-four beds – looks and operates like any other unit in the hospital. Common diagnostic categories include affective, schizo-affective, psychotic and personality disorders. But on our unit, one can hear Mama, the pantry worker in the kitchen, asking, "How many kosher patients do we have?" One hears Yiddish being spoken, prayers being said before meals, and men coming out of their room asking for *tefillin*. Men and women separate instinctively when the activities director does yoga or a relaxation group, just as these Orthodox patients do in their own communities. In the dining room, there is one table for the male Orthodox patients and another for the females, because they would never sit together at the same table. For Shabbat, the tables are moved together but the men and women segregate themselves by sitting on opposite ends. The Jewish holidays are celebrated on the unit, and a hospital staff rabbi gives advice and visits patients every Shabbat. All the staff on Four North have been trained in the culture and the traditions of the community we serve.

My husband, Bruce, was a remarkable rabbi and human being. He had the ability to work with and know people from every ethnic group and be welcomed by them. A Reform Jew, he described himself to the Orthodox Jews with whom he sometimes worked as "a Reform Jew with an Orthodox presentation." He appreciated and respected people who thought differently, and found things to learn from them. He felt he did not have all the answers. We were married for twenty-seven years, and I, too, hold the same values. I am known to the Orthodox patient community as the rebbetzin of Four North. In most Orthodox communities, the rabbi's wife is called on to be as knowledgeable as the rabbi in the realm of women's observances. She can be approached when a woman does not feel comfortable approaching the rabbi, or where the rabbi maybe should not be approached. She is always considered to "have the rabbi's ear." The "First Lady" of the community, she performs social tasks and "outreach" roles, freeing the rabbi to attend to his rabbinical duties. It is certainly not the normal, expected role of rabbinic spouses in liberal Jewish movements today, and probably never was.

I have always liked building things from the beginning. This experience in helping to build the first Orthodox Jewish psychiatric unit in the United States is close to my heart. I am thrilled that people in the community do not have to suffer in silence and that there is help available. I love working with the rabbis and leaders of the Orthodox community and have learned so much more about Judaism than I ever knew, and, through it, my Judaism has grown. I love the traditions and the discussions with fellow Jews about the interpretations of the Torah. Most of all, I have found that my talent lies in listening to patients, understanding them on a deep level and serving as a chaplain, life coach and guide. One of the reasons I was interested in the chaplaincy program in the first place was to expand my knowledge and to grow in my job and my Judaism. This has been accomplished. The more I learn, the more I know I need to learn more...

I have had to make a few adjustments to accomplish success on the unit and to assist in the healing of the patients. First of all, I dress like an Orthodox woman. I am allowed to wear pants as a Reform Jew, but I refrain because it is much easier to break the ice with the Orthodox patients and their families and have them listen to me if I look like them. Ironically, I battled cancer for two years and lost my hair. I, therefore, wear a wig, which has helped me relate to the Orthodox on the unit! It has worked for me. Who knew??

I feel very strongly that without the Orthodox community, the Jewish world might have disappeared after the Holocaust. While I do not agree with everything in their lifestyle, I am grateful to them and find much beauty in their traditions and beliefs.

Sometimes, I find the restrictions problematic. On Friday evening, for instance, when we prepare food for the Shabbat dinner, I am not allowed to use the microwave, because doing so is defined as "work." A non-Jew must push the microwave button. Many of these Orthodox Jews have never seen anyone write on Shabbat, which I must sometimes do in the course of my work. I tell them that a rabbi explained to me that taking care of others is not a violation of Shabbat, and most of them accept this explanation. Of course, I do not tell them that it was my husband, a Reform Jew, who told me that! Obviously, having to write on Shabbat doesn't conflict with what I believe, and I do not feel badly doing so. When Orthodox patients refuse medication on Shabbat, I remind them that endangerment to life is a violation of the Sabbath, and they agree and take the medicine without argument.

Most of the women on the Orthodox unit love having a rebbetzin there, and I think they tell me more than they tell their psychiatrist. They feel very comfortable with me and it is rare when I cannot "reach" them. Most of the women have many children and work, while their husbands study and pray. Life is hard for *haredi* Orthodox women. Many are depressed because they want to look at the outside world a little and are not given the opportunity. It is sometimes a challenge to help them find ways to fulfill their own needs and desires within the Orthodox community context, but most usually manage, and they are very grateful to have talked and, consequently, to have been enabled to heal. Some Orthodox women with ten or more children find the stay at the hospital restful. I give them permission not to feel guilty while others take care of their mothering responsibilities for them.

When women get married in the ultra-Orthodox community, the matchmaker's fee is lower if the prospective bride is thin. This leads to eating disorders or weight gain after marriage, and to bad feelings about themselves. Many of the women question their looks, and I tell them of the beauty they have inside and out. These women would never talk to a rabbi about such matters, but have no trouble expressing their feelings about themselves to me. I can always find beauty in a good person, and have no trouble helping them see it as well.

The men also respond to me as a rebbetzin and a chaplain. An Orthodox male patient spoke extremely loudly and at great length by phone to his mother every day, disturbing others on the unit. I went over to him one day and said, "The rebbetzin is telling you that you must hang up NOW!" He immediately told his mother that the rebbetzin asked him to hang up the phone, and he did it quickly! I had no idea until then that I had such power, and I have since learned how to use it to benefit the unit.

Most of the male Orthodox patients on my unit seem to be helpless without their wives or mothers, and many of them frequently forget to take showers. One day, after I had smelled my seventh male patient as he passed by, I told all the men to come into the living room, where I announced that there was a new Jewish religious holiday called, "Clean-Up Day Without Mama." I got the seven men showered, put clean linen on their beds, and so forth. Just the other day, I was told by another such patient that he would bathe when he "got married"! I told him that I did not know a Jewish woman without a nose, and if he didn't bathe, he would never find a wife! Obviously, these men are ill and their hygiene practices reflect that.

I will continue to learn and to grow through my patients and with my colleagues. I hope to contribute a great deal to the Pastoral Care Department, as well. In the near future, I hope to earn a certificate in life coaching from NYU, which will help in the learning process and make me a better mental health worker, chaplain and rebbetzin.

My husband, Bruce Cohen, was ordained in 1973 by HUC-JIR in Cincinnati. I was the executive co-director of Interns for Peace with Bruce for twenty-seven years and then, after his death, worked for New York Presbyterian Hospital for ten years in the Orthodox unit.

34

A Rebbetzin Remembrance

Diane Steinbrink

One encounter that I will never forget happened in our first congregation when I was a very young rebbetzin. After the service one Friday evening, a woman whose name I will not mention here, approached me and said, "Diannie," (no one had called me that before or since), "you are such a pretty girl. Why do you put that blue stuff on your eyes?" I was taken aback and thought hard for a moment and answered, "Well, I guess I don't think I am as pretty as you think I am." That was the response of me as I was then – a good girl and rebbetzin of the nineteen sixties. The Diane of today would have answered, "Excuse me, but why would you ask me such a question?"

I met and married Richard Steinbrink while he was a rabbinical school student at HUC-JIR in New York; Dick was ordained in 1961. We are the proud parents of David, Carolyn, and Ellen, and enjoy our five wonderful grandchildren. We have lived in Philadelphia since 1970. I was born and raised in Brooklyn, graduated from Midwood High School and have a B.A. in Speech and Drama from Adelphi University. In my early years, I worked as a speech therapist for children, and for seventeen years, I served as

Coordinator of Philadelphia Plays for Living, a socio-drama program, where I also acted. I also produced The Diary of Anne Frank, which was used as a tool for Holocaust education. I currently do theatre lectures, which include the background of famous playwrights and monologues from some of their plays. For many years, I have been active in the National Council of Jewish Women, and currently sit on the board of the local Section. I also serve on the board of the Philadelphia Jewish Family and Children's Service.

35

A MOMENT IN TIME

BONNIE YALES

AT THE AGE OF EIGHTEEN, I MET, FELL IN LOVE WITH AND MARRIED CARY David Yales from Jacksonville, Florida. After our wedding, we moved to Cincinnati, Ohio, where he studied at HUC-JIR. He was ordained a rabbi at the Cincinnati campus in 1967.

Though I was basically a shy person, I loved meeting all the people at the congregations he served in New Iberia, Louisiana; Portsmouth, Ohio; and later Newton, and then Lexington, Massachusetts. During those years, I created visually in the fields of needle arts and fine arts. I began designing needlepoint canvases so that people could make *atarot* (neckpieces) for *tallitot* (fringed garments worn as prayer shawls). Later, I started making the *tallit*, as well, with fabric I would buy in Israel. This allowed me to offer the option of handwoven white or cream-colored *tallitot* which are made for me by Gabrieli or Carine Kleiman in Israel.

In Lexington, I opened a needlepoint shop I called, "The Needle's Eye." I covered the walls with hand-painted needlepoint canvases with all kinds of different themes I particularly loved. During this time, I started painting silk *atarot* so that people who didn't want to needlepoint could have the option of painted silk for their *tallit*.

Cary was always helpful to me and suggested themes for my Judaic work. As time progressed, the architect of our temple proposed that I design a needlepoint tapestry for the temple to be stitched by members of the congregation. That launched my career as a tapestry artist. I created a fourteen foot by six foot group needlepoint project, the theme of which was the prophet Isaiah. And I was at the project's helm. Ninety-three people worked on the ten-panel project, including my husband, Rabbi Yales, who added stitches.

It took us two years from start to finish, and as the concept of the group project advanced, the people who participated became friends with one another. People from outside Temple Isaiah came for b'nei mitzvah, weddings and other events, and everyone who saw the tapestry loved the idea of the group project. My career took off! More than 500 synagogues in the United States and Israel hired me! I continued this work until 1999, at which time I lived at the hospital with Cary for most of the year until he passed away.

I then moved to Jacksonville, Florida, and now live in Ponte Vedra Beach, Florida with my husband, Ray Gibson. After moving to Ponte Vedra, I joined several artist groups. In Florida, I began working for many of the cruise lines as part of their enrichment programs. I taught needlework workshops for them as well as classes in experimental painting. I currently teach mixed media painting at the University of North Florida and in other venues in the area. This year, I won the first-place award at the National League of American Pen Women conference in Daytona Beach, Florida, for my tapestry art entitled, "War and Peace."

My paintings are of multiple styles and designs and are induced by a vision of a peaceful and harmonious world. People say that I excel in mixed media paintings which are influenced by the texture of the tapestry work for which I am universally known. My work is exhibited at and is part of the permanent collection of HUC-JIR in Jerusalem. Additionally, my work is currently displayed in the state capital buildings in Columbus, Ohio, and Boston, Massachusetts.

I feel that my life has been a journey on a path less traveled. I find myself looking forward to each new chapter in my life and to every new adventure along the road.

My late husband, Rabbi Cary Yales, was ordained by HUC-JIR in Cincinnati in 1967.

36

REFLECTIONS OF AN ARGENTINIAN REFORM RABBI'S SPOUSE

INES SONSINO

I WAS BORN AND GREW UP IN BUENOS AIRES, ARGENTINA. MY PARENTS were also born there, but my grandparents came to Argentina at the turn of the century from various countries in Eastern Europe. My father was a physician, and my mother helped him in the office and was busy with my brother and me.

Growing up, my life centered on family and friends, mostly Jewish, but not on synagogues, which were mostly Orthodox. I remember visiting our grandparents for the High Holy Days at their congregation. When I was a teenager, a young Conservative rabbi, Marshall Meyer, came to Buenos Aires, and he was very well-received.

We belonged to Hacoaj, a Jewish social and sports club, and most of our social activities were based there.

My brother was tutored privately and became a bar mitzvah. Jews often rented a synagogue building for all types of life-cycle events. Funerals were done directly at the Jewish cemetery.

Haim Asa, who was sponsored by the World Union of Progressive Judaism and some American Jews who were living there at the time, came to Buenos Aires, and established a Reform congregation called Temple Emanu-El. He stayed for three years. During that time, I was very active in its university group, called Hillel. Once he left, the group dismantled, but the congregation remained relatively active. My parents were not members.

Rifat came in 1966, newly ordained from HUC-JIR in Cincinnati. Being of Jewish-Turkish origin, he spoke Ladino. As he established himself, our Hillel group formed again, and this is how we met. We started dating and were engaged and married within six months. He had already told me he was going return to the USA to pursue his doctorate and that I had to be willing to leave Argentina for our relationship to go forward. I always say that was the best decision I ever made.

I was working at the time, and Rifat would meet me for lunch almost every day. I did not have anyone to educate me or to whom I could ask questions regarding my role as a rabbi's spouse, but I relied on my instincts. I frequently went to services, lectures and activities.

Our son, Daniel, was born two years later, and we were already making plans to get green cards and to have Rifat accepted into a Ph.D. program at a university in the United States. We left Buenos Aires in 1969 for the University of Pennsylvania in Philadelphia. Rifat was studying full-time and teaching confirmation classes at Main Line Reform Temple, where Ted Gordon was the rabbi. That job secured us green cards. Our second child, Debbi, was born in 1971.

After Rifat's graduation in 1975, we went to Glencoe, Illinois, where Rifat became the education director of North Shore Congregation Israel, whose senior rabbi was Herb Bronstein. We left in 1980 and came to Temple Beth Shalom in Needham, Massachusetts, where Rifat became the solo rabbi. We stayed for twenty-five years, until Rifat's retirement.

The role of a rabbi's spouse changed over the years, but I stayed true to myself and supported Rifat and our two kids through the ups and down of the job. I did not take a leadership position, nor did I chair any committees. I was there to give a helping hand to anyone who needed my support and did that with willingness and cheer.

For me, this has been a wonderful journey, and I learned how to be flexible and take full advantage of all the positive things in dealing with issues as they emerged.

Rabbi Rifat Sonsino was ordained in Cincinnati in 1966.

37

BECOMING A RABBI'S WIFE AND RAISING CHILDREN IN THE RABBINATE

HELEN KRAVITZ

NEVER IN A MILLION YEARS WOULD I HAVE IMAGINED I WOULD MARRY A rabbi. Given my upbringing and the very liberal bent of my parents regarding religion, I would NEVER have anticipated marrying a person with of any kind of traditional way of life. However, as fate – or luck, if you want to look at it that way – would have it, I was introduced to and subsequently married my husband. After forty years, we have developed a grand "meeting of the minds," with both of us willing to compromise, each following our own traditions based on the traditions of our respective families.

I didn't know Bob until after he was ordained and already in his first pulpit, so I was out of the loop and not involved in any of the seminary life. But, coming into the relationship, I had no idea what to expect or what would have been expected of me. *Rebbetzin* was a word I had heard, but I never really understood its meaning, certainly not as it might apply to me. I had this image of an older, gray-haired woman with an out-of-date house dress, orthopedic lace-up shoes and a warm, huge hug. I never put myself in that category, so when anyone in the congregation referred to me as a rebbetzin, I always offered the distinction that I was too young to be a rebbetzin. Now, forty years later, I still feel that way.

We'd been married for a year and were in the midst of deciding that we wanted to make not just a congregational change but a climate change as well. Upstate New York was very, very cold, even before the advent of climate change. The only problem was that the first congregation Bob was serving was Conservative, and CCAR placements are for Reform congregations. At the time, it was very difficult to cross the imaginary line from Conservative to Reform, so although the Placement Commission and its director were polite and somewhat helpful, it began to look more and more probable that we would have to find our own placement.

Through a family friend who knew someone in another congregation, who knew... well, you get the picture, we wound up in central Georgia, to interview once again for a Conservative congregation. Since I wasn't at HUC-JIR when Bob was a student there, I found this congregational negotiation-stuff a real challenge. Being the rabbi's wife means you have to maintain relationships with many people, including some whom you would not normally have in your circle of friends.

So when we flew south, I asked Bob what I was supposed to do. He told me I was basically there to be his support and to let the congregation know we were a family. Through the initial interview process, I was open and friendly, answered various questions, told a bit about our history, what I do – all the usual, surface stuff, nothing that I considered other than chitchat. So far this had been a piece of cake. I wasn't nervous, and I felt I hadn't done anything to hinder the process.

Fast forward several hours and the committee asks both of us to come in for further discussion. Now, I'm getting a little nervous. I hadn't thought this was something I was going to have to do, let alone be expected to do. As we sit on one side of the conference table and the committee on the other side, the conversation begins in a pleasant enough way. All seems good until the chairman of the committee looks right at me and asks, "What is it that YOU will be doing for our congregation?" I don't know for sure, but I would assume the look of panic and "deer-in-the-headlights" expression that I gave Bob was enough of a clue that I had no idea how I was supposed to respond, let alone what they wanted me to say.

Without hesitation, Bob turned to the committee members and said that my primary responsibilities were to our family first. Then he added that, because I intended to continue working at my profession (nursing), if there were anything of great importance, I would certainly be available to *help* in the congregation.

At that point I knew just what my rabbi expected the role of his wife to be. Everything I knew and had done until then was because I thought I was supposed to do so. It had never occurred to me – or to us – that my "rabbi's wife" duties needed to be clarified, but in that instant, I also realized that Bob had never expected me to be something I wasn't comfortable being, or doing.

A rabbi in a small community has a lot of responsibility. I don't know how it is today, but in the late 1970s and 1980s, the rabbi wasn't just the person who led services and took care of the life- cycle events of the congregation. He was also the temple administrator, principal of the Hebrew/religious school, main bar/bat mitzvah tutor, Torah reader and occasionally *hazan* as well. Educating folks of other faiths about Judaism was also a key element of the rabbi's job. The occasions our "family time" had to take a back seat to "congregation time" are too numerous to count.

I think our watershed moment about how we were going to raise our family came during a trip to my in-laws' hometown. My father-in-law was celebrating his seventy-fifth birthday, and his shul was honoring him on a Shabbat morning. This was the largest Conservative synagogue in the city, and the one where Bob had grown up. Their rabbi had known my husband and the entire family for decades. As a courtesy to my father-in-law and to my husband, Bob was invited to participate in leading the service and to remain on the bimah.

During *shaharit*, our daughter was getting a little antsy, though not disruptive. When my brother-in-law was invited to go up to the bimah to read a prayer, one of his daughters wanted to go with him. He picked her up and carried her with him onto the bimah. Though he returned to his seat when he finished, all that our daughter saw was that her cousin got to go up and be with her daddy. So, why couldn't she? As she tried to wriggle out of my grasp and off my lap, she used her "outside" voice to let me know she wanted her daddy.

A withering look from my mother-in-law and another brother-in-law did nothing to calm the situation. I knew I had to remove our toddler from the sanctuary, ASAP. As I struggled to gather up this now very angry little person, the rabbi halted the service, threw an extremely irritated look our way and sternly reprimanded me for having the child in the sanctuary. I was mortified.

Needless to say, out we went – not quietly I might add – and once out in the foyer, I had to deal with a complete melt-down, tears and lots and lots of angst. This three-year old did not understand why she was being punished just for wanting to be with her daddy. And truthfully, I couldn't blame her.

Shortly thereafter, we were faced with another life transition. We had moved north from central Georgia, and for a couple of years, Bob had been cultivating a small Reform congregation just outside a large metropolitan area. Jewish families were moving to the area and the camaraderie and excitement were growing. Religious school classes were small. All the children were at the same level, and there was no expectation other than to learn together.

Soon after our son Aaron was born, the congregation's powers-that-be decided to look for land to build a synagogue, instead of continuing to rent store-front space and having a rabbi on retainer.

Again, the opportunity to grow spiritually and professionally was put on the back burner, and we were at the mercy of the Placement Commission. With a toddler and an infant, and our respective families living on the East Coast, we were given the choice of going to Alaska or somewhere in the Pacific Northwest or upper Midwest.

As had happened in a prior search, Bob was contacted by someone who knew of an opening, this time in a UAHC pulpit. It wasn't in Alaska, but close enough to the North Pole that it was by far the coldest place we had ever lived. We moved to that strong community of 110 Jewish families and settled in for what I hoped was our final move. Both kids were getting to the point that they needed to develop friends and relationships in school and temple.

The congregation's expectations for the children of the rabbi always seemed more rigid to the kids than what they understood as our expectations of them, but, as adults, we "played the game." Many times the kids were resentful, because it appeared to them that they were held to a different standard than the others; they were expected to know and speak Hebrew, understand all the holidays and the history of our people, and be perfectly comported Jewish children.

Once, nearing the conclusion of a Shabbat morning service, our then-three-and-a-half-year-old daughter, Miriam, put her prayer book down and announced that she was going up to the bimah to be with her daddy. It should really not have been a big deal, but as she scrambled up the steps, which were pretty steep for her to maneuver, the collective gasp from the congregation was palpable. Bob scooped her up and held her through the closing hymn and continued holding her as he greeted congregants during the kiddush.

Later, she put her little hands around his face and gave him a big kiss. Then, after she attempted her "Shabbat Shalom, Daddy," she told him in as an authoritative voice as possible, that she really wished he could sit with us, like all the other daddies who sit with their kids. In that moment, Bob realized that as much as he enjoyed everything about being a pulpit rabbi, maybe there was a different avenue he could pursue that would allow him to use his expertise and abilities off the pulpit and, at the same time, be the daddy he wanted to be and needed to be, the one who his kids longed for him to be.

We stayed with that congregation for three-and-a-half-years, long enough for our daughter to attend kindergarten and first and second grades at the same school. Aaron was about to begin preschool when professional burn-out finally caught up with Bob, and what Miriam had asked him several years earlier finally really began to bother him. He wanted to spend more time as their daddy, to be able to participate in their lives. A career move would be necessary in order to achieve this.

As luck had it, the position of executive director for an international advocacy and public policy agency opened in the city which we call home. He was hired and so began a nineteen-year adventure. The goal of being more of a daddy was met, and we were settled down for the duration of the school years of both children through college.

It was important for the kids to know that, yes, their dad is a rabbi, it is his profession and it defines who he is. More importantly, he is their dad and he will always love them unconditionally and without reservation. He played a huge part in their religious lives and gave them a basis from which to make informed and positive decisions about their lives. They are a blessing, despite the challenges that we may have faced as a family.

Balancing family, occupation and synagogue is like juggling jello. It's not easy.

An incident from our congregational years has shaped my personal practice to this day. When there was a community event or congregational dinner, the rabbi of our small congregation was always invited to sit at the head table. As his spouse, I was assigned a place at the head table as well. I'm not sure who made the decision, but, as was often the case, we were not placed together.

He was usually seated in the middle of the table to the left or right of the main speaker or guest, while I was placed at one end of the table or the other.

I have never been comfortable drawing attention to myself in any way. So, there we were at a big fund-raising community dinner, the guest speaker was a world-renowned person, and, as usual, I was stuck at the very end of the head table. The person to my left was much more interested in the person to his left, so I spoke to no one and was left to my own devices. I know proper manners and didn't take large bites or chew with my mouth open, so I felt relatively unnoticed and I was fine with that.

Dinner was over, and the speeches were about to begin, as dessert was served. I had caught the eye of a couple of congregant friends of mine and we were silently trying to determine what had just been served to us. It was some kind of frozen concoction that hadn't been adequately thawed. So, as the speakers, one after another, got up and down, I worked diligently on my dessert cup, trying to pry the frozen cherry loose. Just as the main speaker got up to the podium, the frozen cherry flew off the dessert and hit me squarely between my breasts. There I sat, in a navy-blue dress, already uncomfortable being at the head table, and now with a large white spot on the front of my chest. As I looked at my friends, their eyes said it all. I was horrified and embarrassed. Whether anyone else had seen what happened or not, I was mortified. As inconspicuously as possible, I wiped the excess off and, as nonchalantly as I could, kept my arm crossed over my body until the dinner concluded. Then I waited for Bob to come down to my end of the table so we could leave with him shielding me. *That* was the last head table at which I ever sat. From then on, if we were invited to attend a dinner of any kind, I either declined or insisted on not being seated at the head table. If Bob was there to give an invocation or benediction, he made the trek up to the dais when his time came.

Although Bob is no longer in the pulpit, he still works for a Jewish communal agency. We're more comfortable without the pressures of the congregation, but we know that we still represent something bigger than just ourselves. And no one ever complains that I don't do head tables!

When the call for spousal input about living in the fishbowl of congregational life came, these incidents entered my mind as shaping the way I view my position as a rabbi's wife. To me, the tiny victories I made with creating my home, raising our family and working at my profession *before* giving to the congregation, as well as putting the kibosh on sitting at the head table, have made for a successful stint as a rabbi's wife.

I was born in the Northeast and lived in several cities in the Midwest with loving parents, a sister, and a brother. I grew up in Youngstown, Ohio, where my family belonged to Temple Rodef Sholom. After attending nursing school in Albany, New York, I began working at the Upstate Medical Center in Syracuse. The rabbi of Temple Society of Concord played matchmaker and introduced me to his colleague, Rabbi Robert L. Kravitz (C. 1974). We were married in 1976. Our daughter, Miriam, was born in 1979, and our son, Aaron, was born in 1983. We have lived in the Phoenix/Scottsdale, Arizona area since 1987. I knew we were finally "home," when we purchased our first house.

38

FROM INTERVIEWS TO CHICKEN SOUP

ELLEN KLEIN

MY FIRST INKLING OF THE LIFE THAT LAY AHEAD CAME A FEW MONTHS before Rich was ordained. He was in the interview process and was asked to come to the community for a second interview and to bring me with him. Our son was around six weeks old, so my going meant he had to come with us, as well.

The interview was held in a large living room where I sat next to Rich, with Phil in my arms. Fortunately, Phil slept through the whole thing. After the committee asked Rich several questions, they turned to me and asked, "What do you see as your role in the congregation?" I was totally caught off guard, never expecting to be asked anything, so I made some statements about being an active congregant and attending services.

The following Shabbat we attended services at our neighborhood temple, and I told the rabbi's wife about what had happened. She told me what her response would have been, and I've adopted it as my own: "My role is to love the rabbi!" Pretty great answer if you ask me. By the way, I was never asked to participate in an interview again.

I received many phone calls from congregants over the years, but the one that stands out occurred when we were serving our first congregation. I was twenty-eight years old with two little ones, ages two and a few months. The call came from a longtime member of the congregation, many years my senior, who, along with her husband, had made it clear that, to them, Rich wasn't a very good rabbi. The purpose of the call was to ask me for a recipe, although she had never tasted my cooking. Her words ring in my ears to this day, "I'd like your recipe for chicken soup. I figured, since you're the rebbetzin, you'd have the best recipe."

My response: "My recipe is really quite simple. I open the jar of Telma chicken soup powder and add it to boiling water." There was complete silence on the other end. Then a quick thank you and the phone call ended.

I must admit that I'm a pretty good cook and have been asked to share my recipes many times. However, no one has ever asked for something of mine they've never tasted! Oh, by the way, I've graduated from Telma powder to boxed Tabatchnick chicken soup.

Richard and I retired to Sarasota, Florida in July 2010 after Rich, who was ordained by HUC-JIR in New York in 1974, completed serving for thirty-six years in the congregational rabbinate. Our two children, Rabbi Dena Klein and Phil Klein, live in Rye Brook, New York, and Potomac, Maryland, respectively, and have enriched our family with their spouses, Jon and Sarah, and our four amazing grandchildren: Rachel, Max, Eliana, and Jacob. Retirement has allowed me to volunteer in both a local elementary school and at Jewish Family and Children's Service, and to serve as co-chair of our Friends of the URJ Religious Action Center social justice group at our temple. Rich filled his retirement days teaching Torah and Adult Education classes and filling in to lead services in our local congregations. His favorite retirement activity, however, was leading holiday services on many cruise ships.

Unfortunately, our magical retirement life ended in February 2019 when Rich passed away very suddenly. His death, however, provided me with a new understanding of the impact that his life has had on so many. Hearing from a multitude of former congregants from our first days in Cheshire, Connecticut. to our other congregations in Hazleton, and Wynnewood, Pennsylvania, and our final placement in Concord, New Hampshire, where he was named Rabbi Emeritus, helped me and our children and grandchildren realize that Rich's rabbinate made a difference. The overwhelming commonality of the condolence notes that I received was the sharing of specific anecdotes involving Rich or the retelling of his words that had stuck with the writer over the years. People recounted how Rich comforted them in times of sorrow, celebrated with them at times of joy, and inspired them with words of Torah. These recollections alone would have been enough to mark a successful career, but his colleagues shared how they looked to him with respect to chair the Social Action Commission, lead the Board of Rabbis and most recently, to serve as President of NAORRR. His was truly a life well-lived.

Ellen Klein has a B.S. in Elementary Education from Lesley University, an M.S. in Elementary Education from Temple University, and an M.A. in Counseling from Marywood College. She received her School Administrator certification at Plymouth University. Ellen is a retired elementary school principal. She and Richard were married on June 12, 1966.

39

FROM A SMALL TOWN TO REBBETZIN

VIVIAN EHRLICH

ONE OF THE QUESTIONS I AM MOST OFTEN ASKED IS: "HOW DID A GIRL from a small town in northern Indiana meet a rabbi from a small town in southern Georgia?" Irvin likes to joke that he picked me up in a black jazz bar in Cincinnati. I had moved to Cincinnati, where my oldest brother lives, to find a job and meet a husband. I did both in the first week that I was in town! It was not until after we were engaged that I finally realized what my brother had been teasing me about for so many years. He used to tell me to come to Cincinnati to date the boys from the reform school, which I thought was a big joke. Since I was raised in the Conservative movement, I knew nothing about Reform Judaism, so I did not know about HUC-JIR.

The party was a Hillel function, and it was pretty boring. As I was leaving with the girls who came with me, two men from the mixer joined us to go out for a drink. Irvin sat down next to me at the bar, and we chatted as best we could in the noise. Since most of us did not order more drinks, we were asked to leave. It was decided to go to the home of one of the girls. I learned that there was going to be some gathering of young people the next week and I was invited to attend. Irvin said he was taking his friend home and asked if I would like a ride back to my brother's home.

When we arrived, I was surprised that Irvin got out and walked me across the street to the door. He asked me if I would like to go to a concert with him the next Saturday night. I said, "Yes." I had no idea what Irvin's last name was or what we were going to see on Saturday night. But I was happy to have a date. This was on February 11, 1967. On Valentine's Day, Irvin called to see if I would like to go out for coffee on Thursday night, but that was the night that I was planning to go to the social I had heard about. He asked about Wednesday night and I had something planned. I really did, but now I don't recall what it was, so we decided to go out that night. The rest is history. I did not go to the other events; we went out the next two nights but not on Friday, which I could not figure out. After that first coffee date, I said to my sister-in-law when I got home, "I bet he will not kiss me until the third date; and if I am not wrong, I might just have a rabbi for a husband."

It was not until about a week after our Saturday night date that I finally learned Irvin's last name. We were at HUC-JIR, where he was showing a film for his part-time student job. He projected some of the glass slides that were used by his family to advertise the family drug store. I learned his last name was Ehrlich! Those glass slides are now in a shadow box that we made, and it is hanging in our home. One month after we met, my parents came to Cincinnati to meet Irvin, and he proposed on the HUC-JIR campus. That was fifty-one years ago!

Since I met Irvin, he and our life together have always been my first priorities. I knew our children would grow up and leave, and it would be just the two of us after that, so I always worked on having a good marriage. (I have joked that the key to a good marriage is to buy your own gifts!)

I never thought I would marry a rabbi. When it came to the rabbinate, I had to learn as I went along. I knew that the one thing I had always disliked about being Jewish was feeling left out of school social events. My parents only allowed me to date Jewish boys and there weren't any in my school, and I was not included at synagogue, which was forty miles from my home, because I was not part of that social crowd. As a result, my main role as the rabbi's wife, as I saw it, was always to welcome people. I would greet newcomers and try to get them involved. For years, we had large gatherings for holiday meals in our home so that congregants who were alone would have somewhere to feel welcome. We made many wonderful friends. It was a special journey and I feel very blessed.

It was not until we got involved with NAORRR that we learned that our experiences as a rabbinic couple were not unique to us. Throughout his career, Irvin served in small communities, with relatively few Jews, and we felt isolated. In the forty years he served as a rabbi, he attended only a few conventions, and his experiences seemed very different from those of his peers. We had two congregations before Irvin decided to become an Air Force chaplain.

Irvin entered the Air Force after the end of the Vietnam War. We figured the country seemed to go to war about every twenty years, so we hoped that would hold true for us, and basically it did. Our first assignment was in Germany for three years. It was a massive adjustment to the Air Force and being overseas, all at once. We were so fortunate that he did not have any "remote" duty stations in our twenty years on active duty; our family was together at all stations. In addition to Germany, we lived in Colorado Springs at the Air Force Academy; in Bellville, Illinois at MAC (Military Airlift Command) headquarters; in Mildenhall England; in San Antonio, Texas, and then back to the Air Force Academy to finish up his twenty years. The best thing about being in the service was that there was no stigma attached to "why" you left your old position. And the people we served were not our bosses. We were an equal part of our community.

People in the service used to tell me that it was hard not always having a rabbi, or having to become used to each new rabbi coming in. I used to joke that I did not have that problem; I just brought my rabbi with me on each move. Because there was no permanent program at any base, we always had to start from scratch. There was never any support for oneg Shabbat or holiday celebrations, so I would organize the ladies and families that came to the base for services. Slowly, our congregation would grow, and we would create wonderful friendships that have lasted a lifetime. The worst part was having to leave friends after three or four years.

Office support for the Jewish chaplain was not always adequate. That's why Irvin was one of the earliest chaplains to get involved with the computer. If he wanted to send out a flyer, he would have to write out or type all the labels himself. For a while, we got some of the families to come in to help send out mailings, but this got old after a few months. Once he found out that he could build a database and print out the labels, he was "hooked." This was in the early 1980s when a "portable" computer was the size of a portable sewing machine case.

As a small-town girl in the 1950s and 1960s, I never really thought I would get to visit Europe, let alone live there. Looking back on some of the amazing things we got to do, while living a full three years each in Germany and England, seems like a dream come true. We had two young sons while we were in Germany, and they loved to go to the train station to watch the trains. By the time we went to England, we also had a daughter, who came back to the States with a definite British accent. We had the best of both worlds, since we got to enjoy Germany and England and the conveniences of American schools and American groceries on base. In England, we lived off base, and for a while our daughter thought that all Americans were Jewish because the only Americans she ever saw, which was at services, were all Jewish.

One of the most moving events we experienced in Germany happened on the second day of Rosh Hashanah when Irvin held services at the Rashi Synagogue in Worms. Normally, we did not get many people for the second day, but the synagogue was FULL that morning. It was amazing when we all recited kaddish in the rebuilt synagogue. The Jews had prevailed!

While in England, the Prince of Wales, HRH Prince Charles, came to the base to dedicate new windows in the chapel. I got to see him; Irvin got to shake his hand. Sadly, Princess Diana was not with him on the trip.

On Memorial Day, we would go to the Cambridge American Cemetery for services. One year, it was Irvin's turn to do the benediction. Right as he finished, there was a flyover of military jets. It was a very impressive moment.

One Veterans Day observance in England, we were invited to participate in the AJEX (Association of Jewish Ex-Servicemen and Women) Jewish memorial service at the Whitehall Cenotaph. We were in the company of the Chief Rabbi of Her Majesty's Forces, and we got to meet Baron Rothschild. After the service, we walked down Downing Street – which is closed to public traffic – to watch a parade of the AJEX members on the Horse Guard parade grounds.

One day, Irvin got a call to go see the base commanding officer, who wanted Irvin to be on the greeting team for a very important guest. Menachem Begin. The prime minister was flying from Israel to the United States for a meeting, and his plane needed a fuel stop. We drove down to London to pick up some kosher "noshes" since we did not know what level of kashrut he observed and we wanted to be prepared. Unfortunately, this was the flight he took when his wife was so ill and he was very subdued while we served tea and cookies to him and his daughter. We kick ourselves, even to this day, that we did not think to bring a camera to take a photograph with Mr. Begin.

When it became time to consider life after the Air Force, we knew we wanted to stay in Colorado Springs, as we loved it there and I had a very good job that I loved. We knew we could try to get a congregation somewhere that we might or might not like, or where we might or might not be liked, and where I might or might not have been able to find a position as a cancer registrar. As we were talking to a friend, I mentioned that my dream had long been to form a congregation where people joined because they liked the rabbi. Our friend said that if you do not try something, you will never know if it would work. We took their advice and talked to people – mostly civilians who attended services at the Academy to support the cadets – about forming a new congregation. Thirty unaffiliated families came together to form Temple Beit Torah. It was a wonderful challenge, and I continued my role as welcome lady and organizer. The temple grew to over 100 families.

After a few years, I realized that if the sisterhood were ever to stand on its own, I needed to step back from the advisor role and let the other women do the organizing. That was not easy to do. But it worked. Our little "baby" is twenty-six years old now. We are so very proud of the congregation and the people who have worked so hard to keep it going.

Once we both retired, we found that we were always driving back and forth through Kansas to see our children and grandchildren. We really did not like that very much, so we made the move to Madison, Wisconsin, where our daughter lives. Here we found a much larger Jewish community and a temple we felt comfortable in joining. It was our turn to take our own advice – to get involved in temple activities in order to make friends and to enjoy temple life. For the first time, I sat on the sisterhood executive board! It was very hard to say goodbye to our Colorado friends, but when it came to a choice between being close to our own family or not, our children won.

We currently live in Fitchburg, Wisconsin, near our daughter. We have three married children and eleven grandchildren. We do volunteer work for our temple and in the community.

Irvin was ordained in Cincinnati in 1970.

40

RABBINIC MUSINGS

MERYL TATTELBAUM

I GREW UP IN NEW YORK CITY AND MET HARVEY WHEN HE WAS IN his last year of rabbinical school at the New York campus of HUC-JIR and I was studying there for a master's degree in Jewish education. We were married in 1960, the year of Harvey's ordination. After ordination, Harvey went to chaplaincy school, where he was named valedictorian of the class. As a "reward," he was assigned to Parris Island, South Carolina, having been informed that the best in the class got the least desirable assignment. In fact, we enjoyed those two years very much, and I ran the religious school in the Reform congregation in Beaufort, where we lived – close to the Navy/Marine Corps base.

At the end of Harvey's active duty assignment, we returned to Manhattan, where he became the assistant rabbi at Temple Shaaray Tefila on East 79th Street. I was told that it was "inappropriate" for the rabbi's wife to work at the congregation – or at any other congregation, so I found different ways to be active and involved there. And I was also busy raising our three children.

After two years at Shaaray Tefila, Harvey became the rabbi of the Village Temple in lower Manhattan, where we spent the next seven years.

The following thirty years were spent back at Shaaray Tefila, where Harvey was now the senior rabbi. During those years, I became a silversmith with a small business. I also worked at *The New York Times,* bringing book reviews from the late nineteenth century into the new world of computers. We also traveled the world!

One of our great pleasures over the years has come from being part of the extended rabbinic family.

We have been in the same wonderful apartment, near the synagogue, for over fifty years. When you find the perfect apartment in New York City, you NEVER give it up! But living in that neighborhood brought home to me over and over again how peripheral, or do I mean invisible, I was to so many of the members of the congregation whom Harvey and I would run into when we were out walking, or in a store or a restaurant. They were always delighted to see "the rabbi" and greeted him effusively. I, on the other hand, was "what's her name," the virtually ignored spouse at his side.

I suppose I must have mentioned it to a few of our close friends in the congregation because on the evening that Harvey was honored for his (first) twenty years at Shaaray Tefilah with a fancy event at the Plaza Hotel, the high point of the evening came when the double doors of the ballroom were thrown open to the sound of drums and members of the congregation carried a canoe into the room on their shoulders. It was a very thoughtful gift for our lake house. Yet for me, the high point came when Harvey and I were invited to examine the boat closely and read the words beautifully lettered on the side: RABBI AND WHAT'S HER NAME! After the party, as we walked through the lobby carrying the canoe, we asked several people who were standing there and gaping at us where we could find a river! It was very funny! My reason for mentioning it here, however, is that it epitomizes succinctly, in a single anecdote, how I and many of my "rebbetzin" colleagues felt about our role in the congregations our husbands served: we were there but not there, no doubt welcome and loved and yet virtually invisible much of the time to a remarkable number of congregants.

My absolute favorite rabbinic spouse anecdote happened like this:

A member of the congregation who was born in the deep South had come to New York as a child of six or seven. I met her at our temple in her later years, and she still spoke with a carefully cultivated southern accent. She was still the quintessential southern belle. She liked to talk and talk and talk ... and talk. It wasn't sufficient for her to chat at the oneg Shabbat. She frequently called us at home, and we COULD NEVER get her off the phone!! You know the type. "Just one more thing...."

One evening, Harvey was at a meeting when she called. She went on and on. As usual, I tried to be my polite self, but I was seething. Almost unconsciously, I grabbed the large scissors on the table next to me and cut the phone wire in half!! *Mea culpa*! It felt wonderful!!

Just then Harvey returned to the apartment and, instantly grasping the situation, began to laugh. We're still laughing many years later.

Today, we have three adult children and seven grandchildren. We divide our time between Manhattan and our longtime vacation house on Candlewood Lake in New Milford, Connecticut.

41

Ashreinu

RESA S. DAVIDS

INTRODUCTION

As with many great moments of transition, it all began with a frantic, determined phone call to my one unshakable tower of reason and stability: "Hello, Mom. Please call Rabbi Schindler and reserve every Sunday in August. Then call the temple and do the same thing. I just accepted an AEPi pin from a young man who is in rabbinical school!!

"Hang on there, Resa. Are you telling me that all of a sudden you are engaged to be married? I just dropped you off at graduate school in Cleveland three weeks ago."

"No, Mom, just 'pinned,' but the next step will be an engagement, and I don't have any idea when that will happen. The wedding will have to be before he goes back to school in the fall next year, and Alex and the temple get so busy in August, I just want to be ready."

"Have you told the guy this?"

"No, he doesn't have to know about it until we are formally engaged and start to plan the wedding."

And that was my first, not very subtle, step toward becoming a rebbetzin.

◆═◆

I grew up in Malden, Massachusetts in the 1940s and '50s. Malden is not the fancy west side of Boston, with towns like Brookline and Newton, nor far enough north to be part of the fancier northern suburbs like Peabody, Swampscott and Marblehead, all of which are on the water. Malden is just Malden, a blue-collar, hard scruff town with a population in those days of 60,000 people, including about 10,000 Jews.

Our family home was an apartment on the second floor of a rather large house. My father, *z"l*, was a dentist; his office occupied the first floor. Living above the office was a wonderful way to grow up. My mom, *z"l*, and my dad were always around. When my older sister, Rana, was in high school, she worked as a dental assistant in the office. I got to sit in the back room and cut up cotton strips for my dad to use in the office. I also played with the mercury, at that time used in fillings for teeth, not exactly healthy, but no one knew that then.

Every day, after school, I would stop in the office to see Dad before I went upstairs. Inevitably, he would chase me with a needle filled with water and squirt me before I got safely, but a little wet, to the door leading to the stairs. When he had played a bad round of golf, he would give two patients Novocain and come up to the apartment to practice his golf swing while his patients waited patiently for the anesthetic to take effect.

Dad was the head of the U.S. Army Dental Corps during WWII in the China-Burma-India (CBI) theater, stationed at the end of the Burma Road before that road was completed. One of the CBI Jewish chaplains, Rabbi David Seligson, a Reform rabbi, had a very strong influence on my dad, who had grown up Orthodox and knew nothing about liberal Judaism. When my father returned to Malden, after serving for over four years in the Army, the shul that he had attended prior to going off to China had fallen on difficult times. Most of the young men of the community had been away in the military. Dad was asked to take over as president. He taught the families about Reform Judaism and agreed to accept the office if the congregation agreed to turn the shul into a Reform temple. And that is exactly what happened.

At the same time, Dad took over the North Shore Jewish Federation, started the Israel Bonds appeal, built the Malden Hebrew School with the help of Rabbi Joseph B. Soloveichik, and more. Every evening he would come up from the office at 8:00 p.m., change out of his dental gown into a suit and tie, and leave for this meeting or that meeting to solve this or that issue and to move the Jewish community forward. Eventually, after serving for fourteen years as the president of Temple Tifereth Israel, he became president of the New England region of the UAHC. Then he served for many years on the UAHC national board. During these years, he and Rabbi Alexander Schindler, then executive director of the region, built twenty-two Reform congregations around Boston.

Dad was my hero. Mom was a political Zionist and a socialist. In addition to doing the bookkeeping for the dental office, she worked side by side with Dad in all of his activities in the Jewish community. In her own right, she was sisterhood president, chair of federation and president of Hadassah, and was once elected "Man of the Year" by the Malden Trust Bank, of which she was a trustee. This was a title of which she was extremely proud. Together, my parents helped work to build the State of Israel. My sister and I were sorting Federation pledge cards when we were still in elementary school.

Thus, I became a child of the Reform Movement. I was not just Jewish; I was a very proud Reform Jew. Rabbis were hired and fired in our living room. I was invited to some of those meetings as a NFTY representative to the rabbinic search committees. When the time came, I chose to date only Reform Jews throughout my high school and college years. When Alex's wife, Rhea, heard that I was planning to marry a rabbinic student, she laughed and told my parents, "You deserve it!"

I attended Jackson College of Tufts University in the neighboring town of Medford, Massachusetts. As part of the ten percent Jewish quota accepted at Tufts during those years, I, like all of the Jewish students, was assigned a Jewish roommate, and we lived on a floor with only Jewish students. We took that for granted, and never raised a question about the policy.

My most important extra-curricular activity in those years was college NFTY. We ran a Shabbaton in Lenox, Massachusetts, once a year. Participants came from all of the local colleges, including Tufts, Boston University, Harvard, MIT, Smith, Mt. Holyoke and the University of Massachusetts. HUC-JIR arranged for us to have faculty members as scholars-in-residence, and we experienced incredible weekends of shared learning. To the best of my knowledge, this group existed for a total of six years.

When I became an upper-class student and had a single room and a car, I lit candles every Friday night in my room, together with a number of my Jewish friends. Then I drove a carpool from Tufts, via MIT and Harvard, to Temple Israel in Boston to attend erev Shabbat services. Understandably, many of these friends called me "The Rebbetzin." My fate was pre-determined, and I loved it!

Following my graduation from Jackson with a B.A.in mathematics, I entered Western Reserve Medical School and Graduate School to begin a course of studies that was supposed to lead to an M.D. degree and a Ph.D. in biostatistics. I arrived in Cleveland not knowing a soul. During my first week, I attended a mixer at the medical school and met a young man named Gordon. We left the mixer together and went out for something to eat. Over our deli sandwiches, we got into a discussion – or maybe it was an argument – until the wee hours of the morning about the theologies of Reform and Conservative Judaism. The next morning, Gordon called Stan and told him that he had a met a girl from Boston, and she was for Stan, not for himself!

That morning, I went to Fairmount Temple to introduce myself and to get involved in the Young People's Congregation. The associate rabbi, Sam Broude, introduced me to his secretary and asked her to make sure that I meet some of the young people in the community. She called her brother and told him she had just met a girl who was perfect for him. Stan said, "Don't tell me she's from Boston!" We were pinned in short order – or, should I say, he was hooked.

Stan grew up in Cleveland. His father owned a deli and his mother was a stay-at-home mom, entirely devoted to raising Stan and his older sister, Sandi, *z"l*. Stan spent many hours helping his dad in the deli. The highlight of that experience was listening to the conversation around the one very important lunch table in the back room. The customers were many rabbis who were guaranteed a great meal and a private place to talk. Stan listened to their conversations and decided, by age seven, that he wanted to become a rabbi. He loved studying Hebrew at the Cleveland Hebrew Schools and then at the Cleveland Hebrew College. When he entered HUC-JIR, his language and text backgrounds were so strong that he was accepted as a second-year student.

OUR WEDDING

We had a wedding date – August 18, 1963 – a venue, an officiant, an invitation list and a bride and a groom. We managed to offend those who didn't make the cut-off for invitations, those for whom the date and/or location were inconvenient, and those who weren't happy about where they would be seated for the reception. Nevertheless, we were certain we were on track for a beautiful, love-filled, and mostly conventional ceremony. And besides, Alex Schindler was going to officiate at our wedding. What could go wrong?

Alex and Rhea were very close friends of my parents and had known me since I was quite young. As the time came for Alex to speak to us under the *huppah*, he closed his eyes, tipped back his head, and said, "Stanley, you are about to enter your fourth year at HUC-JIR. Soon you will be a rabbi. This is a difficult job, and one that will keep you busy many hours of the day and night. Be certain that you make time in your schedule to be at home with your beloved Rhea!"

Everyone laughed hysterically, including Rhea, who was sitting in the congregation. The *huppah* shook, the wine cup tipped over, the photographer caught the moment, and Alex told this story many, many times. He called it his most embarrassing moment in the rabbinate! I learned then that whatever one might guess could go wrong, most likely won't. It is the unthinkable and the unimaginable that happen.

RONN'S B'RIT MILAH

In 1965, Stan was a member of the fifth-year class in rabbinical school and I was studying biostatistics at the University of Cincinnati Medical School and Graduate School. One of the required courses for rabbinical students that year was Practical Rabbinics, taught by Rabbi Dr. Sylvan Schwartzman and his wife Sylvia at their home. Spouses were expected to attend. On February 9, the topic was how to conduct a wedding. Students were asked to role play: bride, groom, rabbi, parents of the bride and groom, etc. Since I was well along in the ninth month of my pregnancy, the class decided that I would make the perfect bride!

About fifteen minutes into the mock ceremony, I went into labor. Each labor pain was announced with an amazingly strong hot flash. My face was blazing red. Everyone was timing the contractions while the wedding continued. Some students were making swimming motions, waiting for my water to break...which did not happen.

When it became quite obvious that it was time to head to the hospital, there was cheering and teasing. Everyone was hoping the baby would be a boy because they knew it would be catered by Stan's dad and that the food at the *b'rit milah* (ritual circumcision) would be fantastic. (Celebrating a *b'rit bat* – covenantal welcoming ceremony for a baby girl – had not yet occurred to anyone.)

And so it was. Ronn was born on February tenth. Eight days later, the *b'rit* room at the Cincinnati Jewish Hospital was filled to capacity. All of the students and most of the faculty joined us to celebrate. The sights and sounds of the *b'rit milah* made the reality of our being parents for the first time amazingly real. We also knew that it was real by seeing the looks in our parents' eyes. Somehow, Stan and I had actually done something that made all of our parents joyous at the very same time.

STAN'S MILITARY CAREER

HUC-JIR and the other rabbinical schools were each committed to providing a certain number of chaplains to the quota being requested at the time by the National Jewish Welfare Board. Every senior rabbinic student at HUC-JIR had to apply to the military; anyone who did not would be barred from the placement process for a CCAR pulpit. The names of every eligible student were entered in a lottery. In Cincinnati, the names were placed in a military cap, and Rabbi Nelson Glueck, president of HUC-JIR, drew the names of those who had been selected for service.

Stan called me the morning of the drawing and informed me that he was not only first in his class academically, but also first out of the hat! I thought he was joking, but he was not. Since Ronn was only a few months old, we requested stateside service rather than going overseas with a baby and were sent to Fort Belvoir, Virginia, the home of the U.S. Army Engineers, where Stan, the only Jewish chaplain on the post, was assigned to the main chapel as head of the "Jewish rabbis." A high-ranking Catholic chaplain pretty much ran that chapel, which was also served by a Protestant chaplain. The chapel had a rotating platform that allowed the sanctuary space to be a synagogue, a Catholic church or a Protestant church as needed. About 150 Jewish family units were attached to the chapel. Many of the doctors at the DeWitt Army Hospital on the post were Jewish, and there were also many retired career officers who lived near Fort Belvoir and made up the permanent core of the Jewish community. Accustomed to getting a new rabbi pretty much every two years, they took it upon themselves to train the young, newly ordained chaplains who rotated through. Chaplains entered the military as first lieutenants. Medical personnel all came in as captains. But these mentors, who were primarily career Army, either on active duty or retired, all outranked us. (And yes, military wives in those days carried the rank of their husbands.)

I was a stay-at-home mom. The other wives were incredibly supportive of both Stan and me. There were about seventy-five children in the religious school. In many ways, this was a stronger congregation than those of many of Stan's classmates who, as newly ordained rabbis, were not allowed to serve congregations with more than 125 families.

Stan was once asked to bless a newly planted tree on the post. Afterward, he drove by that tree every day to make sure it would thrive. If it died, he was sure he would be sent to Vietnam.

After he wore his uniform to an anti-Vietnam demonstration on the National Mall in Washington, D.C., he was called into the Post Commanding General's office and informed that if such a thing happened again, he would definitely be sent off to Vietnam, where war had recently exploded into the headlines.

THINGS THAT HAPPENED

At Stan's request, a *hanukkiah* was built in front of the chapel. He drew a picture of what he wanted but did not include measurements. The Army Corps of Engineers showed up a few days later with a huge *hanukkiah* made of plumbing pipes and just as tall as the chapel itself.

Stan asked his chaplain's assistants to prepare six dozen roasted eggs for a community seder but forgot to tell them to boil the eggs first. The odor in the chapel when all those eggs exploded in the oven was unbearably excruciating.

Two prisoners, sent from the local stockade to clean up the post chapel, decided to drink all the sweet kosher wine in the storage closet. They wound up incredibly drunk *AND NOTICEABLY ILL* and were hauled back to the brig to sober up.

As the post expanded in response to the Vietnam War, Stan made sure to have several Jewish chaplain assistants at all times. He kept them assigned to the chapel until they were "short-timers," meaning that they had less than nine months remaining to serve and thus would not be sent to Vietnam. One morning, he arrived at the chapel and learned that a yeshivah-trained soldier had received orders to deploy to Vietnam. Stan had the MPs stop him on the New Jersey Turnpike and had him reassigned to the chapel because he was "necessary personnel." And they did.

The greater Washington area had a chaplains' wives club that met occasionally to listen to lectures, have tea and socialize. Many of these women's husbands were serving overseas, and they were alone, living on our post or on other posts in the D.C. area. The club was intended to be a support for them. Obviously, there were no Catholic chaplains' wives, but there were about seventy Protestant women in the group. I was the only Jewish wife. Thus, I was frequently honored by being asked to offer the opening or closing benediction, or to pour the tea. It was a wonderful opportunity to discover that a rebbetzin would often be expected to have some of her husband's expertise. Writing a blessing, speaking in public, answering questions about observance or even textual matters is too often and erroneously assumed to be in the skill set of the rebbetzin, and it takes a level of maturity to realize there's no need to feel inadequate in not knowing answers one shouldn't have been expected to know in the first place.

SHOSHANA

I gave birth to our second child, Shoshana, at DeWitt Army Hospital in February 1967. Total hospital bill: $5.25. A great military benefit! On the other hand, when I left the recovery room and walked to my assigned hospital room, I found sheets, a blanket a pillow and some towels stacked at the end of my unmade bed. Definitely not what I had anticipated. Stan served as an Army chaplain from July 1965 to

June 1967. We look back quite fondly on our military experience, which, quite fortunately, was very positive. Those years also afforded us time to do a lot of growing up.

BIRTH OF AVIVA

Civilian life, at last. Rabbi Dudley Weinberg had invited Stan to become associate rabbi at Temple Emanuel B'nai Jeshurun in Milwaukee, Wisconsin and I joined the faculty of Marquette University Medical School (later renamed the Medical College of Wisconsin). We had two children and a third was on the way.

Aviva was born on a lovely, early Tuesday morning between Rosh Hashanah and Yom Kippur in September 1969. My mom had come from Boston to take care of Ronn, age four-and-a-half, and Shoshana, then two-and-a-half. When Stan brought Ronn home from pre-school that day, my mother opened the door, took one look and asked, "Why is Ronn's arm hanging backwards?" It turned out that he had fallen down the three steps of a small plastic slide and the teachers had failed to notice that he had broken his collarbone! Off Stan went to have Ronn placed in a butterfly splint.

Stan had left the hospital shortly after Aviva arrived because he had an insanely busy schedule far beyond his High Holy Day preparations. There was no time for him to come back to the hospital to see me, because he had to go to the airport with a group of Milwaukee Jewish leaders to greet Prime Minister Golda Meir. And no time to see me or Aviva the next day either, because in addition to preparing for Yom Kippur, he was organizing Milwaukee's first moratorium against the Vietnam War. And he was involved in evening sessions devoted to interviewing young men who wanted to learn about becoming conscientious objectors or going off to Canada.

So, I stayed in the hospital for the five days which were routine then and was pleased that Stan was able to get there to bring the two of us home. It was a Saturday, so after *shaharit* he came with Ronn (in his butterfly brace, of course) and Shoshana, and was the very happy dad of three little people.

When Aviva was six-weeks old, Stan's senior rabbi, Dudley Weinberg, suffered a heart attack. Off Stan went to the hospital, where he sat with Dudley in the CCU and was given a very long list of things that had to be done for this 1300 family congregation. Stan came home a bit nervous about what was going to happen next. In fact, what happened was that he was so nervous he developed shingles on his leg. The doctor insisted that he had to rest for two hours every afternoon. I put the two older children in bed next to him and they all napped together while I had some quiet time with newborn Aviva. No one had told us that shingles is contagious. In short order, Ronn and Shoshana had chicken pox. Aviva evidently wasn't affected, the proof of which was that she and her two-week-old newborn came down with chicken pox thirty-five years later!!

MASSACHUSETTS, AND ESPECIALLY WORCESTER

Although we loved Milwaukee, it was time for Stan to go out on his own, to be in direct touch with his board, to work with his own lay leaders, to put in place the programs that we had been dreaming about. Stan accepted a pulpit in Springfield, Massachusetts, where we would be close to my parents. We stayed at Sinai Temple for six years, and then moved to Worcester, to Temple Emanuel, a much larger congregation. There was a sense among many rabbis in those years that bigger is always better. At CCAR conventions, both spouses and rabbis seemed to assess classmates and others by the size of the pulpit they occupied. It was a dramatically flawed metric, but who knew that then?

During those years, I was first a member of the Public Health Department of the University of Connecticut Medical School and then switched careers, attending Worcester State College to be certified as a math teacher for the State of Massachusetts. I taught math at the middle and high school levels for a number of years before eventually teaching statistics as an adjunct professor at Quinsigamond Community College.

Our kids acquired friends wherever they lived. And so did we. Yet it is Worcester that Ronn, Shoshana and Aviva really consider to be their hometown. Our family had moved from city to city a number of times already, but for Aviva, at age seven-and-a-half, the move from Springfield to Worcester, was a very big adventure, since the move from Milwaukee to Springfield had occurred when she was less than two years old. I sat down with her and explained that we would be living only fifty miles down the road. We would have a new home and a new temple, and it would be a wonderful adventure for all of us. I explained further that, although she did not remember, our family had already lived in four different cities, which seemed like a good way to reassure her. I told her that when Ronn was born, Daddy was a student at Hebrew Union College in Cincinnati; when Shoshana was born, Daddy was a chaplain in the United States Army at Fort Belvoir. And when you were born, I said to her, Daddy was an associate rabbi in Milwaukee. I was sure she understood, and it seemed to satisfy her. Which was not the case, because when Aviva went to her first day of religious school, the teacher introduced her to the students as the daughter of the new rabbi and asked her to tell something about herself. Aviva announced, “I have a brother and a sister, and we all have different daddies.”

SUMMERS IN ISRAEL

With each passing year, Israel became more and more central to our lives. Stan and I believed that the best way to inculcate a love for and an understanding of Israel in our kids was to provide them with ample personal experiences in *medinat Yisrael*. We were sitting with Rabbi Steve Schaefer next to the pool at Kutz Camp and began talking together about the NFTY in Israel program, which existed very much because of Steve's work as NFTY director. Stan and I thought it sounded like a great opportunity for us to be leaders of a NFTY summer program. We had visited Israel only once before, as part of the first CCAR convention in Jerusalem, in March 1970. Now, in the summer of 1972, we were eager to return to Israel but definitely did not have the finances even to consider such a trip.

Steve was hesitant because we had three small children – Aviva was just shy of four, Shoshana was six and Ronn was eight. After many discussions, we were accepted as leaders and assigned to the ulpan program of the Eisendrath International Exchange /Ulpan trip, which meant six weeks at the Ben Shemen Youth Village, including one day each week of in-country travel, and only two weeks of intense touring. That meant that we would have a home base for most of the summer, and it would be easier for our family than a NFTY in Israel program that involved eight weeks of nonstop touring.

Off we went with 40 teenagers in July 1973. We met the group at JFK. The teenagers were a bit surprised to see that they would be traveling with our entire family. Some of their parents were also not sure what was happening as they dropped their youngsters off in our care. When I look at my young grandchildren today, I understand why my mother was not happy about our plans and why the NFTYites and their parents were a bit shocked.

The EIE/Ulpan schedule included four hours of class each morning, study time in the afternoon and various programmed activities as well as a travel day each week. I attended the second level Hebrew class, and Ronn, now eight, attended the first level class. He saw himself as a full participant and took the class very seriously. Shoshana and Aviva went to the local day camp, which gave them full days of total immersion in Hebrew.

And so our summers in Israel began. Eventually, we would lead two more EIE/Ulpan groups in 1976 and 1979, and then led Confirmation class trips in 1981,1982, 1984 and 1985. We absolutely loved these experiences and considered them to be among the biggest benefits available to pulpit rabbis. Unfortunately, few of these NFTY trips are led by rabbis today, and I think it is an unfortunate change both for the students and for the rabbis.

Working with our groups twenty-four hours a day, seven days a week, was our summer vacation. During those summers, we traveled all over Israel – from the peaks of the Golan Heights to the beaches of the Mediterranean to the tip of the Sinai Desert and to the Jordan River. We came to know and love this land of ours, to know Israel in a way rarely experienced by other rabbinic families. Our children grew up surrounded by teenagers and comfortable with the Hebrew language. We saw Israel through the eyes of our children and through the eyes of a few hundred teenagers. Over the years, many of these young people grew into our lifelong friends. Many have become rabbis, cantors and Jewish educators. We like to think that our summers together helped to direct them to choose professions in the Jewish world. I wish we could do it all over again.

MEET DAVID SILVER

We all spent the summer of 1981 in Israel, Stan and I as *madrichim* for the confirmation class trip from Temple Emanuel in Worcester. Shoshana traveled with us as a member of that class, and Aviva was with us in her role as RK. Ronn was a volunteer for the summer at Kibbutz Kfar Blum following his tenth-grade academic year there as a member of the American class.

We'd enjoyed a wonderful summer and were happy to be bringing Ronn back with us to Worcester.

Two hours after we arrived home, the phone rang. It was my mom and dad calling to tell us that our nephew, David, was living with them on a temporary basis and that it would be better if he were to live with our family.

WHAT?????

David was now fourteen years old, just six weeks younger than Shoshana. We sat down as a family and discussed what it would mean if we decided to accept this responsibility, even though none of us had any real idea of what we were talking about – or taking on. Stan and I were incredibly proud of our children's willingness to accept David into our family, and we also felt completely overwhelmed. A few hours later, my mom showed up on our doorstep with David.

Slowly but surely, everything began to fall into place. David joined the routine of our family life. He attended religious school and learned Hebrew. We decided not to worry about planning his bar mitzvah right away. That would occur only after Aviva's bat mitzvah, which was already scheduled for the following May.

The Worcester community accepted David as if he had always been a member of our family. He succeeded in school with the help of some very wonderful teachers. He quickly made friends, participated in sports at the JCC with Ronn, joined the temple youth group and went off to camp at Eisner, in Great Barrington, during the summer of 1982.

David lived with our family for three years. In the spring of 1984, at the age of sixteen, he celebrated his bar mitzvah. The entire congregation turned out to celebrate with us. After that major life cycle event, he returned to California to live with his dad and attend his senior year of high school in Beverly Hills. The Silver family remains close to all of us. In fact, Shoshana likes to say that she has "a brother, a sister and a David." David remains precious to our lives. He taught us so very much about what really matters, and he will forever be a part of our family narrative.

LATER YEARS

In 1986, we moved to New York City, where Stan was named senior rabbi of Central Synagogue, and I worked as a math teacher at The Dwight School. In 1991, Stan became associate director of the Synagogue Council of America, and I continued at the Dwight School. Ronn and Shoshana were attending Tufts University (my alma mater!), and Aviva wound up skipping her senior year of high school and enrolled in NYU. All of a sudden, we had three children in college simultaneously! We began to think that this would be a permanent situation as each one went on to graduate school. And, in fact, the schooling has not ended yet. As I write these words Aviva is studying for her DMin degree at HUC-JIR!

In 1992, Stan became senior rabbi of Temple Emanu-El of Greater Atlanta, Georgia and also was elected national chair of ARZA. In Atlanta, I served as assistant principal of Yeshiva Atlanta for six years and then as the director of the Florence Melton Mini-School of Adult Jewish Learning at the JCC.

In 2004, we retired and made aliyah. We lived in Jerusalem until 2014. During those years, Stan became very involved in the politics of JAFI, WZO, ARZENU and the Labor Party; I studied Hebrew and became the founding chairperson of WRJ-Israel.

One of the great blessings of the rabbinate is that it provides an astonishing variety of ways to contribute to Jewish life. A positive, liberal Zionism is a shared characteristic in our family. To this day, I work to bring a non-dogmatic, but deeply rooted love for Israel to all of my efforts on behalf of the Women of Reform Judaism, on whose board I served for nineteen years. Stan does the same in his ongoing volunteer work. More than fifty years after ordination, he and I are still trying to change our world. I think that my being a full partner in a rabbinic family has strengthened both of us in countless ways.

Many of the people with whom we have shared both laughter and tears over the years have transformed us and have remained defining parts of who we are. I really believe that the rabbinate is unique in the way that it allows barriers of separation to be broken down and for new relationships to take root and to flourish. There are indeed people whom I sincerely wish that I had never met, but their numbers are few and their presence is minuscule when compared with so many other fascinating and loving people who make each new day so rewarding.

Ashreinu. May our lives together continue to be a blessing.

We now live in Santa Monica, California surrounded by Ronn and Aviva and their families. Shoshana and her family live in New York and we spend time with them there and when they visit us in California. Stan has become very active as a volunteer at the University Synagogue in Los Angeles, HUC-JIR, and the Israel Consulate; he was also deeply involved in working for the Hillary Clinton presidential campaign. I've continued in leadership roles on the international, board, district and local levels of WRJ and am currently president of the University Synagogue sisterhood.

42
THE CRUCIBLE
PAM BLUMENTHAL

IN SOUTH ROODEPOORT, A SMALL MINING TOWN IN SOUTH AFRICA where my parents lived for some years, my father was a mining engineer who worked underground in the gold mine, and my anxious mother literally lived on her nerves. Bernard Price was a devoted family man, brilliant and a success at everything he did in life. When I was five, he moved our family to Pretoria and went into business with a family member. I was enrolled at a nearby Roman Catholic convent and my younger brother at Christian Brothers College.

Our Jewish education was taken care of at Temple Menorah, which was founded, built and nurtured by my father, one of four men who began the Progressive movement there under the guidance of the late Rabbi Moses Cyrus Weiler. During the two years it took to build Temple Menorah, we held our services in the Sons of England Hall nearby. The music was arranged by Jerry Idelson, a small fiery man who drove us mercilessly to attain high musical standards; he arranged Kol Nidre for my contralto voice.

One of my earliest memories is listening to my parents recount the academic achievements of Rabbi Walter Blumenthal, whose distinguished school career earned him a Bachelor of Arts degree and then a Master of Arts, both as a scholarship student at the University of the Witwatersrand (Wits) in Johannesburg and as a rabbinical student at HUC-JIR in Cincinnati, where he studied for seven years.

I had an aptitude for languages. I was honored with a national award for an English essay and went on to graduate from Wits, where I majored in English, French and the history of music. I had a year at the Teachers Training College in Johannesburg, then teaching posts at various schools. I studied classical ballet and worked hard every day to further my studies on the piano. Singing lessons followed during my university years.

It was the norm then for young Jewish men to court, and soon marry, suitable young women. Consequently, my work toward my honors degree in English was interrupted by social activities. Overprotected by both my parents, my rebellion took the form of making an unsuitable marriage. Little did I know that my first husband was bipolar. He could be kindness itself and then, for no reason, suddenly erupt into terrifying rages. Our two children, Mark and Bonnie, had difficult childhoods, but they were under the spell of their charismatic father.

Times without number, I warned him that his uncontrolled temper tantrums could result in a coronary occlusion. Bonnie was two when he had his first; his second occurred three years later. His third coronary destroyed three quarters of his heart muscle. He was left brain damaged. His six weeks in hospital were characterized by such violent behavior that the nursing staff avoided him, relying on me to try to calm him. He was sent home in that condition and went frequently to Walter with his troubles.

I could not accept that my marriage was over or that I should deny my children their father until, one day, our family doctor took me aside and persuaded me to leave him. One Saturday morning while he went out, I hurriedly packed a suitcase and drove to a hotel in Pretoria with the children and our German Shepherd Dog. We registered under an assumed name and, together with my parents, hid out there until a protection order could be issued. He died six months later, just one month before our divorce was due to be heard in court.

Although I had shares in the properties he had accumulated, it turned out that in his will he had formally stripped me of my shares, leaving me destitute. After a legal battle overcame that, we returned to Johannesburg, where I went back to teaching and then decided on a career change. I began writing professionally, eventually becoming the opera and vocal music critic for *The Star* and for *Scenario*, an arts magazine with international exposure.

During this time, I had continued to be a chorister at Temple Shalom, the congregation Walter served as rabbi, so he and I had stayed in touch. Some months after I was widowed, Walter's first wife died suddenly and, after an appropriate interval, Walter courted me. We married in the August of the following year. Our honeymoon in Israel was my first experience of travel outside Africa.

After that, we made annual and sometimes biennial trips throughout Europe and the United States. This was at a time when American rabbis' wives' views of their role had begun to change, and I was often asked for my views on the role of the rebbetzin in congregational activities. Some of my interlocutors found what I had to say old-fashioned. My views had their genesis at Temple Menorah. In South Africa, a rebbetzin was expected to work at the side of her husband. For me, it was a privilege, not a duty.

My music reviews continued to be published. When my workload was particularly heavy, Walter saw to our children – his one and my two – whom we had cross-adopted, and to other duties at home. We had season tickets to all the concerts, recitals and other musical events in Johannesburg and Pretoria, and attended the opening of the magnificent State Theatre there.

In South Africa, for the most part, the lay leadership predominates in Jewish organizations. My husband was a brilliant and scholarly rabbi. He had rabbinic ordination, was a Ph.D. and could chant from the Torah. He was outspoken in defense of the important causes about which he cared passionately.

Nevertheless, not everyone agreed with his views, and when

Walter had been in the pulpit of the Johannesburg congregation for twenty-seven years, the leadership of South Africa's Progressive movement suddenly turned on him. They watched him like a hawk, waiting for him to fail. But he never did.

Then, one day in 1986, Walter suffered a heart attack and was admitted to hospital. While he was in his hospital bed, the congregation's leadership barred him from the congregation and summarily dismissed him, without giving him any real explanation after all his years of devoted service. When Walter had recovered sufficiently to leave the house, he went to his office to retrieve his belongings only to be refused entry.

The press got hold of the story, and people across the Jewish community were horrified at how he had been treated. Our whole family tried to comfort him, but to no avail. Labor laws in the new South Africa a decade later would never have sanctioned his dismissal. The congregation would have had to compensate him or rehire him had the case gone to the labor courts.

At its next annual general meeting, the congregation publicly discussed Walter's situation. Our son, Mark, went to the meeting to try and get some answers, and bravely stood up to our adversaries before being shouted down.

A reporter from the now-defunct *SA Jewish Times* who went to the synagogue to try and obtain the story, was unceremoniously thrown out. In an effort to avail herself of the facts, the editor of the paper approached the chairman of the congregation and threatened him with the prospect of a one-sided story that would reflect poorly on Temple Shalom if he did not speak to her. He then agreed to a meeting, which he attended supported by a cohort of fellow congregants who tape recorded every word that was said. They were unsuccessful in their attempt to convince her of Walter's ineptitude, and the *Jewish Times* came out full-square pro-Walter, with editorials entitled, "What Have They Got to Hide?" and "Sweeping It Under the Carpet." None of those actions mitigated the intransigence of the lay leaders.

Walter and I had been married for eleven years at this time. After his dismissal, our family faced a severe drop in income, especially because he was barred from taking a rabbinic position anywhere in the Republic of South Africa. He had no choice but to seek a job in the United States, and accepted a pulpit in Gary, Indiana. I planned to follow him after my elder daughter had obtained her university degree and the younger one had written her high school finals.

Walter was loved and appreciated by the Gary congregation, the members of which kept in touch with me on a regular basis. Then, one unforgettable night, I received a phone call from the States. Walter had been driving to the opera in Chicago when he had a sudden onset of pain in his chest. Forever mindful of others, he had pulled the car to the side of the road, where he suffered a fatal heart attack.

I was inconsolable. To me, it was as if Temple Shalom had struck its final blow.

Walter's remains were flown back to Johannesburg, and he was interred next to his father in the Jewish cemetery. Although Temple Shalom made no effort to honor his memory or make reparations, Temple Israel, the original Progressive synagogue in Johannesburg, with a more caring leadership, arranged a memorial service for him. Not a single member of the Temple Shalom leadership attended. There was, however, a huge representation from the black Lemba tribe, which claims Jewish origins and practices certain Jewish customs. Although they are not accepted as Jews, they have Jewish hearts and souls and were very close to Walter.

Temple Shalom is no more. The next rabbi adopted Masorti observance, and the Progressive movement in Johannesburg diminished to minimal numbers. I am especially bitter, because I have the sense that, in keeping the congregation alive in the face of all the negative efforts of the Progressive leadership, Walter lost his own life.

Years later, the by-then former editor of the *Jewish Times* bumped into the then-Temple Shalom chairman in an elevator in Cape Town.

"Now that Walter is no more and the years have passed, are you at last able to tell me why you fired Rabbi Dr. Walter Blumenthal?" she asked.

"It's simple," he replied. "He just would not listen."

For the past thirty-one years, I have set foot in a synagogue only twice, and that was to attend my children's weddings, which took place in an Orthodox shul in Johannesburg. I have not been in a synagogue since.

From 1962 until last year, my hobby has been the breeding, showing and training of show-quality German Shepherd Dogs. "Once a teacher, always a teacher." For eleven years, my Sunday mornings were spent teaching obedience training at my club. Last year, after I was awarded the bronze, silver and gold medals, the German Shepherd Dog Federation of Southern Africa honored me with Honorary Life Membership in that august institution.

In today's torrid times in this once-wonderful country, riots and protests are the order of the day. Our guard dogs are regarded as a valuable deterrent. The country's infrastructure is in tatters, we are in debt to the tune of trillions of our beleaguered rand, and we are tightening our belts further than the tightest notch with an inflation rate that has gone through the roof. Property values are at an all-time low, with the threat of property expropriation without compensation hanging over our heads.

All we can do is pray for a miracle...

Pam Blumenthal is a lifelong resident of South Africa. Her husband, Rabbi Dr. Walter Blumenthal, z"l, was ordained by HUC-JIR in Cincinnati in 1957.

43

I LOVED BEING THE WIFE OF A RABBI: ALL THE REST IS COMMENTARY

IRENE MELTON PALNICK

My parents were both immigrants to Canada. Because young Jewish boys were being drafted into the army for thirty-five years in Russia (I believe to keep them from procreating), my father and his brother were among many who fled to avoid conscription. They went to Newfoundland, which was then a British protectorate. In 1949, Newfoundland became a province of Canada. My mother was from Vilna. When she arrived at Ellis Island with her parents and six siblings, the family was immediately sent by train to Montreal, rather than being allowed to remain in the United States. Canada has always accepted immigrants. When my father was in his twenties, he determined to look for a bride. As there weren't many Jews in Newfoundland, he moved to Montreal and checked out Schwartz's Deli on St. Lawrence Boulevard, a famous gathering place for Jews. (The deli is still thriving to this day!) My mother worked there. Both spoke Russian and Yiddish, which was my first language, as well. (I still speak Yiddish.) They courted and married.

I was an only child. My parents taught me to be kind and accepting of people – and, because they had lived through pogroms in Europe, they also taught me not to trust Christians. They wanted me to be a good Canadian and always gave me pennies to participate in holidays like Valentine's Day, Halloween and Christmas at school. Schools in Quebec at that time were either French-speaking Catholic or English-speaking Protestant. I went to the Protestant school, as did most of the Jews in Montreal at that time. Our family was what we now called modern Orthodox – we kept kosher, didn't work on Shabbat and went to synagogue on Saturday morning. Although we were poor, my parents scrimped and saved in order to send me to college.

My very best friend in high school was a Reform Jew, whose parents weren't immigrants. My parents told me that family wasn't *really* Jewish, because they rode to shul on Saturday and on the holidays. We remained best friends through high school. In fact, we reconnected in recent years and are best friends once again.

How ironic that I ended up marrying a college graduate who was planning to become a Reform rabbi! My parents were not happy that I was moving to Cincinnati, but they always were kind and accepted Zeke's family without question.

When I first met Zeke, whose full name was Elijah Ezekiel Palnick, we were both at McGill University. At the time, he was a literature major and wanted to go to Oxford for graduate studies. But he was invited to spend his senior year at Mt. Allison University, a United Church school in Sackville, New Brunswick, teaching Hebrew to theology students and literature to engineering students. At the end of the year, the dean of the theology department told him he should become a Reform rabbi and go to HUC-JIR, because all the scholarly footnotes Zeke included in his papers were from books published by that rabbinical school. In fact, the dean had already sent for an application to give to Zeke!

So off we went to Cincinnati in the fall of 1955 for Zeke to study for the rabbinate. I had grown up in Montreal and graduated from McGill with a B.Com. degree in accounting. I was twenty-two years old, quiet and shy – and had no idea about being a rabbi's wife. But I was willing to try, because I loved Zeke. I believe that being at HUC-JIR gave me insight into how hard and long the studies were to become a rabbi, and I quickly came to respect my husband for his knowledge, his caring qualities and his respect for people.

Zeke was ordained in 1959. Our son was born in Cincinnati, and the friends we made with other married rabbinical students is a bond that lasts until today.

One of my vivid memories from the rabbinical school years is going to a course in practical rabbinics at the home of Rabbi Sylvan Schwartzman, who told us never to be close friends with members of the congregation. We all thought that was old-fashioned and that we were different. Well, I found out, by experience, he was correct. I was emotionally wounded by the betrayal of some of my closest friends in the congregation. Being the wife of a rabbi was like living in a fishbowl. It is beautiful to be swimming in the water, except that people on the outside are looking at you and commenting on your tastes and behavior.

Zeke's first pulpit was in Miami, Florida, where he served as the assistant rabbi to Joe Narot. We stayed for a year, during which time we learned that we preferred a smaller congregation. I didn't have anything to do with the congregation beyond going to services. The congregation was huge and didn't need me. I took my turn baking cookies and doing things like that, and I was pregnant with our daughter. But I would have liked to have done more. We left soon after she was born.

◆═◆

The sixties were turbulent times: civil rights and the Vietnam War.

Zeke's next pulpit was at the University of Alabama in Tuscaloosa, where he served as a congregational rabbi, professor and Hillel director. I had never been in the South and was trying to understand what southerners were like. Zeke was on the team negotiating the integration of the university, which was integrated in 1963. He and I were both deeply involved in the civil rights movement, and I was enormously proud of his efforts, especially because he was criticized by members of our congregation for the stands he was taking. I learned from the experience to calm down and stop being hot-headed. As a result, I became a good negotiator. Much has been written about those events, so I will not go into detail here. Suffice it to say, those were difficult, frightening times for us and for our family.

Despite the fact that I was shy, I was a rebel at heart. I worked part-time in an era when most women did not have professional jobs. I discovered that I loved being in the middle of controversy, and that I enjoyed meeting the so-called "power people" in the community.

Almost everyone loved the rabbi, and I was the beneficiary of that. But, from the beginning, in every congregation Zeke served, there was always a group of people who didn't like him because he was active in the broader community – and controversial in the synagogue, as well. He introduced Hebrew into the religious school. It was very hot where we lived, so Zeke wore Bermuda shorts to baseball games. When people objected to that, we stopped going to the games.

Zeke was very much ahead of his time, especially as a rabbi serving a congregation in the south, because he was in favor of performing intermarriages so long as the couple studied with him and agreed to raise any children they might have as Jews. It caused a lot of friction in the congregation. The rightness of what he did was confirmed for me yet again in recent years, because I have heard from a number of those couples who are living Jewish lives and raising their children as Jews.

We moved to another southern community after three years, and Zeke became a congregational rabbi. I was one of the first female CPA's practicing as a public accountant. Clergy wives at that time did not work in our community. The temple board did not like my working, although the backlash was subtle. The important thing for me was that my husband, the rabbi, supported me. He told the temple board that they had no authority over me.

Our life became divided into His, Mine and Ours. Our children were six and three. I was involved in controversial projects such as prayer in the public schools, voter registration for African Americans, and, of course, my work as a CPA. A contentious Catholic priest was a very good friend. He always wore a black suit and collar, but the lining of his suits were wild colors and patterns. I learned from him that it is important to conform on the outside, but it is okay to have your rebellion and controversies on the inside.

Zeke was always busy in the community and at the temple and involved with other members of the clergy. I decided that it was important for me to be involved with Zeke and go with him to as many functions as possible. That meant going out almost every night. We made sure we had wonderful sitters for our children.

I did my share as the rabbi's wife in all three congregations Zeke served: I baked cookies, I participated in every temple function and began the practice of hosting an open house for the congregation on Sukkot. I also taught Hebrew in the religious school and helped prepare the bar and bat mitzvah students. I didn't believe the rabbi's wife should take a leadership position in sisterhood or on other committees, because I didn't want to get involved in the politics and infighting, although because I am a CPA, I agreed to serve as treasurer of the sisterhood. I felt it was much better that congregants assume those roles.

I loved being the wife of a rabbi. In what other profession can you be so involved with your husband's work? You become an important person in the community. You get to meet people of great intellect and character. You learn to entertain visiting lecturers, etc. You get to travel to conventions and rabbis' meetings. And you can do it on the salary of a rabbi. You learn to stand up for what you believe is right and to have an opportunity to help change the community for the better.

Both Zeke and I were very well-respected in the general community. When an Arkansas state senator called Zeke a communist from the Senate floor, the very next day many non-fundamentalist Christian clergy, including bishops, went to the Senate to demand an apology. I couldn't help thinking then about how my parents, trying to protect me, taught me not to trust Christians. I realized that stereotyping people was wrong and that the Jewish teaching of respect and fairness was much more important. Through this incident, I became even stronger in publicly confronting negative comments. I gained a lot of confidence, which also served me well in my profession.

Of course, the fact that we lived in a fishbowl was always lurking in the background – people talking about you and your family. There were constant rumors, but I learned not to be negative. I was proud of what I was doing and proud of my husband. It strikes me funny now, but it wasn't then, when, at a reception for the congregation to meet us, one of the board members told me he didn't think my stockings were appropriate. I was wearing a black suit, a white silk blouse, black high heeled pumps and black patterned hose – all very appropriate and conservative. I politely told him that the stockings were the newest thing in Europe and that he might want to buy some to sell in his many stores. The following week, he sent me a dozen pair of plain hose. I politely thanked him and made no comment. Later, he told me that his stores had had many requests for patterned hose for the holidays, which they weren't able to supply.

Because I was a CPA, I was friends with and often went to lunch with other CPA's and with clients, most of whom were male, as well as with my partner, who was also male and a respected person in the community. I was horrified when rumors started that I was having affairs with some of these men, based on the fact that congregants often saw me eating lunch or going to meetings with them. Once again, I learned to be proud and hold my head up high. Long after the fact, I was told that other CPA's in the congregation viewed me as competition for clients, instead of as a colleague.

Despite the fact that I was the first female public CPA in Arkansas, I was never described in terms of my profession but always as "the rabbi's wife." This was true in every congregation and every community in which we lived. I mention it now because it hadn't occurred to me until recently, when I saw the film *RBG,* that that's how I was consistently defined – and that, as it apparently never occurred to me to question or protest it, perhaps that is how I defined myself as well.

I was also the subject of very hurtful rumors – and it didn't help that none were true. Because I did voter registration, some people claimed that I had an African American boyfriend, because why else would I want to help blacks to vote? My motives were also questioned when I helped start a business through the Environmental Defense Agency to employ poor women of color in sewing dashikis; the company did very well, by the way. The rumors were painful and insulting, but they also made me even prouder of what I was doing, because I knew that what I was doing was the right thing to do.

I believe our children had a hard time being close friends with the children of the congregation, and many of our neighbors did not let their children play with ours. Their friends would repeat what they heard at home about the rabbi and probably didn't realize – or think about the fact that – they were talking about their friend's *father*. To give just one example from years later, when our son was in college, the board of the congregation Zeke was serving at the time objected vocally to the fact that our son wore his hair long.

There was a SAC Air Force base in our town, and Zeke was on the town/base council. When Israeli pilots came to train at the base, the chaplain called and suggested that we meet the visitors and perhaps invite them to dinner, etc. Some even stayed in our home. We became very good friends. Many of the pilots told us they would like to hear black jazz music. Clubs were segregated then, but we talked to our friends, and they arranged for us to go to some African American clubs with the pilots to hear music. These pilots were fighter pilots who had wiped out the enemy air bases in the Six Day War. And the C-130 pilots were the lead pilots in the Entebbe raid to rescue the hostages. New rumor: We were arranging for the pilots to sleep with women of color.

Zeke died in 2005. I now live in Delray Beach, Florida, where I have a full new life.

I could go on and on, but the synopsis is this: Both Zeke and I supported each other through the turmoil. Despite everything I've mentioned above, I loved being married to a rabbi, because I was able to observe and participate in the wonderful relationships he nurtured. I was able to teach our children, by example, about values and tolerance and acceptance and to be proud of who they are. People's lives were changed. These relationships provide me with wonderful memories. My life was changed. Many years later, people still express gratitude.

The "fishbowl theory" is true for all who are in public life. I am delighted to see the changes that have come over the years for rabbinic spouses. Most clergy wives now have careers. It would be interesting to have a dialogue with the rabbinic spouses of generations after mine to discuss how our lives – our roles, expectations and reception – as well as those of our children (and our spouses, too, for that matter), are different from theirs.

Irene Palnick was born in Montreal, Quebec, Canada in 1933. She graduated from McGill University with a Bachelor of Commerce degree in accounting. She and Zeke were married in 1955. Irene has two children, Lazar and Rachelle, and three grandchildren – Oren, Doron and Jacob. Zeke was ordained by HUC-JIR in Cincinnati in 1959. Rabbi Elijah Zeke Palnick z"l died in March 2005.

44

RABBI'S WIFE

NINA PACKMAN

DAVID A. PACKMAN AND I MET AS TEENAGERS IN PHILADELPHIA. We both belonged to Congregation Rodeph Shalom and both of us became extremely active in the youth group and, ultimately, in NFTY. Many of the young friends we met during those years also became rabbis, and we have been lifetime friends.

I always have enjoyed my role as a rabbi's wife despite the fact that it sometimes felt that we experienced both great joy and profound sorrow on almost a daily basis. Perhaps that's why my sleep pattern was permanently disturbed. I frequently worked through the night at home, because I never knew what the next day would bring.

Originally David wanted to pursue a Ph.D. after ordination, but the rabbinical school and Uncle Sam thought otherwise. As a result, David was a chaplain in the Air Force from 1964-1967. We lived in Ramstein, Germany for three years, and our oldest child, Keren, was born there.

We knew that I would have to return to Cincinnati after that, because the terms of the funding for my MSW degree required that I work for two years for the Hamilton County Welfare Department, the agency that underwrote the cost of my schooling.

David also had become eager to obtain an MSW degree. While he was serving as a chaplain, many young servicemen who had either been to Vietnam or would be deployed there came to him with enormous problems and he felt inadequate, ill-equipped in counseling skills because HUC-JIR did not prepare students well in this area. So, David took advantage of our being back in Cincinnati to get his MSW degree, which was a life-defining change in the course of his rabbinate. And I believe that it also positively altered our relationship as a rabbinic couple.

Finally, in June 1969, we moved to Newport News, Virginia, to his first solo congregational pulpit. Our two younger children, Kenan and Jana, were born there, and I remained busy primarily as a mother and, yes, as a rabbi's wife, but mostly as a committed Jew. After the 1967 and 1973 wars in Israel, I became increasingly involved not only in our temple but also in our Jewish federation and in work on behalf of Israel.

In 1976, we moved with our three children to Oklahoma City. I was so busy with child-care and with the Jewish federation's campaign, that I had not accompanied David to his interview in Oklahoma City and was a little shocked when he returned home so enthusiastic about the city and the congregation. We drove out there with three kids and a U-Haul.

With our children all in school, I focused more on my own career. After I had been working for a while with children in foster care, a friend said to me, "Nina, you do great with death and dying. You should be a hospice social worker." And that became the direction in which my journey continued.

My hospice team, which was part of a Catholic hospital system, was incredibly supportive. They got a kick out of it when a patient or family member would ask if I were a nun. I wore little makeup and, with my gray hair, I guess that was a legitimate question. Usually the nurses smiled and simply answered, "No." Many patients knew of my husband, and I believe that was a comfort to them.

Both through my hospice work and as a rebbetzin, I bonded with families in a very special way. David rarely went away without me, thank goodness! And I really only remember two times, years apart, but both occasions were fraught. Naively, I had looked forward to the idea of David's being out of town briefly because I thought my life might be quieter while he was away. Wrong!!

On the first occasion, I received a call that a congregant had died. David was a solo rabbi. The bereaved family was at the hospital, and they asked me to join them there in David's place. Which I did. When I arrived, they were sitting by their dear deceased husband and father, and they did not know what to do. We quietly walked through their initial grief, after which they began to make plans.

The other time David left, another family called. They had decided to take their mother/grandmother off a ventilator, and they wanted David. When I told them that David was on an airplane, they asked if I would come. I was able to talk with David and then I headed to the hospital. My time with this family was incredibly special, as each member of the family expressed their love for a woman who was dying. The ventilator was removed and, peacefully, this lovely lady died. I had the Rabbi's Manual with me, and I hope my presence gave this family some comfort. I did tell David that next time he left town I was going to go with him!

There were also times that he was called back from vacation. I remember at least three occasions when I stayed at a vacation site with the children while he flew back to Oklahoma City. He ultimately managed to get some coverage, which allowed us to begin to travel out of the country.

When David volunteered as a prison chaplain, he decided that the Jewish inmates needed a seder. Freedom from bondage, right? The night before the seder, I dreamed that the prisoners came to the seder dressed in prison garb and they were accompanied by a guard when they arrived. But in reality, they came with a chaplain, and the two men were both wearing polyester suits. In advance of the seder, my daughter asked me if we were going to use our silver. And our son was worried that we were possibly putting our daughter in danger! The prisoners were very grateful, and I sent them back to prison with lots of goodies. And yes, I used our silver. But we never did that again, having convinced David that there were many other needy people, non-prisoners, who needed a seder invitation.

When David retired, we both were delighted with the idea that we would be able to travel extensively – except that he agreed to serve a small congregation in Monroe, Louisiana, an arrangement that lasted for eight years. He went there once a month and, while I stayed home, the congregation at least had the full-time attention of their rabbi.

We were living in Oklahoma City when the Murrah Building was bombed in 1995. Years ago, I wrote about that experience for a Central Conference of Reform Rabbis' publication called *The Spouse Connection*. I was a short distance from the bombing, as our hospice chaplain and I had gone to a prayer breakfast at the Convention Center. I was in my car and was heading back to my hospital when I heard the noise caused by the bombing. Back at the hospital, everyone was on alert to receive patients. Unfortunately, there were few injured, only mortalities. David and I – as well as the whole Jewish community – were involved in helping. The downtown was like a war zone, filled with army tents and rescuers. I remember that it was a very cold day, but, in addition, it clearly was a chilling experience. David stayed at the morgue, as he tried to minister to the staff there. I stayed at the church where families were waiting to hear about their family members. They – and we – knew there were no survivors, but each family wanted some definite information that would help them deal with the reality of death.

People ask: *Isn't this just too depressing?*

Our kids did not want to hear about hospice. And, of course, I never shared personal information. But if family members I was working with chose to be open about my contact, that choice was up to them. I remember our daughter saying to me, "I didn't know you were 'hospicing' with my teacher's mother!" And I said, "I did not know 'hospice' was a verb!"

I regret now that I did not keep a journal so that I could share more experiences. Frequently, the nurses, chaplains and I reminisce about our experience and share special moments.

My social work background and my experience with hospice have given me the opportunity to interact with friends and congregants in a very meaningful way. I don't need to resort to small talk out of discomfort in times of crisis; I am comfortable engaging in intimate conversation at a crucial time in the life of a family.

In 2017, we finally moved to Bethesda, Maryland, where our youngest child lives. From the day we married, we never returned to live in Philadelphia again. As a result, throughout our lives we never had family who lived near us. Our congregants became our family. We always felt the warmth of their care and their love. However, ultimately our children all moved away and settled on the east coast. It made sense for us to move closer to our children. I marvel at the joy I now have in being physically closer to our children and grandchildren.

To summarize, yes, I was a rebbetzin and enjoyed being a rebbetzin, although I know that many rabbis' wives disliked that title. I am sure it helped that I had a career. It was essential to me to define myself in a professional role of my own; yet it is interesting that I chose social work and specifically hospice work, both of which coalesced with my role as a rabbi's wife. While it was very important for me to have my own identity, I viewed my role as my husband's helpmate as a very positive part of my life.

I have had a wonderful life. I started on this journey as a young Jewish teen and now I am the seasoned, contented wife of a retired, emeritus rabbi. All in all, thinking back, I realize that I have been blessed with a very meaningful life, and for that, I am eternally grateful.

My husband, David, was ordained in 1964 in Cincinnati.

45

"SHE NEVER COMES TO SERVICES, AND SHE ALWAYS SITS IN THE BACK"

KAREN SPIEGEL FRANKLIN

THE YEAR WAS 1978. I WAS A 1976 GRADUATE OF WELLESLEY COLLEGE, and was working towards an M.A. in the Department of Religion at Temple University. Simultaneously, I worked at the synagogue in which I had grown up, Reform Congregation Keneseth Israel, in Elkins Park, Pennsylvania, as an assistant to the director of education. My mentor was the congregation's rabbi, Dr. Bertram W. Korn. The associate rabbi of the congregation was Stephen Franklin. I was smitten by him. We were married in 1978. I was twenty-three. He was thirty-seven. Today it would be against CCAR rules to marry your rabbi, but lots of rabbis married their congregants then.

Before I married Stephen, I consulted my Aunt Adrianne Sundheim, the wife of my mother's brother, Frank, to find out just what was in store for me if I were to become a rabbi's wife. She gave me great advice. She said never to believe that the congregation was imposing impossible time demands on a rabbi, and that to some degree, he (at that time, it was almost always a he) had control over his own schedule and priorities.

Altogether, I didn't go into the situation without notice. Stephen proposed to me in front of the open ark at KI, in the darkened, empty sanctuary (it was pretty dramatic – the congregation seated 800), and told me that marrying him was marrying the congregation, and to think about whether I was prepared to take it all on. I said, "Yes. But...."

Eight months after we were married, we moved from suburban Philadelphia to just outside New York City, where Stephen was to become the rabbi of Riverdale Temple, a post he held for almost twenty-five years. While the responsibilities for a rabbi of a congregation of over 600 families were overwhelming, Stephen spent a great deal of time on temple projects of his own choosing – the library and bulletin. And he spent a considerable amount of time on home projects, plumbing and carpentry, leaving endless responsibilities to me. But I did go into the partnership with open eyes.

Within the next five years, we had three sons – Ross, Andrew and Josh. When we first married, the congregational expectations for a rabbi's wife far exceeded those of today, and I gladly acquiesced to every expectation except the ones that would interfere with the raising of our children. While demands of congregations in earlier decades may have taken a toll on the personal lives of rabbis' wives, I suppose I was lucky in living in a transitional time when there was less expected of me. I worked at the temple bazaar, served on the sisterhood board, and participated in various community organizations, but nothing outstanding.

There was, of course, always an eye toward the regularity of my service attendance. I was loath to abandon the boys every Friday evening when they were young, despite strong pressure from Stephen. And when I did attend, I was always prepared to make a quick exit. When Stephen retired, I summoned the courage to inquire from his secretary (that's what they called "administrative assistants" in those days) what people had been saying about me all those years. Her one sentence reply: "They say she never comes to services, and she always sits in the back." I can live with that.

I choose to remember the decades of being a rebbetzin with a few anecdotes. Here goes:

In 1986, I was working part-time at the Hebrew Home for the Aged at Riverdale as Director of its Judaica Museum, a position I held for almost twenty years. As part of my job in those early days, I would represent the Home at lunches sponsored by auxiliary organizations that raised money for the Home. Few organizations like this exist today, with so many women in the work force. I recall a rather wild Knights of Pythias luncheon on Coney Island, where I was introduced to "Chuck a Buck," which was not familiar to me from my childhood in suburban Elkins Park. By the 1980s, many who attended the luncheons, so popular in the 1950s, had only an indirect association with the Home, and likely had not even visited there for many years.

Assuming my responsibilities, I summoned up my rebbetzin skills (still working on them, as they didn't/don't come naturally to me) and decided to greet the guests at each table and thank them for their support of the Home. I was pretty proud of my success until I reached the third table, blurted out my welcome and a lady looked up at me rather quizzically and shot back, "We've been coming here for thirty years. Who the hell are you?" I quietly sat back down, gave my brief remarks at the formal program and called it a day.

In 1988 (or 1989), our middle son, Andrew, was in second or maybe third grade. After religious school class on a Sunday morning, he approached the teacher and announced, "Do you know who I am?" Playing right along she answered, "No, why don't you tell me?" His response surprised us all. "I'm Karen Franklin's son." At the time, I was certain he was proud of my professional activities as a museum director, chair of national and international organizations, and the many boards on which I sat. In retrospect, I realize that it could just as likely have been my role as Cub Scout den mother (do they still call them that?) or as a member of school committees that had engendered his admiration.

The year was 1994. Our sons were ten, twelve and fourteen. Stephen was about to undergo emergency bypass surgery. His situation was critical. As he was being rolled on the gurney into the operating room in the wee hours of the night, his mind was on the temple bulletin, his "proud baby," which was late to go to press because of his condition. He begged me to proofread the text immediately so it could go out on time.

"What?" I shrieked, "you expect me to proofread the bulletin in addition to all the other responsibilities I have at this critical moment? How could you even ask?"

The doctor peeked out from the operating room and said, "Mrs. Franklin, these could be the last words you might want to say to your husband. Are you sure you want to address him this way?"

My response? "Absolutely!"

One never stops being a rebbetzin (and I do hope to remain a rabbi's wife for many years to come). There is no retirement. There may be fewer responsibilities, but people still see me and know me as a rabbi's wife. This isn't the way I define myself or my identity, but I am aware of it. When I make a shiva call or attend a funeral, I am told that my presence is important to the family. For me, this is a responsibility and privilege I do not take lightly. And I try to dress well in public (well, okay, this might be a bit of an excuse for a decent clothing budget).

If I had ever thought that my identity might not be dependent on those who surround me, I've recently come to realize it's a myth. I'm now happily the mother of Rabbi Josh Franklin, of the Jewish Center of the Hamptons. I now have new "rabbi family" responsibilities that again include regular service attendance and, as I've explained to Stephen, an expanded clothing budget.

Our daughter-in-law, Stephanie Whitehorn, has taken a dynamic role in the congregation, a full partner to Josh, and probably more active than I ever was. We are extremely proud of her. Though the expectations for a rabbi's spouse may have changed, it seems to me that Stephanie's genuine enthusiasm and support for Josh and the congregation will be welcomed – even though her active participation may not be "required."

And with a granddaughter in East Hampton, Shabbat on the Beach, and so many other programs at JCOH, I might even become a revitalized grandma-rebbetzin myself. It could happen.

Karen Spiegel Franklin is the wife of Rabbi Stephen D. Franklin, Cincinnati '69. She is Director of Family Research at the Leo Baeck Institute, and jury president and co-founder of the Obermayer German Jewish History Awards. She has served as president of the International Association of Jewish Genealogical Societies and chair of the Council of American Jewish Museums, as well as chair of the Memorial Museums Committee of the International Council of Museums and co-chair of the Board of Governors of JewishGen.org.

46

PART TIME CONGREGATIONAL LIFE

LEE HAAS

MY HUSBAND, RABBI PETER HAAS, WANTED TO PURSUE A CAREER IN academia. With these plans in mind, he decided to take a break between ordination and graduate school. So, after ordination, Peter joined the Army as a chaplain. He spent three years on active duty, the first two at Fort Knox, Kentucky. Most of the Jews at Fort Knox were doctors and dentists who had been exempted from the draft during Vietnam so that they could go to medical school. Now they had to put in their three years of military service. There were a few others in various different professions and some recruits who were going through basic training there. As I recall, only one doctor, an oral surgeon, was making the military his career.

The Jewish community ranged from the unaffiliated to the Orthodox. One of the Orthodox families was active in the congregation and wanted everything to be halakhically correct and done according to tradition. This wore the patience of most of the rest of the congregation, who were from more liberal backgrounds.

While we were at Fort Knox, I became pregnant with our first child. There was a shortage of obstetricians, so only women with high risk pregnancies saw an obstetrician for monthly appointments. Everyone else (I, included) saw midwives. Most weeks, I saw a male midwife. But the Army policy was that if it was your first baby, a doctor should do the delivery. So, the baby was delivered by an obstetrician. In fact, I knew the doctor from the Jewish community; I had been to his house that afternoon for a sisterhood meeting.

Compared to civilian hospitals, the hospital at Fort Knox was rather spartan. Patients made their own beds and the sheets weren't changed unless the patient was there more than five days. Rooming-in was a new concept at the time, so if a patient wanted to have the baby in her room, the baby was with the mother all day and all night. My first baby was two weeks late, and I am small, so I was rather sore. Consequently, rooming-in was difficult.

For our last year in the military, my husband was ordered to Korea. To our dismay, it was an unaccompanied tour. We didn't want to be separated when we had a young baby, so I went to Korea on a tourist visa and Peter got permission to live off post. That enabled the three of us to live together in a furnished apartment. But I couldn't use the commissary because officially, I wasn't there. And Peter couldn't buy baby food, of course, because "officially" he didn't need it. We didn't have a car in Korea, so Peter would go to the commissary to buy items like milk, peanut butter, and coffee and come home in a cab with the groceries. I shopped at the local Korean open-air market for fresh fruits and veggies. I had a baby stroller with a basket in the back.

After our year in Korea, Peter began working on his Ph.D. at Brown University in Providence, Rhode Island. He was hoping to get into a reserve Army unit, but there were no chaplain slots open. One day, I was shopping with the baby at a nearby deli. Suddenly a car pulled up, and an Army general got out. (It is very unusual even to see a general just walking around on an active duty post, so it was exciting to see one in the civilian world). I smiled at him and said, "You're a general!" He said, "I know." I mentioned that my husband and I had recently returned from Korea and that my husband was hoping to get into the Reserves. The general asked what my husband did in the

Army, and I told him he was a chaplain. Then he asked what religious denomination, so I told him Jewish. The general asked for Peter's name, gave me his business card and said that Peter should call him. Peter called the next day and learned that this man was the adjutant general for the Rhode Island National Guard, and he was Jewish. In fact, his brother once was the president of the Jewish Federation in Providence. So that was how Peter became a chaplain in an artillery brigade of the Rhode Island National Guard. It brought in extra money to supplement our G.I. Bill income.

Although Peter has been in academia for most of his rabbinic career, for many years he had small part time congregations in towns near our home. When he was in graduate school at Brown, he led occasional Friday night services and High Holy Day services at a small Reform congregation in New Bedford, Massachusetts. Sometimes Peter would go alone on Friday nights, but sometimes I would hire a babysitter and go with him. For High Holy Days, our daughter Michelle and I both went with him.

The first year, at the long Yom Kippur morning service, Michelle was very restless. The temple did not have babysitting or even a room for kids, only a sanctuary that they shared with a church. I struggled to keep her quiet but was not winning the battle. In the middle of the service, a man I knew from the congregation came over to me and said, "Have you ever seen the Whaling Museum?" When I told him, "No," we left the service together, got into his car, and drove about six blocks to the museum. I spent Yom Kippur looking at whale skeletons and the equipment that was used to hunt them from past and present days of whaling and fishing in New Bedford.

If you don't go with your husband for the High Holy Days, you are on your own for whatever happens. A few years after leaving Providence, we were living in Nashville, Tennessee in the early 1980s. Peter was teaching at Vanderbilt University, but had a part time congregation in Florence, Alabama, over 100 miles away. I was not working but was taking care of our two young children. (Our son had been born while we were still in Providence.) For some reason, we decided that Peter would go by himself for Rosh Hashanah, and all of us would go down for Yom Kippur.

I had a babysitter for erev Rosh Hashanah so that I could go to services at the Reform temple in Nashville. While I was getting ready, the kids were running around in the basement. I remember saying, "Stop running! Someone could fall and get hurt." But the kids were having too much fun. Until my prediction came true. My daughter fell and knocked out her two front teeth (permanent ones, of course).

Our Jewish dentist lived about three blocks away, and fortunately he was still home when I called. He said to meet him at his office. There was a babysitter coming anyway, so she stayed with our three-year-old son. I spent erev Rosh Hashanah at the dentist's office while he bonded Michelle's teeth. I think I had to wait until Peter came home the next day to tell him what happened since cell phones didn't come into use until many years later.

Although my husband was primarily devoted to academic life, the military and the part time congregations gave an added dimension to our lives. We met new people and learned a lot about Army life and small city congregations. I didn't enjoy the Army at the time, but now I'm glad that we had the experience.

Lee Haas was born in 1948 and grew up in Pittsburgh, Pennsylvania. She attended the University of Michigan where she earned a B.A. in anthropology. Lee and Peter met at Michigan. After graduation, she returned to Pittsburgh and earned a master's in library science at the University of Pittsburgh, while Peter spent his first year of HUC-JIR in Israel (his was the first class to do so). When Peter returned from Israel, they married and moved to Cincinnati.

There, Lee worked in the University of Cincinnati library while Peter attended rabbinical school. He was ordained in 1974. The years in

Cincinnati were followed by Peter's three years in the Army as a chaplain, and then several years of graduate school. After Peter earned his Ph.D., Lee and Peter spent nineteen years in Nashville, Tennessee. Lee supervised four synagogue libraries and the JCC library for many of those years, while Peter taught in the religious studies department of Vanderbilt University. In 2000, Lee and Peter moved to Shaker Heights, Ohio. They have lived in Shaker Heights for nineteen years. For eleven of those years, Lee worked part time in the Temple Emanu El library. Peter taught in the religious studies department at Case Western Reserve University. Lee and Peter have two daughters and a son, all now adults. Lee is now retired and does volunteer work for the Shaker Heights Public Library and the Western Reserve Historical Society. Peter is also retired and does a lot of adult education teaching as well as other volunteer work. Rabbi Peter Haas was ordained by HUC-JIR in Cincinnati in 1974.

47

MARRYING RELIGION AND POLITICS

JOYCE FOSTER

IN 1965, WHEN WE WERE MARRIED, STEVE AND I CONSIDERED ourselves partners. Perhaps not exactly equal partners, as I think I was the junior partner (in my eyes, as well as his). You must know that I loved being a rebbetzin. Meeting new people was always pleasant. By joining many of the usual Jewish organizations in the city, I was able to meet women mostly my age. We had a young married group at temple, and one didn't have to be a member of temple to join. Without realizing it, many of the new people I was meeting ended up joining the congregation. It was a bonus, as it really hadn't been my intent to be the sole recruiting arm of the temple. I should have worked on commission, as the numbers were quite substantial.

Many of us have encountered the same experiences: the good, the bad and the ugly. In 2015, the year of our fiftieth wedding anniversary, Steve and I wrote our memoir (with the great assistance of a professional writer).

My life took on a very different direction, which added new facets to our partnership. I was promoted to equal partner, which was a bit difficult for Steve to grasp. After working for Jewish Family Service for sixteen years, I was elected the first Jewish woman to sit on the

Denver City Council and, ultimately, to become its president. Because of term limits in Colorado, I had to retire after ten years. I became a political consultant and joined the Board of JFS (Jewish Family Service), where I became its president, as well.

I had encouraged Steve to think about retiring since he had served Temple Emanuel in Denver for forty years (his only pulpit, except for student pulpits). He sent a letter to the board advising them that he would retire in two years. We wouldn't move, as all of our children and grandchildren live within walking distance of our home (don't hate me for that). He would hope to become rabbi emeritus.

Then the real test of our marriage occurred. I was recruited to run for the Colorado State Senate. I promised Steve it would be for only one term, which consisted of four years, and that I wouldn't seek reelection. He would have two years left as senior rabbi so that would only mean two years of his complaining about my working.

He did get over it...

So now we have a book which documents our life. It's entitled *The Rabbi and Senator Sleep Together: Marrying Religion and Politics*. We were accepted by the Jewish Book Council to tour with the book, which has proved to be an extraordinary experience.

Joyce Foster was a member of the Colorado State Senate from 2008-2013. The first Jewish woman elected to the Denver City Council, she served from 1993-2003 and was Council president from 2001-2002. From 1977-1993, Joyce was Director of Employment Services for Jewish Family Service. Rabbi Steven Foster was ordained by HUC-JIR in Cincinnati in 1970.

48

A SPECIAL RELATIONSHIP: RETIRED CONSERVATIVE AND REFORM RABBINIC COUPLES IN THE GREATER CHICAGO AREA

ROBERTA H. SCHWARTZ

CIRCA 1994, THE LATE AVIVA AND DAVID POLISH AND LILLIAN AND Lawrence Charney discussed the possibility of establishing camaraderie for retired Conservative and Reform rabbis and spouses. But where to begin?

My late husband, Frederick Schwartz, was known for his graciousness and generosity, among other virtues. In response to the request for a central meeting place, he eagerly agreed and gave the group use of his large office. We met every Shabbat morning for services, with Torah reading and *div'rei torah*, followed by a luncheon which the members took turns bringing. This format existed for some years.

The next stage brought us to members' homes. Originally, dinner was included, but with the aging of the group, we moved from evenings to afternoons with snack. Each session had an assigned speaker. We took turns for those assignments, which covered a wide range of topics, and for home hospitality.

As expected, over the years we have not only made changes in format but have experienced the sad loss of colleagues/friends. Those with illness and those who have experienced the death of partners have received comfort and compassion from this group with whom, of course, we have shared many happy times, as well.

We have tried to encourage younger rabbinic couples, recently retired, to join our hevrah. Sadly, it hasn't worked. In most cases, the next generation has a different agenda. As for us, though we grow smaller in number, the group's spirit is impressive. Our future looks good.

I hope other rabbinic couples will choose to emulate our wonderful, shared experience.

Rabbi Fred Schwartz z"l was ordained in Cincinnati in 1955.

49

MY LIFE AS A RABBI'S WIFE

ELAINE ASA

IN ORDER TO SHARE MY EXPERIENCES AS A RABBI'S WIFE, I NEED TO provide some background as to how I came to be a rabbi's wife.

It was the summer of 1959, and I was seventeen years old. I had just finished high school in Los Angeles and was given the opportunity to go to a Jewish summer camp in southern California for a month. Brandeis Camp Institute (later, Brandeis-Bardin Institute) changed my life. It was where I met my future husband, Haim Asa, and where my life as a committed Jew began. After a month of living Jewishly twenty-four hours a day and discovering my Jewish identity, I began a new journey that would shape the rest of my life.

Haim's background was very different from my American Jewish, Ashkenazi, secular one. He was born in Bulgaria in 1931, of Sephardic ancestry, and survived the Holocaust because of many different factors, the main one being that the Bulgarian Orthodox Church, the king, and the government – despite being allied to Nazi Germany – said "NO" to sending their Jews to a certain death. Haim and his father and mother legally left Bulgaria for Palestine in 1944 in the middle of World War II. He had to make the transition from a wealthy child in Bulgaria to an immigrant during very difficult years in Israel.

He came to the United States, in 1954, to continue his studies in agricultural economics, and then, for an MBA, which he did not complete. As do many Israelis who come to the States, he taught Hebrew in local synagogues and was on staff at Camp Ramah for five summers. He always credited the rabbis of the Conservative movement for mentoring him and helping him to reconnect to his Jewish identity as well as maintaining his Israeli identity.

During the 1957-58 school year, he was offered a scholarship to the University of Arizona by the Jewish community there. The community was having problems with Arab students, who were spreading anti-Israel and antisemitic propaganda on campus, and they wanted an Israeli student to speak up for the Israeli and Jewish side. It was during this year that he began to reevaluate his priorities and, upon graduation and his return to southern California, to think about going into the rabbinate which, for a non-Orthodox Israeli of that period, was something very foreign. He interviewed at both JTS and HUC-JIR and, for many different reasons, including the input of Rabbi Alfred Gottschalk *z"l*, who was the dean of the California campus of HUC-JIR at the time, decided to continue his rabbinical studies at HUC-JIR, first in California and then in Cincinnati.

It was when Haim was serving as a student rabbi in his first pulpit in southern California, in 1959-60, that he and I began to date each Friday night. That was when I began to understand Jewish synagogue life, since my parents didn't belong to a congregation when I was growing up. I became known in the synagogue as "the girl who came along for the ride and became the bride." I began my Jewish rabbinical life at the very young age of seventeen, and I am thankful for that year of dating and learning at the same time.

Haim and I were married in June of 1960, and off we went to HUC- JIR in Cincinnati for the last three years of Haim's studies. He had a series of student pulpits, but I really didn't participate most of the time. I continued my education at the University of Cincinnati until our first daughter, Aviva, was born in 1962. Haim received *s'mikhah* (rabbinic ordination) in June 1963, in Cincinnati.

Haim was a recipient of a YES scholarship from the National Federation of Temple Sisterhoods (NFTS) during his years in rabbinical school. This obligated him to serve the cause of Reform Judaism for three years somewhere outside the United States. We chose South America, because Ladino was Haim's first language. Haim became the Director of the World Union for Progressive Judaism in South America, headquartered in Buenos Aires. It was a big title with very little support from the World Union. When we arrived in Buenos Aires, he began speaking his form of Spanish, and I took a private tutor to learn proper Argentine Spanish.

The World Union initially sent us to a congregation that was officially affiliated with the Reform movement, but in essence was really a German-speaking congregation of Jews who had been lucky enough to get out of Germany before the Shoah. Their rabbi was Hungarian and Orthodox, which came as a bit of a shock to us, because we certainly hadn't expected an Orthodox rabbi to be leading a Reform congregation. What we realized very quickly was that the congregation wanted the new rabbi to serve as their youth leader. Haim felt that his mandate from the World Union was to direct the Reform movement in South America, which he could not fulfill by working within the confines of this congregation. He decided he needed to create something new and separate, for which he had to get the blessing of the World Union.

Under duress, but with the strong support of Jane Evans, who was then the Executive Director of NFTS, the World Union agreed to give Haim one year to create this new entity – or else! And so, literally within a year, *we* – and I mean *we* – established Congregación Emanuel de Buenos Aires, which began in our own backyard in the Buenos Aires suburbs.

As soon as Haim found a piece of property to rent for Emanuel, off we went to build a community with the support of many forward-looking Argentine Jews who wanted new leadership and a new kind of Judaism that would be native to Argentina, not imported from Europe. We began working with the young people. We established a school to teach them about Judaism, in which I was one of the teachers. We opened a summer camp where Haim trained future youth leaders, and I became their Jewish role model for involvement in creating community. And we started a youth group, which would ultimately have a great impact on the next generation of Argentinian Jews.

I was an equal partner with Haim in creating this new community. I hosted people at our home. I helped translate Haim's sermons from Ladino into proper Spanish. I was actively involved with the youth programming through my presence at their activities and by counseling them when they needed a sympathetic ear. And, by working with the youth and getting them involved, Haim and I brought their parents along – and they became the founders of Congregación Emanuel.

It was a lonely endeavor for both of us without colleagues who could have shared our concerns and eased our isolation. When I look back on that time – 1963 to 1966, when I was only twenty-two to twenty-five years old – I realize what a challenge we took on: a new country, a new language, a new Jewish community that was different from the American Jewish community we knew.

And besides all of this, we now had a second child, Ariel, and I had to learn how to raise a baby without prepared baby food or disposable diapers. I was young, so I adapted easily to all of these new experiences, which ultimately prepared me for my life as a rabbi's wife in the United States, with all of the multitasking necessary to balance everything.

After creating a new community from scratch, we needed to determine if we were going to remain in Argentina beyond our three-year commitment to the World Union. In the end, we decided that it was time to return home to the United States now that I was pregnant with our third child, Liora. I am eternally grateful for our years in Buenos Aires and for the lasting friendships we made, and to know that we are part of the ongoing history of the Argentine Jewish community.

We were fortunate that upon our return to California, Haim was hired as the rabbi of Temple Beth Tikvah in Fullerton, where we helped build a Jewish community from sixty families when we arrived in 1966, to close to 400 families when Haim became rabbi emeritus in 1996. Coming back to Jewish life in America was a piece of cake compared to the challenges that we faced in Argentina. The most obvious was that Temple Beth Tikvah was already an organized synagogue with a president and board members. We didn't have to create it; we just needed to nourish it, which we did.

In the beginning, in order to meet the members, we invited a different group of five couples every Friday night to our home after services to get to know them better. As the congregation grew, and we had more b'nei mitzvah, it was my idea to host every family prior to their child's bar/bat mitzvah for a Shabbat dinner, which I did for many years. I also hosted a brunch for the students who returned from college during the holiday vacation. Our home was always open.

I did these things, not because they were expected of me, but rather because I felt that was how to build a Jewish community. I never felt I had a role imposed upon me; it would not have worked if I had. My choice was my own, and whatever I did was because of my own commitment to Judaism. When our children became b'nei mitzvah, we always included the entire congregation. I never took a leadership position either in the synagogue or in the sisterhood. I saw myself in a supportive role. If they needed me for something, I was always there to help.

There came a point in our lives when I made the decision not to go to b'nei mitzvah receptions because I hated to leave my children for the entire day on Shabbat. I needed to choose between the BAR and the MITZVAH so I chose the Shabbat morning service over the reception, and it worked: no one complained or seemed to be insulted, so long as I didn't go to *any* family's reception.

Haim eventually joined me in this practice, but it wasn't an easy decision for him to make because he felt it was important to be with families for their *simchas*. He wrote a letter to the congregation explaining why he was not going to continue to go to receptions, and someone told me that one of the professors at HUC-JIR used that letter in teaching the class in practical rabbinics. I hope it helped some other rabbis make those important choices for their own families.

During those thirty years and beyond, I always felt blessed that I had the opportunity to raise our children (our fourth child, Eliana, was born in Fullerton) as part of a Jewish community that gave them the foundation for living Jewish lives. At this point, our children are married. Two of the four live in Israel; three of the four are Orthodox. I have fourteen grandchildren – and now, great grandchildren as well. It's a bit overwhelming for me at times, but I do manage to keep up with all of them.

Haim died in May of 2014. I am proud to carry on his legacy, continuing to help create a caring Jewish community for *ahm Yisrael*.

There certainly were challenges but, in looking back at the big picture, I don't think I would change any of it. I am thankful that I am able to continue to be part of the Jewish story that has played such a meaningful role in my Jewish life's journey.

As an addendum to my story, I want to say that the present rabbi of Temple Beth Tikvah is an Argentine, Israeli-trained Reform rabbi who is a product of the Reform movement, both in Buenos Aires and in Israel. The Argentine synagogue in which he grew up merged a number of years ago with Congregación Emanuel, and so, indeed, my Jewish worlds have come together once again.

I still live in Fullerton and participate in the congregation as a regular member. My interests revolve around my family and traveling to see them in Israel, in Atlanta and in Los Angeles. I keep busy with connecting with friends and community. I especially try to visit homebound members who can't get out anymore. Since Haim died, I have become a member of the local YMCA and try to go to the gym daily, which keeps me in shape.

50

WE'RE A FAMILY: IN IT FOR THE LONG HAUL OR, SOMETIMES WE DISAGREE, BUT ALWAYS ARE CONNECTED

BETH WALDORF

MY HUSBAND, FRANK, IS THE RABBI EMERITUS OF TEMPLE SINAI IN Brookline, Massachusetts, having served the congregation for thirty years. We are very happy in this community and it feels like an extension of our family.

However, the thirty-year journey has had bends and twists and a "palace coup."

After we were there for seven years, one bright, sunny, early July morning the president of the congregation informed Frank that his contract would not be renewed. So, in slightly less than a year, we would no longer be part of Temple Sinai.

We were shocked and surprised, especially since we had just entertained board members at our home only a few days prior to the president's telling Frank of the board's decision.

Our emotional responses ranged from shock to anger, and –for me – mostly shame.

What had we done? But my sense of shame lasted only a short while. In its place came the realization that we had done nothing wrong, that we were still the same people, and that, while we were in this community, we should continue to be ourselves. This meant greeting people, as always, interacting with everyone, as we generally would do, dissenters included, and not letting the impending termination define us. We took the position that there are disagreements within families and the family members continue on, sometimes changing positions, sometimes agreeing to disagree. We had to live as part of the community for however long we were in Brookline.

At first, we shared our feelings only with family members. However, the termination was revealed about two weeks later, when we were canoeing with friends, and they told us how delighted they were that Frank would be the rabbi steering their daughter through her bat mitzvah. We felt we had no choice but to tell them what had happened. The whole story of Frank's dismissal was out, and with it we learned that the buildup to the board meeting had been carried out by a small group meeting privately, with no input from the larger congregation.

At that point, the secret attempt by some members of the board to oust Frank became public, and – after a thorough public evaluation of Frank and his rabbinate – there was a new congregational meeting at which seventy-four percent of the congregation voted to keep Frank. What I remember saying during those hectic weeks was that Temple Sinai was like a family, with its conflicting pulls and tensions.

Much to my surprise, many years later, one of the very people who was part of the secret meetings and decision to ask Frank to leave told us how beloved Frank was and how much Frank had helped him and encouraged his growth and his taking on greater roles within the Jewish community. Then he added: "Temple Sinai is family. Sometimes we disagree, but the warmth and caring keep us together."

I was born in Evanston, Illinois to Bea and Elliott Ruttenberg. My brother, Frank, was born seven years later. During school years, we moved several times: to Stoneham, Massachusetts and then to Cincinnati, Ohio and from there to Northport, New York. I attended the University of Cincinnati where, at the UC Hillel fall open house, I met an attractive rabbinical student, Frank Waldorf. Over the months, we fell in love and were married in June 1961. Frank was ordained by HUC-JIR in Cincinnati three years later. Within six years, we had three children: Josh, Ellen and Deb. Frank and I also moved many times: from Cincinnati, to Frankfurt, West Germany, and from there to Boston, Massachusetts, then to Baltimore, Maryland and back to Brookline, Massachusetts, where we finally stayed at Temple Sinai for thirty years and turned Frank from rabbi to rabbi emeritus. Anne Berman joined up with our son Josh. They have two children, Sam and Lily. Wyatt Gotbetter married Deborah; they also have two children, Sarah and Mimi. Ellen is a single mom; her daughter is Lucy. My pursuit of a doctorate in early childhood education marked an important shift in my life. I found new loves: child development, and emerging literacy. My dissertation on the pre-alphabetic strategies young children use as they come to understand the written English code allowed me to continue to teach professionals and parents about the concepts young children have of what a word is, the way speech is mapped to print, and the shift from young children's use of a personal to a conventional writing style. These workshops continue to the present. Although retired, we are not retired. Frank and I were Executive Vice Presidents of NAORRR for four years, Frank teaches at Temple Sinai, and I continue on the Caring Committee there. We live in Newton, Massachusetts.

51

YOU'RE WELCOME

JANET ENGELHART GUTTERMAN

AS I SAT THROUGH THE ENDLESS INTERVIEWS FOR THE FEDERATION Executive Director's position nearly eighteen years ago, there was one recurring question: "Do you have any personal questions?"

I had traveled from Pittsburgh to Providence over two hot days, prepared with professional answers. But regarding personal questions? Not really.

Umm...yes, I had one: "Is there a social life for a single woman (in this seemingly multi-generational, family-oriented community)?"

Umm... "Yes. I can think of two, no three, single professional women you would like."

Ummm...A small voice inside wondered, *"Is this the community for me?"*

What I didn't know then, but found out later, is that most people sitting on those interview panels were thinking, "Have we got a match for you!" Especially when I described myself as having been a Reform Jew from early childhood on, with parents who co-founded our temple on Long Island in the 1950s.

Shockingly to me, the phone call came a month later, offering me the position. What? Put my money where my mouth is? But just a month later, with my household goods packed, I set out by car to my new home.

I traveled with my bichon frise pup across Pennsylvania to my daughter, in Philadelphia. Then up the New Jersey Turnpike to my sister in New York City. Then, really scared for the first time, I convinced my sister to drive up Route 95 with me to Providence, Rhode Island.

The voices in my head were now pounding......*What am I doing? I know no one there. How do I ever head an organization for the first time? Will there really be only two or three potential friends in the new town?*

"Well, at least I'm not going for a job with IBM," I remember thinking. "Jews. My community. They'll welcome me."

I was unaware of the welcome I was about to get.

My second week in town, the Federation president took me to the Jewish Family Service annual meeting. Installing the incoming Family Service president was a rabbi, a funny rabbi, who not only remembered his installee's bar mitzvah Torah portion but also part of his long-ago bar mitzvah speech. *This is a rabbi?* He certainly had my attention! We met briefly afterwards, and, as Les is wont to do with any new professional in town, he asked me out for coffee.

It was a Tuesday afternoon. We went to the best pastry bakery in town. Apple turnovers with coffee. And we talked. Or,I talked and talked and talked. He bought me an Italian bread. "Here. You can always use this." I returned to the Federation office aglow. His bright blue eyes. His lightheartedness. His interest in me. His uncensored comments. I was already smitten.

Coffee and dinners followed. *A rabbi? Who would ever imagine I would date a rabbi?* But he was funny and interesting and seemingly loved by everyone in this small state. Yes, I was falling in love.

It was an awkward time. Les had lost his beloved Julie just eighteen months before. He was devoted to his two daughters, who were still grieving their mother's untimely death. He was a very public man. And I was a public woman. I had come to succeed at a politically challenging job, and I was dating one of the rabbis? We went to out-of-the-way places and stayed very quiet.

But in a community of 17,000, staying quiet is not so easy. I remember a drive we took around our neighborhood one afternoon, when we ran into a very well-connected congregant who was out taking a walk. "Hi," Les said. "I'm just showing our new Federation director our neighborhood." She smiled broadly.

Or the Jewish education lecture that we both wanted to hear one evening. Even though we parked about a block away. Les at first wouldn't get out of the car. "What will people think?" he asked. I answered, "I think it's time for them to think or not think. But we can go." Oh, around that time, they indeed started thinking!

After only a few months, it was obvious that we were getting serious. We began to talk of marriage. Marrying a rabbi as a Jewish professional? Becoming a *rebbetzin*? I'd grown up in the Reform movement and was also a feminist. How was I going to deal with being a rabbi's wife? And deal with the leadership expectations of my own constituency? It would be a tough balance.

But I was smitten, and it was obvious where we were heading. The only hurdle was having our daughters accept the idea of their mom/dad remarrying. Les is a cautious man. He served one congregation for forty-five years and lived in one house for almost that long. We were continually together, yet it was nearly four years before we married.

◆═◆

What has it been like these fourteen years? I still remember the overwhelming outpouring of joy and affection from both of our communities. We were married on the weekend of *Shabbat Shira*, with songs and flowers and lightness. And nearly 1,000 well-wishers at our oneg Shabbat. We never had to worry about the community's reaction. They were thrilled that their beloved rabbi had found a second love. And I guess I was acceptable – right age, right religion, interested in every person in my new life. I know that I had an easier time being married for the last eleven years of Les's rabbinate. He was not building a career; he was capping it. I was used to being a public person, so the interrupted dinners and endless phone calls, while not always welcome, certainly felt familiar. The hardest part for me was the large number of calls from people dealing with illness and death. For someone not used to the rabbinic world, it sometimes felt overwhelming. As if the entire world was ill, because so many people in ours were.

My life with our quite well-blended family and my new community has been enriched beyond imagination. The love and well wishes that I get to this day in the supermarket or the cleaners or the bakery are heart-warming. Seeing Les still honored and being called upon fills my heart. Clearly, after nearly eighteen years, I'm still smitten!

Janet Engelhart Gutterman, a retired Jewish Federation Executive, lives in Providence, Rhode Island with her husband, Rabbi Leslie Yale Gutterman, ordained in Cincinnati in 1970. She is the proud mom and stepmom of Allison, Rebecca and Elizabeth, and joyful grandma of Daniel, Jonah and Benjamin. Besides time with her family and continuing involvement with the community, Janet is particularly dedicated to arts education for inner city children and serves as a docent at the Rhode Island School of Design Museum of Art.

52

RICH MAN, POOR MAN, BEGGAR MAN... RABBI????

LINDA STARR

I WAS TWENTY-NINE YEARS OLD WHEN ARTHUR COMPLETED HIS ARMY service and we moved from El Paso, Texas to Manchester, New Hampshire. It was a lovely congregation, with members from infants to people 100 years old. We brought our two young daughters with us, and three years later, had our third daughter. I taught mid-week religious school classes, which I loved. Like most of the other wives in Arthur's class, I had no training for the "job" of rebbetzin. When I told our friends what my husband did for a living, I explained that, unlike the childhood game in which you pointed to the buttons on your shirt and asked, "Who will I marry? Doctor, lawyer, Indian chief, rich man, poor man, beggar man, thief?", rabbi was not one of the choices. I married a wonderful man. All I remembered from when I was growing up was that my rebbetzin wore a black hat to temple, slipped into a seat on the side aisle at the last minute and didn't stay for very long at the oneg Shabbat. Unlike her, I sat in the middle of the congregation with our children. I baked for the oneg Shabbat, attended all sisterhood meetings and board meetings, and, later on, I expanded and ran the Judaica shop and taught religious school for twenty years.

THE YOUTH SHALL SEE VISIONS

I was nine-months pregnant when Arthur went to Manchester, New Hampshire to interview, so I did not go with him and, therefore, did not know what to expect. I knew it was an established congregation and that the previous rabbi had been there for seventeen years. There was a button on the bimah to open and close the ark electrically. I teased Arthur that the button was the reason he chose the congregation.

We rented a congregant's home for six weeks, while we looked to purchase our own. One afternoon during our first week, we got a phone call that went like this (in one breath): "Hi. I belong to the other temple, and I want to come over and meet a rabbi who is younger than I am." Thirty minutes later, she showed up with some of the baked goods for which she was known, and we became friends.

In the early days in Manchester, I wore gloves to services every week. After a number of years, I stopped wearing them. That first Friday without gloves, a member said, loud enough for everyone to hear, "Look, the rebbetzin isn't wearing gloves!" I felt as if I was dressed in the emperor's new clothes.

Every year on Sukkot, we hosted an open house for the entire congregation with wine, hors d'oeuvres and dessert. For economic reasons, I made everything, but hired a caterer/waitress to serve and clean up. One year I overheard a congregant say to the caterer, "You made wonderful things for this party." The caterer answered, "Thank you," without ever giving me credit. That was the last time I used her services.

After about five years in Manchester, happily serving the congregation, Arthur came home from a board meeting, while I was taking a relaxing bath. He came into the bathroom and sat down across from the tub, facing me and said, "I have something to tell you." A well-respected lawyer had been appointed personnel chair and told Arthur that it was time for him to move on to "bigger and better things," that he had so much potential and was not being fired or let go; it was for his best interests. Twenty-five years later, at Arthur's retirement from the Manchester congregation, that lawyer and Arthur were still friends.

Over the years, the congregation doubled in size. Arthur was highly respected in the interfaith community, had his own television show and was quoted as the spokesperson for the Jewish community in New Hampshire.

I was sitting next to a visiting family during services one Friday, when their five-year old son turned to his mother, pointed to Arthur, and asked, "Does God have any children?" The mother replied, "That's the rabbi, not God." Just then, the service continued with Arthur reading from the prayer book, "I am the Lord your God, who brought you out of the land of Egypt..." The child said, "See, mommy, I told you he was God."

Our kids had funny experiences, too. At our oldest daughter's bat mitzvah, to which the entire congregation had been invited, she remarked, "It looks like Rosh Hashanah, and I know if I do a good job, people will think it's because I'm the rabbi's daughter, and if I mess up, it will make the rabbi look bad. I can't win."

THE OLD SHALL DREAM DREAMS

Retirement didn't last long. Since our children were all married and living at a distance from us, we considered accepting the pulpit in St. Thomas, in the United States Virgin Islands. When Arthur asked me what I thought, I said, "You brought me to cold, snowy New Hampshire and we loved it, so why not warm, sunny St. Thomas!?!" Sitting on the beach after the interview, we saw that our cell phones worked, and we could connect with our children. We called them and asked what they thought about our moving here, and they all replied, "We're getting tickets now for a visit!" Since I had been selling fine jewelry in New Hampshire, I was assured there was a job for me and, in this tax-free haven, there were several offers.

We bought a condo overlooking the Caribbean, which I loved, and on day five, I started working. It was my contact both with the tourists and with the locals. Arthur fit right in, greeting the thousands of visitors to our synagogue and sharing with them its incredible history, and working with the interfaith community and the local Rotary Club.

There were some challenges, though. While we had always had Shabbat dinner at home as a family in New Hampshire, many people in St. Thomas went out to dinner after services. We went home, disappointing people that we wouldn't join them, although we often included some of them at our Shabbat dinner table. Shopping and preparing the dinner was a challenge, too, since it took trips to several different stores to get everything I needed, and I always went to services first. After a few months, we began to change our pattern, and the congregation appreciated our sometimes joining them for dinner. Change isn't always bad, but it was an adjustment for us.

Living on an island provided unique opportunities. *Tashlikh* (the symbolic "cleansing of sins" by casting bread crumbs on flowing water) on Rosh Hashanah was always well-attended, bringing almost everyone to the service. We held it at Magens Bay, one of the ten most beautiful beaches in the world, according to *National Geographic* magazine. We held an annual Shabbat morning service on the beach on St. John and an annual flotilla of boats joined together in the bay.

In our second year, I was asked to chair a silent auction, a new component of the annual fundraiser, which was an art-and-antiques auction. I agreed and chaired the event, raising $7,000 the first year and increasing every year to $20,000, five years later, when we retired. I also coordinated bar/bat mitzvah and wedding arrangements since St. Thomas was a destination place for both. It was very appreciated because it was personal for the guests and I was able to guide the families to save money at the same time as we made some money for the synagogue. During our last two years in St. Thomas, we started Make a Wish of the Virgin Islands and granted eight wishes to children with life-threatening illnesses. This was a very rewarding experience for us and has had lasting impact on the community.

After Arthur was ordained in Cincinnati in 1969, we moved to Fort Bliss, Texas, where Arthur was one of thirty-three chaplains. From 1971 to 2002, we lived in Manchester, New Hampshire. After Arthur was named rabbi emeritus we moved to St Thomas, United States Virgin Islands, for ten years. Arthur was rabbi at the historic synagogue there for six years. We now reside in West Palm Beach, Florida, from which we travel for several months each year as Arthur serves as the on-board, cruise-ship rabbi. We spend our summers in the Berkshires of Massachusetts. Our three daughters are married and have given us six wonderful grandchildren.

53

DON'T CALL ME REBBETZIN!

BARBARA ROSENFELD

I MET HARVEY WHEN WE WERE BOTH IN HIGH SCHOOL. IT TOOK HIM several years to decide to become a rabbi; he also had considered careers as a lawyer or history teacher. Opposition to the Vietnam War along with a love of Judaism influenced his decision. In 1974, Harvey was a newly ordained rabbi and I was his wife.

Rebbetzin was not a term I found particularly endearing. My image of a rebbetzin was that of an older, small woman dressed in mostly dark clothing including a long skirt with black dowdy shoes and a hat or *sheitl* covering her head. I certainly did not dress like that, nor did I want to! I had my own identity and I did not want to be an appendage of my husband, similar to the "Frau Doktor" who gained her stature from her husband's profession. The "rebbetzin" honorific was not one I had earned, nor did I want it.

I think that most of the wives of the rabbis in Harvey's class were of a similar opinion when it came to taking on the title *rebbetzin*. We were college educated. We were willing to participate in synagogue life to the extent we would be comfortable, but we didn't think this meant taking on an office, such as the sisterhood presidency, merely because we were married to the congregational rabbi. We did not want to be taken for granted. (Does anyone?) We wanted to be appreciated for our own talents. Hence, our dislike of the term.

Each of my parents had been fortunate to escape Nazi Germany in 1939. Neither of them had had a college education, but it was an expectation that both of their daughters would. We were reminded of this often. My mother's mantra was, "They can never take away your education." My mother grew up in a comfortable home in Germany and was not wanting for anything, but she came to the U.S. with only a little money, clothing, and some household goods. She was not permitted to take anything else. She was not fluent in English when she arrived, but she managed to find work and learn the language. What I found amazing, therefore, was that my parents didn't want me to work after marriage. Their expectation was that my husband would take care of me. That was common thinking at the time, when ideas of the feminist movement were still fairly new. Yes, they wanted me to have an education, a career, but it was supposed to be for back up in case of an emergency. I disagreed. After all, I had worked hard to become a teacher and I was ready and willing to try it out. I went to college to earn my B.A., and I was determined to use it to help children learn.

I taught while Harvey was in rabbinical school, making me the main provider during that period. Many of us rabbinical spouses had worked while our husbands were in rabbinical school. We were used to being paid professionals. I believe the feeling was that our husbands (at that time there was only one ordained female rabbi) were the paid professionals serving the congregation; we spouses should not be mandated to participate as substitute religious leaders at the caprice of the congregation.

I was fortunate in that I never was asked to play a role in which I was uncomfortable. There were no expectations of me as a rabbinic spouse in any of the four congregations in which Harvey served. It was clear that he was the paid professional. If I volunteered, it was because I wanted to take part. To that end, I gladly chaired community Passover seders and organized a community play group for our youngest children. I taught in the Sunday School. I helped out with congregational meals and contributed to potlucks whenever asked. I worked at rummage sales, bazaars, gift wrapping, and other fundraisers. I continue to volunteer. I believe the importance of congregational members getting together for a common purpose should be heavily underscored. Not only do these communal events often help the congregation financially, but they also enhance the bonding of members that leads to lasting friendships.

To this day, I prefer not to be called rebbetzin. I didn't earn it. Congregants occasionally introduce me using this term, giving me a knowing wink as they do so. They are aware of my preference, but use it anyway, just to tease or, perhaps, to be annoying. However, I am better at brushing off this perceived insult now because I know that many people consider the term to be one of endearment.

If I must have a title, I prefer "professor," one that I earned. Just don't call me late for dinner.

Barbara Rosenfeld was awarded a Ph.D. in Curriculum and Instruction by the University of Missouri in Columbia, where she also earned a Specialist degree in education. She received her B.A. from the University of Bridgeport and her M.Ed. from William Paterson University. Harvey was ordained in the class of 1974 at HUC-JIR in New York and served Temple Beth El in Hollywood, Florida; Congregation B'nai Abraham in Hagerstown, Maryland; Congregation Beth Shalom in Columbia, Missouri, and Congregation Beth Am in Teaneck, New Jersey. The Rosenfelds have two children, Daniel and Michael, and three grandchildren, Shalva, Oriel and Amalya.

54

CONGREGATIONS WE SERVED DURING OUR RABBINIC LIFE

FRANCES DOBIN

A NOTE FROM THE EDITOR:

WHILE LIVING AT THE REUTLINGER COMMUNITY FOR JEWISH LIVING in Danville, California, the late Frances Dobin wrote about her years as a rabbi's wife. The essays appeared in the Reutlinger newsletter. The Dobins moved to RCJL in 2007, following his decline in health, and lived there together until his death in 2012. She wrote these stories in the years that followed. Frances Dobin died in 2017. We are grateful to her daughter Deborah for sharing them with us. What follows are excerpts from those essays.

- *Naomi Patz*

ROCHESTER, NEW YORK 1954-57

IN FEBRUARY 1954, WE TRAVELLED TO ROCHESTER, NEW YORK WITH our infant son, Louis, for our first permanent rabbinic pulpit. Rabbi Harry Orlinsky, one of his professors at HUC-JIR, came to install Rabbi Joel as the assistant rabbi to Rabbi Philip Bernstein at Temple

B'rith Kodesh.

At our first High Holiday services in 1954, Rabbi Joel and Rabbi Bernstein met together to discuss the services, which were held at the Eastman School of Music. Erich Leinsdorf, then Director of the Rochester Symphony Orchestra, was a member of the temple, and he conducted the music for the service with the choir singing.

At that time, the temple blew a trumpet instead of a shofar for the High Holy Days, as did many other Reform temples. Rabbi Joel did not like this and requested that he be allowed to blow the shofar. Rabbi Bernstein agreed, but insisted that Joel stand behind a curtain on the balcony so he wouldn't be seen. The congregation responded with awe to the sound of the shofar, and it was used ever since.

After Rabbi Joel took over his duties, Rabbi Bernstein left for six months to be head of the Jewish chaplaincy, under the direct supervision of General Dwight Eisenhower. While Rabbi Bernstein was gone, Rabbi Joel officiated at every service. One member of that year's confirmation class was George Astrachan, who later became a rabbi. Upon Rabbi Joel's death in 2012, Rabbi Astrachan sent me a letter stating that his decision to become a rabbi was largely based on Rabbi Joel's role model and teachings.

I was always held to a high standard as the rabbi's wife. One day, a temple member who was our neighbor called Rabbi Bernstein to complain that she had seen me from her window hanging laundry in my backyard – wearing shorts, which she thought was inappropriate for me to wear. We were always under scrutiny as the rabbi and his wife.

Our life was very full, and in 1955, our daughter, Sarah, was born. That was a very exciting year; we met Abba Eban, then Prime Minister of Israel, and we also met Israel's Commander of the Navy.

The congregation invited Rabbi Joel to become associate rabbi when his contract was up, but he turned down the offer. He felt he had a mission to support the civil rights movement, and accepted a pulpit in Alexandria, Louisiana. The Rochester congregation asked him to reconsider and told him that he wouldn't be able to make a significant difference in the South, but he wanted to go and try. As it turned out, it was very difficult to make progress in that part of the country; the warnings of the Rochester congregation had been correct.

ALEXANDRIA, LOUISIANA 1957

We moved to Alexandria, Louisiana, in May 1957. We settled into our new home, which we had had built, just in time to get ready for the High Holy Days. The change was traumatic; we were not used to living in the southern culture. We were asked to join a country club and declined; congregants were critical of this and wondered aloud if my husband would know which utensils to use for dinners at the club. There wasn't much socializing among the congregants, and families kept to themselves.

We were able to get a housekeeper, Louella, to help with the two little ones, which worked out pretty well, although congregants began to complain because they thought that her weekly salary of twelve dollars for five-and-a-half days of work was too much to pay a person of color. When we left town, Louella said that, if she didn't have to stay to see her son through college, she would have come with us.

In the fall of 1957, President Eisenhower sent troops into Little Rock to integrate the public schools. At Rosh Hashanah services that fall, Rabbi Joel spoke about how the president was following the laws of the land by integrating the schools – and the entire congregation stood up and walked out of the service. I was the only person left in the temple with my husband! After that, we received phone calls from temple members saying that their rabbi could only speak out in favor of segregation, and that we'd better leave town. They said that we were in trouble and people would "get to us." It was a painful, frightening time for our family.

And a financial burden as well. We had needed a $3,000 down payment to build the house, which we got from my in-laws. When we started getting threatening phone calls, we decided to leave quickly and essentially fled between Rosh Hashanah and Yom Kippur. The Jewish Post newspaper said that the rabbi had left because he was "too Jewish." Among other aggravations, we never got our $3,000 back. Years later, when we visited Alexandria and the current rabbi apologized to us and asked for a picture of Joel for their "wall of rabbis," Joel told him he'd send the picture when the temple returned the $3,000. End of story.

We went back to Trenton to live with my widowed mother while Joel thought about whether he wanted to stay in the rabbinate. While we lived in Trenton, Joel worked in his father's Children's Supermart, which sold children's furniture, clothing, and toys.

BUTLER, PENNSYLVANIA 1957-1959

In November 1957, Joel received a call from Butler, Pennsylvania, asking to speak to the man who was too Jewish for the congregation in Louisiana. He asked if Joel would be interested in coming for an interview. My husband asked if the congregation was a member of the UAHC, and the man hesitated. Joel met with them, then we both went to meet with them. It turned out that they weren't members of the UAHC, but they promised they'd join. Rabbi Joel decided to give the rabbinate another try, and he took the job. We stayed in Butler until it became apparent that they were not going to join the Union; they hemmed and hawed for more than two years. Our daughter, Deborah, was born in January 1959, while we were there. That summer, we told them we were very sorry, but if they weren't going to become a Reform congregation, we wouldn't be able to stay.

NIAGARA FALLS, NY 1959-1962

We got to Niagara Falls in time for the High Holy Days in 1959. We had a good life there. Our daughter, Rachel, was born in August 1962, and we completed our family of six. Niagara Falls was beautiful; we would visit the famous waterfall and the floral clock, where the numbers were made of flowers. We went to Louis' Restaurant downtown, which was kosher.

Unfortunately, the economics of life in Niagara Falls had gone downhill, and the temple couldn't afford to pay Joel's salary, so we had to move again. We took a pulpit in Malden, Massachusetts, a suburb of Boston.

MALDEN, MASSACHUSETTS 1963-1964

In Malden, things went very well, and we became well situated in the community. In the summer of 1964, after we'd been in Malden less than two years, there was a conflict in the congregation. Two congregant families, whose children were getting married, asked Rabbi Joel to perform the wedding on Tisha B'Av; they had set the date with the previous rabbi. Joel explained that Jewish weddings weren't performed on Tisha B'Av, and told them they'd have to change the date. One of the families, which was quite wealthy, picked a new date that conflicted with an already-scheduled wedding. There was a disagreement over who would get the date of their choice, and the temple board and president wanted the wealthier family to get their way. Joel objected, and as a result, his contract wasn't renewed.

BAY SHORE, 1964-1981

In 1964, Rabbi Joel accepted the pulpit at Sinai Reform Temple in Bay Shore, on the south shore of Long Island. Joel and I entertained the whole congregation on the first day of Rosh Hashanah. We held an open house and were helped by many of our new friends. I did all the baking, and our friends contributed melon, apples and honey, and challah. It was a really festive time.

Rabbi Joel became active in the community very quickly. He started a group for the local clergy of all denominations, and they learned together. Every Shabbat, we had guests for dinner, either members of the congregation or visiting guest speakers. Joel started a program for the young teenagers where they created their own Shabbat services. He took the first class to see the musical *Hair* in New York City, which created a stir among some of the parents. Many of these teens went on to NFTY, through LIFTY – the Long Island Federation of Temple Youth. LIFTY had a choir, which would travel around and sing at services in the area. Our son, Louis, sang in the LIFTY choir and later became very active in NFTY as well.

One weekend, a group of LIFTY teens came to Bay Shore and brought all their instruments and songs to sing at temple. By Sunday, there was a snowstorm, and we ended up with twenty-three teens staying overnight at our house. We had a big five-bedroom house, and we had kids everywhere – upstairs, downstairs, under the dining room table, on the recliners, everywhere. Joel and I were supposed to go to the Amish country for the weekend, but we couldn't go because of the weather. I cooked for everyone, including six kids who were staying with our neighbors. I had ordered a side of beef before the weekend, and I ended up feeding everyone all weekend. After that weekend, we received a gift from all the kids who stayed over – a night away in the Amish country. Three or four years ago, at a LIFTY reunion, those fifty-somethings talked fondly about their weekend at the Dobin's.

When we first moved to Bay Shore, I didn't have a job, but when the women's movement came around, I went to work for the local Head Start program as a part-time employee. When the program closed, I worked for the Bay Shore public schools, in the curriculum office. Later, I worked in the library in the high school from which all our children graduated.

We stayed in Bay Shore until 1981, when the temple decided not to give Rabbi Joel tenure. They were concerned that, if Joel died, they would have to take care of me – and they didn't want to take on that responsibility. Although Joel left in the summer of 1981, I stayed in Bay Shore until late in the fall, so that I could get in my ten years with the public schools and qualify for a pension and health insurance. With our children out of the house, we started the next part of our lives in Florida.

PORT ST. LUCIE, AMARILLO, AND LIVERMORE 1981-1995

Rabbi Joel moved to Port St. Lucie, Florida, and took a pulpit in nearby Fort Pierce in early 1981 and I joined him there several months later. After I was in Fort Pierce for a while, I saw an advertisement for a job in the public library in town, and I was hired as the night supervisor on the basis of my experience in Bay Shore. I worked from 4:00 to 9:00 p.m. and closed the library for the night. We bought a nice house in Port St. Lucie, after having lived in the temple's house in Bay Shore for so many years.

Rabbi Joel was given a six-year contract. Within the first two years, he found out that his secretary (who had been there for many years) was going through all his mail and reporting its contents to the president and board of the congregation.

The board member who had helped finance the temple had been in partnership with the contractor who built the temple. One Sunday morning, the president came to Rabbi Joel and asked if Joel would let a group use the temple on Sunday mornings for services. A young friend of the contractor, who had been in Israel, wanted to have a meeting there. It turned out that the young man was from Jews for Jesus, and they wanted not only to hold their services in the building but also work toward converting members of the temple. Rabbi Joel told them that they couldn't use the temple for this purpose. Because of that, he was asked to resign his position. We hired a lawyer, but the temple leadership put pressure on him, and he dropped our case. Some members of the temple split off from the main group and held weekly services in a building in Port St. Lucie. Rabbi Joel conducted services for them *pro bono*.

After a while, money became a problem. Rabbi Joel's difficult experiences in his last few congregations made him look at another possible line of work. He took the exam to become a stockbroker and passed, and we relocated to Fort Lauderdale.

Joel was a stockbroker for three years. Although he made more money as a stockbroker, he wasn't happy – he didn't like giving financial advice that he didn't entirely believe in, and his heart wasn't in it. I suggested that he consider going back to the rabbinate, and he contacted the UAHC Placement Committee. With two of our children living in Texas, we chose to take a pulpit in Amarillo. After a couple of years there, Joel was almost ready to retire, and we moved to northern California, where our daughter was living, and took a half-time pulpit in Livermore.

RETIREMENT

I never in my life thought I would experience such wonderful times as when Rabbi Joel and I first retired and he took over the position of cruise director for NAORRR for the Norwegian Cruise Lines. Rabbi Erwin Herman and his wife, Agnes, had held the position previously. Norwegian Cruise Lines had a relationship with NAORRR to place retired or about-to-retire rabbis on cruises during key Jewish holidays: Rosh Hashanah, Yom Kippur, Passover, and Hanukkah. In those years, at least, the rabbi was invited to travel for free and conduct Shabbat and holiday services on the cruise. The rabbis gave lectures and explained Reform Judaism to the people of all religions who came to these shipboard events. We also acted as escorts on excursions and daytrips off the ship. Joel's job was to give out the cruise assignments – and it was a good job. Of course, for doing the job, we got to pick our cruises first! Over the years, we went to Hawaii more than once, Europe (including Italy and France), Vancouver and Alaska, Russia, China, Japan, Turkey and Australia. Rabbi Joel had a colleague who did the same job for Cunard Cruise Lines, which was repositioning a ship from the Pacific to the Atlantic during a fifty-eight-day cruise. The cruise went to the South Pacific, and lots of other places. Joel's colleague needed a rabbi for the voyage, and we volunteered. It was our longest cruise.

It was a great period of my life, an opportunity for my husband and me to have interesting and fun experiences all over the world. I remember it fondly.

Rabbi Joel Dobin was ordained at the New York School of HUC-JIR in 1954.

55

DREAMS, DISAPPOINTMENTS AND FULFILLMENT

PAULA BLUMBERG

AT FOURTEEN, I WAS WELL ON MY WAY TO BECOMING A "BUM" – hanging out on street corners in Queens with a slicked-back DA and a cigarette hanging out of my mouth – when my parents threatened me with a choice between attending boarding school or going to the youth group at the new temple they had just joined. Needless to say, I chose the temple. My life was about to change, as I walked down the stairs to the youth room. That night, I met a wonderful group of young people who were to become the first building block of my NFTY family. An only child with two parents who worked and played long hours, I didn't know quite how lonely I had been. The embrace of this new world allowed me to exhale and ultimately be empowered as an evolving person and as a young leader.

NFTY became my family and Priscilla Marks my adult anchor for the next years. Priscilla, who later married Rabbi Leonard Poller, was the regional director of the Greater New York Federation of Temple Youth. (GNFTY). She was a beautiful, warm young woman from Boston, with an extraordinary ability to draw teens in and inspire them to become committed to social justice and social action, as well as to one another. I wanted nothing more than to *be* Priscilla Marks!

I rode Sam Cook's NFTY train! (Rabbi Samuel Cook was the creative genius who directed NFTY.)

I took part in TYG activities, became LIFTY regional president, a NFTY national board member and participated in GNFTY conclaves at a private boys' camp in Honesdale, Pennsylvania. You had to have experienced those gatherings, which included a GNFTY Pilgrimage to HUC-JIR in Cincinnati, and work to realize the dream of "A Camp of Our Own," to understand their power for us. Four short years later, we had that camp. I was privileged to go with my friends, the leaders of the Greater New York Federation, to form the first staff of the Joseph Eisner Camp Institute for Living Judaism in Great Barrington, Massachusetts. Many decades later, I became a member of the board of the camp, whose motto is "A Summer to Last a Lifetime." Today, our family counts three generations of camp involvement.

Priscilla remained my role model. But I had no real Jewish background and wanted the educational skills to enable me to do the kind of group work Priscilla did so well. I shared my interest with Rebecca Lister, mother of my Eisner friend, Sheila Lister Bamberger. At the time, Rebecca was teaching in HUC-JIR's School of Education. She picked up the phone to call the dean of the New York school and told him, "You have to see this girl!"

To my surprise, he not only agreed to see me, but made me an offer. I entered HUC-JIR as the first undergraduate in a newly created Bachelor of Jewish Studies program. I would take sixty-four academic credits elsewhere (I already had a jump on that) and sixty-four credits in the rabbinical school, since, at that time, there were no undergraduate courses. Hoping this would be the beginning of a counterpart to the JTS-Columbia program, the school issued me a full scholarship and made it possible for me to complete my academic classes at Columbia. I loved those classes and I loved competing with fifth-year rabbinic students and sometimes besting them. My mentor was a young Rabbi Eugene Borowitz.

Herman and I first met when I was a high school student on a "pilgrimage" to HUC-JIR in Cincinnati. He was a first-year rabbinic student in charge of the "pilgrims" who had come from New York. Those visits were a recruitment vehicle for the College-Institute, and it surely worked on me. We met again two years later at Eisner Camp and started dating the summer he began his chaplaincy training. We were married the following March 1962, two days after the completion of my last classes. Herman was ordained that May.

I think the dean of the New York school had hoped I would become the first woman rabbi. He was so angry with me for getting married and choosing to follow Herman to his chaplaincy post in El Paso, Texas that he punished me by insisting I could not graduate without taking a comprehensive exam, a non-existent requirement. I was lucky enough to succeed in spite of him, but his vindictive behavior gave me problems for fully fifteen years.

In Texas, Herman was a rabbi. I had much of the same training, but no credentials at all. We argued over theology and the like, but that was a little loaded and soon stopped.

In El Paso, I sought employment as a social worker. There was none to be had so I applied for a provisional teaching certificate in the Ysletta public school system. I was accepted, despite my utter lack of training. I was handed an armful of books and told to read ahead of the kids.

Despite my disappointment that there was no job available in social services, it was a good year in the classroom. Half of the kids were Army children whose fathers left in the night to respond to the Cuban missile crisis; the others were dirt-poor Mexican children who didn't always have enough to eat. We did good work that year, including holding regular barbecues at our home to add food to their bellies and some fun to their lives.

And then came a make-or-break Christmas issue. A tree was delivered to the door of my classroom. I refused to put it up. Or lead

Christmas carols or be involved in preparing a Christmas pageant. A staunch believer in the separation of church and state, I took the issue up the chain of command to the superintendent of schools. A meeting of my students' parents was called. All I asked was that they try taking Christmas out of school for one year, while celebrating fully at home and at church. The vote went in my favor. I was able to complete the year, teach my kids an important lesson and acknowledge the bravery of those families who had never before thought about this issue. I was twenty-two.

After the Army, I felt too young to settle down as the wife of a congregational rabbi. I remember attending a wives' meeting at a CCAR convention where a panel of senior women was teaching us younger wives how to pay hospital and *shiva* calls with our husbands as well as what our role in sisterhood should be. One young woman raised her hand and said, "The president of the sisterhood called to ask me to do something and I told her I was diapering the baby and couldn't talk because my hands were full of shit." The place erupted in applause and rebellion. The panelists could not regain control and ultimately walked out. I was neither ready to fit into their mold nor to fight the fight for a new model.

I talked my husband into applying for the Peace Corps. I was young and idealistic, and, at the time, it truly spoke to me. We received an assignment to work in Africa but didn't take it. Instead, we hopped on a freighter with one suitcase between us, spent three and a half months touring Europe and then sailed to the port of Haifa.

During those months in Israel, I made an attempt to follow the next part of my plan. I sent for applications to schools of social work and secured the promise of a scholarship from the Jewish Welfare Board. But, if I didn't hurry, I would be past twenty-five before starting a family and, in those days, two more years of graduate school and two years after that working to fulfill my obligation to the JWB, felt unacceptable. My career would have to wait.

Two months before my twenty-fifth birthday, I gave birth to a beautiful baby girl in Providence, Rhode Island, where Herman had accepted an assistantship in a 1200-family congregation, Temple Beth El. And now I was the rabbi's wife.

A word about my background: I grew up in an antiseptic Reform family where bacon was the staple for breakfast, shrimp cocktail was a weekly delicacy, a carefully decorated "Hanukah bush" graced our house and, every year, an Easter basket with chocolate bunnies appeared in the living room. Seders, where the table was beautifully set, started with my father saying, "Now let's open the book; now we close the book. Let's eat." My richest Jewish memory was of watching my maternal great grandmother, Tziporah, light the Shabbos candles she had brought with her as a young woman from Stockholm, Sweden, and smelling the delicious chicken soup bubbling on her stove. My youth group and HUC-JIR experience deepened my love for, and knowledge of, Judaism, but had not, at this point, had an impact on my personal practice.

When we moved to Providence, the senior rabbi, William Braude, a renowned scholar of midrash, indicated his bottom line for our dietary practice: biblical kashrut, at least in public. Herman had no problem with this. I was aghast and challenged this formidable man, face to face. How hypocritical to adhere to something that had no meaning to me, just because someone else decreed it! Rabbi Braude took me for a long walk. He gently introduced me to the concept of *na'aseh v'nishma* and cleverly got this twenty-four-year old upstart to agree to try it, without making me feel as if I had lost my pride. I have never again eaten those things.

I loved Providence, made some lifelong friends and had three children in the six years that we were there. The wife of the senior rabbi, Pen Braude, was clearly not of the "old school." Little was expected of her by the congregation, and even less of me. Of course, some of the older women were anxious for me not to forget my hat or my gloves, when coming to the temple. It was a small price to pay until one evening in the lobby of the synagogue, when Herman, bursting with joy, publicly announced the news that we were expecting a third child. A woman came marching across the lobby with her finger pointed at me and said in a very loud voice, "I will allow you this one, and then I am going to teach you something about birth control!"

While in Providence, I became active in the nascent natural childbirth movement. Traditionally, women were routinely drugged, and neither they nor their husbands were allowed to be part of the birthing process. That had to change. We threatened the doctors that we would go elsewhere, and Herman and I drove sixty miles to Concord, Massachusetts weekly for a prepared childbirth class. I was determined to be drug-free and to participate in this delivery. The doctor acquiesced, set up a mirror and I was present as my miracle baby, with a shock of dark hair, emerged. We stayed home for most of the second labor, so we could be together. By the time of my third pregnancy, things had progressed so that the hospital allowed us to stay in a private room together until the baby was about to be born. I was also active in supporting women who chose to nurse their babies, something not done yet by most of our mothers, nor by most of our peers. Support was critical. Change comes slowly, but we worked at it and eventually changes occurred. We had made a difference.

During those years, child rearing was my primary focus, although I did find time to work with Herman to create one of the first curricula for teaching about the Holocaust to tenth graders in Reform religious schools, and I taught it to the Confirmation class. I developed and presented to these bright and eager young people a course in personal ethics. The work was personally fulfilling. I also studied painting, returning to an earlier interest. The six years that we were in Providence were truly happy ones for me.

A small congregation opened up in Wellesley, Massachusetts, and now it was time to leave. Herman beat out the significant competition and was invited to Temple Beth Elohim. He was thrilled. It was hard for me to leave the community and the work and friends that had become important to me.

We spent a number of months looking for a house in Wellesley, a wealthy, suburban Boston community. The town was slowly allowing Jews to move into some sections of the community. One or two tracts in the more modest section (one of them across from a subsidized housing complex) were open to Jews; other, more upscale neighborhoods allowed no more than one family to a street. I wasn't sure I wanted to live in that kind of town. Besides, housing was expensive, more than we could afford.

Three businessmen from the temple offered to help us purchase a house. We soon found a lovely Dutch colonial, not too far from the synagogue. The men toured the property and said, "Go for it." We signed a purchase-and-sale agreement and put our own money down. Happy to be looking forward, I had stationery printed with my new Wellesley address.

Then the call came. The board had decided that they didn't want to be in the real estate business, after all. The offer of financial assistance was withdrawn. We were unusually lucky to get our money back. With the window before we were to leave Providence closing quickly, Herman and I chose one of the three houses we were shown in Newton, just next to Wellesley, and a little closer to our budget. Certainly, it was a confusing and unsettling beginning!

The rough start became even more painful when we gathered for the closing. It was one day before we were to leave for Israel on a trip the Providence congregation had given us as a parting gift. Our belongings were packed on a moving truck. The bank officer entered the room where all parties were gathered and informed us that the title to the house was not clear and, as far as the bank was concerned, there was "no deal." We all cried. The owners were flying to California to meet their furniture, our van was to arrive that day and we were to leave the following day for Israel. Our lawyer promised to find a new bank that would give us a mortgage before we got back from our trip. The owners let us move into the house we did not own. The lawyer was true to his word, but the interest rate had gone up. It took a year to clear the title.

This community was very different from anything that I, from Queens, had ever known. Upscale, houses with "function rooms," lots of tennis, golf and French maids worthy of extended chatter. It was not the kind of congregation or community I was used to, and I was uncomfortable.

Herman was a spunky young rabbi who threw himself into the work of transforming this quiet congregation into a "cutting-edge beacon" of a new type of synagogue. He worked extraordinarily long hours. I missed him; our children missed him. The pace he set for himself was ultimately unmanageable and, after a few short years, he began to burn out. When an opportunity arose to become the headmaster of the Solomon Schechter Day School in Newton, where we had chosen to send our children, he took it. For him, it was an exciting move. He envisioned a school with families coming together in *hevruta* to celebrate and live a Jewish life. When he joined Schechter, I stepped down from my short presidency of the school's parent association.

In those Wellesley/Newton years, I was immersed in life with my children, whom I adored. I did find a couple of hours a week to take painting classes at the DeCordova Museum in Lincoln. It was totally fulfilling! And the only time in the week that I wasn't preoccupied with the children. Soon, they would all be in school and it was time to begin to think of myself. Social work! I had a transcript that showed the completion of the proper number of college credits for graduation, with excellence, but no degree. Three schools of social work refused to talk to me. James McCrackin, dean of admissions at Simmons School of Social Work, said on the phone that the school accepted only applicants who were college graduates, but agreed to see me. He ultimately brought my case to the Admissions Committee, which, surprisingly, admitted me to an innovative, part-time program open only to "eight women with children." I loved my four years at Simmons, had wonderful placements and gathered an extraordinary foundation of knowledge from fine and committed professors. Herman was most flexible and helpful with the children, all of whom managed well, since one of us was always home.

As those years at school were coming to an end, Mr. McCrackin called me into his office. My transcript at Simmons was impeccable and he thought it was time my undergraduate school, which for a variety of reasons had denied me my degree, finally granted it. He had prepared a letter to that effect that he promptly handed to me. I will always be grateful to him. I called the New York school. The dean would not discuss the matter on the phone and insisted that I go to New York and meet with him in person, bringing the letter with me. His final stipulation: "You must come to graduation ceremonies and walk in the processional." So, two weeks after I received my MSW in clinical social work I finally received my bachelor's in Jewish studies from HUC-JIR. Mission completed. I was then lucky enough to be hired by Jewish Family and Children's Service, a premier social service agency that served a diverse Boston Jewish community. Couldn't be better!

The next years were good for me. Herman was on a twelve-year hiatus from congregational work, so the only expectations for me were to be the best mother I could be to our three children, and to grow in skill and passion for my work as a clinician. The agency office to which I was assigned, located in a lower middle-class Jewish community, was exactly where I wanted to be. Many families, some struggling financially, others with every manner of life-problem, filled the waiting room. Many had grown up in the same milieu and knew each other. As a clinical social worker, I was expected to take the next case that came through the door, be it a whole family, a couple, an individual, adolescent or child, and be excellent at it. To its credit, the agency supported this philosophy by providing years of intense post-graduate training and fine supervision. During those years, the local rabbi received a Federation grant to place a social worker in the synagogue to be available for "advice, evaluation and referral." I did that one day a week for several years. The program was an overwhelming success, clearly a model that other synagogues could follow.

At Jewish Family and Children's Service, I served as the president of the staff association. In this capacity, I met with the agency director monthly and negotiated three contracts. It was great fun partnering with our labor lawyer, and I learned a lot.

I stayed with JF&CS for thirteen years, committed to the community and its people, many of whom were seen on a significant sliding scale. After some years and with a new administration, the agency changed. The office was moved off the bus line to sleek new space clothed in gray and mauve. Clinicians were told to raise the minimum sliding scale and to close those cases that could no longer afford the new fee structure. This was incredibly sad for me. I could have stayed there, poorly paid, for the rest of my working life. In 1990, I left to start my own private practice dedicated to all, regardless of their capacity to pay the modest fee. In the years that followed, I found great satisfaction in my clinical work. It has been a privilege to share people's lives at moments of crisis by facilitating healing, strength and resolution. It was also important to me that I could participate fully to enhance the economic security of our family.

My work has been private, not like the public job of a rabbi, but no less important. Quietly, it has made a significant difference in the lives of many, person by person.

When Herman reached his fiftieth birthday, he returned to the active rabbinate to serve Shir Tikva, a small, young congregation in Metro West Boston. We did not have to move. He is a brilliant, dynamic, creative, dedicated, hard-working rabbi, and that sleepy place could hardly believe what hit it. Within a very few years, it grew exponentially and was the darling of the synagogue community. I loved that we were there and finally felt at home Jewishly. Unlike my earlier experiences as "the rabbi's wife," I now knew who I was, I had a most satisfying career and allowed myself to become part of the community and to cherish the connections.

Our daughter, Naomi, who is married to a Conservative rabbi, reflected on my relationship with Shir Tikva as, "participating, being present, making other people feel welcome, making others feel that you are interested in hearing their stories. Walking the fine line of being friendly with congregants, while still protecting the privacy of your own family." No doubt she saw this as a model for herself as a rabbi's wife.

In 2001, Herman was granted a sabbatical. I walked away from my practice for six months, not knowing if there would be anything to return to. My choice for us – Herman went along with my decision – was to spend the first month in South Carolina at Sea Island Habitat for Humanity, working on the building of three houses. Eight hours a day for me, six days a week. Exhausting, exhilarating, and a fulfilling taste of what the Peace Corps might have been like. The work was inspiring, and, when we continued the sabbatical in the Berkshires for Herman to focus on developing his skill as a storyteller, I chose to work with Habitat of Pittsfield one day each week.

Luckily for me, it didn't take long after my return to Boston for my clinical practice to become robust once again.

During those sabbatical months, I also immersed myself in learning to sew, and a new craft, quilting. It became the creative medium for me to explore my love of color and form. In the last fifteen years, I have become proficient in turning fabric into art. My portfolio now numbers over forty quilts that have become a legacy for my children and six grandchildren.

We were at Shir Tikva for nineteen years, a long enough time to become fully woven into the fabric of the synagogue and to be in relationship with its people. I considered this an extraordinary gift. Together, Herman and I took tenth graders, by ourselves, to experience Jewish New York, hosted graduating seniors at our home, visited college students at their universities and invited everyone to Sukkah parties. I attended services regularly, not only to be supportive, but because, at that point in my life, I found them deeply fulfilling. Behind the scenes, Herman used me as a sounding board for sensitive community and personal issues, and shared his important sermons, which often ended in useful rewrites.

Finally, at age seventy, Herman retired from congregational life. Herman took an "interim position" that lasted a few years, and, after that, we shopped around for a satisfying synagogue experience. We settled on a "Shabbat Alive" service at the large Conservative synagogue in our town. I liked the rabbi and enjoyed the music, but it wasn't home. Ten years later, we once again began attending worship services and social events at Shir Tikva and were welcomed with open arms. It felt good to be home.

Being a rabbi's wife comes with sacrifices that I think none of us could have understood when we were young. You are always sharing your partner with an unending line of others. There are often anticipated and unanticipated obligations that keep the rabbi from family, vacations that get interrupted, and telephone calls that take precedence. Herman learned to understand the impact on our relationship and on our family. We worked hard to communicate about these matters. In large part, I believe these issues were responsible for Herman's twelve-year hiatus from congregational life. That time allowed me to grow as a woman and to be ready to partner with him with comfort and understanding. In those years, we always had our "date night" and arranged our evening schedules in tandem. The ongoing process worked for both of us. We continue to refine the sharing of feelings and needs in order to be the best partners we can be for one another. How lucky are we!

At this writing Herman (HUC-JIR, Cincinnati, 1961) and I have been married for fifty-six years. We have three married children and six grandchildren, all living near us in the Greater Boston area. I have worked as a clinical social worker since 1977. I love my work and feel privileged to be allowed into the intimacy of people's lives. I continue to find great joy as a quilter.

56

A MAINE STORY

ESTHER SALTZMAN

THE YEAR WAS 1967. OUR FAMILY HAD JUST COMPLETED TWO WEEKS at a Christian-sponsored summer camp in Bangor, Maine. Our kids, Debra, Josh and Oren, aged ten, eight and six, respectively, bunked with their camp contemporaries. I was the camp manager's assistant to the assistant. Before leaving home, I had made reservations through the local Chamber of Commerce for a cabin near the Maine beach. As we excitedly pulled up to a small group of weathered cabins, Murray went to the reservation clerk to check in.

The clerk looked at us and the children and blurted out, "Sorry, there must be a mistake. We are completely booked."

I had made the arrangements myself in May and was not going to be denied. Tired and frustrated from driving, Murray whispered, "Let's get out of here. There are lots of other places, I am sure."

Not me! I was not going anywhere. Hadn't we spent two weeks hearing and talking "brotherhood and good will" in an interfaith program?

I insisted that we go to the local Chamber and get that cabin which we had rented.

When we got to the Chamber and recounted our experience, the manager was embarrassed. She called the clerk at the cabin and asked if there were any cabins available. The response on the other end was that they had several vacancies left. "That's funny," the manager continued. "A family was looking for a rental and was just told that everything was taken."

There was a moment of silence and then the clerk replied, "Well, look at this, I just found a cancellation."

The manager hung up the phone and was very apologetic. "Let me check something." She came back moments later and said, "How does a beautiful house right on the beach, with lots of special amenities, like a salt-water pool and sailboat sound to you? A friend of mine with such a house is away for a while, and he would be delighted to let you stay at his place."

And that's how our family spent two weeks at the home of William Burroughs, the well-known American writer and wordsmith.

In 1956, Murray graduated from HUC-JIR in Cincinnati. We moved to Milwaukee, Wisconsin, for his first pulpit. I did not take a job while we lived there. When we moved to Chappaqua, New York, I began working as a substitute teacher for the junior and senior high schools. After seven years in Chappaqua, we moved to Indianapolis, Indiana, where I became a full-time social studies and English teacher in an inner city junior high school where most of the students were poor and underserved. It was during the time of the burgeoning civil rights era. I was in charge of a program for civil rights and integration for the middle grades in the district. Also, during that time I received my master's degree in history.

In 1978, we moved to Baltimore, Maryland, where I began teaching social studies to junior high school students, after which I moved to another school to teach high school social studies. Eventually, I left teaching and became assistant director of the women's division of the Baltimore Jewish Federation. During that time, I also worked as a job developer for the placement service of the Federation to help find jobs for Jewish Russian immigrants to the United States. In the

1990s, I became director of development for the Mt. Washington Pediatric Hospital, a long-term care facility for children in Baltimore. We raised over $15,000,000 for the construction of a new hospital. It is still in existence today, thriving as a center for long term care of children with multiple illnesses and disabilities. I ended my career as director of volunteers at the Mt. Washington Pediatric Hospital.

In 1997, Murray and I retired to Sanibel Island, Florida, where I became very involved as a volunteer in ZONTA, a professional women's organization similar to a Rotary club, but for women. I also became a trustee for the Katherine Ames Foundation, which distributes funds to needy organizations in Israel and the Palestinian territories for the purpose of enhancing relationships between residents of those areas. I only just recently resigned as a trustee of that foundation.

57

SO, YOU ARE GOING TO BE A REBBETZIN

MARY GENDLER

"SO, YOU ARE GOING TO BE A REBBETZIN," SOMEONE SAID TO ME UPON hearing of my upcoming marriage.

"What is a rebbetzin?" I asked, never having heard the word.

"It's the name for a rabbi's wife," she said.

"Does this imply the traditional rabbi's wife who is expected to do all sorts of things in the synagogue, like chairing the women's division?" I asked. "If so, the answer is no! I will never be a rebbetzin. Just because I fell in love with someone who happens to be a rabbi doesn't mean I am going to be a free adjunct to his job!!"

I was suddenly transported to my home temple and memories of going to services and watching the assistant rabbi's wife and children walk down the aisle to the front row after everyone else was seated. "Oh, those poor kids," I thought. "How embarrassing! I would never want to do that to my children...or myself, for that matter."

And I didn't.

I first met Everett in 1963 in my hometown, Kansas City, where, at my father's urging, I had returned after my second year in France. My plan was to complete a master's degree in English literature at the University of Kansas and then work my way around the world.

As it had been two years since I graduated from college and my friends had left Kansas City, I did not have much of a social life. I started going out with the assistant rabbi of my classical Reform temple, B'nai Jehudah. One day, he called me to see if I would like to go hear Everett Gendler, a rabbi who had been in the South with Martin Luther King, talk about his experiences there. My friend had learned of this from a woman he knew in New York who, it turned out, was also a friend of Everett's. In those days (early 1960s), there was not a lot going on in Kansas City, and this sounded like the most interesting thing to come along in years. Because of their mutual acquaintance, after the talk we went out for tea with Everett and his brother-in-law. As we were leaving, Everett and I exchanged addresses and began to correspond. He invited me to visit him over the winter vacation. I had been planning to go skiing in Colorado, so I was torn. Finally, I said yes, and told my parents I was going job hunting in New York. Little did I know then how close this was to the truth! I just did not know what kind of job.

The visit was magical, literally life changing. When I returned ten days later and announced that I was getting married, quite understandably my parents were shocked. "To whom?" they asked.

Fair enough. I had not been dating anyone seriously, and they had heard zilch about Everett. Knowing how strongly my father felt about Reform Judaism, I decided to give him a hard time. I told them that he was a rabbi, that his beard reached down his chest, his side curls hung down the sides of his face and he had a wonderful fur hat.

My father looked mildly apoplectic.

Then I had mercy and told him I was teasing him, but the fact that Everett was a Conservative rabbi ordained at the Jewish Theological Seminary was bad enough. For my father who, as president of B'nai Jehudah, used to torture the rabbis by complaining that too much Hebrew was used in the service (including the songs), this was a mixed marriage! I wonder if he would have preferred my Polish Catholic boyfriend at college who wanted me to marry him and convert to Catholicism? Probably not. But as I had never before talked about getting married, they knew this was serious.

My own exposure to Judaism was quite solid in the way of classical Reform in the 1940s and 1950s. I went to Sunday School for many years, culminating not with bat mitzvah, but with confirmation. At religious school, we learned about the history and customs of Judaism and about the holidays, but we did not learn Hebrew. Our family went to services on the High Holy Days and celebrated Passover with another family and the rabbi from the temple. I vividly remember sitting next to the rabbi one year, and his taking all four of my cups of wine. I also remember the pregnant cat coming in when we opened the door for Elijah. They were wonderful celebrations, and sometimes lots of fun. We also observed Hanukah, lighting candles every night and sometimes placing the menorah on the mantel next to the Christmas tree!

Despite our dilutions of traditional customs, I always felt very Jewish. One year at my school, I was asked to play Jesus in a Christmas play. I refused. Instead, the other Jewish girl in my class and I played a couple eating at a table, and we quietly recited the prayer over bread in Hebrew. Our rabbi, Samuel Mayerberg, was a big influence on me. He was very involved in social justice work, and when he stood at the lectern dressed in a black robe with his hair streaming out behind him and preached about the need to confront social wrongs and political misdeeds, I was mesmerized. To me, he came to embody Judaism, so it is no wonder that of all the ten "blessings of faith" that we had to recite at confirmation, my favorite, and the one I remember to this day, is "*tzedek, tzedek tirdof* – Justice, justice shalt thou pursue."

I went to Princeton, where Everett was living, a couple of times that winter, and Everett came to Kansas City during the months when I was finishing an M.A.in English Literature at the University of Kansas. The wedding was set for the end of May. During one of Everett's visits to Kansas City, he and my father started talking about the wedding ceremony, which rituals should and should not be included in the ceremony. The resemblance to fathers' negotiating the bride price in India was astonishing! I hardly knew what they were talking about, as I had never been to a Jewish wedding that I was old enough to remember. I had no idea of the rituals and customs involved. One thing that was very important to Everett was the *huppah*. His insistence upon this meant that we would not be able to have the wedding ceremony at our temple, because no *huppah* was allowed! Then there was more discussion about the seven blessings and other rituals. Finally, I think all the traditional elements were included, except the breaking of the glass.

At that time, Everett was the rabbi of the Jewish Center of Princeton. He had been there for two years and was much beloved. He was technically a Conservative rabbi, having been ordained at the Jewish Theological Seminary, and I, on the other hand, was raised in a "*glat*" classical Reform congregation where the particular list of the unspoken "shalt not" commandments included: Thou shalt not speak too much Hebrew; Thou shalt not wear a *yarmulke*; Thou shalt not wear a *tallit*; Thou shalt not have a bar or bat mitzvah... You get the idea. So, although I had a very strong Jewish identity, I had a very meager knowledge of many of the customs and traditional practices outside classical Reform Judaism. Everett, however, had some rough times explaining that the girl he was marrying was Jewish, even though her name was Mary!

And so, at the end of May 1964, I got married and left home to enter a whole new world. This world contained none of my old friendship circle and little of my former way of living. I was madly in love but stunned by my new life. I had been quite a free spirit, traveling around Europe on my own while going to school to learn French in Grenoble, France, one year, and teaching English conversation to French students in a high school outside Paris two years later. I was used to being on my own, going where I wanted to, when I wanted, and basically being my own boss, accountable to no one. My obligations were limited to the school where I taught. It was already a stark change when I returned home to Kansas City in 1963, but I was still planning to work my way around the world when I got my M.A. Instead, I found myself a rabbi's wife in New Jersey! In my wildest imaginings, this had never been in my game plans. As a friend so aptly put it, "So you gave up the world for Everett!" I had not thought of it this way before, but moving to Princeton, New Jersey, as the wife of the rabbi of the Jewish Center of Princeton was an entirely a new thing. I had entered an entirely new world and left my old life, friends and institutions, behind.

I knew no one, there was no one near my age (I was twenty-three at the time), and I did not know what to do in relation to the congregation. Everett and I had discussed the rebbetzin issue beforehand and had agreed that the unwritten part of our ketubah was that being the rabbi was his job, and my role was to be only what I wanted it to be. This was put to the test soon after my arrival, when I was approached by the head of Hadassah, who, in my memory, was a substantial and imposing woman. She asked me if I wanted to give the opening prayer at the Hadassah meeting. I sort of stuttered and said that prayers were my husband's department and that I would not feel comfortable doing this. "Oh," she said, "we assumed he would write it." "Thank you, but no," I said, and, to their credit, I was never approached again.

The highlight of that first year was our trip to Selma. Although this was the march where Dr. King turned back rather than crossing the bridge, it was an exciting and moving experience.

I was lonely in Princeton, despite the fact that there were many interesting people, both in the congregation and at the university. It was a fairly young congregation; many members were in their thirties and had children. But as I was a good ten years younger and, at first, had no children, I was very much alone. I was the only person age-wise between the youth group teenagers (all of whom had mad crushes on Everett and were furious with me for getting him), and the older members of the congregation. The first year, I taught school, which kept me busy during the day, but was alone most evenings, as Everett had the usual parade of meetings he was expected to attend. Another problem was that when we were – infrequently – invited to gatherings or parties, as soon as we entered, the conversation turned to religion, as if this was the only thing in which Everett might be interested. We gradually became friends with three couples, two of whom had young children, and are still in touch with them now.

Our first child was born a year-and-a-half after we got married. I was no longer teaching school and became a full-time mother. Our newborn was a very lively, alert, busy child who, from birth, took only three twenty-minute naps a day! I had not spent any time with babies, and like many first-time mothers, had no idea of what to do. So, there I was, with no one from my former life around, with no vestige of how I had lived in my former life, and a baby who was awake most of the time and whom I had not the slightest idea of how to parent. Everett was busy at the temple, and, since I knew so few people, I was alone. No wonder I got depressed.

We stayed in Princeton for four years after we were married. Everett was very happy with the congregation and they with him. But he knew how unhappy I was and suggested that we leave and go off to something new. Among the myriad things we had in common were travel and our commitment to doing something to help others. Although short on many traditional practices and customs, my religious background was deeply rooted in the prophetic tradition. Rabbi Mayerberg was very active in the community in Kansas City and served as a wonderful role model. And clearly Everett was dedicated to social justice, as well. That was how we met, and it was one of the things which drew me to him.

So, we thought, let's go somewhere in South America, where we may be able to find a worthwhile project to help people. I was pregnant with our second child at the time, so rather than go immediately to a needy area, we spent the first year in a town in

Mexico called Cuernavaca. A radical priest named Ivan Illiech had a school there for learning Spanish, and it also served as a magnet for priests and others who wanted to challenge the old order and give more rights and opportunities to the poor and dispossessed. We thought that through him we might meet someone engaged in a project which would fit us.

Our year in Cuernavaca included not only the birth of our second child, but many surprises. Life in Third World countries is different from life here. For example, we had to have a cook who would also guard the house all the time, as it was dangerous to leave it unattended. There were no teenage babysitters for the children. I did not like being the *patrona*. Our maid's child got worms from eating dirt. In addition, there were political problems which led to violence in Mexico that year. And Mexico was the only democracy in Latin America! By the end of the year, it became clear to us that our desire to serve in a poor or needy community was totally incompatible with having two very young children. We would either have to subject our children to an extremely basic lifestyle or live like the upper class. We decided that the risks we could take on for ourselves would not be fair to impose on our children.

We returned to the United States and spent two years as staff at Packard Manse, an interreligious and interracial retreat center a few miles outside Boston. Although there were many interesting workshops and we met many people who were involved in social justice work like those we had hoped to meet in Mexico, Everett was missing rabbinical work and the Jewish community. At the end of two years, he found a small, liberal congregation, Temple Emanuel, in Lowell, Massachusetts.

Filled with dropouts from some of the more traditional synagogues, this small, off-beat congregation of around 100 families proved to be an ideal place for us. Unpretentious and unprestigious, it was a magnet for people from all over the area who did not like the feel of larger synagogues, with all the jockeying for power. I was never asked to do anything, and the closest I came to walking down the aisle after everyone was seated, as in my home temple, was chasing our two-year old daughter who ran to Everett calling, "Daddy, Daddy" in the middle of a Yom Kippur service!

For Everett it was perfect, as the members were open and responsive to new rituals and practices. The congregants were respectful to Everett, but they also saw him as a person, as well as a rabbi. They were friendly and entirely undemanding of me. We made some really wonderful friends with whom we are close even today, twenty-five years after retiring. One amusing incident illustrates this point. As we were preparing to leave the temple, I told Everett I wanted to have a few people from the congregation over for dinner, and I named them. He responded "Sure," and then asked if I realized I had just named the synagogue board. Amazing! Had I been required to invite them, I would have balked.

When we returned to the United States in 1970, the women's movement was in its budding stages. I had continued to feel depressed and unhappy, though I felt guilty for feeling so. I had a wonderful husband, two lovely children and a good life. But something was missing. Little by little, I realized that what was missing was ME! The bottom line was that I no longer knew who I was. Yes, I was the wife of a rabbi and the mother of two children, but somehow, somewhere along the line, I had lost myself. I wanted more but did not know what. Like other women, I became aware of being angry. I was angry that I had become trapped in the mother/wife role and had no time for myself. I was angry that I had to do most of the child-tending and the cooking and cleaning. The first time I went into Boston to take some classes, I made sure to cook the dinner and get a babysitter to help Everett feed and put the children to bed!

Women's support groups were forming, providing a place to express our problems and concerns, and an opportunity to get feedback and help from other women in questioning the life and roles in which we found ourselves. Was it wrong to develop a career? To become a professional? What about the children? The housework? Should our husbands be asked to share some of the responsibilities? And was it right to demand my own time, when doing so interfered with the important work Everett was doing in the world? These are some of the things we talked about. The sharing with other women was very helpful, and, slowly, I began to feel myself emerging.

Little by little, I developed a project. My choice of direction was undoubtedly influenced by having married a rabbi and finding myself involved Jewishly in a way I would not have been, had I not married him. I began writing articles about women in Judaism. The first, published in Response magazine of 1971, was a seminal article about Jewish women, their inclusions and exclusions within the history, liturgy and practice of the tradition. In subsequent issues, I went on to explore the lives and actions of some of the women in the Bible, concentrating on unheralded figures, such as Lilith and Vashti – strong, independent women we needed to reclaim as models. I also created new rituals for girls, which I wrote about in Lilith magazine. The less controversial was a ritual to celebrate a girl's first menstruation. The more radical was my proposal for a female counterpart to the *brit milah* for a boy, the idea of which horrified even my lefty friends. Rabbi Levi Kelman (now Weiman Kelman), whom I saw shortly after the article was written, told me he had just been at a Jewish gathering where people joked, "Hide your baby daughter. Here comes Mary Gendler!" I had become Lilith! As my articles were published, I began receiving invitations to speak on women in Judaism. I had never spoken in public before, so this was a stretch for me. I soon got used to it and enjoyed the opportunities to share my thoughts and learn about others. I was intensely involved in this work for about a decade.

Fast forward ten or so years. Our children were growing up, and Everett, in addition to his work at the temple, was also now the Jewish chaplain at Phillips Academy, a boarding school in

Andover, Massachusetts. I had gradually pulled back from the public speaking and found a new interest. At age forty, I decided to go back to school and get a doctorate in psychology. I commuted from our home in Andover to Boston University and finished my program in three years. I began a private practice and, for a period, was also clinical director of a Jewish Family Service in Lawrence, Massachusetts.

In 1987, when our children were in and past college, it was "payback" time. Everett got sabbaticals from the temple and school, and we spent one entire year wandering around the world, mostly in Asia and the Middle East. It was worth the wait. So, I both lost the world and then regained it in spades!

In 1995, Everett felt it was time to retire from his work at Phillips Academy and the temple in Lowell. He was sixty-seven. I am twelve years younger and, at fifty-five, I was not at retirement age, but I was not going to continue working when he was free. Neither of us was clear about what we should do next, but we decided to take a year and travel. As we had loved Asia, we decided to return there. Our wanderings led us to visit Tibet, a country I had long wanted to see and whose people, in their strong dedication to their religion and family, led me to view them as the Jews of Asia. We were moved by their plight, their land having been invaded and taken over by the Chinese, who were in the process of destroying the Tibetan culture and religion.

We knew that the Dalai Lama had told the Tibetans that their struggle to regain their freedom must be nonviolent, but that they were having little success. When we had an audience with the Dalai Lama in Dharamsala the following month, we suggested that the Tibetans might have more success if they learned new ways to struggle nonviolently. He liked the idea, and so began a project which has lasted so far for over twenty-three years, during which we have traveled to all the different Tibetan settlements in India and spoken to thousands of Tibetan monks and nuns, students, administrators, business people, and others about how to make their nonviolent protests more effective. About ten years ago, we founded ANEC – Active Nonviolence Education Center, a Tibetan-run, non-governmental organization, to continue this work in India. We have commuted to India for this project almost yearly since the program began.

Our life together, initiated by our mutual concerns about injustice and our commitment to nonviolence as a way to effect change, has come full circle in our post-retirement years. It has been wonderful working together on this project and has brought us even closer than before.

So how has my life been shaped by marrying a rabbi? *Totally!* I have no idea, of course, how my life would have turned out, if instead of marrying Everett, I had followed my plan to work my way around the world after I finished my master's program at the University of Kansas. I strongly suspect I would have been less Jewishly involved, though I would have joined a temple and raised my children as Jews. I most likely would not have experienced the richness of celebrating the Jewish holidays as intensely as we do. I would not have had the fun of building a sukkah every year and eating in it every night, often with guests. I would not have gone to NFTY encampments and learned the rousing songs and felt the wonderful energy there. I would probably not have devised new rituals for Jewish women or researched and written about Lilith and Vashti. Involvement in our small temple in Lowell was a deeply meaningful experience that I might not have had elsewhere. At home, we always light candles and say the blessings on Shabbat. Everett always recites a prayer before we eat. I would not have done that on my own.

We raised our children in a decidedly Jewish home. They complained about not having a Christmas tree, when they were small, but they had other compensations, for example, presents every night of Hanukkah. They both became bat mitzvah and were involved with NFTY. They both went to Jewish summer camp at Eisner, and their own children have followed suit at the same camp. Despite very demanding careers, both of our daughters have been on the boards of their respective temples, which is more that I can say for myself. All of our grandchildren have become b'nei mitzvah. Our older daughter joined a synagogue in New Haven, which was started by my great-grandfather. Neither she nor I knew this when she joined. My own grandfather helped found our temple in Kansas City, and (as I said earlier) my father was president there for a stretch. Perhaps it was not so far out that I ended up marrying a rabbi.

Everett introduced me to a warm, embracing, sustaining Judaism that I probably would not have known, and, at the same time, kept his pledge to protect me from getting involved in temple activities that I did not want. I never felt I *had* to be a rebbetzin. Despite some of the difficulties in the early years, our life together has been rich and full. I guess my father was right after all. It's a good thing I spent that year in Kansas City! Thank you, Dad, and mostly, thank you, Everett, for the life you have helped me live.

Mary Gendler, a retired psychologist, lives in the Berkshires of Massachusetts, with her husband, Everett. In the '70s and '80s, she wrote some of the earliest articles "outing" and lauding Lilith and Vashti, two of the earliest feminists in Jewish lore. She helped create new rituals for women's involvement in Judaism, from rituals that acknowledged the female experiences of menstruation and menopause to ceremonies for welcoming Jewish baby girls that would have the same power and significance that circumcision has for Jewish boys. She spoke widely to different groups, especially women, about the importance of treating women as equals in Jewish practice, of modifying the language in prayers to include "she," and of referring to God as both male and female. She also stressed the importance of women becoming rabbis. She has been a member of B'not Esh since its inception. Still an avid feminist, Mary Gendler is thrilled to see the many changes and opportunities for women in Jewish liturgy and practice. She is also an avid gardener and photographer. Her husband, Everett Gendler, a member of the Central Conference of American Rabbis, was ordained at the Jewish Theological Seminary, in 1957. He has served congregations in Mexico City; Brazil; Princeton, New Jersey and Lowell Massachusetts.

58

THE CONVERSION OF MISS KNOW-IT-ALL

COCHAVA PRYSTOWSKY

I DIDN'T MARRY A RABBI. I MARRIED A STUDENT. I HAD NO IDEA WHAT I was getting myself into. I was young, I was eager to learn, I was naïve...

I came to New York City in the end of the 1950s, fresh from Israel, after having served in the army and gone to Bezalel Art School for just over a year. I was looking for a new adventure in the big wide world. I had met some American students in Israel who had convinced me that an exciting experience would be spending my junior year in a college in America. I applied to Hunter College in New York, since I heard it had an excellent art program, and got accepted. My family agreed. I packed my bags and was on my way.

New York was a big and overwhelming city, but I had enough friends who were guiding me and helping me negotiate life there. I was having a wonderful time at Hunter, learning and paying attention to the differences between American and Israeli students. I found that, compared to my experiences – Israeli Army, growing up during the war, the simple life – the Americans were spoiled, childish and naïve. I did not realize at the time how naïve I myself was.

My plan for this adventure was to come to New York City only for one year. The Hunter administration, of course, was not aware of that and accepted me as a fulltime student. Since Hunter was a "no tuition" city college, it limited its acceptance of foreign students to ten people, and I was one of the lucky ten. I met a lot of American and Israeli students my age, and mostly went with groups of friends to different activities. Life was fun.

And then came my first (and only) blind date ever. In Israel, in those days, blind dates were not the norm. I had never even heard of the concept. A distant relative gave my name to someone who gave my name to this guy. When he called, I told him I would not go out with a "stranger." But when the conversation on the phone continued for more than an hour, he convinced me that he was no longer a stranger. He threw in some Hebrew words. He showed me that he cared about Israel. The conversation was interesting, and he was not only a student himself but also a Hunter graduate.

Finally, I thought, "*Oh, what the heck!*" That was *THE* fateful thought of my life.

Our first date was short, as I had requested, since I was not sure that I wanted to go out with someone I had not met "normally." He stopped at my place for half-an-hour on the way to a Hebrew school class he was teaching nearby. We argued about Ben Gurion for most of the time, but I liked how he argued and how much he knew. We set up our next date. The rest came swiftly. We were talking marriage after three months of knowing each other and decided to get married after six months. I would continue my studies and graduate from Hunter, and he was planning to get another degree and consider coming to live in Israel. That's all I had to hear. I was madly in love.

I had come from a traditional family in Israel. If I had to classify it in today's terms, I would call it "conservadox" – a very lenient, observant family. My father went to synagogue on Shabbat and we didn't ride that day. But who had cars then, anyway?! Since buses didn't run on Shabbat in Jerusalem, there was no chance of riding even for the non-observant. Switching on the lights was not encouraged, but if the lights went out, putting them back on was not considered a big deal. My siblings and I had gone to a secular school (Gymnasia Ivrit in Jerusalem). We learned in school about Jewish traditions. Some of us would practice them at home, and some of us would just know them in theory. The background of the student body was mixed. I had some close friends who went to a Tzofim Datiyim youth group (modern Orthodox scouts), so I joined there as well, which gave me the privilege of knowing and feeling comfortable with both "religious" and "non-religious" kids.

Religiously speaking, therefore, I was flexible and ready to hear, listen and learn. Sim was a wonderful teacher, particularly since he himself had come from a traditional home and was understanding of my questioning. He had the answers that I was seeking. We talked a lot about different religious approaches, and after a while I found that I had not known as much about Judaism as I thought I had. I knew a lot about the Hebrew sources, having been an attentive student in school, but I had been limited in my knowledge of the more liberal approaches to Jewish thinking. I had been exposed mostly to an Orthodox point of view, the only known approach taught at the time in schools in Israel. I did have a Bible teacher in the upper grades who was considered somewhat of a heretic, and from him I got a glimpse into liberal thinking, which attracted me. Unfortunately, he left later to teach at Hebrew University. Most of our teachers instructed us only in the traditional sources. One has to keep in mind that I am speaking about the educational system in Israel in the 1950s. Today's approach is probably much different.

I could not quite get it when Sim told me that he was considering becoming a congregational rabbi. That called for a lot of explaining for me. A rabbi to me was a guy with a white beard, usually much older, very Orthodox and old fashioned, and his wife a "yenta" with a head covering and dark, unattractive clothes. "What does this have to do with you???" I wondered.

I was not yet aware of the "other" types of rabbi in America. I learned the difference very quickly. And when I sent a message to my family in Israel that I had met this wonderful guy and was planning to get married, I had to do a lot of explaining in order to avoid having a bombshell explode. "Cochava is marrying a rabbi!" they exclaimed. "Who would have believed that this fun-loving gal went to America only to marry a rabbi, no less." I had to explain that a Reform rabbi in America is not like a rabbi in Israel, and that here, a rabbi is a community leader, a social worker and a teacher of Judaism. I also told them that Sim came from a Zionist family, too.

The first year of marriage was "playing house." We were both students. I was finishing my BFA at Hunter, and Sim was completing his rabbinic studies. So far, so good. I got my degree first; Sim still had another six months to finish his studies. During that year, every other weekend we left for Connecticut, where Sim led services and taught a course at a student congregation. Driving up together was always fun. We stopped on the way for my favorite soft ice cream which, in those days, Israelis called "American ice cream." Driving back and forth to Connecticut, with his arm around me (in the front bench seat), Sim taught me how to drive a car, too. It was, for me, a treat and fun. For both of us, the whole experience was part of being newlyweds.

I certainly did not fully comprehend at that point what my role as the wife of a rabbi was or was expected to be.

Then came the ordination ceremony at Temple Emanu-El in New York. To me, it was like a grand graduation. It was getting a beautiful dress for the occasion and being proud of my husband for insisting on his principles and being the only one in the class to wear a *kipah* at the ceremony. Being fresh out of Israel, I couldn't understand his classmates. "How can you be in a synagogue without a head covering??" I wondered. I still didn't get it!

The following two years also were fun and games. Sim served as an Army chaplain at Fort Lewis, Washington, and, of course, I went along. We lived in the officers' quarters, facing the grand Mt. Rainier from our living room picture window. We traveled a lot, took "Army hops" to Japan, Hawaii and the like, camped and took gorgeous hikes. and enjoyed the World's Fair in Seattle to its fullest. Basically, we got the travel bug into our blood. And the best thing was getting the idea of New York City being the center of the universe out of Sim's head. He came to love the outdoors as much as I did. I continued enjoying playing in this vast playground called America. I really loved it. To me, it was heaven. Still, I did not realize what I had gotten myself into.

When his military service came to the end, the question was, "What now?" Since Sim wanted to pursue his studies toward a Ph.D., he looked for synagogue openings near major universities. Luckily, there were a few opportunities in the Philadelphia area. He interviewed, and we settled in Lafayette Hill, with a fairly small congregation that allowed him time to pursue his studies at Dropsie University.

In the congregation, I realized that I was referred to as, "The Rabbi's Wife." I made it clear from the beginning that I did not like to be called "The Rebbetzin" and that I had a real name, Cochava. I had no role models for guidance and did not know how I was supposed to behave or appear in the new position. I pretty much paved my own way. Sim did not want me to teach Hebrew or any other subject in our congregation's religious school. He told me that he did not want me to be under pressure, that if someone disapproved of something I did or did not do as a teacher, he would be put in the middle. And I agreed. So, for a short time, I taught Hebrew and Jewish art in a neighboring Conservative religious school in the Philadelphia area.

I loved the fact that when, during his interview to be rabbi of the congregation, Sim was asked what he thought his wife's role should be, he answered, "To keep the rabbi happy." Not only did I love the answer, but they loved it too. My position in the synagogue had started to gel for me. I was always there beside Sim at services and events, but never took a position of leadership even though my nature was to be a leader. In Israel, I was always involved with committees, always leading songs and games and chairing programs. I realized that I had to give all of that up for the sake of keeping out of Sim's way. The synagogue was his community to lead, not mine. I sometimes thought that if my friends in Israel could see me in the congregation, they would not believe how quiet I had become.

We were very much involved in the social fabric of the community, going to dinner parties and hosting them. Those were the days that dinner parties for eight-to-twelve people were a weekly affair. There was little "going out to dinner" socially. I used to prepare some Israeli delicacies that people loved, but they always used to say that they were "invited to the rabbi's house for dinner." My name was not mentioned, even though I had done all the preparations and cooking. "Oh, well," I thought and smiled. I got used to that oversight on their part.

Once, at a party, one of the congregants crudely came up behind me, grabbed and squeezed my butt and exclaimed loudly, "I always wanted to know what a rabbi's wife's *tush* feels like!" I felt like slapping him and showing him some Israeli Army tactics, but of course, I stood there dumbfounded, not knowing how to react, worried that my response would jeopardize Sim's position. I looked around for Sim to come to my rescue, but he was nowhere to be seen. Fortunately, a lovely assertive young woman yelled at him, reprimanding him in front of everyone. He must have had a bit too much to drink, but I was so uncomfortable I just wanted to disappear. I am not sure if I did not react because I was the rabbi's wife or because I did not know yet how to respond appropriately to this kind of behavior in this country. Needless to say, I disliked this fellow from then on.

During the next ten years, our family grew from two to four. I took care of the kids and had a part-time job, while Sim was completing his Ph.D. and leading the congregation. On his sabbatical after ten years with the congregation, we moved to Israel for six months, something I really looked forward to. We wanted to have a reality check on whether or not we could live in Israel, long-term. We rented an apartment, not wanting to live with my family, as we had on our other, shorter trips. Our children attended public schools, and we wanted to see if we could "make a go of it." After a few months there, we realized that, as much as we tried, it would not work for us. Israelis were not ready for a new approach to religious Judaism in the 1970s, and Sim would have to spend his days fighting the system. I was not ready for that kind of existence. There were a few Reform rabbis trying to do just that, and their life there was strained. We came back to the States, to the congregation to which we had become attached, where we had made a lot of friends and had been treated very well. To make it more attractive, the congregation offered Sim tenure and allowed him the time to become certified as a family therapist.

So, I came to accept the life we had established in the synagogue. It gave our kids a steady place and home without having to wander from community to community. I felt comfortable in the position of the "rabbi's wife" that I had established for myself. I joined the Fine Arts Committee in the synagogue (as a member only), because that's where my interests lay. I made sure that Sim pronounced Hebrew properly, and put in my two cents when I did not care for something he said (but did so only in private, of course.) I did not view Sim's position as a "job," and I came to feel part of it, too. I hosted (oops, the rabbi hosted), an "open house" on Rosh Hashanah for years, because I liked the people. I continued to attend services and congregational events and learned how to be gracious the American way. All in all, I learned to enjoy my life as a rabbi's wife, even though, when asked if I would have had it any other way, I would answer that I would have liked to have had a more private life and been less in the public eye. Otherwise, I certainly enjoyed a good life and grew to be happy with my role.

You could say that this Israeli had certainly converted to being a

Reform rabbi's wife pretty successfully.

Cochava Prystowsky, a fifth-generation sabra, was born and raised in Jerusalem. She attended high school at Gymnasia Rehavia, and after serving two years in the army, studied at the Bezalel School of Art. She met her husband, Sim, when she came to the States to spend her junior year studying art at Hunter College in New York. Sim swept her off her feet and she became his wife. After completing her BFA degree at Hunter, Cochava pursued a career as a commercial designer for more than ten years. She began sculpting in paper in the 1990s and enjoys working in paper and cellulose, a medium that allows unlimited variations in results. She has lived in the Philadelphia area for the last fifty-four years, where she and Sim raised two children. They now have four grandchildren. Sim was ordained at HUC -JIR in New York in 1961.

59

ALONG FOR THE RIDE: A LEARNING CURVE

WALLIS CHEFITZ

IT WAS MEANT TO BE. I WAS ATTRACTED TO MITCH. I HAD ARRIVED IN Israel a few days earlier and had taken a bus from Jerusalem to my ulpan in Arad, and there was a rainbow in the sky as we traveled south. It was October 1969, the year I graduated from college. Mitch was tall, had dark eyes and a lot of dark hair, and he was wearing his khaki Navy uniform shirt. He had been an officer in the waters off Vietnam and was also stationed in the Mediterranean during the Six-Day War. He was six years older than I was. We had a lot in common, but he did not look like anyone I had ever dated.

I saw him the first night at a gathering in someone's room where he was playing his flamenco guitar. No one seemed to be paying attention to him but me. Then we met at the bulletin board and talked about where to take the laundry. Then we ate lunch at the same table and stayed on to talk after lunch was over. On the first Shabbat, we met on the patio of the ulpan, and he asked me if I wanted to read the book that he had written. We traveled to Jerusalem and talked about our families and sat in Gan HaAtsmaut. We made picnics in the wadi with pita, cheese and fresh dates. When I read the chapter of his novel about a boy and a girl whose hair was flying, I was even more interested. And then it seems like the next day he asked me to marry him. By the end of the second week we were engaged. We took the bus to Beersheba for falafel or sometimes to a restaurant that had steak. It was a great time.

He and I had lived and gone to camp in the same areas of Massachusetts and Maine just a few years apart. I knew of his rabbi, Roland Gittelsohn, and when we were on our honeymoon, I took him to meet my teacher, Shlomo Bardin, in Los Angeles. And Mitch had studied in Berkeley. It was *bashert* ("meant to be"). I had mentors in New Orleans who pushed me in the direction of Bardin's Brandeis Camp Institute, Honey Brener and her daughter, Anne, my good friend since third grade. Anne became Rabbi Anne Brener and is still in California where she inspires everyone she meets.

Mitch had planned to apply to HUC-JIR in New York before he had left for Israel, and later he did apply and was accepted. We were in the same beginner Hebrew class in the ulpan until Passover, 1970, and then lived in Boston with his family. My parents had some reservations, but let me marry this exotic man and made a beautiful wedding in their backyard in Metairie, Louisiana. After the wedding, we returned to Jerusalem and studied together in the first year of the new HUC-JIR Rabbinical program. I was welcome to learn in the school's ulpan.

In our program in Arad, we had Hebrew and Judaic learning and Orthodox services and a week on a kibbutz. HUC-JIR was filled with adventures in the Sinai with the other students and some of our teachers. I sat on the bus next to Dean Ezra Spicehandler. At Mt. Sinai the guys played cards and I remember going into the monastery and wishing that I could bring one of the many unused refectory tables home. I was not yet clever enough to figure out how to do that. I walked to the Hebrew University and studied in English and in Hebrew and then worked at the Ministry of Health as a secretary. I liked that job because it was across the street from HUC-JIR.

We were invited to the home of Chanan Brichto, one of the professors who lived in Jerusalem with his wife and older sons. He blessed the sons and we took note of it. We bless our three sons every week, even by phone, if necessary. Today I see our son, Josh, blessing his children. It was a pivotal moment for us.

I had grown up in a comfortable family in New Orleans. We went to Temple Sinai, and though my parents sent us to Sunday School, they did not put much energy into anything Jewish. My mother's mother was spiritual. We would draw Jewish stars together, and she took me to Touro Synagogue for the children's services. After the summer at Brandeis, I was twenty-years old and took my grandmother to dinner and erev Shabbat services at the Conservative shul. They did not have a minyan and we were the only women. We all just sat in the very small circle. My mother, and her sister and many great aunts spoke some Yiddish words that were funny and saying them always made my mom happy. She had her own Yiddish *patois.* One Sunday morning when I was in sixth grade, I felt ill and declined the pancakes that my father was making. He was disappointed, so I ate some but then got sick in class. I was taken to the rabbi's study where Julian Feibelman allowed me to lie down on his sofa and he covered me in his black robe. It was so cozy, and his kindness made me like Sunday School and him from then on. I taught first grade in that Sunday school when I was a junior at Newcomb.

When we got back from Israel, I taught Sunday School in the temple in Clifton, New Jersey where Mitch was doing a lot of teaching. We lived in a nearby community, then called West Paterson (now Elmwood Park). During those years, Mitch also taught confirmation classes in Livingston, New Jersey and Chappaqua, New York. He had a student congregation on weekends in New Milford, Connecticut and spend the High Holy Days in Cranston, Rhode Island. He was busy with all of that and with his studies at HUC-JIR.

I remember that he was asked a question about the purpose of prayer by a friend in the Connecticut congregation, and I did not think that he had given a good answer. Driving in the dark with snow coming down, I gave him a rough time about it. He took the discussion seriously enough to pursue it further and write his HUC-JIR thesis about the early *hekhalot* literature (Jewish mystical texts) and compare it to the theories of Carl Jung. After sitting on our big faux leather chair one day and going over words that seemed to make no sense, he discovered by accident what the mystics were doing. He found that he was in a trance and could now understand prayer. He wanted to maintain that kind of kabbalah intimacy for himself and seems to have found a way to let others connect, as well, through our decades together. He does this with stories that he creates. In New Jersey, I volunteered at Overbrook, a large old mental hospital with weeping beeches and locked wards. I learned woodworking and about greenhouse plants and decided to go for a degree in occupational therapy. Then we had our first baby.

I was glad that we had moved to Miami after ordination; it was more like home. Mitch was an assistant rabbi at Beth Am with at least one other assistant. He formed *havurot* at Beth Am, because, in California, he had learned about their vibrancy from Rabbi Harold Schulweis. After five years at Beth Am, he started and directed Havurah of South Florida, which kept us busy for more than twenty years. Our home was the center of much of the activity. It was like an old model of the rabbi's home, with lots of guests all the time. Over those years, I felt tempered like silver and learned to be as gracious as I could. Much of my time was in the – luckily open – kitchen, where I was busy making tofu and bean cholent. Havurah was on the map, and people who came through Miami visited us. World-class teachers taught and stayed in our home, including David Zeller and Zalman Schachter and their families. One Friday morning, Zalman (then "Reb Zalman") taught me how to make cholent with barley, tofu, seitan, tempeh, chili powder, cumin, caraway, pinto beans and oil until it had "eyes." Shlomo Carlebach came several times and sang and taught. We bought and renovated a big old house that could hold as many people as came. The new National Havurah Committee was beginning its summer institutes when we started in 1980. We went to the summer programs and our world expanded. By then, we had two, almost three, children. That week each summer was full of creativity, stimulation and learning. I loved the arts and the literature and movement and dancing. My body was made to dance Jewish dances. Mitch took and then started teaching the heavier text classes and soon became involved in the organization, later becoming chair and going to New York often.

Although he hadn't wanted to do a start-up, we liked Miami and it had become home. He spoke to Rabbi Narot at Temple Israel and wanted to do there what he had seen in California. But Rabbi Narot died before Mitch's plan could materialize, and Mitch was told that he needed to formally apply for the position in order to do what he wanted. However, the CCAR placement rules had been changed and Mitch did not have the seniority level to apply. Synagogues at that time were territorial and the establishment seemed to us to be cold and easily threatened. I am sorry that Mitch felt the need to leave the Reform movement as a result. But even so, Temple Israel needed help and he taught and conducted some services there while keeping a very low profile. Because he did not want to call attention to himself, he did not start a havurah program there as he had planned. He became a (Reform) counterculture rabbi. We met all kinds of very differently practicing Jews, and he was broadened by Talmudic University, in Miami Beach. We held retreats on the beach at the old Art Deco hotels before they were gentrified. We had wonderful Purim festivities and anyone who wanted could give a one-minute sermon on Yom Kippur since we had all day. We raised money and Mitch and I went to the Lower East Side in New York and bought a Torah scroll. I picked out the *rimmonim* for the scroll.

To this day, we have friends who were so kind to us and our children in those years. As a family, we had freedom to be ourselves. I had the audacity to do crazy songs and dances and skits and costumes on Purim, and to deliver "sermons" about the "invisible in the body" that I was discovering in my new Feldenkrais studies. Laurie Horn, the *Miami Herald* dance critic, taught me how to belly dance and we performed at Purim. One person walked out because of one of my costumes. But I grew up with Mardi Gras, and I could be on the wild side.

After twenty-one years, Havurah was a big organization. Mitch was recovering from meningitis and needed a sabbatical. I was an occupational therapist working with various populations. Our kids were out of the house. We decided to withdraw from the havurah and were pleased when the group found a new rabbi to lead it. The havurah continued for a number of years; a few of the old members still meet now and then.

It was 2001, and Temple Israel again wanted a rabbi, but this time no one wanted to take the job. There were many fewer members and the area was no longer safe. Gentrification had not yet happened. I was ready for the opportunity to get out of the kitchen and take some of the things I had learned into the temple. I encouraged Mitch to go for it, and it was as though time turned back to him. I became part of the sisterhood and, with my friend Ellen Kempler, created a committee and programs that were fun and successful. The temple grew, because Mitch and his team were popular; Mitch would plan the services at dinner beforehand, together with his cantorial soloist, Karina Zilberman, and the music director, Dr. Alan Mason.

On Saturday mornings, in addition to the service, there was a study session called Joseph's Table, which is still thriving. When we came there in the early 2000s, we met a hero of a man, Joe Grosbard. He came to every Friday night service as well as to Saturday morning study. Mitch introduced hasidic texts to learn on Saturday, and just happened to choose the teachings of the Sefat Emet (the Gerer Rebbe) from Poland. Joe did not say anything during the sessions. After several months, Mitch asked him what he thought of the new learning, because it was different from what they had been doing in previous years by studying the Torah portion of the week.

Joe said, "You don't know? I am from Ger, and I thought these teachings had died with the Jews of my town. I wasn't there the day the Nazis came, and when I returned, everyone was gone."

He said the son of the Gerer Rebbe had taught in his house. Joe was generous and always happy. He brought bagels, cream cheese and sweets every Saturday, cut the bagels and toasted them. We named the sessions Joseph's Table in his honor. He had a double kiss for everyone, men and women, and for me he also would say, "Smile, Rebbetzin."

I asked him after several years if he loved me for me or because I was the rebbetzin, and he said "Both." He wanted to keep doing the same texts the following year. "They were the same," he said, "but we were different." Time had turned back for him, too.

Mitch was feeling the effects of psoriatic arthritis and wanted less work. When the temple hired a new rabbi, Mitch stayed on as "scholar-in-residence." During that time, he wrote three novels, two books of short stories, a memoir and poetry. I took classes in sculpture at the local college.

But Mitch also wanted to give up the title "rabbi." He felt it was an impediment, that people saw the title and not the person. For the last several years, he has been retired and happily writing and feeling stronger. We sold our house and moved into a down-sized apartment. We love our new neighborhood in Coconut Grove. I had always loved Coconut Grove but never imagined that I would live here; I just had too many reasons to stay in the house we owned. Mitch was asked to teach kabbalah at Beth David, not as "rabbi," but as Mitch. We fell in love with Beth David's monthly Shabbat Pasio'n service – high energy, live Latin music to the liturgy, with some of the songs composed by their talented, amazing rabbi, Julie Jacobs. Beth David is about to reinvent itself by tearing down its old huge edifice and building a new community center, school and synagogue on the campus. Exciting things are happening in Miami.

And now we have come full circle. As I write this, Temple Israel is again looking for a rabbi. They needed help for the High Holy Days, and asked Mitch to serve as an interim until they find someone. Three times, Temple Israel has called. It is a leitmotif in our lives. We have changed each time, and so has the congregation. It is smaller again and still struggling, but still very spirited and friendly. Mitch has ideas for its success, as do I. So far, I have plans to get in the kitchen (!) and teach hallah-making, starting with the Sunday school parents. I hope to teach Israeli dance to the kids. Mitch will enlist help and altogether we will turn it around. I could feel it during services on the High Holy Days. The congregation will have more outreach into the gentrified community, be more lay-led, with more text learning, more emphasis on culture and hands-on activities, and more open to the Jew-*ish* as well as the more religious aspects of Judaism.

I am finally comfortable with being me, and with being a rebbetzin and the wife of a revolutionary guy who knows something about how a progressive Jewish life can be authentic. Today there is a new paradigm for living a Jewish life. Things are different. I feel that the old model of rebbetzin is an antique, as is the old model of "rabbi." To me, being rebbetzin is like living a dance in a costume. The new rabbi will be a facilitator coach, encouraging others to learn and to teach, providing ways for them to live their primary Jewish lives.

Wallis Adler Chefitz was born in New Orleans in 1947. She graduated Newman High School and Bradford Junior College and received her B.A. from Newcomb College. She earned an M.A. at New York University in occupational therapy. She and Mitchell Chefitz married in 1970. Their three children are Walter, Josh and Adam. She and Mitch have lived in Miami, Florida since 1975. Wallis has worked as an occupational therapist, Feldenkrais practitioner, sculptor, Israeli dancer, and co-founder of the Wednesday night Beth Am Israeli Dancers. Rabbi Mitch Chefitz was ordained at the New York School of HUC-JIR in 1975.

60

EZER K'NEGDO

NAOMI PATZ

I'VE BEEN INTRIGUED FOR A VERY LONG TIME BY THE EXPRESSION *ezer k'negdo*, usually translated as "his helpmate" or "helpmeet," because its literal translation seems to me a contradiction in terms. *Ezer* means "helper," but *k'negdo* suggests opposition (*neged* = "against"). At the same time, it has always struck me as a concise description of my relationship to Norman's career and, in fact, to the pattern we have established over the fifty-six plus years of our marriage. I am his fiercest critic and proudest ally. And he is mine. I recently read that "helpmate" or "helpmeet" is no longer the desirable – or possibly even accurate – translation, that *ezer* is now being understood as *equal*, and *k'negdo* as "opposite," as in *partner* and even occasionally "lifesaver" (according to Robert Alter). Either way, it perfectly fits Norman's and my relationship.

Although I never wanted to be a rabbi, my upbringing and career path have had an intense Jewish focus. As a result, Norman and I, in many ways, have had a professional Jewish partnership. At the same time, I believe that I have been a dedicated, if not totally traditional, congregational rebbetzin. Combining professional, remunerated work with "work" as a rabbi's spouse and the congregation's rebbetzin, combined with volunteering in the community, turned out to be easier – although much more exhausting – than I might have anticipated if I'd given it any forethought, which I most definitely did not do.

On my mother's side, I come from a bunch of fiercely liberal Yiddishist Zionists, who loved to argue, even over things about which they all agreed. Their experiences, filtered through my mom, informed who my siblings and I became. I was raised in the Conservative movement, active through high school in the Leadership Training Fellowship (LTF), the national "elitist" (intellectual? nerdy?) youth organization of the Conservative movement and spent many summers at Camp Ramah. I went to Israel on the Machon Kayitz in the summer of 1958, before entering college.

During high school, I not only did a great deal of Israeli and international folk dancing, but also studied modern dance with the full-time ballet students at the American Ballet Academy in Newark, New Jersey. It all gave me the background I needed to work for several summers as dance specialist at Camp Ramah in Nyack, New York, in its first years as an overnight camp.

I met Norman in October of my senior year at Barnard, and we were married that April. He was in his second year at HUC-JIR in New York. There was no sense of *hevruta* there. In fact, I had no idea until fairly recently of the relationships among the students, and especially the wives of the rabbinical students, in Cincinnati. In New York, there was no campus, there were no dormitories, no student lounges. Unlike what I understand took place in Cincinnati, in Norman's years in rabbinical school, at least, no one gave the spouses of the students on the New York campus any insight into what we might expect or what might be expected of us, or what we should do about either, once our husbands were ordained.

Students lived all over the greater New York City area, including in New Jersey. And most had a heavy load of Hebrew school teaching midweek afternoons and on weekends. Yes, we went out to dinner occasionally with other couples and with Norman's single classmates, but in no way were we – or our spouses, for that matter – a cohesive group. And Norman's class did give a reception for the faculty at the end of the fifth year on the tenth floor of what was then the UAHC building at 838 Fifth Avenue in New York City, something we hoped future classes would emulate. (They did not.)

We wanted to spend Norman's third year of rabbinical school studying in Israel, but, despite the fact that he was already a graduate of the Hebrew Teachers College in Boston and far more advanced in many areas of study than his classmates, the dean brusquely told him "no credit," and we were cowed. In addition, because he'd spent a semester in Israel during college, he had graduated a year behind his Harvard classmates and felt pressure to move on with his career. We were too unworldly to realize how little difference it would have made in the long run.

In New Milford, Connecticut, the location of Norman's student pulpit for his final two years of school, I learned through experience how to become my way of being a rabbi's wife. And Norman and I learned together how to make our marriage and the rabbinate a partnership.

My two favorite stories from New Milford both took place on Friday nights. The first was a conversation I had with one of the older women in the congregation, someone probably much younger than I am now. I'm not sure how we got on the subject, but I was talking about the way Norman and I divided our household responsibilities, especially given the schedule that had us leaving the city right after I finished work on Friday afternoon and returning late in the evening on Sunday. Apparently, I mentioned taking out the garbage. Horrified, my interlocutor gasped, "You don't let the rabbi take the garbage out, do you?" "Oh no," I answered immediately. "My husband does that." "Good," she said. And, of course, it was!

The other came when Norman announced to the congregation that he had won the lottery (a questionable victory) and was going to enter the United States Navy as a chaplain. "But can you *shvim*?" asked Nathan in his thick Yiddish accent. "Nathan," Norman responded, "in the Navy, the idea is not to have to swim!"

In New Milford, I determined that I had no problem being a rebbetzin – in fact, enjoyed it – so long as it wasn't my only identification. That realization has served me well over the years.

After ordination, we moved to Newport, Rhode Island, where Norman attended Naval Chaplaincy School, and I was terrified of the hats, white gloves, calling cards, teas with cucumber sandwiches and polite, stilted conversations until I came across a book called *The Naval Officer's Wife*, which detailed each appropriate response to every conceivable occasion. Once I knew what was expected and when I was flouting protocol rather than just being gauche, I managed to survive – and even thrive.

Debby was born during the year we were in Norfolk, Virginia, Norman's first naval assignment. I also edited the Tidewater Jewish Federation newspaper, did the coursework toward my M.A. in English literature at Old Dominion University, and taught an undergraduate course there. In September, just after Yom Kippur, Norman got orders to report to the Second Marine Division in Camp Lejeune, North Carolina.

Our first Naval address in the military was on Purgatory Road, in Newport; our second was on Timothy Avenue, in Norfolk; our third was a garden apartment in Cardinal Village in Jacksonville, North Carolina, while we waited for housing on base. When we moved to Paradise Point for the final few months of Norman's active duty, we knew it was time to separate from the service.

After the military, Norman accepted an assistantship in Cherry Hill, New Jersey. In our second year there, the senior rabbi went to Israel on a full year's sabbatical. We were on our own in a 750-family congregation. Norman said he was only minding the store and not changing the stock, but we were frustrated with what we saw as the aridity and lack of warmth in the congregation. We held receptions at our house for the executive board, the administrative staff and faculty, and for the youth group. I wrote the service for Confirmation, which included a Ruth midrash with musical accompaniment by a very talented confirmand. And we began our years-long tradition of spending at least two weeks every summer at UAHC Camp Harlam.

Norman knew he couldn't resume being the assistant when his senior rabbi returned, so we began the search process. We were certain that we didn't want a mega-congregation, but, rather, a place where we could know everyone who wished to be known and Norman could be involved in the broader Jewish community. Although we had very little idea of the rest of the country (and might have thought differently if we had visited some of the cities we'd dismissed out of hand), we were sure we wanted to stay in the New York area – close to the culture we loved and to our families. There wasn't much available.

Norman interviewed at a congregation in central New Jersey, which expressed a great deal of interest in him. The search committee insisted that I be there, which I didn't mind because I was curious about them, too. They didn't ask me any questions but, while I sat there, they asked Norman questions about me. My favorite: "If the rabbi's wife could sing, would she insist on singing the solos on the High Holy Days?" Norman chuckled and said something to the effect that "The way my wife sings, I can guarantee you that you're safe on that score." It wasn't enough for them. "But *if* your wife could sing, would she insist..." For that and many other reasons we decided that congregation was not for us, and Norman turned down their offer.

We went together to the interview in Cedar Grove, New Jersey, where the search committee members were truly *menschlikh*: wonderful, warm, welcoming, intelligent and eager for Norman to be their rabbi. There was a beautiful rosewood ark in the sanctuary/social hall. And, except during rush hour (as I came to know well during the fifteen years in which I commuted to New York City), it took barely more than thirty minutes to get into Manhattan. Norman took the job. We thought we'd be there for five years, but we never left. And we have never regretted it.

I was newly pregnant with our second child when we arrived. Aviva was born on the Saturday morning before Pesaḥ, *Shabbat HaGadol*.

The congregation was incredibly supportive when our nephew, Etan, disappeared in 1979 and during the painful years that followed. And again in 2015 and 2017, when we endured the two trials that resulted in the conviction of his murderer.

Norman retired in 2006. We still have many dear friends from our more than fifty years associated with the congregation. We've lived in the same house since 1982 and occasionally go to services, even when Norman does not conduct, which he is invited to do several times a year. And, with his successor's agreement, he officiates at weddings, baby namings and funerals for longtime congregant families who ask him to do so. We conscientiously try to abide by the prayer for the czar in *Fiddler on the Roof*: "May God keep the emeritus far away from us!" On the whole, it seems to work well.

For years, I was afflicted with a personal malady that Norman dubbed "Septemberitis." I realize now that it was a form of depression and that its cause should have been obvious. Because my mother had moved to Florida in the early 1970s after my stepfather had suffered a couple of heart attacks, the job of making the annual seders for our large extended family fell to me. Soon after Pesaḥ, I would write each year's confirmation script, basically a review of the material that Norman covered during the year presented in a relatively dramatic form, with excerpts from the kids' essays inserted, as appropriate. Then we'd head off for six weeks in Israel – and, after a few years, to Amsterdam on the way home – with the confirmation class. When we got back, it was time for me to write or rewrite the alternate liturgy for the second day of Rosh Hashanah, a tradition we'd started the year we arrived in the congregation, which observed two days of the holiday. I'd bake for days for the dessert reception for the entire congregation we hosted in our yard. Then everyone else went back to work and school, and I didn't know what to do with myself.

I realized that I wanted to write, and to do so in the Jewish field. Although I felt fairly confident that I could research whatever I needed , I decided it would be wise to go for a second master's degree, both to bolster my own sense of security in what I would be doing and to give me the credentials that might make other people want to hire me and/or read what I wrote. I enrolled at HUC-JIR and took a couple of courses a semester, overlapping with a great many rabbinical and education students for almost ten years.

In the summer of 1970, when Norman was dean of the NFTY Summer Institute at Kutz Camp, we became good friends with Jim and Jane Perman. Over the next few years, Jane and I collaborated on and co-wrote *In the Beginning, The Jewish Baby Record Book,* which was published by NFTS and is, sadly, now out of print.

Rabbi Eugene Borowitz was my thesis advisor, and he kept badgering me to finish working on it. As soon as the thesis was (finally) submitted and accepted, Gene asked me to be his coauthor on the book that became *Explaining Reform Judaism*, published by Behrman House. Rabbi Kerry Olitzky and I then created the *Teacher's Guide* and a *Workbook*.

For seven years in the 1980s, I edited what came to be called the "Judaica Series" for the Young Leadership Cabinet of the national United Jewish Appeal. It provided basic information on a sophisticated level to highly intelligent, generous, Jewishly committed but, for the most part, Jewishly uninformed men under age forty, for them to study and to read as relevant with their families at the Shabbat dinner table. Each unit was prepared by a different member of the UJA Rabbinic Cabinet – Reform, Conservative and Orthodox rabbis –and I provided continuity, structure and the necessary supplementary text so that the series had coherence and the depth we were seeking. Norman was the Rabbinic Cabinet liaison to the project, and my unofficial advisor and proofreader. It was a very interesting challenge.

Beginning in 1972, Norman and I led twelve confirmation class trips to Israel. A groundbreaking aspect of our program was the people-to-people component we developed, through which the confirmands spent a full week living with families on moshavim connected with the *Lamed Ayin* (Independent Liberal) party, of which the husband of our tour organizer was secretary general. Well do I remember getting on the bus at our temple one day at the end of June with thirty-six hormonally challenged teenagers and hearing a mother call out, "Have a great vacation, rabbi!"

The year we and Larry and Robin Rubinstein, who co-led the trip with us for many of those years, coped with seventy-eight kids, we climbed Masada via the Roman ramp with our sleeping bags and spent the night on the top. It was no doubt totally illegal and decidedly not safe to be clambering around the archeological site in the dark, but it was most definitely an awe-inspiring experience. So were our trips into Sinai, which included sleeping in the open, climbing Mt. Sinai and eating perfectly dreadful food. We loved (virtually) every minute.

My familiarity with Israel and my involvement with the UJA Young Leadership Cabinet were responsible for my becoming the director of a new entity called the North American Jewish Forum that matched key Jewish leaders, all of whom were forty and under, with an equal number of their Israeli peers who had founded the Israeli Forum. After a few years, we involved young Jewish leaders both from Western European countries and countries still under Communist rule and took part in four European Jewish Forum conferences. Norman was a particularly active player in those events. I traveled to Israel five or six times a year for the Forum, and then as director of a new program being developed by UJA and the Jewish Agency called Partnership 2000 (P2K). A peer-to-peer successor to Project Renewal, it paired federations in this country with regions in Israel for educational, medical, business and other partnering activities, including fostering personal and social relations. Thus, both the Forum and Partnership 2000 strengthened Israel-Diaspora relations by creating long lasting friendships, significant working relationships and mutual understanding among business people, academics, members of Congress and the Knesset, rabbis and Jewish communal leaders and key professionals on the national level, and introduced influential Israelis to liberal Judaism in positive ways, something of which I am very proud.

I retired from P2K (now Partners Together – P2G) when Aviva became pregnant and moved from Manhattan to Montclair, New Jersey, fifteen minutes away from us, because she wanted to be near her support network – and what kind of support could I provide with the kind of travel I was doing? I loved my work and my colleagues in Israel, and the amount of time I could spend there, but retiring was the right thing to do.

Since 1975, upon securing a Czech Holocaust Torah on permanent loan to our congregation from the Memorial Scrolls Trust, Norman and I have been involved with Czech Jewry, a connection that has grown deeper and more complex over the years.

During the 1980s, we traveled a great deal in Western, Central and Eastern Europe. We brought busloads of congregants to rallies outside the United Nations headquarters in New York City and to the Soviet Jewry rally in Washington. Going to the USSR was the logical next step. I kept a journal of our trip, which the National Conference on Soviet Jewry sent to Sir Martin Gilbert, who was extremely active in England on behalf of Soviet Jewry, and I was greatly honored that he chose to meet with me on one of his trips to New York.

Because Norman served for several years as missions chair for the UJA Rabbinic Cabinet before becoming its national chair, we were privileged to travel through Central and Eastern Europe, Israel, Turkey, Egypt and Morocco with members of the Cabinet. I got to know many Rabbinic Cabinet members very well through editing their work for the Judaica Series and because so many of them joined us on the missions. Only in recent years – and in some cases not until we began attending NAORRR conventions – have I had the pleasure of meeting and becoming friends with their wives.

For two years, I edited ARZA's *Journal of Reform Zionism.* In recent years, I wrote *The Jewish Holiday Treasure Trail* for Behrman House and monographs on the destroyed Jewish communities from which the Czech scrolls now in our New Jersey and San Juan congregations come. I also wrote the Shabbat prayer book our congregation has been using for fifteen years and, at the request of the congregation, edited a volume of Norman's High Holy Day sermons as a surprise gift to him just before his retirement.

Early on, I understood that my success as a rebbetzin depended on Norman's success and that whatever I did would be seen through a rabbi-centered filter. If they loved Norman, they'd love me – or pity him for having such an awful spouse. If they didn't love him, they'd have even less use for me. Through my love for him, my love for Judaism and my inability to be sedentary, I made it my business to be as good a partner and helpmate as I could on my terms. The girls and I regularly attended Friday night services, with them often falling asleep in the pews. In addition to what we then called "creative services," I put together a Women's Haggadah and led the women's seder each year (actually, I still do that). I wrote the scripts for every temple show – mostly musical parodies of congregational life. I was the behind-the-scenes organizing force for the extremely well-attended *shabbatons* we ran every few years: intensive weekend programming beginning with a dinner before services on erev Shabbat and concluding at the end of the afternoon on Sunday – lectures and workshops, activities for kids, and meals and snacks and lots of singing and Israeli dancing and total exhaustion for pretty much everyone by Sunday night. And then we did it all again a few years later!

For a while I was our congregation's ARZA liaison and, since the early 1970s, have been the motivating force for our participation in the Celebrate Israel parade in New York City. I went to few sisterhood meetings over the years, but I did advise the president and/or her committee on programming if they wanted my help (and very happy when they didn't need me), and brought back unique pieces of Judaica for the sisterhood to sell in their shop. For many years, I led a synagogue book group of devoted, marvelous readers, most of them retired English teachers. I have curated our synagogue's small museum case, which displays books, artwork and ritual Judaica from our own collection plus occasional loans from congregants – four to five different exhibits per year for close to fifty years.

Since 2007, Norman has been one of the retired rabbis serving the Reform congregation in San Juan. Temple Beth Shalom was founded in 1967 by young Jewish Anglo families who'd come to the island to take advantage of Operation Bootstrap (a U.S. government program that gave significant tax breaks to manufacturers who moved their companies to Puerto Rico), together with others who felt disenfranchised because the Conservative congregation on the island had been taken over by very territorial Cuban exiles. Operation Bootstrap is gone and most of the congregants of those years have left the island to be near their children and grandchildren (very few of whom stayed in Puerto Rico) and/or entered retirement communities in the States or are no longer alive. A couple of years ago, it seemed that the synagogue would have to close, but, instead, we have been blessed with many native Hispanics who want to become Jews. They study for two years for conversion. They go to the mikveh (ritual immersion) in the Atlantic Ocean. Some of the men choose to be circumcised and they all undergo *tipat dam*. And their friends who are already Jews-by-choice come to the conversion ceremony to cheer them on. They learn to read Hebrew; they learn all the music and readings in the service and, when they have been converted, many serve as cantorial assistants throughout the year and as lay leaders in the summer months, when there is no rabbi in residence. We now even have a tiny religious school! It is very exciting. Less exciting was the devastation caused by Hurricane Maria on Rosh Hashanah, 2017, when we were on the island, and the painfully slow recovery that still drags on. We are awed by people's resilience and persistence.

My most recent project is the filmed performance of *The Last Cyclist*, a play I reconstructed and reimagined in 2008 based on an almost-forgotten cabaret by a young Czech Jewish avant-garde dramatist, Karel Švenk, which he wrote and rehearsed in the Terezín Ghetto in 1944. It is an absurdist comedy that pits a group of lunatics who have escaped from their asylum against everyone who owns a bike, rides or sells bicycle gear, or whose relatives were cyclists going back several generations. *The Last Cyclist* was banned after its dress rehearsal because the Jewish Council of Elders of the camp deemed its allegory too overtly anti-Nazi. Švenk died on a death march in 1945 at the age of twenty-eight, a few weeks before the end of the war in Europe. The play was later described by the only actor in the cast who survived the Holocaust as "our most courageous production." My adaptation has been performed since 2009 in community theaters, at universities (at four schools, it is on the syllabus of courses devoted to "theater and genocide"), and in high schools, as well as at Yom HaShoah (Holocaust Memorial Day) commemorations. It has been presented twice in Mexico City in a Spanish translation, and in New York City in a well-reviewed, off-off Broadway run. *The Last Cyclist* is particularly relevant today, because of the horrifying rise of anti-Semitism, bigotry and bullying. Norman and I are the film's producers. As I write this, in 2019, we dream of it being screened at Jewish and secular film festivals, shown on educational television, in schools, synagogues and churches, and on Yom HaShoah. The staged play continues to be performed here and abroad, and I travel around the country to lecture about theater in Terezín and participate in question and answer sessions following performances.

In reflecting on my years as a rabbinic spouse, I have come to realize that I've never thought of myself as a member of the congregation, and certainly not as an (unpaid) member of the staff, but rather as a specific "other" – the rebbetzin, I suppose, to give it a title. I have worked hard on behalf of each of our congregations, but only by doing what I've chosen to do. It isn't my style to be out front, and I am not a "joiner" (although I am a life member of a number of Jewish women's organizations); I spent too many years directing organizations for that to give me any pleasure, and I prefer to let others take the visible leadership roles.

The years have been rich and full, and neither Norman nor I is yet ready to slow down more than our bodies force us to, or give up on our Judaica projects, our deep involvement with friends and family – and theater, concerts, travel, thinking, reading, aggravating over the news and bickering with one another (well, maybe Norman could give that up). We have truly been a team, and I hope we will have many more years in which to enjoy our partnership.

Norman was ordained in 1965 by HUC-JIR in New York. We have two daughters, Debby and Aviva, and four granddaughters – Natasha, India, Sadie and Dahlia. They are the joy of our lives.

IN CLOSING

THIS PROJECT BEGAN NEARLY FOUR YEARS AGO, AT A WORKSHOP SESSION at that year's NAORRR convention, when Judy Maslin presented the idea of a book of essays to be written by rabbinic spouses. It took a while for the project to get going, but once the realization that we really did have something to contribute took hold, an impressive number of NAORRR members began writing – and were amazed not only by how much they had to say but, even for those who chose only to share one or two anecdotes, by how much there was to remember and reflect on and evaluate and be impressed by – and pleased and saddened and embarrassed by – and proud of, too. In short, there indeed was something special, something unique to each of us as individual rabbinic spouses as well as things we all shared because we were/are married to rabbis. So, we wrote.

We are a self-selected group. There is great variety in what we chose to write about and the length to which we discussed the things that were on our minds. Some of us were more reflective than others; some of us found humor in situations that made others feel uncomfortable. We represent a broad variety of individuals. Our experiences are informed but not limited by our backgrounds; by the size of our congregations or the nature of our spouse's non-congregational rabbinate; by the geographic locations in which we lived, and the number of years we spent in each; by the situations we found ourselves in and how we coped with them; and by the degree to which each of us responded to the then-burgeoning women's lib movement which changed so many of our lives.

Although I was already acquainted with most of our essayists, it has been my great pleasure to get to know all of them so much better through their words, and to learn about them as individuals as well as about the many different ways they chose to be a rabbinic spouse in our era. I find myself wondering what I might have done differently as a result of these insights. I know that Judy Maslin, my new soulmate, shares these feelings as well.

Judy and I hope that those of you who have read this book and known our writers as your rabbi's spouse are enlightened and even inspired by what they have written, that those of you for whom this is a new subject gain insight into the joys and complexities of rabbinic family life, and that those of you who are yourselves currently involved in the active rabbinate will find our narratives not only instructive but also entertaining and occasionally even worth emulating.

Being married to the rabbi has been a remarkable journey!

Naomi Patz
co-editor
Winter 5780

GUIDE TO ABBREVIATIONS

CCAR – Central Conference of American Rabbis

D.H.L. – Doctor of Hebrew Letters

HUC-JIR – Hebrew Union College-Jewish Institute of Religion, the Reform movement's rabbinical and cantorial, education and nonprofit management schools. HUC-JIR has four campuses: Cincinnati, New York, Los Angeles and Jerusalem.

JCCA – Jewish Community Centers Association

JDC – Jewish Joint Distribution Committee

JFS – Jewish Family Service

JTS – Jewish Theological Seminary, rabbinical school of the Conservative movement in Judaism

JNF – Jewish National Fund, known in Hebrew as *Keren Kayamet l'Yisrael*

M.A.R.E. – Master of Arts in Religious Education

NAORRR – National Association of Retired Reform Rabbis, an organization open not only to rabbis but also to all spouses and widowed survivors of retired Reform rabbis

NFTS – National Federation of Temple Sisterhoods, earlier name for Women of Reform Judaism

NFTY – The Reform movement's high school youth program (the acronym has been retained from the organization's earlier name:

North American Federation of Temple Youth)

ORT – Women's American Organization for Rehabilitation Through Training

PAAR – Pacific Association of Reform Rabbis

RK's – Rabbis' children; also, sometimes, PK's: preachers' kids

UAHC – Union of American Hebrew Congregations, former name of the Union for Reform Judaism

URJ – Union for Reform Judaism – the congregational arm of the Reform movement

USY – United Synagogue of American Youth, the Conservative movement's national high school youth program

WRJ – Women of Reform Judaism, the Reform movement's women's organization

z"l – *z"l* is an abbreviation for the Hebrew phrase *zikhrono/ah l'vrakhah* – "May his/her memory be for blessing."

CPSIA information can be obtained
at www.ICGtesting.com
Printed in the USA
FSHW010250151219
64979FS

9 781734 393002